AMERICA'S FIRST ALLY

France in the Revolutionary War

NORMAN DESMARAIS

CASEMATE

Philadelphia & Oxford

Published in the United States of America and Great Britain in 2019 by
CASEMATE PUBLISHERS
1950 Lawrence Road, Havertown, PA 19083, USA
and
The Old Music Hall, 106–108 Cowley Road, Oxford OX4 1JE, UK

Hardcover Edition: ISBN 978-1-61200-701-4
Digital Edition: ISBN 978-1-61200-702-1

A CIP record for this book is available from the British Library

Printed and bound in the United States of America

For a complete list of Casemate titles, please contact:

CASEMATE PUBLISHERS (US)
Telephone (610) 853-9131
Fax (610) 853-9146
Email: casemate@casematepublishers.com
www.casematepublishers.com

CASEMATE PUBLISHERS (UK)
Telephone (01865) 241249
Email: casemate-uk@casematepublishers.co.uk
www.casematepublishers.co.uk

Front cover: Top image: Reenactors. (Courtesy of author)
Bottom image: Second battle of Virginia Capes. (Wikimedia/US Navy)

Contents

I should be wanting in the feelings of gratitude, did I not mention on this occasion, with the warmest sense of acknowledgment, the very cheerful and able assistance, which I have received in the course of our operation from his Excellency the Count de Rochambeau and all his officers of every rank in their respective capacities. Nothing could equal the zeal of our allies, but the emulating spirit of the American officers, whose ardor would not suffer their exertions to be exceeded.

George Washington to the President of Congress
19 October, 1781
The Writings of George Washington
collected and edited by Worthington Chauncey Ford
(New York: G.P. Putnam's Sons, The Knickerbocker Press, 1891),
Vol. IX 1780–82, p. 387.

Introduction

France and Britain were rivals for domination in Europe and wherever they had colonies throughout the eighteenth century. British North American colonists saw France as a natural ally in this struggle for independence. France influenced the American War of Independence in a variety of ways, including intellectually, financially, and militarily.

The French Enlightenment thinkers, called the *philosophes*, provided the ideological foundations for both the American and French revolutions. Charles-Louis de Secondat, Baron de La Brède et de Montesquieu (1689–1755), developed the idea of the separation of powers and the need to divide power among the executive, legislative, and judicial branches of government in his works, particularly *The Spirit of the Laws* (1748).

François-Marie Arouet (1694–1778), better known by his pen name, Voltaire, used sarcasm and irony to advocate intelligent political authority based on the rule of law. During his entire literary and professional life he advocated freedom of thought in all of its forms and the ability to ensure that social and political organizations do not silence voices, particularly those of dissent. Most of his political views were based on the ideas of John Locke (1632–1704) and Isaac Newton (1642–1726/27). He distrusted democracy, which he saw as propagating the idiocy of the masses and was very critical about other people's ideas. He essentially believed enlightened despotism to be the key to progress and change. Only an enlightened monarch or an enlightened absolutist, advised by philosophers like himself, could bring about change, as it was in the king's interest to improve the power and wealth of his subjects and kingdom. He considered the French bourgeoisie to be too small and ineffective, the aristocracy parasitic and corrupt, the commoners ignorant and superstitious, and the church a static force useful only as a counterbalance since its "religious tax," or the tithe, helped to create a strong backing for revolutionaries. Voltaire was a firm advocate of secular rule.

Jean-Jacques Rousseau (1712–78) was the most celebrated of the French political philosophers. His works, particularly *The Social Contract* (1762), developed the principles of the general will and the importance of a social contract between people and government.

The increasing absolutism of the French monarchy was an important factor shaping French political philosophy. The role and influence of representative institutions in France were diminishing at a time when the British Parliament was gaining political power and the importance of legislatures was growing in the British North American colonies. While the Americans, and even many Britons, adopted the ideas and concepts that would shape the democratic ideals of the American Revolution, there were few practical outlets for corresponding antimonarchical views in France. This became important as French adherents to the philosophies of Montesquieu and Rousseau, such as Marie-Joseph Paul Yves Roch Gilbert du Motier, Marquis de Lafayette (1757–1834), and Mathieu Dumas (1753–1837) traveled to the colonies to fight for democracy.

The British and French were rivals for domination in Europe and around the globe, where the two nations had established colonies throughout the eighteenth century. The Treaty of Paris that ended the Seven Years War (commonly known as the French and Indian War in America) in 1763 marked the end of French territorial ambitions in North America and the emergence of a mainly European foreign policy in regard to Great Britain. France lost Canada, which was officially called the Province of Québec after 1763. Nearly all of its population of about 85,000 were of French ancestry, except for 2,000–3,000 British or American newcomers. Thus, France lost control of North America to the British. This included all the territories explored by the French in the Ohio and Mississippi River valleys. These territories were annexed to Canada, which now extended all the way to Louisiana.

The loss of all their North American territory dismayed and embarrassed the French. They yearned for revenge, but King Louis XV did not want to commit to another war. His successor, King Louis XVI, thought differently and began preparing the country for war. While some colonists saw the French as a natural ally in their struggle against Great Britain, most were distrustful of the French because the colonists were British subjects and shared Britain's hatred for the French. The English and Americans had been taught to despise the government, religion, and culture of France in the years preceding the American War of Independence. They had been enemies during the French and Indian conflict.

The French were predominantly Catholic. Many colonists came to America in search of religious freedom and, particularly, to escape the Inquisition run by the Catholic Church. Consequently, there was a strong distrust and hatred of Catholicism in the colonies in the eighteenth century. Yet, despite the continuing rhetoric of hostility, the Americans continued to conduct clandestine, illegal trade with France and the French West Indies.

The trade laws of the period were based on an economic system known as mercantilism, which exploited the colonies for the benefit of the mother country. France reasoned that any steps that loosened the bonds between the colonies and the mother country would naturally diminish British power. Adam Smith (1723–90), in his famous treatise, *An Inquiry into the Nature and Causes of the Wealth of Nations*, opposed mercantilism and advocated free trade.

When the war began between Britain and her American colonies, the colonists thought the French would welcome an opportunity to retaliate and regain their country or possibly become a 14th colony. The concentration of British troops (only about 800) in southeastern Canada and the fluid and undefended borders invited raids from both sides. Some thought that France might try to recolonize areas of North America if the British were defeated.

The French people supported the American cause long before the country was ready to join the war and become America's first ally. Antoine-Jean-Louis Le Bègue de Presle Duportail was the first of four officers authorized by King Louis XVI to go to America. The recently promoted brigadier general wrote to Claude Louis, Comte de Saint-Germain, the Minister of War, on November 12, 1777 to report on the situation in America. In his letter, he noted "There is a hundred times more enthusiasm for this revolution in a single café in Paris than in all the united colonies."

This book attempts to chronicle and detail the contributions the French government and people made to secure American independence. We briefly discussed the intellectual and ideological contributions of France to the American and French revolutions above. We will now turn our attention, in chapter 1, to the covert aid France supplied to America before her official entry into the war. Chapter 2 will cover the French merchants and outfitters who provided much-needed military supplies to the colonies. Chapter 4 will discuss French naval assistance, particularly the privateers who harassed British shipping and contributed to increasing shipping rates, chiefly insurance, which added to Great Britain's economic hardships. Chapter 5 will discuss France's military involvement in the revolution. This will not only cover the contributions of individual French officers and French troops but also include engagements involving people of French descent in areas explored and settled by the French, which were part of British possessions following the peace treaty of 1763. The American colonists believed that France would be eager to regain some of those possessions, particularly New France. Their attention, early in the war, was concentrated on Canada, hoping to annex her as a 14th colony. Chapter 3 will discuss the engagements in Canada related to that campaign. Meanwhile, Congress sent delegates to France to negotiate for financial and military support.

After the surrender at Yorktown, there were a number of contests fought in the West Indies. France allowed American privateers to use her ports and those of her colonies in the West Indies as safe havens to bring the prizes they captured at sea. The West Indies were also used as main ports for receiving supplies from France and transferring them to the American colonies. These actions and the engagements in the East Indies, where Great Britain and France fought for domination of the spice trade, are too numerous to cover in this book and must be included in another volume.

CHAPTER I

Covert Aid

King Louis XVI appointed Charles Gravier, the Comte de Vergennes, as his foreign minister in 1774. One of his priorities was to reduce British power, both as revenge for the humiliation of the Treaty of Paris in 1763 and as a way to make France's own position in Europe stronger so that it could deal with challenges from several nations. Vergennes, however, was patient and wanted to ensure that France did not take action too soon, because the Treaty of Paris of 1763 prohibited France from aiding and abetting any of England's enemies. Any such act would be considered an act of war and France could not risk entering another war without some reasonable expectation of victory.

The Comte de Vergennes was also concerned that a new government in London might resolve the problems with the colonies, leaving the British free to concentrate their power against the French.[1] Attempts to tax the colonies (the Stamp Act, the Townsend duties, and the tea tax) to replenish the treasury for expenses incurred for the French and Indian War caused much protest that often turned to riot. This was the first time in the colonies' 150-year history that the colonies were being taxed for revenue. This was setting a precedent that the colonists feared and disliked because they had no representation in Parliament. The Quartering Act created further animosity by mandating that soldiers would be quartered in private homes instead of incurring expenses for the construction of barracks. The colonies were in a state of economic depression after the French and Indian War. Jobs were scarce and the inhabitants competed with off-duty soldiers and sailors who tried to supplement their meager income. This caused further tension and strong hostility toward the military. The British assured the French that their remaining colonies in North America and the Caribbean were safe as long as France remained neutral, but should Versailles decide to enter the war, these possessions would be subject to attack by British forces.

The Comte de Vergennes carefully monitored the correspondence of his agents, both in London and in the American colonies during the early years of the American War of Independence. He sent Achard de Bonvouloir on a secret mission to America in September 1775—he was instructed to meet with colonial leaders and to assess the chances for the success of America's rebellion. However, he was ordered not to commit the French government in any formal way. Bonvouloir's report arrived in February 1776 and advocated support for the Americans. Vergennes recommended to King Louis that France begin to offer substantial support to the rebellious colonists.

French economist and statesman Anne Robert Jacques Turgot, Baron de l'Aulne (1727–81),[2] minister of the navy, commonly known as Turgot, opposed the foreign minister because of the potential cost, but the king overrode these objections and, on April 22, 1776, ordered the military to begin preparations for war, including the construction of new ships for the navy and new equipment for the army.

France would not officially enter the American War of Independence until 1778, although many Frenchmen sympathized with the American colonists long before then. However, France began providing covert aid to the Americans two years earlier, largely due to the efforts of Pierre-Augustin Caron de Beaumarchais.

Beaumarchais was the son of the king's watchmaker. He was better known as a playwright, primarily as the author of *The Barber of Seville* and *The Marriage of Figaro*. He also taught music to the king's daughters. Beaumarchais wrote a lengthy memo to King Louis XVI on February 29, 1776 outlining why France should help America. He concluded that "the saving of a few millions to-day would surely result in the loss of more than 300 million within two years."[3] He also emphasized the Americans' need for arms and powder but especially engineers. He stressed that, without engineers, the Americans could not even defend themselves let alone win.[4] However, France could not send them without a commission and such a commission would soon become publicly known.

Meanwhile, the Congressional Committee of Secret Correspondence appointed Silas Deane to the Secret Committee of Congress (then composed of Benjamin Franklin, Benjamin Harrison, John Dickinson, John Jay, and Robert Morris). He was commissioned, on March 2, 1776, "to go to France, there to transact such business, commercial and political as we have committed to his care, in behalf and by authority of the Congress of the thirteen united Colonies."[5]

Deane was instructed to apply first to the French government to secure certain military supplies, and, if he was refused, to purchase the supplies from private sources. He arrived in France on May 4, 1776, and, according to Benjamin Franklin's instructions, immediately wrote a letter to Dr. Edward Bancroft in London. He also contacted Dr. Jacques Barbeu-Dubourg in Paris. Dubourg introduced Deane to Charles Gravier, Comte de Vergennes, the French Foreign Minister, on July 10, 1776. Vergennes referred him to Beaumarchais. Beaumarchais then collaborated exclusively with Deane.

Dr. Edward Bancroft was Deane's close friend and secretary, but he was employed by both Congress and the British government. He had the key to Deane's correspondence and immediately reported to David Murray, Lord Stormont, the British ambassador, everything he knew about Beaumarchais's and Deane's activities. Neither Deane nor Beaumarchais ever suspected that Bancroft was planted to ensure the leaks of their operations to the British government.

The Comte de Vergennes also supported aid to America. In his undated document, entitled *Réflexions sur la Nécessité de Secourir les Américains et de se Préparer à la Guerre avec l'Angleterre*,[6] he noted that "There is no obstacle, and it is even necessary to aid the insurgents indirectly by means of munitions or of money... We are to make no agreement with them until their independence is established. The aid must be veiled and hidden, and appear to come from commerce so that we can always deny it." He proposed to station an intelligent, faithful, and discreet representative in each of the ports where the American vessels would come to land their cargoes. He would treat directly with the captains and "would mask the shipments to prevent the reproach of the court of England."

Roderigue Hortalez et Cie.

Beaumarchais, on the other hand, presented his plan to the King of France in a memo in October or November 1775 or February 1776. The plan was not accepted for several months and only after many modifications. He proposed to establish a new trading house which would essentially act as a front for the French government, concealing, from all the world and even from the Americans themselves, the participation of France in the operations.[7] The company name would be Roderigue Hortalez et Cie. Roderigue refers to the hero of Pierre Corneille's play *Le Cid* who avenges his father's honor and becomes his country's defender. Historian Antoinette Shewmake thinks that Hortalez was selected because it signified "exhort them" to a French ear, but it is more likely that it comes from the Calle de Hortalez where one of Beaumarchais's family friends lived and where he spent much of his time while in Madrid.[8]

The plan was finally accepted in early June 1776. The company would receive 1,000,000 livres[9] from France and another million from Spain, the value of which was expected to triple.[10] The alliance between Spain and France was very important for securing aid for the American colonists. First, it ensured that France did not risk being the sole target of British retaliation. Second, since Spanish participation increased the amount of aid provided to the Americans, the strained French budget would not be quickly overwhelmed. Finally, the Franco-Spanish alliance magnified the military power of the French and made its military involvement in America more likely. The Spanish made it clear that while they were not interested in recognizing American independence, they were willing to go to war with Great Britain if France participated. The French were initially hesitant to commit to open war. When France was ready to enter the war, Spain was preparing to go to war with Portugal.

Beaumarchais would also solicit the cooperation of private individuals and would have to shoulder all the risks and perils, but he would benefit from any eventual profits.

M. Duvergier, Vergennes's 15-year-old son, delivered to Beaumarchais the Comte de Vergennes's voucher for one million livres tournois on June 5, 1776, a month before America declared its independence. Beaumarchais cashed it on June 10. Two months later, on August 11, Spain advanced a similar sum and Beaumarchais had received contributions from numerous private individuals in France and elsewhere, so his first shipment to America exceeded three million livres.[11]

However, the French government only promised "a certain tolerance... Which would be curtailed at the first sign of publicity."[12] Roderigue Hortalez & Cie. "will provision the Americans with arms and munitions, and objects of equipment and whatever is necessary to support the war."[13] The French arsenals would supply these things. As the French army was undergoing a complete change in equipment at this time, the arsenals and forts were filled with munitions of war which the government was willing to dispose of at a nominal price.[14]

Terms of repayment

The Americans would repay Hortalez & Cie. in tobacco or other commodities because they had no money or it was worthless. The importation of tobacco was the monopoly of the Fermiers-Généraux (Farmers-General), the tax collection agency. The Farmers-General agreed to purchase the tobacco from Hortalez at a good price. They would then sell it at the going rate in Europe and pay the royal treasury only a predetermined sum of taxes collected.

The prices of the tobacco and of the goods would depend on the amount of care, effort, and expenses involved in getting them to their destination. Congress would choose either to pay for the goods at their usual value at the time of their arrival or to receive them according to the purchase price plus the costs of delays, insurance, and a commission in proportion to the efforts required.

Beaumarchais wrote to Arthur Lee (alias Mary Johnston) on June 12, 1776, advising him that he established a company to provide munitions and powder in exchange for tobacco and that the supplies would be sent to Cap François (Cap Haitien), the main port of commerce.

Deane wrote to Beaumarchais on July 20, 1776, noting that his instructions were to acquire 200 bronze cannons and arms and clothing for 25,000 men, but he thought Hortalez & Cie. should seek to obtain a larger quantity, given the probability that part of the cargo would be captured.[15] Beaumarchais responded two days later that his means for helping the united colonies were not as extensive as his desire to do so, that he needed to be reimbursed so he could improve his cash flow to purchase additional supplies, and that not all of the supplies requested could be obtained as quickly and as easily as desired and that they might not satisfy the quantity and the quality desired. He was doing his best but the items would arrive in ports unevenly and it might take several shipments to complete the order. The American vessels would have to take whatever was available in the warehouses and the merchandise would have to be apportioned to the troops only after all the goods arrived in America.[16]

Secrecy is essential

Beaumarchais's main concern was to maintain secrecy so as not to attract the attention of Lord Stormont, the English ambassador, and not to alarm the ministers through that ambassador's complaints. He did not yet know that Dr. Bancroft was already reporting his business to the ambassador.

Deane wrote to Beaumarchais on July 24, telling him that he learned that the shipping of cannons, arms, and other military stores was prohibited and could not be exported in a private manner. This gave him much apprehension, as he could not have those things shipped publicly or purchased openly without giving alarm. That could prove fatal to the operation. Beaumarchais would have to resort to various deceptions. Deane acknowledged that Lord Stormont was aware of everything he did and that his spies watched his every movement and would probably watch those of his business partners, not knowing that his own secretary was the spy.[17]

Roderigue Hortalez & Cie. wrote to the Committee of Secret Correspondence on August 18, 1776 to tell them that the company was founded for the sole purpose of serving them in Europe, to meet all their needs there and to see that all the goods, cloth, canvas, powder, munitions, guns, cannons, and even some gold to pay the troops could be obtained rapidly and under concession. Whenever possible, Beaumarchais would remove any obstacle that European politics might present. He also told them that he had procured about 200 pieces of bronze 4-pounders which he would send at the earliest opportunity, along with 200,000 pounds of cannon powder, 20,000 excellent guns, some bronze mortars, bombs, cannonballs, bayonets, plates, cloth, linen, etc. to clothe the troops and some lead to make musket balls. He also found an artillery and engineer officer who would leave for Philadelphia before the arrival of the first shipment. He would be accompanied by lieutenants and officers, artillerymen, gunners, etc.[18]

Beaumarchais complained to Vergennes on November 21, 1776 that he learned that the king's warehouses stored more than 19,200,000 pounds of powder and that he could not even get a small amount. He had acquired enough supplies, artillery, and gear to fill six ships which remained unloaded, costing him great sums of money. He limited himself to five: two at Le Havre (*Amphitrite* and *Seine*), one at Nantes (*Mercure*), and the other two in Marseilles (*Heureux* and *Amélie*). He expected that prudence would hold back the artillery but that he would not have difficulty obtaining the powder.

He said that if the Minister of War was really short of powder, it would be better for the minister to ask for a supplement than to have him, Beaumarchais, looking for suppliers. They might get curious and uncover the secret operation.[19]

Beaumarchais began with a fleet of six ships: the 480-ton *Amphitrite*, Captain Nicolas Fautrel; the 350-ton *Seine*, Captain Stephen Morin; the 317-ton *Mercure*, Captain John Heraud; the *Amelie,* Captain Desmoniers de Barras; the *Heureux*, Captain Pierre Landais; and the *Marquis de Chalotais*, Captain de Foligné Deschalonge. The fleet would be increased to include the schooner *Marie Catherine* (also referred to as *Marie* or *Catherine*); the *Concorde*; the *Comte de Vergennes*, renamed the *Thérèse*; the *Hippopotame*, renamed the *Fier Roderigue*, Captain de Montault; the *Zephir*, and two Bermudian vessels. Beaumarchais requested the vessels be re-loaded as promptly as possible and returned to him to ensure uninterrupted supplies. "By the beginning of March 1777, Beaumarchais had ten vessels sailing to America loaded with military supplies."[20]

Even before Roderigue Hortalez & Cie.'s first shipment, French privateers preyed on English ships and there were many actions involving French and English vessels. Brigadier General Louis Lebeque de Presle Duportail came to America in February 1777 and Major General Marie Jean Paul Joseph du Motier Marquis de Lafayette, often referred to simply as "Lafayette," arrived in June. They were the first of many Frenchmen who volunteered to serve the Continental Army.

The Marquis de Saint Simon commanded a body of 200 volunteers and Major General Vicomte François de Fontanges recruited 2,979 "Europeans" and 545 "Colored: Volunteer Chasseurs, Mulattoes, and Negroes" at St. Domingue (Haiti). The Volunteer Chasseurs, called the Fontanges Legion, included young men who would become famous in the Haitian revolution, most notably Henri Christophe, future King of Haiti.

Amphitrite

Captain Fautrel's 20- or 26-gun *Amphitrite* sailed from Le Havre for Dominica (Haiti) on December 14, 1776 with 39 officers and 56 private artillerymen and artificers. Her cargo included:

- 52 bronze guns (4- and 6-pounders), their carriages and fore-carriages, &c.;
- 20,160 4lb. cannon balls;
- 9,000 grenades;
- 24,000 pounds of lead balls;
- 10 pistols;
- 255,000 gun flints;
- 5,000 worms;
- 12,648 iron balls for cartridges;
- 345 grapeshot;

- 12,000 pounds of gunpowder;
- 925 tents;
- clothing for 12,000 men;
- and 5,700 stands of arms.

The *Amphitrite* was obliged to put into Port Lorient, where she was detained for a short while and then released. She arrived in Charleston, South Carolina by March 6, 1777 after a tiresome crossing of 85 days. She then proceeded to Portsmouth, New Hampshire, where she arrived on April 20, 1777.[21]

The *Amphitrite* took only part of the artillery. The rest was sent to Marseilles and Dunkirk along with between 100 and 200 tons of bronze with workmen to cast it into large cannons. The guns sent previously were all 4-pounders. All, or the greatest part, of this cargo was to be loaded aboard two brigs and brought to St Pierre, Martinique, to be transferred to America. One of the brigs had already sailed on June 10, 1777 with a train of field artillery and a large quantity of entrenching tools on board. She returned to Lorient on November 14 with a cargo of almost 1,000 barrels of rice and 20 barrels of indigo. Captain Pierre Landais's *Heureux* would bring the rest of the artillery.[22]

Mercure

The 14- or 16-gun (3-pounders) *Mercure* sailed from Nantes on February 4, 1777, loaded with 11,987 stands of arms; 1,000 barrels (50 tons) of gunpowder; 11,000 flints; 57 bales, four cases and two boxes of cloth; 48 bales of woolens and linens; nine bales of handkerchiefs; thread, cotton, and printed linens; two cases of shoes; one box of buttons and buckles; one case of sherry, oil etc.; one box lawn, and one case of needles and silk neckcloths; caps, stockings, blankets, and other necessary articles for clothing the troops. She arrived at Portsmouth, New Hampshire, on May 17, 1777, after a crossing of 40 days. There, she took on masts and lumber for France.[23]

Lord Stormont, grossly exaggerating, complained to Lord Weymouth on July 2, 1777 that the two ships *Amphitrite* and *Mercury* transported no less than 30,000 stands of arms, 400 tons of gunpowder, 5,000 tents, and 64 pieces of field artillery.[24]

Seine

Captain Morin's 14-gun and 37-men *Seine*, formerly the *Andromide*, sailed from Le Havre on February 19, 1777. She was loaded with:

- 317 cases of muskets;
- 154 bales of tents or tent covers;
- 2 barrels of flints;
- 2 barrels of gun worms;
- 359 bombs;

- 2 cast iron mortars;
- 1,000 pounds of matches;
- 6,000 pounds of gunpowder;
- 10 cases of musket balls.

She also carried nine large pieces of bronze ordnance, clothing for 10,000 men, and 10,000 tents. She arrived safely in St Pierre, Martinique, on March 18 where she landed most of her cargo which was transferred to the Continental Navy sloop *Independence*. The *Independence* brought to Maryland:

- 10,000 tents;
- 7,000 stands of arms;
- 10,000 blankets;
- 12,000 gun locks;
- 10,000 suits of clothes;
- 4,000 bushels of salt;
- 10,000 pairs of stockings;
- 400 barrels of powder;
- a quantity of lead and other articles.[25]

William Bingham shipped 15 bales of cloth and tents and 15 cases of arms on board Captain McIlnoe's brigantine *Chance*. The *Chance* was bound to North Carolina or any other port in the 13 United States and the shipment was addressed to the Continental Agent or Committee of the district where the vessel may arrive. He also shipped, on board Captain Jarvis's fast-sailing Bermudian brigantine *King Tamany*, 26 cases of fusils, 20 bales of tents and cloth, and 48 cases of muskets (totaling 1,164) from the *Seine*'s cargo.[26]

The *Seine* was ordered to proceed to Prince Ruperts Bay, Commonwealth of Dominica, on March 31, 1777 to resupply with wood and water. The Comte d'Argout, who was the governor of Martinique and the Continental Agent there, concocted a scheme to prevent the *Seine*'s falling into enemy hands. He wrote a letter to the governor of Miquelon to conceal the real destination of the vessel, pretending she was heading to the Isle of Miquelon with military supplies. The captain threw his letters overboard before being captured, but the pilot kept some papers which disclosed the real destination: Boston.[27]

Captain John Colpoys's HMS *Seaford* captured the *Seine* off Martinique on Monday, April 5, 1777, the morning after she left Martinique. Captain Morin steered into the channel between Martinique and Dominica where he was more likely to encounter patrolling British vessels. He allowed a fire to burn in his caboose the whole evening. Captain Colpoys sighted this little light at 1 AM on April 5 and chased the *Seine*. He fired two guns at 2 AM to stop the *Seine* which made no resistance. He put a prize crew aboard and took her to Roseau,

Dominica, at 1 PM where she was moored. The British estimated she had a value of £30,000 in goods.[28]

The Comte d'Argout sent a memorial to the governor of Dominica demanding the restitution of the vessel as the property of King Louis XVI. However, England could not restore her without showing an excessive degree of weakness, and France could not relinquish her claim and still preserve her dignity.[29]

Seine was tried and condemned on April 28, surveyed on May 9, and sold to the Royal Navy, for £2,200 on June 12. She was renamed the HM Sloop *Snake* and fitted to mount 16 6-pounders.[30]

Amélie

Captain Desmoniers de Barras's ship *Amélie* was loaded by February 28, 1777. Her cargo included:

- 19 bronze guns with their carriages & fore-carriages, &c.;
- 19 bronze guns without their carriages;
- 6,561 cannonballs;
- 288 bombs;
- 200 barrels of powder each of 100 pounds;
- 120 bars of lead;
- 20 cases of musket balls.[31]

She was sent to Hispaniola (Haiti), as the season was too far advanced for the ship to go directly into an American port. Beaumarchais instructed Mr. Carabasse, his correspondent at Cap François, to buy three or four Bermudian vessels to ferry the cargoes of the *Amélie* and *Thérèse* and their returns between the Cape and the Continent and to transfer the whole load onto those vessels upon the *Amélie*'s arrival in that port. The *Amélie* arrived on May 18, and her cargo was distributed among several American and Bermudian vessels and immediately sent out again.[32]

Comte de Vergennes/Thérèse

The last ship loaded was the *Comte de Vergennes*. While Beaumarchais thought the name was a good omen for a superb cargo, he realized that the English might make the connection between the name and the use of the ship, so he asked the Comte de Vergennes if he wanted the vessel renamed. Even though it was hard for Beaumarchais to do so, the vessel was renamed *Thérèse* before April 1, 1777. She set sail from Mindin (opposite Saint-Nazaire), on the estuary of the Loire, on April 26, 1777, after many obstacles and delays.

The ship waited for two mail deliveries from the Paris post office, in spite of Beaumarchais's precautions and recommendations. He suspected that everything was opened and copied, delaying the packages from Monday to Friday. The ship set sail without its letters, after waiting for them for four days and having risked the weather 10 times. He complained that those who received the ship would not know what use to make of its cargo, and the ship which carried the papers of the first one may be delayed three months or it may go under.[33]

The *Thérèse* carried between 60,000 and 70,000 livres of goods, which the American commissioners purchased, in addition to Beaumarchais's cargo. Everyone agreed that she should sail to St. Domingue instead of Boston. This would be the safest route at this time of year, despite the much longer time for the goods to arrive on the Continent. She would also have seven officers and two servants as passengers. Although her cargo manifest showed a large quantity of cordage, sailcloth, and anchors which were consigned to Mr. Carabasse, Benjamin Franklin noted that she carried stores for fitting out two 36-gun frigates. He wrote to John Jay, President of Congress, on October 4, 1779, more than two years after the arrival of *Thérèse* at St. Domingue to tell him that he learned that the naval stores had never been called for and were still in Carabasse's warehouses. He suspected that due to "the miscarriage of Letters the Navy Board never heard of those Goods being there."[34]

Marquis de Chalotais

The frigate *Marquis de Chalotais* sprang a leak and damaged her rudder in a storm after leaving Hispaniola. She put into Charleston, South Carolina, for repairs on May 4, 1777, accompanied by three other French ships.[35]

Heureux/Flamand

The 400-ton, 80-man *Heureux* remained in Marseilles until Beaumarchais could obtain more money. She would mount 18 guns, though pierced for 20. She would sail for Martinique, but her real destination was New England or any safe port in North America. She would carry a double commission: an ostensible and a secret one. The ship would have a French captain (Pierre Landais) in the service of the Congress, and one with a commission from the Congress (Joseph Hynson) who would have the direction of the expedition. But it would be several weeks before they could be gotten ready for sea.[36]

Heureux met with a number of delays and finally sailed on June 3, 1777 with a cargo of "44 Barrels of oil, 19 Slabs of marble, 5000 Packages of figs, 25 thousand of Soap and 2000 olives to put in oil." Actually the cargo included:

- 40 Swedish-style bronze cannons, 4-pounders, with their equipment and carriages;
- 20 bronze mortars with their equipment;
- 20,000 4-pound balls;

- 3,000 grenades;
- 3,000 bombs;
- 20,000 pounds of gunpowder
- 150,000 flints;
- 25,000 pounds of lead in ball;
- 6,000 muskets with their bayonets;
- 1,000 officers' muskets with their bayonets;
- 500 pairs of pistols, trimmed in copper.[37]

Heureux was forced to unload and reload at Marseilles. She was renamed the *Flamand* and sailed on September 26, 1777 with 25,000 muskets, saltpeter, etc. "for the French Islands." She passed the Straits of Gibraltar on October 1 and arrived at Portsmouth, New Hampshire, on December 1, 1777, after a fatiguing passage of 66 days. The *Flamand* also brought Beaumarchais's secretary, Jean-Baptiste-Lazare Théveneau de Francy, to America to manage Beaumarchais's affairs with Congress. He returned to France in the spring of 1780. Friedrich Wilhelm Ludolf Gerhard Augustin Baron von Steuben, General Quarter Master Lieutenant, and Aide-de-Camp to his Prussian Majesty, and two other officers were also on board. The American commissioners also hoped to send between 20,000 and 30,000 suits of clothes before the winter.[38]

News of the arrival of *Heureux* reached Valley Forge on December 21, two days after the Continental Army established its camp there, greatly improving morale.

Marie Catherine

The schooner *Marie Catherine* (also referred to as *Marie* and *Catherine*) sailed from Dunkirk for Martinique on July 12, 1777. She had a cargo of 34 bronze 4-pounders with their carriages, 16,872 cannonballs, and 2,700 hand grenades. The cargo was reshipped to America early in September. Sixty-six large bronze cannons (from 12- to 32-pounders) and about 60 fieldpieces (4-pounders) with their carriages and accoutrements were also shipped from Dunkirk about the same time.[39]

William Bingham shipped the remainder of the *Marie Catherine*'s cargo on board Captain Lamb's brigantine *Irish Gimblet*. The vessel was bound to New London where the cargo was to be delivered to Nathaniel Shaw, Jr., Continental Agent for the State of Connecticut.[40]

Hippopotame/Fier Roderigue

Captain Montault's *Fier Roderigue* was the former French Navy 30-gun frigate *Hippopotame*. The *Hippopotame* was preparing to sail from Rochefort on September

15, 1777 to transport 700 or 800 militiamen to St. Domingue. She would carry no arms or ammunition and her cargo "consists of soldiers' ready-made clothing, of cloth and blankets, etc." Yet, she mounted a total of 100 bronze cannons (four 33-pounders, 24 24-pounders, 20 16-pounders, 12 8-pounders, and 40 4-pounders).[41]

Beaumarchais conceived a plan to have one or two American privateers sent to the latitude of St. Domingue. One of them would send a shallop to Cap François or signal with a white pennant and three cannon shots. Mr. Carabasse would then go on board with Captain Montault, of the *Fier Roderigue*. They would arrange for the American vessel to capture the *Fier Roderigue*, under some pretext, and take her away. Captain Montault would protest and write a complaint to Congress which would publicly disown the cruiser and free the *Fier Roderigue*. In the meantime, the cargo would be landed, the ship filled with tobacco and promptly sent back to France.[42]

All of the vessels sent by Roderigue Hortalez & Cie. reached their destinations. Only the *Seine* was captured with a small portion of her cargo.

The supplies from France helped the Continental Army secure its victory at Saratoga. That victory convinced France that the Americans, with adequate support, could defeat the British. It also induced France to join the war as America's first ally and King Louis XVI pressured Spain to also support the Americans.

France enters the war

King Louis XVI signed the Treaty of Amity and Commerce and the Treaty of Alliance on February 6, 1778. Beaumarchais was not part of the negotiations nor was he even informed of them. Once France entered the war, there was no longer any need for the services of Roderigue Hortalez & Cie. but Beaumarchais continued his support. On December 6, 1778, he sent the cruiser *Zephir* with news that he was ready to launch a fleet of 12 vessels under the leadership of the *Fier Roderigue*. That fleet would contain between 5,000 and 6,000 tons of military supplies.[43]

However, Beaumarchais faced bankruptcy and needed reimbursement for the goods he had shipped. He wrote to Congress on March 23, 1778 to identify himself as the person they knew only as Roderigue Hortalez. He told them that, long before Mr. Deane arrived in France, he planned to establish a commercial house to supply munitions and merchandise for clothing the American troops. He then proceeded to describe all the services he provided to support the American cause.[44]

A full year later, on June 5, 1779, Congress considered various invoices from Beaumarchais totaling 4,547,593 livres (about £198,957) for cargoes shipped. These did not include commission or insurance but did include interest to March 31, 1779:

Amphitrite,	782,827 livres;
Seine,	687,515;
Mercure,	700,594;
Amélie,	230,174;
Thérèse,	985,317;
Mère Bobie,	66,750;
Marie Catherine,	148,075;
Flamand,	545,416.

They also included 115,000 livres for Mr. Carabasse, at Cap François, for purchasing Bermudian boats, 141,400 for demurrage (charges incurred by delays in loading and unloading vessels), and 144,525 advanced to Silas Deane.[45]

Congress refused to pay the invoices. Beaumarchais made several unsuccessful appeals. The matter was finally closed in 1837 when Beaumarchais's heirs received 800,000 francs, which only covered the cost of the cargo of the first shipment.

CHAPTER 2

Outfitters and Suppliers

The rebellious colonies knew they could not defeat Britain on their own. Most of the weapons were manufactured in Europe. The British Army was confiscating gunpowder in all the colonies. The Americans sought help from European countries, particularly Britain's arch-enemies, France and Spain. While Beaumarchais was busy setting up a front to channel covert government funds from France and Spain to the American colonies, the colonists were already dealing with European agents by the end of 1775, particularly those in France. They preferred firms in Nantes and Bordeaux which were a distance from the English Channel. Nantes was in the western center of France and accessible to all parts of the country by rivers. Bordeaux was the southernmost port on the Atlantic and thus, the farthest French port from the English Channel.

Shipments of arms and powder could be loaded secretly, at night, aboard vessels bound for North America at these ports. They would then be sent to the West Indies where they were transferred to smaller vessels bound to the United Colonies to circumvent the royal prohibitions.

> Lisbon and Nantes soon became favored transshipment ports for contraband munitions, since they already furnished arms for the slaving trade to Portuguese and French plantations in Brazil and Saint-Domingue. Slaving was an incredibly violent trade that annually absorbed thousands of the guns manufactured in Liège and other centers, many of which were then traded as currency for the slaves themselves. With so many arms being loaded onto so many ships, it was fairly easy to smuggle guns and powder onto American-bound vessels.[1]

Jean Peltier-Dudoyer and Jean Joseph Carrier (Carié) de Montieu

Beaumarchais's preferred supplier was Jean Peltier-Dudoyer who had worked with Jean Joseph Carrier (Carié) de Montieu, an arms manufacturer who employed more than 1,100 workmen at St. Etienne. Saint-Étienne, near Lyon, was the largest of the three manufacturers of French muskets. The other two were Charleville and Maubeuge in the north. Saint-Étienne produced about 20,000 muskets per year, most of them the 1763 and 1766 models (69 caliber). Foundries run by the Maritz family in Lyon, Strasbourg, and Douai used advanced solid casting and boring techniques to produce standard infantry cannon, the most common of which were the 1732 and 1740 models of 4-pounders developed by Jean-Florent de Vallière.[2]

Montieu managed to obtain an exclusive right to manufacture arms for the French military in 1769, but his principal activity was the purchase of obsolete light arms from the government. By early October 1776, Montieu had promised Beaumarchais to ship 1,600 tons of supplies to America and to return with a cargo of like size "laden equally on account of the Congress… and of Messrs. Hortalez & Cie. for a fee of 200 livres per ton."[3] Peltier-Dudoyer would now act frequently as an agent for Roderigue Hortalez, and his name appears frequently in Benjamin Franklin's correspondence. He became the most important supplier at Nantes between 1778 and 1782.

Philippe Charles Jean Baptiste Tronson du Coudray, a leading figure in the French artillery, was on an inspection tour of France on September 18, 1776 when American envoy Silas Deane and Montieu were having dinner with Beaumarchais to finalize the terms of the contract that would ship 1,600 tons of surplus muskets, cannons, and other military supplies to America. Montieu then chartered a fleet of eight ships from the shipping firm of Jean Pelletier-Dudoyer. Montieu had often done business with the firm to transport his arms to the French colonies. Deane and Beaumarchais thought that the arms should also be accompanied by French officers who knew how to use them, but it was impossible for the French government to send commissioned officers to America and still maintain secrecy. So Deane, who had no authority to grant commissions, nevertheless granted them to officers who were not commissioned in European armies and who wanted to go to America, usually at their own expense.

Deane signed the contract with Roderigue Hortalez and Montieu on October 15 and the suppliers agreed to deliver the first shipments by the following month. Beaumarchais purchased the surplus muskets directly from Montieu. He also procured as many cannons from the royal arsenals as Coudray and the Minister of War would allow to be sent to America. Although the cannons were provided free, shipping costs would amount to more than the total price of the muskets.[4]

Beaumarchais advised Deane that, since he was a novice in France, he should "not attempt to buy cannons or other arms" except through him. Deane did not want to enter into a monopoly agreement and Vergennes was also wary of an arms monopoly. He suggested another source of military supplies to Deane: Beaumarchais's former boss Jacques-Donatien Le Ray de Chaumont.

Between 1771 and 1786, Peltier-Dudoyer outfitted some 45 vessels. They include: *Diligente* (1771), *Belle Nantaise* (1773), *Boynes* (1773), *Orage* (1773), *Amitié* (1775), *Amphitrite* (1776), *Andromède* (1776), *Anonyme* or *Anonime* (1776 or 1778), *Elizabeth* renamed *Franklin* (1777), *Fier Rodrigue* formerly *Hippopotame* (1777), *Mercure* (1777),[5] *Duc de Choiseul* (1778), *Duchesse de Choiseul* (1778),

Duc du Chatelet (1778), *Mouche* formerly *Montgomery* (1778), *Thérèse* formerly *Comte de Vergennes* (1778/1782), *Amphytrite* (1779), *Jeune Héloïse* (1779), *Pallas* (1779), *Union* (1779), *Zéphir* (1779), *Appolon* (1781), *Arlequin, Aventure, Belette, Belle Eugénie* (*Eugénie* or *Aimable-Eugénie,* named after Beaumarchais's daughter born January 5, 1777), *Bonhomme Richard* 1779), *Drake* (1779/1783), *Ménagère* (1781), *Petit Cousin* (1781), *Persée* (1781), *Comte d'Angevilliers, Comte d'Estaing, Dauphin, Duchesse de Gramont, Emilie, Flamand, Lyon, Majestueux, Marquis de la Chalotais,* and *Mars.* The British captured 13 of his vessels, including *Zéphir* which Peltier-Dudoyer armed to accompany *Fier Rodrigue.*[6]

Roderigue Hortalez & Cie. chartered two more ships in February 1777. *Romain,* renamed *Amélie,* and Captain Joseph Varage's 14-gun ship *Hardi* which carried a cargo of 18 cannon, three mortars, and 3,263 muskets with bayonets and gunpowder supplied by Montieu.[7]

The American commissioners contracted with Montieu on June 6, 1777 to supply 10,000 uniform coats, half in royal blue cloth and the rest in brown cloth with red facings and trimmings, white buttons, vests and breeches of white double milled cloth at the rate of 38 livres per complete suit; 100,000 pounds of red copper for casting cannon; 20,000 pounds of fine English tin; 200 tin cases or boxes; 22,000 pounds of copper in sheets and in nails suitable for sheathing ships; 4,000,000 flints; 4,255 soldiers' muskets and bayonets; 8,000 soldiers' muskets and bayonets similar to those of the French infantry; 10,000 pairs of knitted woolen stockings to be delivered to Jonathan Williams, Jr. by the following September. Williams also ordered, from Montieu, copper, flints, and "All the Arms and Furniture repaired and unrepaired in the magazine" before July 9, 1778.

Paul Wentworth wrote to the Earl of Suffolk on July 17, 1777, advising him that the government of France had two ships at Marseilles, one bound for South Carolina and the other for Congress under the command of Captain Landais. Mr. Montieu's ship *Anonime* was ready to sail from Nantes with 100,000 pounds of copper and 30,000 stand of arms (10,000 by Beaumarchais and 12,000 by Montieu). The vessel would also bring Charles François Sévelinges, Marquis de Brétigny, and 13 officers along with arms and clothing for a corps of German troops he intended to raise for the congressional service. Two more ships were ready to sail for Le Havre with linen, clothing, lead, steel, and other materiel. Negotiations for another ship were also under way with Mr. Holker at Rouen, who supplied the means to procure 30,000 suits of clothing for laborers and had an order for 150,000 pounds of brass to be shipped at Marseilles. He expected to soon receive an order for a quantity of sail cloth, cordage, anchors, etc. for three ships of the line.

James Van Zandt, alias George Lupton, wrote to William Eden on August 20, 1777 that French merchants at Paris were planning to send five 40-gun and two 64-gun ships to America in September or October. These vessels, owned by Desegray, Beaugeard fils et Cie., would sail from Lorient and Brest, respectively. They would be cleared out for the East Indies but would proceed directly to America where their cargo would be unloaded.

Lord Stormont wrote to Lord Weymouth on December 3, 1777 to report that he had reason to believe that "a vast quantity of arms purchased for the use of the Rebels, is going to be shipped on board of the American Privateers [*Raleigh* and *Alfred*] that are at Nantes and L'Orient." He estimated the quantity to be no fewer than 50,000 stands of arms but acknowledged that he had no "direct positive proof what share m. de Montieu has in all this." In another letter, dated the same day, he further exaggerated the number to 80,000 weapons.[8] The English lodged an official complaint to the French minister and demanded the vessels be unloaded. They were unloaded and, later, reloaded and sent to America.

Beaumarchais wrote to Montieu in Nantes in November 1778: "I noticed that your appetite is growing as you eat," because Montieu had added ships to the squadron. Beaumarchais admitted he was nervous about the tremendous outlay required by this fleet of at least one dozen ships that included the 300-ton *Aimable Suzanne*, the 196-ton *Zéphyr*, the 220-ton *Deux Hélènes*, the 350-ton *Thérèse*, the *Pérou*, and the *Comte de Sabran*. The ships were to sail in a convoy from Nantes to Martinique with flour and other provisions and some goods for sale in America. When the convoy arrived in the West Indies, the French governors there could purchase what they needed and the remainder would be sold on the open market. The fleet would then return to France with tobacco and other goods while the fully armed *Fier Roderigue* would escort some of the ships to the Chesapeake Bay and then back to France.

Beaumarchais's financial resources were stretched to the limit and he was concerned that the slowness of the returns to France could create great difficulties for him. Meanwhile, Montieu ordered a new ship, the 700-ton, 100-man *Franklin* which delivered 32 cannons on February 3, 1779. He was also preparing for sea the 80-ton *Bonhomme Richard* and the 90-ton *Belette*.[9]

Jacques-Donatien Le Ray de Chaumont

Chaumont, now one of France's richest shipping magnates, had connections with Antoine Raymond Jean Gualbert Gabriel de Sartine, Comte d'Alby, the Minister of the Navy. He ensured that Chaumont received the lucrative contract to supply the colonies of Martinique and St. Domingue and finance the naval fleet in India. Deane met with Chaumont about the same time he was negotiating with Beaumarchais. He requested 50 tons of saltpeter, 200 tons of gunpowder, and a load of bronze 12-pounders on credit against a future payment in tobacco.[10]

Congress ordered 40,000 uniforms in February 1777 and cloth to make another 40,000. The American commissioners in France acknowledged the order in late April and agreed with Chaumont, on April 27, to furnish 10,000 uniforms. Chaumont had learned, during his long career, which firms could be relied upon, and he guided the Americans accordingly. He steered the contract for the manufacture of the Continental Army uniforms to the textile firm of Sabatier Fils et Després on May 9. Jean Holker, another textile merchant and one of the inspectors general of French manufacturers, would supervise the quality. Half of the uniforms would be blue and the other half brown at a cost of 365,373 livres tournois. The clothiers were to deliver 2,000 uniforms on July 1, 3,000 on August 1, and 5,000 on September 1. Franklin and Deane paid Sabatier 10,000 livres in early June and ratified and signed the contract on the 12th.

Holker made another agreement for an additional 5,000 uniforms with Sabatier on August 10. Half of these would be blue and the other half brown, all with red facings, linings, and collars. Sabatier delivered the 15,000 uniforms to Deane between July 30 and October 25. Another order for 10,000 uniforms was signed on August 6. A 60-gun ship at Rochefort and an East Indiaman, pierced for 60 guns, and belonging to Mr. Chaumont, Holker, Sabatier, etc. at Lorient were being loaded with merchandise in early October. Chaumont also sent 10 vessels loaded with salt in addition to the several vessels of clothing and other merchandise. Montieu and associates shipped six or eight valuable cargoes, Mr. Buat of St. Malo and his associates (the Comte de Vaux, the Vicount Narbonne Pelet) sent four, Mr. Jauge of Bordeaux shipped 10, and Mr. Basmarein also shipped several cargoes.[11]

Chaumont also solved the problem of financing these purchases by introducing Franklin to his long-time business associate and neighbor in Passy, Rodolphe-Ferdinand Grand. Grand was part of a Swiss family of bankers that extended from Amsterdam to Cadiz and was the Paris agent of the bank Horneca, Fizeaux et Compagnie, based in Amsterdam. The bank was very experienced in freight insurance and managing French government bonds. Grand was also a longtime confidant of Vergennes, so he quickly gained Franklin's trust. Franklin never let any other European bank touch the financial affairs of the Continental Congress, despite later protests by his fellow commissioners and Robert Morris.[12]

Chaumont submitted a bill to Franklin for repairs to the packet the *Mère Bobie* on June 12, 1777 and helped John Paul Jones who repeated his desire for a ship on November 1, 1778. Jones arrived at Lorient on the evening of December 6, 1778. Within the week, he told Chaumont to arrange the purchase of the *Duc de Duras*. Negotiations took almost two months. Sartine wrote the official letter on February 4, notifying Jones that the king was giving Jones command of the ship with orders for her complete armament and consented to change the name to *Bonhomme Richard*.

On January 1, 1779, Franklin authorized payment of two bills of exchange for 50,000 and 20,000 livres, which Jonathan Williams, Jr. charged to Chaumont who sent Franklin a promissory note for 30,000 livres to be paid on the 30th of the month and another note for 20,000 livres to be paid at the end of February.[13]

On January 12, 1779, Williams reported that one of his richest ships blew up with her cargo and more than 100 men. Chaumont lost more than 100,000 livres in this accident and Mr. Montieu probably lost more than twice as much.[14]

By late September 1780, clothing for the troops of the Continental Army was at Lorient, Chaumont had obtained cloth for the officers' uniforms, and John Bondfield[15] had promised to supply cannon. Desegray, Beaugeard fils et Cie., at St. Malo, had been requested to dispatch saltpeter, which was subject to special provisions when exported by anyone but the king. Franklin appealed to his old friend and fellow scientist, Antoine-Laurent Lavoisier, *régisseur des poudres et salpêtres* and son-in-law of Jacques Paulze, a prominent member of the Farmers General,[16] to cut through the red tape and secure the necessary passport.[17]

Franklin wrote to Bondfield on September 11, 1780, inquiring about the cannons he had procured to be cast and if he still had any of them, or any other military stores belonging to the Congress. He requested that the materiel be shipped immediately on board the *Marquis de la Fayette*, formerly called the *Breton*. Less than a week later (September 16), Chaumont informed Franklin that Bondfield had no 12-pound cannons but only 28 18-pounders and 28 24-pounders ready to deliver. He requested Franklin's order to send the 18-pounders to replace those he had delivered to Lorient to ballast the *Alliance*. Bondfield reported on September 19 that he had 56 cannons (28 18-pounders and 28 24-pounders) to load aboard the *Marquis de la Fayette*.[18]

Jonathan Williams, Jr. ordered uniforms for soldiers and officers amounting to 25,551 livres 19 sous from Chaumont in October 1780. Chaumont ordered the soldiers' uniforms but the officers' uniforms were purchased on Mr. Holker's account.[19]

Sabatier Fils & Després

The Americans began doing business with the clothiers Sabatier Fils & Després (or Desprez) in Montpellier in mid-December 1776 to purchase clothing for Washington's troops. The transaction was recorded in the Sabatier Fils & Despres "Cloathing Department" folio, the first of 19 needed for that line item. Another volume for "Prisoners, American" contains 31 folios for that line item. An entry in one of their documents records the sale of 15,000 uniforms in July 1777 and other clothing from July 30 to October 25, 1777 totaling £3,529 18d 6p. The Americans also purchased furniture for the merchant ship *Marquis de Lafayette* for £134,000.[20]

Montaudouin Frères

Beaumarchais also did business with the Montaudouin family, which had been established in Nantes for almost a century (1694–1792). They would dispatch perhaps as many as 450 ships across the Atlantic. Montaudouin Frères was run by Arthur Montaudouin and his brother Jean-Gabriel (or Jean Montaudouin de la Touche) who was a consul of Nantes, an intellectual and author of economic treatises, a member of the Academy of Sciences and of the Academy of Fine Arts, Sciences and Arts of La Rochelle, and a friend of Voltaire. (He even named one of his vessels *Voltaire* in 1774.)

The Montaudouin brothers were also associated with Jonathan Williams and Jean Daniel Schweighauser in the sale of prizes. The leading slave-trading firm in Nantes, they used their trade connections in Philadelphia "to conceal covert arms shipments, aboard ships whose names like *Jean-Jacques* (after Rousseau) and *Contrat Social* (a reference to Rousseau's political rights manifesto, *The Social Contract*) revealed the family's Enlightenment leanings toward the American cause."[21]

Beaumarchais wrote a letter from London on April 16, 1776. It arrived at Riverside on Sunday the 21st, the day before the decision to give secret aid to the Americans. It said that Captain William Meston's 250-ton snow *Dickinson* sailed from Philadelphia under orders from Congress on March 1. The captain, according to instructions, opened his orders only after they were at sea. He was instructed to sail to Nantes to pick up a cargo of arms, gunpowder, ammunition, and military stores from the house of Montaudouin Frères. Aware that such purchases were illegal, the mate and crew mutinied, overpowered Captain Meston, took command of the snow, and took her to Bristol, England—the first British port where they could moor—where they turned over to the authorities the letters and papers which were on board.[22]

The *Dickinson*'s cargo consisted of 2,221 barrels of flour, 260 boxes of spermaceti candles, 13 casks, one bag of beeswax, and 5,600 barrel staves. The cargo was valued at nearly 6,000 livres and the vessel was worth more than 1,500 livres. She was instructed to load: 1,500 stands of arms, with bayonets and steel ramrods; 15 tons of good gunpowder or the same quantity of saltpeter, with 15 pounds of sulfur to every hundred pounds of saltpeter. If these items were not available, the *Dickinson* was to return with specie from the sale of her cargo for the use of the Continental Army.

Captain Thomas Rawlins's ship *Sally,* Captain Robert Collins's *Neptune,* Captain Checky's *Aurora,* three brigs (under captains Montgomery, Bethel, and Martin), and many other vessels sailed at the same time as the *Dickinson.* They were all bound for different ports in France and on the same business. As the *Dickinson* was a very swift sailer, she left them soon after they put to sea. The Comte de Vergennes received a letter from the Montaudouin brothers on May 2, 1776 disclaiming knowledge of the *Dickinson*'s mission.[23]

The same day that the *Dickinson* departed Philadelphia, a French vessel laden with powder, ball, and small arms, arrived there.[24]

Pliarne, Penet & Cie. and Jean Jacques Barthélémy Gruel

Prior to 1778, Congress preferred to deal with Pliarne, Penet & Cie. in order to obtain all arms and supplies for the colonies. Emanuel Michael Pliarne and Pierre Penet (most of the documents refer to them simply as the "two French men") arrived in Providence, Rhode Island, from the West Indies in Captain William Rhodes's sloop *Victory* on December 10, 1775. They made contracts with Nicholas and John Brown and received a letter from Governor Cook of Rhode Island, who wrote, "M. Penet comes extremely well recommended to our committee for providing powder from a merchant of character at the Cape (Cape François)."[25]

Pliarne and Penet met with General Washington during the siege of Boston and presented him with an elaborate plan for supplying the colonies with powder and arms. They declared that these stores were available in France and that no one was better equipped than they to get muskets and ammunition into the hands of the American soldiers. General Washington, not thinking he was authorized to make a contract with them, sent them to Philadelphia to make their proposal before the Secret Committee of the Continental Congress.[26]

The Secret Committee of Trade handled dealings with private merchants, while the Committee of Secret Correspondence channeled all direct assistance from the French and Spanish governments. The five committee members, including Benjamin Franklin and John Jay, met with Julien Alexandre Archard de Bonvouloir, a secret French envoy to the American colonies, in one of the upstairs rooms of Carpenters Hall. He was with Francis Daymon, a French émigré serving as librarian for Franklin's Library Company of Philadelphia. Daymon knew Bonvouloir from his earlier voyage and would translate for them. John Jay described Bonvouloir as an "elderly lame gentleman" even though he was only 26 and four years younger than Jay.

During this and two subsequent night meetings, Bonvouloir assured the committee members that if they wanted arms, ammunition, or money "[they] shall have it" and that he would pass along the requests to the French government. He transmitted the requests to Adrien-Louis de Bonnières, duc de Guines, by writing in the blank spaces of an innocent-looking business letter with an invisible milk-based ink. De Guines would heat the message over a chafing dish to make the writing appear. De Guines had just been recalled to Paris, so, as one of his last acts, he recopied the secret report and gave it directly to Vergennes.[27]

Mr. Penet, born in Alsace, the son of an artillery store keeper, embarked for France on February 8, 1776 after Congress signed a contract for Pliarne, Penet & Cie. to supply 15,000 stands of arms and powder. He found the means to collect a considerable quantity of stores, part of which he had shipped. Meanwhile, Silas Deane arrived in France with instructions to apply for arms and clothes for 25,000 men, and for 100 field pieces, with ammunition and stores in proportion. He hoped to obtain these items directly from the French Ministry, but they evaded the request, forcing Deane to try to procure them through the agency of Mr. Chaumont and Mr. Beaumarchais.[28]

Chaumont provided massive amounts of his own money to purchase weapons, supplies, and clothing for the Continental Army. He was asked by the American government to take charge of the equipment and management of the combined French and American naval fleet. He worked closely with Admiral Jean Baptiste Charles Henri Hector d'Estaing, the commander of the French fleet.[29]

Providence, Rhode Island, merchants John and Nicholas Brown sent three vessels to Europe in 1776 to obtain materials under government contract. The first was sent to Bilbao, Spain, but eventually landed her cargo at Bordeaux, France. The second, Captain Joshua Bunker's schooner *William,* sailed to Nantes to the care of Pliarne, Penet & Cie. with orders dated April 12, 1776. After discharging her cargo of oil, spermaceti, candles, codfish, and staves, she was to load powder, sulfur, saltpeter, arms, gunlocks, Russia duck (a fine white linen canvas), and various kinds of cloth or blankets in that order. Captain Gideon Crawford's brigantine *Happy Return* sailed for Nantes on April 24 with a cargo of oil and spermaceti. The Browns also dispatched Captain Samuel Avery's 112-ton schooner *Sally* shortly afterward. She sailed on May 23 with a large quantity of oil and spermaceti. The Browns hoped that the oil could be exchanged at Nantes for about 6,000 blankets and some 6,000 yards of broadcloth.[30]

The *Happy Return* brought, from Nantes, 1,820 yards of brown cloth, 1,810 yards of blue cloth, and small amounts of yellow, green, red, white, gray, and dove cloth for facing the uniforms of brown and blue. She also brought 96 pigs of lead, 12 boxes of sulfur, a small quantity of lead "bullets," 1,500 gunflints, 40 dozen blankets, and some salt.[31]

The sloop *Liberty*, which the Brown brothers dispatched on their own account, was lost with all her cargo on her return voyage from Nantes.[32]

The *Sally's* cargo consisted chiefly of brown and blue cloth, with small amounts of yellow, green, and white facing. The total was about 2,400 ells (an "ell" is equivalent to around six hand breadths). She also carried a quantity of salt. Her return cargo included 6 tons of lead, 200 stands of arms such as those used by the French infantry, 500 double-bridled locks, each with its bayonet, scabbard, and steel ramrod, and 5,000 pounds of gunpowder. Pliarne & Penet also paid for books, utensils, and instruments for the Chevalier de Vraicourt, engineer and officer of artillery and son of the Count of Vraicourt, Director-General of Engineers, which they shipped on the *Sally.* The *Happy Return* and the *Sally* arrived from Nantes late in 1776. The *William* was seized by the British on her homeward-bound journey. Her cargo, loaded at Bordeaux, consisted of 30,000 pounds of lead, 110 pieces of Russia duck, about 5,500 ells of "Bretaigne" cloth, 500 bayonets, a large quantity of nails, and 18,000 pounds of powder.[33]

Dr. Jacques Barbeu-Dubourg, appointed to act as secret intermediary to the Americans, wrote to Benjamin Franklin on June 10, 1776 informing him that he received a promise from Mr. de la Tuillerie, representative of an arms manufacturer, to deliver 15,000 muskets, model 1763, for the infantry. He also received a letter from Mr. Penet about procuring 12 6-pound cannons for the colony of Virginia. He said he would try to find some but this caliber was not common in France.[34]

Pliarne & Penet wrote to Silas Deane on July 30, 1776 offering 20,000 wool blankets at a price of four to six livres each. They also noted that they made arrangements for 30,000 muskets for 12 or 13 livres each. They said that these muskets were similar to those which they had sent to Congress and were quite reliable. They also advised Deane to beware the Irish and Scottish firms in Bordeaux and elsewhere because they charged twice as much for inferior weapons. Pliarne & Penet also claimed that they were expecting six private vessels from the northern colonies which they would fill with military supplies.[35]

Comparing the cargoes with the terms of the contracts shows that the four voyages yielded only 9 of the 36 tons of gunpowder authorized by the Committee of Secrecy. The vessels brought approximately one half of the 30 tons of lead, 40 dozen of the 10,000 "good striped blankets," and about 300 of the 1,000 bolts of Russia duck which the contract called for. None of the 1,000 stands of "good arms" and the 1,000 double-bridled gun locks was forthcoming, although 500 bayonets appeared. Of the sulfur and saltpeter to be imported in default of gunpowder, only a small amount of sulfur was shipped. On the other hand, the ships brought somewhat more than the 10,000 yards of cloth mentioned in the contracts. The scarcity of military stores at St. Eustatius undoubtedly accounts for the *Polly*'s slender cargo. The low price of candles and oil, high duties on these articles, heavy interest charges, and other costs so reduced the net proceeds of the three cargoes sent to France that the funds were not sufficient to purchase all the goods stipulated in the contracts.[36]

Pierre Penet wrote to General Washington on August 3, 1776 to ask him to appoint him aide-de-camp. The general transmitted the request to Congress on October 7 and the brevet was granted on October 14. Pliarne & Penet also wrote to Benjamin Franklin on August 3 to advise him that they had shipped powder and muskets to the Brown brothers aboard the *Sally* and that they were ready to ship a cargo of muskets, saltpeter, powder, tin, and lead valued at more than 60,000 or 70,000 livres.[37]

Pliarne, Penet & Cie. wrote to the Secret Committee of the Province of New York, the President of the Virginia Council, and other state committees in October 1776, claiming that only they were able "to furnish you at demand with cannon and gunpowder, saltpeter, sulfur, lead, iron and brass Cannons of all sizes, muskets such as we have sent the Congress, being of the last mode for the Infantry of France, proved, well finished and perfected, with double bride [bridle] locks" at a cost of

12 to 22 livres each, "with bayonets and steel ramrods, and bores suitable for ball of fourteen or sixteen to the pound" and ammunition, cloth, clothing, blankets, and military supplies. They referred to their business with the Brown brothers and Congress.[38]

James Warren, President of the newly constituted Massachusetts Board of War, wrote to Jean Louis Poncet & Son (also associated with Jean Jacques Barthélémy Gruel, a prominent merchant in Nantes) at Bordeaux on December 3, 1776, requesting that "good effective Fire-Arms and Bayonets, such as are us'd in the King of France, his Army" be shipped aboard the *Montgomery.* If the muskets were unavailable, he specified other articles he wanted:

- Five hundred well made Gun Locks, with what the English call good Bridles—
- One hundred & fifty thousand good Flynts, cost 3 ½ to four Livres pr Thousand—
- Fifty pounds Borax purificata, cost in London about five shillings pr pound—
- Ten good Brass Cannon for Feildpeices carrying three pound Ball, if not too dear—

If any thing remains after these purchases, please to send it in good Ravens Duck fit for Soldiers Tents, it generally costs from 22/. to 27/. Sterling a peice of 38 yards 7/8 of a yard wide.[39]

Samuel Phillips Savage, President of the Massachusetts Board of War, wrote to Jacques Gruel & Co. a month later, on January 7, 1777, advising them that they entered into a contract with Mr. Pliarne to supply them with up to £80,000 of military supplies and other articles. They had sent Captain Nicholas Bartlett's brig *Penet* as the first vessel of their agreement with a cargo to sell in exchange for the desired goods. They promised to dispatch Joseph Chapman's ship *Versailles* a few days later loaded with logwood and mahogany.

The ships also included the following:

- 20,000 good firearms with bayonettes;
- 30 4- & 6-pound brass field pieces;
- 1,000 barrels of powder;
- 300,000 flints;
- 70,000 yards of wool for clothing;
- 132,000 yards of coarse linen for soldiers shirts;
- 40,000 pairs of shoes.[40]

Two months later, on March 14, 1777, the Massachusetts Board of War ordered Captain Jonathan Haraden of the Massachusetts Navy brig *Tyrannicide* and Captain John Fisk of the Massachusetts Navy brig *Massachusetts* to apply to Messrs. Jacques Gruel & Co. to "take in as many Arms & other warlike stores as you can conveniently stow, together with such Masters & Mariners of Vessels, fitted out by this Board & sold there, as you can accomodate, & return to Boston, or other safe port in this State immediately." He was also ordered not to chase any vessels or run any risk of being captured, as the articles he would bring back were of great importance for the defense of Massachusetts.[41]

Thomas Morris, half-brother of Robert Morris, the financier of the revolution, became associated with Pliarne, Penet & Cie. in 1777. They partnered with Jean Jacques Barthélémy Gruel, a prominent merchant in Nantes and owner of Captain Peter Young's slave ship the *Marie-Séraphique*. The company's office in Bordeaux was in the hands of Reculès de Basmarein & Raimbaux. The company recommended a Mr. Vanhammé, on June 4, 1777, as a man of many useful skills, among them a quick and effective way to make saltpeter. Mr. Pliarne died in 1778 and the firm of Pliarne, Penet & Compagnie dissolved. Mr. Penet then formed the new firm of Penet, d'Acosta & Compagnie.[42]

Penet, d'Acosta Frères had sold arms to Arthur Lee for Virginia. Lee wrote them on November 29, 1778 to procure a quantity of arms and military stores and to introduce Jacques Le Maire de Gimel, who was sent to France by the Virginia Congress to assist Lee in procuring arms and ammunition for Virginia. The letter also complained that the firm had promised goods by the end of September, but Lee had not yet seen a single article. The delay caused the state of Virginia to miss a favorable shipping opportunity and Lee demanded that the firm pay all damages. The firm responded on December 12, upholding their honor and challenging Lee's honesty. They argued that the articles were being manufactured as quickly as possible and offered the use of their own ship, the *Courier de l'Europe*, to transport the goods. However, Lee's temper caused several manufacturers to refuse dealing with him. Franklin could not rectify the situation and avoided meddling with Lee's affairs.

The American commissioners were distancing themselves from Jacques-Barthélemy Gruel, Benjamin Franklin's first host in France, perhaps because of his connection with Pierre Penet, whom they had come to distrust. Gruel wrote a note to Benjamin Franklin on Christmas day 1778. If it was an attempt at reconciliation, it did not have the desired effect. Gruel declared bankruptcy in the spring of 1780.[43]

Reculès de Basmarein & Raimbaux

Reculès de Basmarein & Raimbaux (Pierre-Jacques Reculès de Basmarein and his brother Pierre and le sieur Raimbaux), in Bordeaux, were also partners of Pliarne, Penet & Cie. They dispatched 10 ships to the West Indies between 1774 and 1777. They were in contact with Benjamin Franklin and Silas Deane since 1776 and became one of the first French outfitters to propose supplying vessels, at their own expense, to aid the Rebels. They had several packet boats built to carry their dispatches and offered their services to the Continental Congress to transport anything they wanted to consign to them. A packet would sail every four weeks.[44]

The first of Basmarein and Raimbaux's ships to sail carried a cargo that had cost $90,000 at Nantes and had sold for $240,000 in Boston. They sent a ship to America early in 1777 and, shortly afterward, Silas Deane purchased a whole magazine of stores and arms to send to America. It included 87,000 stands of arms, pikes, pistols, swords, and cutlasses. In the early stages of the war, eight of the nine cargoes shipped from France direct to American ports arrived safely. But the proportion of captures increased markedly as the British fleet became more vigilant. Between February 1777 and August 1778, the British captured 38 of 65 cargoes dispatched by Basmarein and Raimbaux, 27 of them taken while France was still officially neutral. They supplied provisions, arms, munitions, and other military supplies (uniforms, shoes, etc.) totaling more than 5.6 million livres tournois (more than $8,050,000). However, more than half of the ships never arrived at their destination. Four were shipwrecked in addition to the 38 captured by the British. The fleet of 65 ships, totaling 13,000 tons, were armed with 381 cannons and 1,550 crewmen.[45]

At the beginning of 1777, Basmarein and Raimbaux outfitted the *Duchesse de Mortemart* (450 tons, 18 guns, and 60 men under Captain Decamp), the *Meulan* (260 tons, six guns, and 30 men under Captain Laguehay), and the *Victoire* (220 tons, six guns, and 30 men under Captain Le Boursier). (The latter was dispatched in March 1777 and brought the Marquis de Lafayette and 14 other officers to America. Lafayette paid a deposit of a quarter of the 112,000 francs and the balance over the following 15 months.) These vessels were loaded with muskets and supplies for the insurgents, volunteers, and men ready for combat such as: Lafayette; de Kalb; Mottin de La Balme, founder of the American cavalry; and Charles François Adrien Le Paulmier, Chevalier d'Anmours, who was appointed the first French consul at Baltimore in 1778. The *Duchesse de Mortemart*'s cargo, valued at 448,464 livres 8 sous and 2 deniers, sold for 1,200,000 livres in America. The *Meulan*'s cargo was valued at 279,982 livres and 17 sous. Basmarein and Raimbaux also sent 46 other vessels from Bordeaux to North America before March 1779 and armed 13 ships in New England for the West Indies or France.[46]

Reculès de Basmarein & Raimbaux armed three privateers (*Vengeance*, the schooner *Cherche-Bruit*, and Captain Loisel's 750-ton, 32-gun and 335-man frigate *Marquise de La Fayette*) in 1778 to replenish its funds, depleted by debts and losses. Despite the auspicious beginnings of the four prizes taken by the 400-ton privateer *Vengeance*, the recovered funds did not compensate for the enormous financial losses which continued to mount. Unable to repay its creditors, the five-year-old company went bankrupt in 1779 and 35-year-old Reculès de Basmarein had to flee to England to escape his creditors. He died in misery in 1806 at a house near the Pantheon in Paris. Half a century later, in 1831, his heirs were still appealing to Congress for compensation.[47]

Jean-Jacques de Lafreté had business dealings with the firm of Reculès de Basmarein & Raimbaux. When they declared bankruptcy, Lafreté drew up a power of attorney on February 19, allowing Jean Holker, the French consul in Philadelphia, to do whatever was necessary to salvage his assets in America. Those assets were in the hands of Sieur Roulhac, Basmarein & Raimbaux's representative in America, but his whereabouts were unknown, even to his relatives.

Lafreté requested that Franklin write letters of recommendation on his behalf so he could ship some packages. Two copies of the document, dated Passy (a village outside Paris where Franklin resided), October 22, 1779, are at the Yale University Library.[48]

Jean Daniel Schweighauser

When France declared war against Britain in 1778, there was no longer any need to maintain secrecy in assisting in the American war effort. Several firms emerged to provide their services. Mr. Jean Daniel Schweighauser became the Continental Agent in France in 1778 and served as consul at Nantes at least until 1800. Together with his son-in-law, Pierre-Frédéric Dobrée, they ran the firm of Schweighauser. Dobrée continued the business after Schweighauser's death in 1781. He was appointed Vice-Consul for the United States of America at the port of Nantes in 1794.

Jonathan Williams, Jr. sold his gunsmith's business to Mr. Schweighauser in 1778 and Captain Charles Forest's brigantine *John* or *St. John* was sent to Schweighauser. The brigantine's cargo of flour and other products was to be exchanged for things of another nature to be sent to St Domingue.[49]

The American commissioners instructed Schweighauser, on September 13, 1778, to sell the cargo of the *Thérèse*, transmit an account, and hold the proceeds in abeyance until the settlement of Roderigue Hortalez & Cie.'s accounts with Congress. They also informed him that M. de Sartine had arranged for a cartel ship to come from England to Nantes and Lorient with American prisoners to exchange for all the British prisoners in France captured by American warships and privateers.[50]

The commissioners' action over the cargo of the *Thérèse* began a quarrel with Beaumarchais, similar to the dispute over the *Amphitrite*'s goods in the winter of 1777. At that time the commissioners ordered Schweighauser to sell the ship's cargo and informed Beaumarchais that the proceeds would be held. But they were too late. Beaumarchais's agent in Nantes, Peltier-Dudoyer, had already disposed of the goods. Schweighauser, encouraged by the commissioners, took legal measures against Peltier. When Beaumarchais returned to Paris after a three-month absence and learned of this action, he launched a bitter counter-attack and demanded payment of 269,400 livres, which were due him since October 1776.[51]

John Bondfield concluded agreements with Mr. Schweighauser for the public freight of the *Governor Livingston* and the *Chasseur* on November 12, 1778. As these two ships were very valuable and would not sail without a convoy, they proceeded to Paimboeuf to await a convoy. Schweighauser notified the American commissioners in mid-December that many vessels had been ready since the end of November to ship their order and were still awaiting a convoy. A letter from the Minister of the Marine indicated that an escort would not go beyond Cape Finisterre. Schweighauser replied that a convoy that only went that far was not worth his attention.[52]

The American commissioners instructed Cornic, Veuve Mathurin & fils, of Morlaix, on January 2, 1779, to have Schweighauser dispose of the cargo of Captain Benjamin Gunnison's brig *Morris*, and to settle any demand for disbursements on her account.[53]

Jonathan Williams, Jr. sent to Franklin Schweighauser's receipt for the arms magazine on January 23, 1779 and noted that he awaited a further receipt from him for the remainder of the gunstocks to allow Williams to pay the man who repaired them.[54]

Benjamin Franklin instructed Schweighauser on February 17, 1779, to comply with the Orders of the Navy Board, respecting the fitting of the *Alliance* for sea but cautioned him not to furnish more than is absolutely necessary, as the captains of frigates were wont to demand extravagantly. He also accepted Schweighauser's bills for 30,000 livres.[55]

Schweighauser sent Franklin another bill, dated February 18, 1779, for 58,407 livres 14 s. 0 d. as the balance of his account and enclosed an invoice for 300 hogsheads of tobacco, which arrived in the *Bergère*.[56]

Captain Landais acted against Franklin's positive and repeated orders in making purchases for the *Alliance*, also disregarding Schweighauser and Puchelberg & Cie. This created a number of problems for everyone involved. Captain Landais also intimidated suppliers to the point that they dared not refuse him.

When Schweighauser presented Franklin with bills for payment, Franklin refused to pay them because they lacked significant details. They included:

- 1,551 livres to Arnous, a timber merchant, for sundries, not mentioning what these sundries were, nor the price;
- 1,194 livres. 14. 6. to La Rivière (Jean-Baptiste Rivière, Chargé d'affaires for Saxony in Paris?), for rum, flour, butter, etc. with no mention of quantity or price;
- 1,158 livres.16. 0 to Beauvais (Louis-Marie-Daniel de Beauvais), a grocer, not even saying for what goods;
- 2,650 livres to Blodget (Nathan Blodget, Purser on the *Alliance*), for shirts with no mention of the number or price;

- 1,673 livres. 5. 0. also to Blodget for linen jackets and stockings with no mention of the quantity or number or rates.

Most of the articles may have been for specimens only and many probably were unnecessary. Franklin also complained that Schweighauser was charging a 5 percent commission when Franklin thought it should be 2½ percent.[57]

The American Commissioners instructed Jonathan Williams, Jr. on July 10, 1778, to order any goods available, including 63 barrels of beef, to be delivered to Mr. Schweighauser.[58]

Puchelberg & Cie.

Jean-Daniel Schweighauser appointed the Lorient merchant firm Puchelberg & Cie. to oversee American affairs there in 1778. Puchelberg handled a number of prizes for Mr. Schweighauser's account. Captain S. Tucker's frigate *Boston* arrived at Lorient on July 2, 1778 after capturing four prizes. He brought three to Mr. Schweighauser (Puchelberg) at Lorient and was astonished to have to deal with someone who spoke no English. He would have preferred to work with James Moylan, who told Tucker that he would furnish whatever he needed until he received instructions from the American Commissioners.[59]

Captain Tucker sold the three prizes with cargoes of fish to Mr. Puchelberg, who advised him of the high duty. Consequently, Tucker permitted the sale of the fish and the three vessels for 30,000 livres, a sum far below their true value had provisions of the treaty with France been observed. Captain Tucker would then load the *Boston* with whatever he could take, particularly as much lead as he could carry and which Schweighauser could supply.[60]

Puchelberg primarily handled prizes, leaving Moylan, the American agent in Lorient, to deal with prisoners. However, the firm occasionally arranged for prisoner exchanges, particularly those brought in by the *Black Prince*. Benjamin Franklin explained the terms of the prisoner exchange arranged with Puchelberg & Cie. in a letter to William Hodgson on February 26, 1780. He further explained to Hodgson on April 11 that he had sent the prisoners in exchange for the Frenchmen brought by the *Happy Return*, on the understanding that France would furnish prisoners for the next British–American cartel.[61]

Puchelberg & Cie. outfitted the American frigate *Alliance*, so the officers and crew authorized Puchelberg as their lawful attorneys and agents to receive all the money due to them for their prizes. Several officers needed money and applied to Puchelberg for it before the allotment of the prize money. The officers of the brigs *Fortune* and *Mayflower* did likewise in June for their part of the prize ships *Serapis* and *Countess of Scarborough*.[62]

Berubé de Costentin

Schweighauser appointed Berubé de Costentin to take care of the American vessels and prizes at Brest and requested instructions on August 24, 1778 about what to do with 140–150 prisoners taken on the *Patience* by the frigate *Ranger* and jailed at Brest for several months. When the *Patience* left in company with the *Providence* and the *Boston*, these prisoners were left under a small guard which wasn't posted regularly. Some of these prisoners revolted and would have captured another ship anchored near them in the harbor had not another nearby ship of the king come to her assistance.[63]

Desegray, Beaugeard fils

The firm of Desegray, Beaugeard fils & Cie. (Pierre-Marin Beaugeard) had long been known to the American commissioners who placed an order with them on July 9, 1778 to deliver 1,520 bags of India saltpeter weighing 216,475 pounds to Mr. Schweighauser to be shipped to America as soon as possible. However, Mr. Schweighauser did not have an opportunity of doing it conveniently, so Mr. Desegray offered one of his ships to take it at Lorient if it could be forwarded there by land as soon as possible.[64]

The ship was already being loaded by October 29, 1780 and the longshoremen were loading seven wagons with 263 bags of saltpeter with lead. They hoped to continue loading the rest of the 1,520 bags as more wagons arrived. They had loaded nine wagons (41,000 pounds) by October 31 when a letter from Gourlade & Moylan forced them to suspend the expedition by November 2 due to complaints from the Farmers General.[65]

Mr. Desegray was so impressed with a Mr. Van Zandt,[66] who was posing as an American businessman, that he proposed a joint shipping venture and offered to send the agent to any port he pleased. Van Zandt left St. Malo promising to consider the offer. From there, he traveled to Rennes before returning to Paris in M. Girard's chaise.[67]

Jonathan Williams, Jr. wrote to Messrs Desegray & Co. at St. Malo on September 26, 1780 requesting them to send the saltpeter to Lorient as soon as possible, as it was intended to be used for ballast. He also notified Mr Schweighauser to send arms.[68]

Lavaysse & Cie.

Lavaysse, or La Vaysse, a merchant at Lorient, was an acquaintance of Jacques-Alexandre Gourlade. Forsters Frères, of Bordeaux, charged him with the advertising of Captain Röache's ship *Three Friends* from Dublin, which was brought to Lorient by Captain Landais of the American frigate *Alliance* in July 1779. Captain Landais caused the owner unnecessary delays in capturing her and, even worse, she sank in the harbor. Lavaysse requested that Captain Landais be ordered to restore the ship and its cargo in good condition and to pay for the repairs and to compensate the owners for the harm he caused.

In 1785, Lavaysse unsuccessfully attempted to join a firm headed by Gourlade, which obtained a passport for the ship *Jean Tarrade* to go to China. He then went into partnership with Schweighauser's former associate Puchelberg.[69]

John Diot & Co., Gourlade and Moylan and Samuel Petrie Pothonnier & Cie.

John Diot was formerly a clerk of John Torris but seems to have established his own company in Morlais before January 6, 1780, when Edward Macatter, commander of the *Black Princess*, came into Morlais harbor. He had captured the brig *Betzey*, loaded with beef and butter, in the road of Brest and the ship *Camden*, loaded with timber, in the road of Perros near Lanion. The *Camden* ran aground, but Diot expected to get her off. One prize of Captain Patrick Dowlin's privateer *Black Prince* arrived at Morlaix the previous week. She was the *James and Thomas*, from Dublin bound to London, with beef and butter. Diot represented the *Black Prince*'s owners and dealt with the prisoners.

Diot must have transferred the account to Gourlade and Moylan, who notified Benjamin Franklin, on January 19, 1780, of the arrival of the *Black Prince* and her prisoners. The prisoners were confined in the king's prisons until exchanged.[70]

Gourlade & Moylan is the commercial house formed by Jacques-Alexandre Gourlade and James Moylan around November 1778. John Bondfield, Amercian commercial agent at Bordeaux, certified on August 5, 1779 that the four 24-pounders he purchased on Benjamin Franklin's authority had arrived at Bordeaux and were to be forwarded to Lorient and consigned to Gourlade & Moylan in February 1780.[71]

When Captain Jones's *Alliance* arrived at Lorient on February 10, 1780, he applied to Gourlade & Moylan for repairs and to supply that ship with whatever she needed. Gourlade & Moylan were also to pay the wages due the surviving seamen and soldiers of the *Bonhomme Richard*. Samuel Petrie Pothonnier & Cie. also worked with Gourlade & Moylan to outfit the *Ariel*.[72]

Jean-Hans Delap

Jean-Hans Delap and Samuel Delap were partners in a Bordeaux firm that served as agents dealing with prizes taken by privateers. Lord Stormont protested to the Comte de Vergennes on December 25, 1777 that Mr. Delap "has found means to sell an English vessel captured by the rebels and taken to Bordeaux. He sold this vessel almost publicly with its entire cargo; and he openly says that he will sell similarly every English vessel which may be captured by our rebels and sent to him for that purpose."

Delap sent a remittance to Jonathan Williams, Jr. in mid-1778 and forwarded a request from Captain William Hill Sargeant for a letter of marque commission and pledged his firm "as Guarantee that no improper use will be made of same."[73]

Poreau, Mackenzie et Cie.

Taverne Demont Dhiver, burgomeister of Dunkerque, planned to outfit a brigantine under the command of the Comte de Maurepas with 14 4-pound cannons and wanted the firm of Poreau, Mackenzie et Cie. to do the work. He wrote to the American Commissioners on February 22, 1779 for two commissions: one for this vessel and one for a second vessel to sail under the authority of Congress.[74]

Mr. Cossoul, Leonard Jarvis and Russell, Cottin fils & Jauge, Fleury & Demadières, Tessier George & Co.

The Americans also did business with a Mr. Cossoul, from Nantes, who eventually went into partnership with Elkanah Watson and formed the firm of Watson & Cossoul. Jonathan Williams, Jr. ordered arms, cloth, and medicines from Holland, sabers and uniforms from Mr. Cossoul on June 10, 1780. Five days later, Cossoul wrote to Franklin about payment for several orders that provided no details. They include an order placed with Leonard Jarvis and Russell for $36 countersigned by the Deputy of Pennsylvania, two orders for $24 each countersigned by the Deputy of Rhode Island, one for $60, one for $30 and two for $24 countersigned by the Deputy of Massachusetts on order for Charles Chauncy, three for $18, and two for $12.[75]

Franklin had extensive dealings with the firm of Cottin fils & Jauge (Jean-Louis Cottin and Théodore Jauge) of Bordeaux. Franklin's son William Temple Franklin had a friendly relationship with Jauge. The firm had sent several vessels to North America since 1777 but many of them were captured. Théodore Jauge wrote to William Temple Franklin on July 4, 1778 to tell him that one of the vessels had anchored in Albemarle Sound and sent for a pilot who refused to come at any price. "The next day, when a frigate appeared, the crew cut their cables, ran aground, and escaped; their ship was looted and burned." The 300-ton vessel was lost with a rich cargo. Another vessel was taken in the Chesapeake and sent to New York. On June 19, 1782, he requested William Temple Franklin get his father to authorize five expeditions to America.[76]

The Orléans firm of Fleury & Demadières supplied wine to Benjamin Franklin between 1780 and 1783 and offered to sell cloth, stockings, and other articles of clothing at a good price. Tessier, a merchant at Cadillac sur Garonne, paid jail fees for imprisoned American sailors. He considered emigrating to America after the war. This man may be different from Tessier George & Co. to whom Captain John Patterson, of the brig *General Lee*, consigned a cargo of tobacco when he arrived at Bordeaux on September 18, 1778.[77]

Marie Louis Amand Ansart de Marisquelles

The rebelling colonies had a pressing need for artillery and gunpowder which the suppliers and outfitters could not adequately satisfy. Some French volunteers sailed to America to provide assistance. One of them was Marie Louis Amand Ansart de Marisquelles, a French aristocrat and military officer. He arrived in Boston on December 6, 1776 and immediately went to the General Court of Massachusetts at the State House to present his credentials.

He offered to share his technique for making cast iron cannons and to supervise the making of all cannons if Massachusetts would pay the expenses for all land, buildings, machines, and all other materials needed to establish the foundries. Instead of casting cannons with a cylinder, which always leaves little holes or cavities which frequently cause bursting, he proposed to cast solid cannons and bore them. He would produce them at the rate of one every 24 hours. In exchange, he requested $300 in cash to reimburse him for his travel expenses to America and payment of $1,000 a year until the end of the war and "after that time the sum of 666 2/3 dollars yearly" during his life. He also requested an appointment to the rank of colonel without pay or command to give him legitimacy. Massachusetts not only appointed him to the rank of colonel but also made him Inspector of the Foundries of Massachusetts.

Although Ansart stated that he expected no command, he requested permission to go to the front when the Rhode Island campaign was organizing. The Board of War sent him to General John Sullivan on July 31, 1778. He was appointed one of General Sullivan's aides-de-camp. After serving for a month, General Sullivan sent him to Admiral Comte d'Estaing on August 31 to erect defenses for the French fleet which went to Boston harbor for repairs after the battle. Ansart was injured in the battle which incapacitated him for the remainder of the war.[78]

Nicolas Fouquet

Nicolas Fouquet and his son, Marc Antoine, arrived from France in August 1777 with Tronson du Coudray, Inspector General of Military Manufacturers with the rank of Major General. Coudray had a particular interest in saltpeter and considered Nicolas Fouquet the best gunpowder manufacturer in France. Nicolas was well acquainted with the process of extracting and refining saltpeter, making gunpowder, and constructing powder mills on the best principles. In short, he was familiar with everything relating to the manufacture of gunpowder. The southern regions of the United Colonies supplied saltpeter in abundance, and the arrival of this excellent specialist permitted the insurgents to no longer rely on the importation of foreign powder. The son aided his father and both names appear on the contract signed with Silas Deane, not as powderers but as a captain and lieutenant of bombardiers. The Congress gave them commissions as artillery officers and sent them to New England to instruct the people in the manufacture of gunpowder.[79]

The Fouquets were employed as powder makers and examiners of powder magazines at the beginning of 1778. Robert Troup, Secretary of the Board of War, transmitted bills of exchange for 900 livres tournois on their behalf to Congress on October 16, 1779, along with a note to pay them 900 livres tournois in addition to the sum of 6,000 livres tournois stipulated in their contract with the Board of War and Ordnance.[80]

King Louis XVI recalled Nicolas to France in 1780 and he returned to France without having been paid. Nicolas appealed to Benjamin Franklin on August 2, 1780, to intercede on his behalf for payment. He included his expenses for his return to France. Just as with Beaumarchais, Fouquet's bills hadn't been paid and his heirs had to appeal to Congress in 1872 and 1880.[81]

CHAPTER 3

Canada: The Fourteenth Colony

The French explorer Jacques Cartier was the first European to reach the Gulf of St. Lawrence in 1534. He claimed the surrounding area for France and Samuel de Champlain founded Québec, the first permanent settlement in Canada, in 1608. He named it New France, which became the base of France's colonial empire in North America and remained so until 1763.

By the early 1700s, New France included three colonies: Canada, Acadia, and Louisiana. When the British defeated the French in the Seven Years War (French and Indian War, 1756–63), they gained possession of New France, which now consisted of the province called Canada. It was officially called the Province of Québec after 1763 and the Québec Act of 1774 enlarged the province to include what is now Québec, Ontario, and the Midwestern United States (Ohio Valley). Nearly all of the province's population of about 85,000 were of French ancestry, except for 2,000 to 3,000 British or American newcomers. The Whigs thought the French would welcome an opportunity to retaliate and regain their country or possibly become a 14th colony. As a result of the Québec Act, however, the Catholic bishops threatened to excommunicate anybody who took part in the rebellion against Britain. This quelled opposition to Britain in Canada and eliminated the possibility of an uprising to support the Americans. However, a number of Canadians would join the Continental Army enough to form two regiments, one of them appropriately called the Canadian Regiment.

The concentration of British troops (only about 800) in southeastern Canada and the fluid and undefended borders invited raids from both sides. Fort Ticonderoga was the gateway to Canada.

Fort Ticonderoga

Fort Ticonderoga, originally called Fort Carillon, an outpost of Crown Point, was built in 1755. Located at the north end of Lake Champlain, it was a strategic point for the defense of Canada, as it lay on a main water route into the territory.

It consisted of squared-off timbers laid horizontally and backed by embankments; but the wood eventually rotted and was replaced by stone. As the fort's outer entrenchment was nearing completion, the British attacked it on July 8, 1758 with 15,000 men—the largest British Army yet fielded in North America. Louis-Joseph de Montcalm-Grozon, Marquis de Saint-Véran, did not wait for the attack. He ordered wooden fortifications built in the woods three-quarters of a mile west of the fort. Unlike stone, which shatters and acts like shrapnel when struck by artillery, wood was better able to withstand artillery fire and could be easily repaired. The British lost 2,000 men killed and wounded in an unsuccessful attempt to penetrate the defenses. The French lost only 300 out of 3,500.

General Jeffrey Amherst, Baron Amherst, returned the following summer to find the fort's garrison drastically reduced. After a four-day siege, the French blew up their powder and evacuated the fort. Amherst had the damage repaired and renamed the fort Ticonderoga. The British occupied Fort Ticonderoga for the next 16 years, but with the French removed from eastern North America it no longer had any military importance, so it was only guarded by a few men and fell into disrepair.

Early in May 1775, the Massachusetts Committee of Safety authorized Captain Benedict Arnold to recruit a company of 400 men to capture Fort Ticonderoga from the British. About the same time, the Connecticut assembly made a similar offer to Lieutenant Colonel Ethan Allen and his Green Mountain Boys. When Arnold learned of this, he rode to Castleton, Vermont, to confront Allen, but the Green Mountain Boys refused to serve under anybody but Allen. So Arnold and Allen agreed to share the command.

Allen, Arnold, and 83 men boarded the only boats available, a couple of scows, at Hand's Cove on the east shore of Lake Champlain near Shoreham, Vermont. By the time they landed, it was too light for the boats to return for the remainder of the assault party which totaled 200 to 300 men. With less than one-third of his total strength, Allen decided to attack the fort about 3:30 AM on Friday, May 10, 1775. They caught the garrison by surprise and both the commanding officer and the second-in-command were asleep in bed.

With swords drawn, Allen and Arnold climbed the wooden outside stairs leading to the top floor and demanded the fort's surrender. Allen shouted something like "Come out, you damn old rat!" He later embellished the statement in his memoirs, published in 1779, where he recorded he called for the surrender "In the name of the Great Jehovah and the Continental Congress." The second-in-command described Benedict Arnold as requesting surrender in a "genteel manner." He described Ethan Allen as highly agitated, brandishing a sword, and demanding the keys of the fort.

The fort's position was not as critical as the cannon and ammunition stored there. Many of the guns were in such bad condition that they were useless, but there were at least 78 useful ones. They ranged from 4-pounders to 24-pounders (18th-century artillery is classified by the weight of the shot fired) and included six mortars, three howitzers, thousands of cannonballs of various sizes, 9 tons of musket balls, more than 30,000 flints, and a large quantity of miscellaneous supplies, all of which Allen, Arnold, and the raiding party captured at Ticonderoga and Crown Point (about 12 miles further north), which they seized the next day. The captives were marched to a prison in Hartford, Connecticut.

General George Washington sent Colonel Henry Knox, later to be his chief of artillery, to Fort Ticonderoga to remove the artillery he needed so badly. Knox arrived on Tuesday, December 5, 1775 and began the task of loading 43 cannons and 16 mortars—119,000 pounds of artillery—for the journey to Boston. He also took 2,300 pounds of lead and a supply of flints. The train of 42 heavy sledges pulled by 80 yoke of oxen traveled 300 miles, despite the poor or nonexistent roads in icebound western New England. They arrived at Framingham (20 miles from Cambridge, Massachusetts) by Thursday, January 25, 1776. The guns were eventually installed on Dorchester Heights, overlooking Boston, in March, and contributed greatly to convincing the British to evacuate the city of Boston.

Saint-Jean (or Saint-Jean sur Richelieu)

Saint John the Baptist is a popular saint among the French. There are several cities and towns in Canada bearing his name that must be distinguished further so as not to confuse them with each other. The ones that concern us are this one in Québec and another in Nova Scotia.

St. Johns was a frontier Canadian post on the Richelieu River about 23 miles north of Lake Champlain and 10 miles south of Chambly. The present city or town is currently across the Richelieu River from Iberville. It was strategically located near the navigation route from Lake Champlain.

As a background for understanding the military deployment involved with St. Johns, Ile aux Noix, and Chambly, General Sir Guy Carleton concentrated most of his troops at Fort St. Johns in 1775 to forestall an invasion from the south. It took the Rebels two months to take the position from their base at Ile aux Noix. While the delaying action cost Carleton most of his best troops, it may well have been decisive in saving Canada.

Four days after the capture of Fort Ticonderoga in New York, Captains John Brown and Eleazer Oswald took possession of a small schooner named the *Liberty* at Skenesborough, New York. They joined Lieutenant Colonel Benedict Arnold and 50 men who enlisted along the way on Wednesday afternoon, May 14, 1775. They proceeded toward St. Johns and arrived within 30 miles of the fort at 8:00 PM on the 17th. They boarded two small bateaux with 35 men and arrived at St. Johns at 6:00 AM, surprised the defenders, and captured a sergeant and his party of 12 men, the British sloop *Asia* (subsequently named the *Enterprise*) with two brass 6-pounders and seven men, and a total of 70 prisoners.

Arnold and his men set sail for Crown Point, New York, with the sloop *George III* and four of the king's bateaux two hours after arriving at St. Johns. They destroyed five other bateaux, leaving none for the king's troops, Canadians, or Native Americans to cross the lake if they so intended. They arrived at Crown Point at 10:00 AM on Friday, May 19.[1]

Lieutenant Colonel Ethan Allen and 90–150 men left Crown Point for St. Johns shortly after Arnold. Arnold met Allen and his men about 6 miles south of St. Johns. They saluted each other with three volleys each. Allen boarded Arnold's sloop and learned that St. Johns had already been taken and that its garrison was held prisoner and the fort abandoned. Arnold supplied Allen's starving men with provisions. Meanwhile, some 250 Regulars from Fort Chambly[2] had been sent out to reinforce Crown Point and Ticonderoga. Allen decided to ambush them and sent out scouts. However, his men, tired after three days and nights with little sleep and little food, dissuaded him. When the king's troops arrived within 2 miles of him, Arnold withdrew across the river, where his exhausted men lay down to sleep. A volley of grapeshot from six field pieces startled them. They rushed to their boats, leaving three of their company behind. They exchanged shots with the Regulars as they rowed out of range.[3]

In June 1775, the Continental Congress ordered General Philip Schuyler to march his army into Canada. As Schuyler marched north from Crown Point, Arnold was to advance through Maine to Québec. General Richard Montgomery, a former British Army officer living in the province of New York, joined Schuyler's force of some 1,500 men in late August, took command in mid-September, and lay siege to St. Johns on the Richelieu River on November 2, 1775, opening the way to Montréal.

Captain Noble Benedict and a reconnoitering party encountered some Mohawks, Regulars, and Canadians in a boat near St. Johns on Monday, September 4, 1775. The scouting party lost Captain Remember Baker and killed several of the whites and two Mohawks. General Richard Montgomery set out for St. Johns with 1,200 men and planned to muster at Ile aux Noix with Major General Philip Schuyler's force of equal size.[4]

General Schuyler, who was "very much indisposed … with a bilious fever and violent rheumatick pains" on September 5, ordered his forces to leave some of their supplies behind under guard, and to continue advancing on the Richelieu River toward the small fort at St. Johns. General Montgomery led the party, which went ashore 1½ miles from the fort and attempted a flanking movement through the heavily wooded marsh. Captain Tice, a New York Loyalist, commanding 60–100 Native Americans, ambushed them in a deep and muddy stream. General Montgomery's men drove them back, killing five and wounding five others. They lost eight men killed and nine wounded in the skirmish.

An informant reported to General Schuyler that the fort was "complete and strong and plentifully furnished with cannon," so Schuyler went back to his encampment on Ile aux Noix to make further preparations and to await the arrival of reinforcements. Colonel Benjamin Hinman's 300 Connecticut troops and 400 of the 2nd New York Regiment arrived by September 10, bringing the forces at Ile aux Noix to approximately 1,700 men—more than twice the number of British Regulars in all of Canada.

General Schuyler was now ready to launch a second attack on the fort at St. Johns, now defended by 500 British Regulars of the 7th and 26th Regiments of Foot, later reinforced by an ensign and 12 seamen, 100 Canadian militia, and 70 men from the newly raised unit of Royal Highland Emigrants. However, Schuyler's flanking party of 800 men feared a second ambush in the dark. When they believed themselves threatened, Schuyler's men turned and ran. The second attack on the fort failed, and the forces retreated to Ile aux Noix. While Major General Schuyler was making his second attempt to take the fort at St. Johns, General Richard Montgomery led 800 troops northward from Ile aux Noix on Sunday, September 10, 1775. They were attacked from boats and breastworks near Fort Chambly, a safely entrenched and well-supplied garrison. They killed two enemy and sank a boat with 35 men aboard.[5]

General Montgomery's little army opened three batteries at Fort St. Johns on Sunday, September 17, 1775; but, the land being flat, they found it impossible to overlook the fort so they laid siege to it, entirely surrounding it on Monday, September 18, 1775. The fort was defended by Colonel Templer and about 600 Regulars and some Native Americans. The garrison fired eight bomb shells and 30 cannonballs. General Montgomery's batteries returned fire with 44 12-pound shots, some of which struck a bateau and an armed schooner several times. A large schooner of 16 guns lay within half a mile of the fort but she could not get into Lake Champlain to annoy Whig troops due to a large boom stretching from Ile aux Noix to the opposite shore. General Montgomery sent Major John Brown to engage the enemy. He cut off an escort of 13 wagonloads of provisions, rum, and brandy intended for St. Johns, killed eight Native Americans, and lost two men wounded.[6]

The Crown forces sent out a bateau as a spy on the 20th; but Captain William Douglas fired four 12-pounders, struck her, and drove her back. Three women captured a British sergeant in disguise who was spying in the area. They brought him to the Whig army in a horse cart. The Crown forces continued a smart fire between 10 and 11 PM that night in retaliation for the repulsion of some of their troops who went to take some cattle and hogs near Major Brown's camp.

The garrison at Fort St. Johns resumed fire at 2 PM on the 21st and continued until night. The following day, Friday, September 22, 1775, they kept up an alternating fire without doing much damage. At 7 PM, they began a very heavy fire of balls, grapeshot, and bombs. The exchange killed one of the besiegers. The following day, the defenders kept up a brisk fire all day, launching between 30 and 40 shells that slightly wounded one man. The garrison lost seven men taken prisoners that evening.

The garrison resumed firing at sunrise on Sunday, the 24th, and continued all day. The Whigs fired four cannon at an armed schooner at 5 PM on Monday, with two shots going through her, driving her to shore. They fired four cannons again at 4 PM on Tuesday, the 26th, which the defenders returned. Both sides engaged in a brisk fire the whole day on Wednesday, the 27th. The attackers lost a gunner killed by an enemy cannonball.[7]

Montréal

Lieutenant Colonel Ethan Allen set out from Longueuil on Sunday morning, September 24, 1775 with about 80 men. They headed to La Prairie and then intended to go to Brigadier General Richard Montgomery's camp. They had not gone 2 miles when they met with Major John Brown, who requested that they halt so he could communicate something important to them. Major Brown proposed, "Provided I would return to Longueil and procure some canoes, so as to cross the river St. Lawrence a little north of Montréal, he would cross it a little to the south of the town, with near two hundred men, as he had boats sufficient; and that we would make ourselves masters of Montreal." Colonel Allen and his advisers agreed to the plan and returned to Longueil, "collected a few canoes, and added about thirty English Americans to my party, and crossed the river in the night of the 24th."[8]

Colonel Allen's force of 110 men, consisting of about 80 Canadians and 30 Connecticut troops, spent most of the night crossing the river because they had so few canoes that they had to pass and re-pass three times to get everybody across. Colonel Allen set his guards soon after daybreak on Monday, September 25, 1775, while he reconnoitered the best ground to defend, expecting Major Brown's party to be on the other side of the town. However, two hours after sunrise, he still had not received the signal that they had arrived. As Allen could only cross one-third of his men at a time, he decided not to risk re-crossing the St. Lawrence. A band of 500 Regulars and militia sent out by General Sir Guy Carleton attacked Allen's force at Montréal. They wounded seven and captured Allen and 45 of his men. Most of the Canadians, about 55, deserted. The Regulars lost three killed and two wounded.[9]

Meanwhile, more than 200 French Canadians allied with the Whigs began constructing an entrenchment on the east side of the lake opposite the upper fort about 450–550 yards away from Fort Chambly. They constructed a small breastwork on Tuesday, October 3, 1775. A party from Fort Chambly skirmished with the work party and killed about five.[10]

The Regulars attempted to cross Lake Champlain in a row galley or floating battery about 10 AM on Wednesday, October 4, 1775, to drive Colonel Timothy Bedel's party of Whigs and Canadians from their entrenchment and breastwork on the east side of the lake. They fired cannon and small arms; and both sides engaged in sharp fire for a while. The Regulars eventually returned to the fort. Colonel Bedel had one man wounded.[11]

The following evening, a mortar called the "Old Sow" arrived from Ticonderoga with shells. She was placed on a bomb battery on Friday, the 6th, and fired seven shells at the forts that evening. The garrison at Fort St. Johns returned fire with 24 shells.[12]

The Regulars at Fort St. Johns fired on the Whig besiegers on Wednesday, October 11, 1775. A shell wounded Seth Case, of Captain Mead's Company, who died the next day.[13]

Lieutenant Colonel Seth Warner's troops met a party of Crown forces from Montréal near Fort St. Johns before Friday, October 20, 1775. They killed some and captured five Canadians prisoners but lost one man killed.[14]

One man of the 1st Battalion of Yorkers was killed with a cannonball in the camp at Fort St. Johns on Wednesday, October 25, 1775.[15]

About the same time, Major John Brown with 50 Americans and Captain Henry B. Livingston with 300 Canadians forced Major Stopford to surrender Fort Chambly on Tuesday, October 17, 1775. A party of General Montgomery's troops with some Canadians took possession of the fort at 8 AM on Thursday, October 19, 1775 after a siege of 48 hours. They took 83 Regulars, one major, two captains, and 90 women and children at Chambly and 180 Regulars, women, and children belonging to the garrison at St. Johns prisoners. They also captured three small mortars, 11 swivels, 130 full barrels (6½ tons) of powder, and a considerable quantity of artillery. The Canadians brought the artillery down past Fort St. Johns in bateaux. They sank a schooner and a large row galley.

Captain Richard Cheeseman and a party of 300 men later raised the schooner and the galley and found that neither had received much damage. The schooner had her stern port knocked off and nine shots fired through her hull and three in her mast. The galley had about five shots in her hull.[16]

Longueuil

General Sir Guy Carleton tried to land at Longueuil with 34 boats full of Canadians and Native Americans on Monday, October 30, 1775. Lieutenant Colonel Seth Warner's Green Mountain Boys and the 2nd Regiment of Yorkers repulsed them, inflicting heavy casualties, burning three Native Americans, and taking two others and two Canadians prisoners—all without having a man wounded.[17]

General Richard Montgomery's battery of four 12-pounders on the east side of the Richelieu River fired on Major Charles Preston's garrison at Fort St. Johns on Thursday, November 2, 1775. The British surrendered after losing 25 killed during the siege. Some prisoners whom Lieutenant Colonel Seth Warner captured from Longueil on October 30 arrived that evening. General Montgomery sent one of them into the fort to inform Major Preston of the circumstances of the action. Realizing that he had no prospect of receiving reinforcements, Major Preston surrendered the garrison.[18]

A party of troops was stationed at Point Sorel and another at Le Chien, hoping to intercept General Sir Guy Carleton on Wednesday, November 8, 1775. British ships fired on Major John Brown's troops on shore.[19]

Québec

While Major General Philip Schuyler's and Lieutenant Colonel Seth Warner's troops were attacking the forts along the Richelieu River, on their way to Montréal, Colonel Benedict Arnold was preparing to march to attack Québec. He set out on Wednesday, September 13, 1775 with a force of about 1,100 men. They left Cambridge, Massachusetts and planned to head up the Kennebec River and down the Chaudière to Québec. Colonel Daniel Morgan's riflemen refused to serve under Colonel Christopher Greene, a Rhode Islander, so Arnold had to keep them together in a single division. They led the march, leaving on September 11, with the other companies departing two days later.

They boarded 11 sloops and schooners at Newburyport on September 19 and reached Gardinerstown on the Kennebec below Fort Western (Augusta, Maine) three days later. Arnold had 200 bateaux waiting here—all built in 18 days—of green lumber (the only material available). Many of them were poorly constructed and smaller than specified but Arnold accepted them, as he had no alternative. He also ordered another 20 to be built. He sent two reconnaissance parties from Fort Western up the Kennebec on September 24. The main force followed a few days later. It took them two days to cover the first 18 miles to Fort Halifax.

At Ticonic Falls, Arnold's men had to carry the 400-pound bateaux and about 65 tons of supplies a half mile. They encountered other falls at Five Mile Ripples (or Falls), a half mile from Skowhegan Falls: the Skowhegan Falls themselves, the Bombazee Rips, and the three Norridgewock Falls. They then headed into the wilderness where they could no longer get supplies until they were well into Canada. They rested three days after passing Norridgewock Falls and repaired their badly battered bateaux. They then headed to Caratunk Falls, the next major portage, which they reached on Monday, October 9. Two days later, Arnold and an advance party arrived at the Great Carrying Place—an 8-mile portage and 4 miles of rowing across three ponds—to get to the Dead River, west of the Kennebec. After rowing 30 miles up the Dead River, they came to a 4¼-mile portage ("the Terrible Carrying Place") across the Height of Land that separated the watersheds of the Kennebec and the Chaudière.

The weather was getting cold and severe, particularly getting the boats past obstacles in the cold rivers. They also had to endure heavy rains and a hurricane on

Monday, October 21, that swelled the river from 60 to 200 yards wide. A division of about 300 men quit the expedition at the first Carry Pond on the 25th, taking stragglers and the sick from the other divisions.

The expedition was running out of food. The men had to eat shaving soap, pomatum, lip salve, candles, and the leather of their shoes and cartridge boxes to survive. Their "greatest luxuries now consisted of a little water, stiffened with flour."[20] The remaining force proceeded up the Dead River to another portage of 4½ miles and to Seven Mile Stream. They sloshed through icy swamps to Lake Megantic and arrived at the Chaudière on Tuesday, October 31, with only a few bateaux left. The expedition marched north to the St. Lawrence, arriving at Point Levis, opposite Québec, on November 9, 1775.

When Colonel Arnold and his troops crossed from Maine into Canada on Saturday, November 4, 1775, the first village they came to was Sartigan at the mouth of the Rivière Famine. His advance detachment had gathered provisions here. Some of the men, compensating for their hardships and deprivations on the march, gorged themselves on cooked food. Three of them ate themselves to death. Natanis and about 50 local Native Americans joined Arnold's forces here. The expedition followed the Chaudière River to Ste. Marie (the original settlement of Montréal). When they left Ste. Marie, they traveled overland toward Point Levis through snow, mud, and knee-deep water.[21]

The expedition, now down to 675 of the original 1,100 men, arrived at Point Levis, opposite Québec, on Thursday, November 9, 1775. After traversing 350 miles of wilderness in 45 days, they were ready to attack Québec's 1,200 defenders. Captain Thomas Mackenzie's HM Sloop *Hunter* exchanged fire with some of Arnold's troops on shore at Wolfe's Cove. Within a day, Arnold had located canoes and dugouts, acquired supplies of flour, and had the men prepare scaling ladders. A hurricane which lasted until November 13 prevented him from crossing the mile-wide St. Lawrence which was full of British naval vessels.

After the fall of St. Johns on November 2, 1775, General Montgomery sent an advance detachment of Whigs and Canadians toward Sorel the next day. They encountered light resistance. The main body of Montgomery's force set out on Monday, November 5 and crossed the St. Lawrence River upstream from Montréal on Saturday, the 11th. As General Sir Guy Carleton only had about 100 troops and a few militiamen to defend the town, he spiked his cannons and embarked his men on a few small vessels during the night of the 12th. The following morning, General Montgomery's troops entered the town with no opposition.

Everything was ready for Arnold's troops to embark on Monday, November, 13. The first division set off at 9 PM, a very dark evening. The canoes passed undiscovered between the 14-gun *Hunter* and Québec and landed safely at Wolfe's Cove. They made three trips across the river before everyone had landed around daybreak. The men who had crossed marched up the hill and formed their lines. About 3 AM, one of the birch-bark canoes fell apart in the river. The occupants lost their muskets and all their gear but were dragged ashore by other canoes. They built a large fire in a house in Wolfe's Cove to dry themselves.

The *Hunter*'s guard-boat was traveling from the *Hunter* to the 23-gun frigate *Lizard* about daybreak while some of the boats were crossing. This made the Whigs uneasy. They hailed the guard-boat as she came near the shore and some riflemen fired on her, contrary to orders, killing a sentry. Some of the troops on shore could hear some of the men cry out they were wounded. They pushed off and immediately alarmed the whole garrison.[22]

Arnold's troops waited a little while until the rest of the men crossed the river, except for a guard stationed at Point Levis. They marched across the Plains of Abraham at daybreak and took possession of some houses 1½ miles from Québec, including that of Major Caldwell at Sainte-Foy. When they noticed some teams loaded with beef, vegetables, and other provisions heading into the city, they surrounded the house and captured the major's servant. They posted a strong guard and retired. The Regulars seized one of the sentinels and took him prisoner. Arnold's army immediately marched toward the walls, where they came under fire with some heavy shots. They picked up a number of cannonballs, gave three hearty cheers, and retired to their quarters.

A deserter from Québec advised Colonel Arnold that the Regulars were preparing their field pieces to attack him. Arnold convened a council. They determined that they had too few muskets, no bayonets, and no field pieces. Moreover, they only had an average of four rounds per man. They decided to withdraw and proceed about 20 miles or so up the St. Lawrence River. Arnold sent an express to General Richard Montgomery to inform him of his situation and ordered his men to break camp at 8 AM on Saturday, November 18, 1775.

The camp at Point Levis marched upon the south side of the river. Eyewitnesses Isaac Senter and John Joseph Henry note that the troops withdrew to Point-aux-Trembles, which is about 140 miles away from Québec but only about 10 miles from Montréal. (What they refer to as Point-aux-Trembles is the village of Neuville off Provincial Highway 138.) Here, they waited for General Montgomery's column which arrived from Montréal on Saturday, December 2. Montgomery and Arnold's combined force of about 1,000 returned to Québec three days later.[23]

Meanwhile, General Montgomery sent troops to Sorel and Le Chien to block the garrison's escape route. They turned back the garrison's retreat twice at Sorel after the evacuation of Montréal on Sunday, November 12. Governor Carleton disguised himself as a Canadian on Sunday, November 19. He boarded the armed scow *Fell* and reached Québec the next day. Brigadier General Richard Prescott surrendered most of his garrison and his flotilla of small vessels, headed by the six-gun brig *Gaspée*, on Monday, November 20.[24]

Two Massachusetts-based privateers, sent to intercept British ships carrying arms and supplies to Québec, landed in the undefended Charlottetown harbor (Prince Edward Island) on Friday, November 17, 1775. They kidnapped the colonial administrator and one of his clerks, and took the colonial seal, known as the Silver Seal of the Island, which has never been recovered. Before returning to Massachusetts, they looted homes and storehouses and damaged or removed valuables, including the settlement's winter provisions.[25]

Colonel Arnold's troops rested at Point Levis almost a week, preparing to cross the St. Lawrence River to Québec. They purchased birch canoes at Neuville and carried them by land, as the Regulars at Québec had burned all the vessels near them as soon as they learned of Arnold's advance. They also positioned the men-of-war to prevent a crossing of the river. The Rebels fired several shots into the town on Sunday, December 10. HM Sloop *Hunter* fired some shots at them and some shells at their battery.[26]

On Tuesday December 14 (some authors give it as the 13th), the Regulars tried unsuccessfully to capture a second sentinel. The little army immediately turned out and took possession of a nunnery in the suburbs, within point-blank range of the garrison. They posted a strong guard there and began to set up a battery of five 12-pounders and a howitzer. The *Hunter* fired several shots and shells at the work party throughout the day.

The battery began firing on the town before sunrise the following day (the 15th) and continued for about an hour. General Montgomery sent a flag to the town to request surrender but it was refused admittance. The battery resumed fire and the mortars launched some 50 shells into the town. The Regulars returned fire. One shot struck the battery and killed two and wounded five of the gun crew, damaged one of the guns, and dismounted the howitzer. There were five others killed or wounded that day, including four Frenchmen.[27]

General Montgomery's army had two alarms on Wednesday, the 15th. They expected a battle to occur; but it only consisted of a cannonade. A party crossing St. Charles on Thursday evening came under fire. A Pennsylvanian was wounded in the leg by a cannonball. The leg was cut off as soon as possible, but he had lost so much blood before the doctor could see him, that he expired the next morning and was buried on the Plains of Abraham.[28]

A cannonade on Thursday evening, December 16, struck Colonel Arnold's quarters several times, forcing him to seek other quarters. One man was shot through the body with a grapeshot. A council of war met that evening and decided to storm the garrison of Québec "as soon as the men are well equip'd with good arms, Spears, hatchets, Hand granades."[29]

Henry Dearborn's artillery fired 30 shells into Québec Friday night, December 29. The Royal Artillery returned a few shells and some grapeshot. The garrison began a very heavy cannonade early the following morning and continued throughout the day. About sunset, they aimed a gun at the guard house and knocked down the guard house's three chimneys in 15 minutes, but they could not get a shot into the lower rooms which housed the guards.[30]

General Montgomery and Colonel Arnold made an unsuccessful attack upon the city on Sunday night, December 31, 1775. General Montgomery's cannon were too light to breach the city walls, so he planned to scale them as they were quite extensive and the garrison was weak. He planned to attack the upper and lower town at the same time. However, several of Montgomery's men deserted to the enemy and reported on his intent. Discovering that the Redcoats were aware of his plan, General Montgomery divided his small army into four detachments and ordered two feints against the upper town.

Colonel Brockholst Livingston led the Canadians against St. John's Gate, while Captain John M. Brown and a small detachment attacked Cape Diamond. General Montgomery and Colonel Arnold led the two principal attacks against the lower town. General Montgomery and the New York troops advanced against the lower town from the west at 5 AM. They found the garrison ready when they reached the place. Montgomery pressed on and passed the first barrier. He just began attacking the second barrier, a battery of several cannon loaded with grape shot, some of which were fired and mortally wounded the general and his aide-de-camp, Captain John Macpherson, in the first volley. Captain Shearman, and three or four privates, also went down. The guards turned and ran after firing. Colonel Donald Campbell assumed command but ordered a retreat instead of taking advantage of the guards' flight.

Meanwhile, Colonel Arnold's 350 men and Captain John Lamb's company of artillery had passed through St. Rock's Gate (on the north side of the city) and approached near a two-gun battery at the head of Rue du Sault-au-Matelot without being discovered. Arnold attacked the well-defended battery of two cannons behind an 11-foot picket and took it after about an hour. However, he had his left leg splintered by a musket ball that entered below the knee and lodged above the ankle. Arnold was carried to the hospital by two men and Colonel Daniel Morgan assumed command of the detachment. They proceeded to a second barrier a few hundred yards ahead (at Rue de la Barricade) that blocked the road to the upper town. The detachment paused to wait for stragglers to catch up and for Montgomery's troops to arrive from the opposite direction.

When General Montgomery's troops withdrew after his death, the Redcoats went to reinforce the division under attack by Arnold's detachment. A party sallied out from Palace gate (on the north side of the city) and attacked them in the rear. The detachment sustained the whole force of the garrison for three hours. Surrounded, outnumbered three to one and with no hopes of relief, Morgan surrendered about 10 AM. The rest of the army retired about 8 miles from Québec and continued the blockade, waiting for reinforcements. Arnold reported 73 men killed and wounded and 387 captured. Only 210 escaped. The British lost seven killed and 11 wounded.[31]

On Wednesday, March 13, 1776, Captain Thomas Mackenzie, of the HM Sloop *Hunter*, saw some Rebels strolling near Cape Diamond. He sent Captain Littlejohn and a party of 20 men after them. Their advanced sentry fired at the seamen from under a hill and ran away. The landing party marched a little distance further and saw a party of about 40 workmen, fired at them, and rushed them, killing three of them.[32]

A week later, on Thursday, March 21, a number of men were working at the old works on the south bank of the St. Lawrence River, 8 miles east of Point Levis, about 1,500 yards from the garrison. Artillery from the Grand and Queens battery fired upon them all afternoon. The following day, their work was raised about two fascines and a trench of snow had been constructed before it during the night.[33]

Major Lewis DuBois led 100 New Yorkers to attack an enemy advance guard downriver from Québec on Monday, March 25, 1776. They killed seven, wounded four, and took 38 prisoners, including 17 officers, without losing a single man. The officers were sent to Montréal.[34]

A party of Whigs attacked a force of Canadians under John Couillard at St. Pierre Parish around March 27, 1776. They suffered three killed, 11 wounded, and about 36 captured.[35]

The Whigs launched some fireships against Québec and set them on fire Friday evening, May 3, 1776. However, they acted too late. As the fireships traveled against the tide, they had little effect. They tried again about 10 o'clock the following night, sending a fireship to burn the lower town and to set fire to the ships while American Brigadier General David Wooster prepared to attack. There was a brisk fire of cannon and small arms which caused great consternation in the city. General Wooster's troops approached the city with their ladders, ready to scale the walls when the lower town was set on fire. The fireship failed and the attack did not occur.[36]

Two days later, on Sunday, May 5, Captain Thomas Mackenzie's HM Sloop *Hunter* dispersed some Rebels on shore at Québec. His crew also took several pieces of cannon, some howitzers, and a quantity of ammunition at different places.[37]

General Sir Guy Carleton, supported by ships of the Royal Navy, led an attack the following day, Monday, May 6, at 1 PM against Major General John Thomas's troops who were besieging Québec. His 800 Redcoats forced the Continentals to retreat upriver with the ebb tide, losing one man killed and 109 captured. As the tide began to change, Captain Charles Douglas, of HMS *Isis*, detached Captain John Linzee's HMS *Surprise* and Captain Henry Harvey's sloop *Martin* and a provincial vessel to harass the retreating Rebels and to "take or destroy their Craft on the Water, & intercept any Stores or cannon expected from Montréal." The ships prevented General Thomas's troops from joining the others fleeing toward Montréal. The British captured some undischarged cannon, ammunition, scaling ladders, entrenching tools, provisions, and many muskets. The crew of the *Isis* took the artillery at Point Levis, which included two brass cannon captured at St Johns, as well as all the ammunition, stores, and provisions from that post and several prisoners. General Thomas's men retreated in disorder to Deschambault, 40 miles upstream from Québec. They then rallied and marched back to Sorel.[38]

The Rebels formed in large bodies in different places at Québec at 10 AM on Wednesday, May 8. Captain John Linzee, of the HMS *Surprise*, manned and armed all his boats and made a feint landing to draw the Rebels down, within cannon range. The decoy worked and the *Surprise* fired a number of guns as the Americans formed to attack the Redcoats. The boats returned at 11 and the *Surprise* resumed firing at 1 PM, firing a number of shots to annoy the Rebels intending to board her. Captain Linzee prepared to receive them, placing puncheons of water on the gang ways for a barricade.[39]

The HMS *Surprise* headed up the St. Lawrence River on Saturday morning, May 11. Captain Linzee launched a manned and armed barge with the general's aide-de-camp at 11 AM to observe enemy movements. The barge returned at 2 PM after rowing close to Portneuf, where about 200 Rebels came down to the shore and fired at them. The seamen also observed that the Rebels were entrenching themselves on Point de Chambeau (now Deschambault, about 45 miles west of Québec and about 3½ miles south of Portneuf).[40]

The following day, Sunday, Captain Henry Harvey's sloop *Martin* fired several shots at the Rebels on shore at Point Plator (probably what is now near the town of Donnacona about 7 miles west of Neuville). He sent a midshipman and some men in an armed schooner to Point aux Trembles to get the brig *Gaspée*, which the Rebels left there.[41]

Les Cèdres

Colonel Timothy Bedel, of the New Hampshire Rangers, occupied the small fort at Les Cèdres in April 1776. He received intelligence that Captain George Forster and 40 Regulars of the 8th (King's) Regiment, 100 Canadians and 500 Native Americans under Joseph Brant, Mohawk Chief Thayendanagea, were advancing against him with no artillery. They had left the mouth of the Oswegatchie (now Ogdensburg, New York), under the pretense of going to Montréal for reinforcements. Captain Forster's troops surrounded Colonel Bedel at Les Cèdres on Friday, May 17. The site was a Native American portage site to bypass the Coteau Rapids between Lake St. François and Lake St. Louis.

Unable to get any supplies, Bedel sent an express to Lieutenant Colonel Benedict Arnold, commanding officer at Montréal, for reinforcements and provisions. However, he had to surrender before any assistance arrived. Arnold, unaware of the surrender, sent Major Henry Sherburne with 100 men and three wagons loaded with provisions. When they arrived at Fort Anne, about 30 miles up the St. Lawrence River, they crossed over and began marching toward Les Cèdres, which was about 3 or 4 miles from the opposite shore. The Mohawks, alerted to their advance, lined the woods and bushes alongside the road, close to a small bridge and about 2 miles from where they landed. The Mohawks sent a party to destroy their boats and take the guards prisoners. When Major Sherburne's men came opposite to the place where the Mohawks were concealed on Monday, May 20, the Mohawks arose, made their war-whoop and poured a tremendous fire upon them.

Sherburne's men fought for more than two hours and killed a number of Mohawks, including several chiefs. He lost about 60 men killed and many more wounded, 390 prisoners, and two cannons. Major Sherburne was eventually forced to give up, whereupon the Mohawks began to strip the prisoners of their clothes, striking the wounded on the head with their axes and tomahawks and scalping the dead. The prisoners were taken to Les Cèdres and confined in an old stone church (which burned in 1780). Arnold negotiated their release and brought them to Montréal for later exchange, if they promised that they would not fight anymore.[42]

La Chine

A few days after their victory at Les Cèdres, the Crown forces under Captain George Forster began marching toward Montréal, where two-thirds of the troops were infected with smallpox. As the Crown forces had only 21 canoes, each capable of carrying an average of eight or nine men, Lieutenant Colonel Benedict Arnold sent 400 of his 900 men in bateaux to Ile-Perrot in an attempt to cut off their retreat. He pursued Forster's men with the rest of his troops, leaving a small number to guard the city. The Crown forces, consisting of 40 or 50 men of the 18th Regiment, 250 Canadians, and 300 Native Americans and two captured cannons, came within 3 miles of Colonel Arnold's camp, about 12 miles from La Chine, during the night of Friday, May 24, 1776. They expected to find the post undefended; but, hearing that Arnold had a large body of men, they retreated. Arnold's advance guard had not gone more than 2 miles beyond the city when they saw three Mohawks in the road coming toward them on Saturday. The Mohawks gave the war-whoop, threw down their guns and blankets, and fled into the woods. Arnold sent a scouting party after them and his troops arrived at La Chine that evening.

About 10 or 15 minutes after the scouts arrived at a two-room stone structure at La Chine, they heard the Mohawk war-whoop. A few minutes later, the house and the entire road were filled with Mohawks heading, as fast as they could, toward Fort Anne, about 12 miles away. They had all passed about an hour later without discovering the scouts who pursued them all the way to Fort Anne. The scouts returned to La Chine near daylight to inform Colonel Arnold of the enemy movements.

The troops soon mustered to pursue the Mohawks. They set out about two hours after dawn along with a party of 200 Native Americans that had joined them after their arrival at La Chine. They approached the opposite shore about half an hour before sunset when they saw a naked man up to his waist in the water as they passed a small island. They rowed toward him and took him aboard and learned that he was one of their own men who had escaped from the Mohawks at Les Cèdres a few days earlier. Anxious for his revenge, the man guided the troops to the location of the Mohawks. They came within musket shot of the shore at Les Cèdres where woods covered the landing-place. Behind every tree, three or four Mohawks fired heavy volleys at the approaching troops. As it was now sundown, Colonel Arnold gave the signal to retreat to the other side of the river.

The Regulars brought their two captured fieldpieces to the shore and began to fire at Arnold's men. Arnold ordered his troops to light a great number of fires after landing, to give the impression that they had a large number of men. The Crown forces, directly in sight of them on the opposite shore, sent a flag of truce, about midnight, to surrender, as they knew that Arnold intended to attack them the next morning. The Crown forces agreed to give up all their prisoners on condition that they not return to active duty for seven months. They released the prisoners the next day and Arnold released some of the officers he had captured.[43]

Vaudreuil

When the British received intelligence, on Friday, May 24, 1776, that Brigadier General Benedict Arnold positioned his troops at La Chine, Captain George Forster's 8th Regiment marched to attack him. He was later informed that Arnold's troops numbered 600 and would be almost trebled on succeeding days; so he thought it prudent to retire to Vaudreuil. General Arnold advanced up the river on Sunday, May 26, with 700 men to attack the British.

Captain Forster immediately formed his men into three divisions and placed them on three points of land that stretched a little way into the river. The Native Americans occupied the left point, which was rather swampy and covered with wood almost to the water's edge. Captain Forster took the center point, which was open ground. A body of Canadians took the right point located at the head of a dangerous rapid. Another body of Canadians was placed on Ile-Perrot, opposite the right point (now part of the mainland).

Arnold's troops attacked the left point and were repulsed. They then tried to land on the central point but were prevented from doing so. Next, they tried to land on the right point with the same success. Arnold abandoned the attack and returned to St. Anne's on the island of Montréal. Captain Forster, encumbered by the number of prisoners, negotiated a prisoner exchange with General Arnold but Congress later broke the agreement.[44]

Trois Rivières

General William Thompson and between 2,000 and 3,000 Congressional troops planned to surprise Brigadier General Simon Fraser's troops at Trois Rivières before sunrise on Saturday, June 8, 1776. He intended to attack the city from four directions with 300 men in each division but was delayed by poor ground, great fatigue, and losing the way. He did not get near the town until after sunrise.

Captain Henry Harvey, of the sloop *Martin*, received intelligence a little before 3 AM that a large number of bateaux had crossed from Nicolet and "landed a great Body of the rebels, at the Point of the lake, & were on their march towards Three rivers." He immediately sent a boat to reconnoiter. A party of Rebels fired at the boat about 2 miles from the *Martin* off Point Batti. The boat returned to the ship very soon afterward and Captain Harvey sent the 29th and 47th Regiments ashore. He positioned the *Martin* close to the shore to protect them.

A large body of Congressional troops, passing along the edge of the woods off Point Batti and heading toward the town, appeared opposite the *Martin* about 5 AM. The *Martin* fired several shots at them at 6 AM, sounding the alarm. The riflemen fired on the ship and drove her off into the stream while the rest of the troops took shelter in the woods. They attacked the advance guard of the British troops about 6 AM but the line of infantry, posted in an advantageous position, returned fire and dispersed the Rebels.

General Thompson re-formed his men and decided to continue with the attack, thinking only 800 troops defended the settlement. He was unaware that General Fraser had received reinforcements on June 6 and 7 and that the vessels in the river had landed their troops. When the Rebels came within range of the 17 vessels anchored along the shore for about a mile or a mile and a half above the town, the vessels began a brisk cannonade. The troops turned to what they thought was a point of woods to get out of range. The area was a swamp that took them about three hours to cross in knee-deep—and sometimes deeper—water.

Most of the British infantry had disembarked and formed by 5 AM. A force of about 1,100 of the king's troops with two 6-pounders and local militia were positioned on high ground near a wood and a mill dominating the lower city. They were ready for the Rebels when they emerged from the swamp at 7 AM. General Thompson tried to form his troops at a mill about three-quarters of a mile from town. The British fired on the mill and into the woods where the Rebels were and prevented them from forming for battle.

Claude-Joseph Boucher, sieur de Niverville, commander of the local garrison, and 12 militiamen surprised and captured seven or eight of General Thompson's troops about 8 AM. General Fraser's troops began very heavy fire with muskets and two field pieces, sometimes loaded with grape and sometimes with round shot. The 62nd Regiment and militia maintained continuous fire for about two hours. After repeated attacks, General Thompson's troops gave way and withdrew, in confusion, along the river and through the nearby woods.

The sloop *Martin*, anchored 3 miles above the town with some armed vessels and transports full of troops, fired many shots at the Rebels at the edge of the woods, while General William Nesbit and a large body of troops from the ships pursued them. The *Martin* sent her boats to assist the army in the afternoon and fired several shots at some Rebel boats. The Crown forces pursued the Rebels as far as Rivière du Loup (Louiseville).

General Thompson lost 50 men killed, 21 wounded, and 236 captured, including himself and his adjutant, Brigadier General William Irvine. The Crown forces lost two killed and 10 wounded. The wounded were taken to the Ursuline hospital and the dead were buried in a temporary cemetery in front of the powder magazine near the hospital.[45]

Sorel

The Crown forces took advantage of the fair wind and sailed for Sorel, arriving on Friday evening, June 14, 1776, the night after the Rebels had left. Thinking the Rebels were still there, the British fired several shots against the fortifications. Brigadier General Nesbit landed immediately with the grenadiers and light infantry and part of his brigade. The rest of the troops went ashore the next morning and Lieutenant General John Burgoyne assumed command with instructions to pursue the Rebels up the Sorel River to St. Johns. The rest of the fleet sailed for Longueuil and might have arrived that night if they had favorable wind.

Meanwhile, Brigadier General Benedict Arnold and his troops were retiring from Montréal. The next day, they landed and marched toward St. Johns by La Prairie. The Crown forces arrived at Montréal just after Arnold's men had left.[46]

Ile aux Noix

The Northern Army had safely retreated to Ile aux Noix, about 15 miles south of St. Johns, together with all their artillery, baggage, and supplies. A party of 12 of them went to the western shore of the lake, about a mile from the camp, to fish on Monday, June 24, 1776. Some Native Americans observed them and surrounded them while they were at a house drinking some spruce beer. They killed four of the soldiers and captured seven. When a party came from the camp to their relief, two of the prisoners escaped. The others were brought to the Regulars at Montréal. The Native Americans scalped about six other soldiers about 6 miles north of the island.[47]

St. John River, New Brunswick

Captain George Collier's HMS *Rainbow* drove off a Rebel force raiding a settlement along the St. John River in New Brunswick in July 1776.[48]

Isle La Motte, Lake Champlain

The schooner *Liberty* was cruising off Isle La Motte in Lake Champlain on Friday, September 20, 1776 when a Frenchman came down and signaled to be taken on board. The captain suspected him and approached the shore cautiously with his boat stern in, swivel guns pointed, and match lit. The Frenchman waded about 15 feet from the shore. When he found he could decoy the boat no closer, he made a signal, whereupon 300–400 Native Americans, Canadians, and Regulars emerged and fired on the boat, wounding three crewmen. The *Liberty* returned fire with the swivels and small arms. She also fired several broadsides of grapeshot. Several men fell and the rest dispersed. As the *Liberty* proceeded to guard the return boats and bring down the medicine, the crew discovered about 200 or 300 Native Americans on the western shore and a large number of light birch canoes, which the Native Americans could use to pass the larger vessels in the night and secure the canoes in the bushes during the daytime. Several Native Americans and Canadians lined the shore to observe the *Liberty*'s movements.

A party went ashore that evening and saw a man on the top of a house looking at them. They pushed forward through a swamp, found fresh tracks, and saw wigwams and fires. They pursued the Native Americans for some distance and took a fine horse and saddle which belonged to some Regular officer. However, the darkness of the night prevented them from overtaking the Native Americans.[49]

Fort Cumberland

Nova Scotia was poorly defended in the early stages of the American War for Independence. The residents of the eastern regions feared an American-led uprising and reinforcements began arriving at Halifax in 1776. Fort Cumberland, formerly Fort Bonséjour, seized from the French in 1755 and abandoned at the end of the Seven Years War, was in deplorable condition. Lieutenant Colonel Joseph Goreham arrived in August 1776 and his garrison of Loyalists did what they could to restore the fort's defenses; but they were not adequately provisioned and lacked everything from food to uniforms.

Colonel Jonathan Eddy considered poorly equipped Fort Cumberland's dilapidated condition and weak defenses as prime reasons for attacking the fort. Moreover, the Fencibles (a militia unit) were not expected to put up much of a fight. He began to make plans with his officers. They decided on tactics, checked small arms, and arranged special equipment such as shovels for trenching, saws, and scaling ladders for breaking the palisade.

He left Machias, Maine, with 28 men by mid-August 1776 and picked up a few men at Passamaquoddy, Maine. When he arrived at Maugerville, he had "two officers, 25 men and 16 Indians." When he left Maugerville (near Fredericton), he had a combined army of 72 Whites, Native Americans, and Nova Scotians. They traveled in whaleboats and canoes, arriving at Shepody, New Brunswick, a small British outpost, on Friday, October 25, 1776. They caught the outpost off guard and captured 14 British soldiers before heading to Memramcook where some French joined them. Eddy's party then "marched 12 miles through the woods to Sackville" where Eddy focused his attention on the sloop *Polly* which lay in the mudflats below Fort Cumberland, loaded with provisions and other necessities for the garrison.[50]

Colonel Eddy could only muster "about 80 men" of his 200 troops for the attack which, despite the fort's condition, appeared a daunting task for inexperienced troops. Moreover, the defenders outnumbered the attackers. Colonel Eddy thought they numbered about 100 when, in fact, they exceeded 200.[51]

Colonel Eddy "sent off a small Detachment which marched about 12 Miles through very bad Roads to Westcock" on the Aulac River. They found a large stack of wood—"40 cord on the marsh"—with the barrack-master's boat nearby. Realizing that the wood was destined for the fort for fuel, the militiamen heaved all 40 cords into the river and seized the barrack-master's boat along with other boats taken further down the river. Eddy's real target was the provision sloop *Polly* anchored in Cumberland Creek, about a mile along the basin shore. He placed a guard with the boats until the tide could refloat them and went after the *Polly* resting on the mud at low tide. (The tides in this area are the highest and lowest in the world.)

Lieutenant Colonel Joseph Goreham, in command at Fort Cumberland, discovered several boats full of men coming from Westcock along the shore at Fort Cumberland on Thursday morning, November 7, 1776. He ordered to beat to arms and detached Captain Grant and 50 men to cover the provision. They hauled one of the cannon on the parapet, as there was no embrasure. The men "rushed Resolutely towards the Sloop, up to their Knees in Mud, which made such a Noise as to alarm the Gentry who hailed them and immediately called the Sergeant of the Guard!"

The *Polly* had a night guard of a sergeant and 12 men on board. When the sergeant ordered his men to fire at the band of 30 attackers, he was told that if they fired one gun, every one of them would be put to death. They surrendered without firing a shot. Unable to board without the crew's assistance, the men on the *Polly* lowered ropes for the attackers to board. They waited until daybreak for the tide to rise, refloated the sloop, and sailed out of musket range. They also captured nine men and more than 30 others from a work party that came from the fort to the *Polly*. They were captured almost as fast as they came down the hill, in the thick fog, and ordered aboard the vessel. As the fog cleared about 7 AM, Lieutenant

Colonel Goreham saw the loose sails on the sloop and thought they were drying. When Captain Grant returned and notified him that the *Polly* had been captured, Goreham realized that the *Polly* was under way, in barely enough water to float, and ordered a 9-pounder to be taken to the dike to fire on the sloop and the boats. They fired several cannon shots and a party of 60 men marched down to shoot at the sloop which was already out of range. The *Polly* sailed for the Leplanche River and then to Fort Lawrence.[52]

Colonel Eddy began the attack at 4 AM on Fort Cumberland on Wednesday, November 13. He divided his force into three parties. The first party, mostly Acadians, made a diversionary attack, while the second party carried ladders and tools to scale the outer palisades. The third party assaulted the fort from different directions. Eddy also sent a man, a Maliseet, to sneak into the fort to try to unlock the main gate during the confusion of the diversionary attack and before an all-out attack.

Eddy's party marched down the Baie Verte Road that cloudy morning and occupied the hillside north of the fort. They then crept along old trenches built in 1755. Eddy hoped the diversionary attack against the flagstaff bastion would draw most of the Fencibles to that point, while he attacked in force "the Curtain opposite the Bakehouse between Prince's and Howe's Bastion which was the weakest part of the Fort." He would then storm the fort, force his way inside, and demand Goreham's surrender.

The diversionary force opened up a heavy fire that did not surprise the garrison which was on alert since Eddy's ultimatum expired on Sunday. When the Acadians began to fire at 4 AM, the Fencibles in the flagstaff bastion, a relatively strong point, returned a heavy fire of their own. Goreham placed his main force at the weakest point of the garrison, with the main guard kept as a reserve in front of the bakehouse to reinforce as needed. The main attack came against the curtain wall in between the Prince bastion on the left and the Howe bastion on the right. Eddy's main force began a fusillade directly in front of the curtain wall and the Maliseet managed to get inside the fort in the darkness and confusion of battle. However, a Fencible spotted him just as he reached the main gate and began to remove the bar that would open the gate. The Fencible drew his sword and slashed the man's arm, maiming him and securing the fort.

Eddy's men advanced in a frontal assault when the cannon fired, frightening the main body of attackers with concentrated fire from the fort's six heavy guns in "a furious Cannonade." A few of the assailants succeeded in getting close to the fort walls. Isbrook Eddy, Colonel Eddy's 22-year-old son, saw large log rollers above him at the edge of the parapet ready to be cut loose on anyone ascending the glacis—a memory that haunted him for the rest of his life.

"After a heavy firing from their Great Guns and small Arms without intermission for 2 Hours, which we Sustained without any Loss (Except one Indian being wounded), who behaved very gallantly, and Retreated in good Order to our Camp,"

Eddy decided to withdraw. Goreham observed that they "received such heavy fire that they threw down their Scaling Ladders, Saws, and other implements for cutting down the pickets, [and] quitting some of their arms fell flatt on the ground and scrabbled off." The garrison suffered no casualties.

The HMS *Vulture* landed two companies of marines (400 men) at Fort Cumberland on Tuesday, November 26 to relieve the fort and route the invaders. They disembarked that day and the following day. A party of about 200 Crown troops sallied out of Fort Cumberland on Friday night, November 29, and got behind Colonel Jonathan Eddy's guards. They rushed the barracks where his men were quartered about sunrise. The men had just enough time to escape out of the houses and run into the bushes. The Crown troops proceeded about 6 miles into the country to the place where they thought Colonel Eddy's supplies were stored. Along the way, they burned 12 houses and 12 barns, some of which stored most of the supplies. Eddy decided to retreat to the St. John River.[53]

Lieutenant David Prescott and seven men arrived at Shepody on Monday, December 9, 1776 and took four prisoners at civilian Mr. Peek's house. Mrs. Peek and the prisoners informed Lieutenant Prescott that three men-of-war and two transports had arrived at Cumberland on November 26 and that a reinforcement for the fort arrived on the 29th.[54]

Colonel Jonathan Eddy's troops made night attacks on Fort Cumberland on Sunday and Monday, December 22 and 23. They succeeded in burning several buildings, but were again forced to desist. In the campaign against Fort Cumberland, 13 Fencibles were captured and one killed at Shepody. The guard on the sloop *Polly* was taken as were the work party and "spies and others taken and decoyed." They included a captain, lieutenant, chaplain, surgeon, three sergeants, and 42 privates—a total of 49 men who, added to earlier losses, amounted to 63 men—a quarter of the garrison![55]

The Liverpool, England privateer *Terror* captured a French packet bound from Nantes, France, to Boston, Massachusetts, about Friday April 13, 1781.[56]

A French fleet of 19 ships of the line and 70–80 transports sailed from Brest, France in 1781. British Admiral Kempenfelt's fleet fell in with them but did not attack because of his inferior strength. He had only 12 ships of the line and only one 50-gun ship. Nonetheless, he managed to capture 33 transports which had 1,190 troops on board and great quantities of military stores and clothing. The HMS *Agamemnon* captured an additional five and privateers captured 10 more. The rest of the French fleet returned to port.[57]

Bay of Fundy

Four British warships arrived in the Bay of Fundy in December. The HMS *Vulture* had been sent up earlier; HM Schooner *Hope* and the HM Schooner *Diligent* arrived on December 2; and the HMS *Lizard* arrived on the 15th. The *Nancy*, a large victualing ship from Halifax, and the *Independence*, a captured privateer with 14 guns and 100 men, also arrived on the 2nd. The guns of the *Independence* were removed and mounted at Fort Cumberland.

A party of Rebels surprised the jolly boat of Lieutenant Thomas Farnham's HM Brig *Diligent* in the Bay of Fundy on Tuesday, December 10, 1776. The raiders took four muskets and four cartridge boxes with ammunition. The increased British naval presence also frustrated privateering in the region.[58]

Captain Jabes West, Lieutenant David Scott, 12 men, and a Native American with a birch canoe were sent to capture Loyalist fur traders living at the mouth of the St. John River, New Brunswick, on Monday, June 2, 1777. They proceeded from Manawagonis at daylight and arrived at Fort Cumberland at 9 AM after capturing Messrs. James White and William Hazen.[59]

Three men-of-war, two tenders, and a sloop of the Royal Navy landed 120 men, at one Peabody's, at Manawagonis Bay at the end of June 1777. They marched 2½ miles through the woods; but the militia received advance warning, called in their guards, and retreated. They left Captain Charles Dyer and 12 men to observe the enemy's movements. The Crown forces sent their main body to a place above the falls called Great Bay to secure their boats.

Captain Dyer let the main body come within musket range then fired, killing nine men, and retreated. As he retreated, he fell in with the enemy's flank guard. The guards, under Major Studholm, fired at Dyer and his men from 10 or 12 yards' distance, killed three, and slightly wounded two who got off with Captain Dyer. Dyer's party retreated up the river and was seen 25 miles up river at 1 PM. The Crown troops followed Dyer's party upriver the following day, but only proceeded 20 or 30 miles.

Rebels from Machias, Maine had embarked in several small vessels intending to descend near the St. John River. Sir George Collier, of the HMS *Rainbow*, immediately ordered Captain James Hawker's HMS *Mermaid* to proceed to St. John along with the sloops *Vulture* and *Hope*. The *Vulture* arrived first and found the Whigs in possession of the town. The Rebels fired at the landing boats and killed or wounded six men. They abandoned the town and took a post in the nearby woods when the *Mermaid* anchored. Captain Hawker prepared to dislodge them when a detachment from Fort Cumberland arrived. The combined forces drove out the Whigs with considerable loss. They retreated up the river, above the falls, and escaped across the river in whaleboats. The next day, 200 Crown troops came up the river and, after securing several Whigs, went in search of Captain Dyer.[60]

Sir William Barnaby's HM Frigate *Milford* arrived at Halifax, Nova Scotia, on Wednesday, October 8, 1777 after a cruise in the Bay of Fundy. She brought in with her three prizes: Captain Thomas Player's Marblehead, Massachusetts privateer *Daphne*, with 10 guns and 63 men, returning home; a large French brig bound from Nantes, France, to Boston laden with salt; and a large Whig schooner from the West Indies.[61]

The British frigate *Le Bruin* captured several vessels from the French between Boston and Halifax during the first weeks in June 1778.[62]

The HM Frigate *Garland* captured a French privateer in the St. Lawrence River about Saturday, June 20, 1778.[63]

Miramichi Bay

Captain Augustus Harvey's HMS *Viper* was sent to protect the settlers of Miramichi Bay and to punish the Miramichi tribesmen allied with the Congressional forces for their riotousness. Seamen from the *Viper* captured 15 tribesmen at Miramichi Bay on Monday, July 19, 1779. The Micmac chief, Caiffe (or Cive), fled and was proclaimed a Rebel. Captain Harvey and John Julian, who was then declared Chief of the Miramichi, concluded a peace treaty on July 20. John Parr, Governor of Nova Scotia, granted John Julian and his tribe a license of occupation to a 20,000-acre tract of land lying along either side of the North West branch of the Miramichi. This tract extended from a point below the mouth of the Little South West branch, past the mouth of the Sevogle River and other tributaries of the North West.[64]

A party of 26 French Canadians and Native Americans under Captain Lunier, probably an Indian trader, captured Captain De Badier and Colonel Lowder and four Penobscots on the Penobscot River on Tuesday, October 12, 1779. They arrived at the Penobscot village occupied by only two Penobscots about an hour before Colonel Lowder. Captain Lunier's party learned that the Penobscots were on their way to join Colonel John Allan at St. John, Nova Scotia. They sent a canoe with a wampum belt and invited them to Canada with great promises and threatened them if they refused.[65]

St. Lawrence River

The Québec fleet sailed from Torbay, Newfoundland on May 30, 1780. It consisted of 38 vessels under convoy of two British frigates. They were richly laden with provisions, ordnance and military stores, valuable merchandise, and all kinds of supplies for the province of Canada, the British Army there, and the Indian trade. The convoy contained most, if not all, the supplies for that quarter of the year. Three days later, a French ship-of-the-line fell in with the convoy and took seven vessels and probably more and scattered the entire fleet.

A number of Whig privateers then met the fleet and captured 19 more vessels. Whig cruisers then pursued the remainder of the fleet. Each prize was valued at an average of £20,000.[66]

Expedition to the Gulf of St. Lawrence

Admiral Louis, Comte de Barras, dispatched Captain de Latouche-Tréville's 36-gun *Hermione* and the Comte de la Perouse's 32-gun *Astrée*, to form a fast squadron under La Perouse to attack British commerce in the Gulf of St. Lawrence and to return to Boston by August 20, 1781. The *Hermione* and *Astrée* left Boston on June 23, 1781 and reached the region of Sable Island on June 30. They then went past St. Pierre and Miquelon, to enter the Gulf of St. Lawrence through the Cabot Strait north of Nova Scotia where they began to take a number of prizes.

The lookout of the *Hermione* sighted a vessel in the south at dawn on Tuesday, July 17. Captain de Latouche signaled the *Astrée* and they immediately gave chase. They reached the mouth of Aspy Bay at 8 AM. The *Hermione* hoisted British colors at 9 AM and the chase did the same. When the *Hermione* came within cannon range at 9:45, she fired two chase shots. The vessel came about and struck her colors. Captain de Latouche sent his boat to take possession of her. She was Captain Thompson's 120-ton brig *Friendship*, pierced for 16 guns but carrying only 12 3-pounders. She was bound from Barbados to the island of St. John with sugar, rum, and coffee. She had a crew of 12 and had been out 25 days. Captain de Latouche sent a prize crew of four men and a pilot to take command of her. The frigate *Astrée* also sent four men and the prize was sent to Boston.[67]

The following day, *Astrée* hailed Captain de Latouche's *Hermione* at 1:30 AM to turn about and follow the shore to come athwart a vessel she had spotted. The *Hermione* lost sight of the vessel in the thick fog. When the fog lifted, the *Astrée* hoisted British colors and the vessel came toward her. When she came within speaking range, the vessel was ordered to strike her colors and the *Astrée* took possession of her. She was Captain John Papplay's 70-ton sloop *Phoenix* pierced for 14 guns but carrying only eight 4-pounders. She had a crew of 19 and was bound from New York to Québec with salt, coffee, and tobacco. She departed New York on July 6 and left the British fleet of seven vessels anchored at Sandy Hook, New Jersey. Captain de Latouche sent his pilot and a helmsman to take command. The *Astrée* transferred nine prisoners to the *Hermione*.[68]

The *Hermione* and *Astrée* encountered a convoy of 20 ships escorted by five small British frigates in Aspy Bay at the northern end of Cape Breton Island at 10 AM Saturday morning, July 21, 1781 and chased it. They soon perceived two frigates bearing down upon them and waited for them. When the frigates approached the French vessels, they made some signals which were ignored. A third vessel which appeared to be a sloop-of-war joined the enemy. The *Astrée*, in turn, chased the fleet, which was about four leagues' distance to the windward and too close to the harbor to attack.

The enemy vessels of war were joined by three other vessels from the fleet. They consisted of the 28-gun *Charlestown*, formerly the *Boston*; the 24-gun *Allegiance*;

the 24-gun *Vernon*; the 20-gun *Vulture*; the 14-gun *Jack* or *Saucy Jack*, of Salem, Massachusetts; the 18-gun *Thompson*, and Captain Tucker's 20-gun privateer ship *Thorn*. The commodore gave the signal for them to wait to receive the *Astrée*, which continued to approach them with all sails set. The first gun was fired about 7 PM. The *Astrée* advanced to the leeward of the small squadron with the *Hermione* about 50 yards behind to prevent their escape. The small British squadron fell into disorder. The *Vulture* crowded sails to escape after an engagement of about 10 minutes.

The *Jack* struck her colors at 8:15. The *Charlestown* also struck her colors, having lost her main topmast. She later escaped in the thick fog. The other vessels fled with all the sail they could spread. The British recaptured the *Friendship* and *Lockard Ross*. The prisoners reported that the vessels of the fleet were empty and were going to Spanish Bay to load with coal. The *Hermione* had three men killed and 14 wounded, six seriously; the *Astrée* had three killed and 15 wounded. Both frigates had considerable damage to their rigging.[69]

The *Jack* was sent to Boston, where she arrived on Saturday, August 4. She had been captured by the British about 12 months earlier and was cruising in consort with the *Charlestown*, formerly the *Boston*, which surrendered at the same time but took advantage of a thick fog to escape. They had been out of Halifax for only a few days and had taken nothing. They were bound to Spanish River (Sydney), Nova Scotia with a cargo of provisions.[70]

Captain Samuel Tucker's Massachusetts privateer ship *Thorn* arrived at Boston on Friday, August 3, 1781. Captain Sir William Young's HM Frigate *Hinde* captured her five days before she fell in with the French frigates *Hermione* and l'*Astrée* which retook her.[71]

The French frigates l'*Astrée* and *Hermione* captured a brig with about 250 hogsheads of rum and sugar in the Gulf of St. Lawrence and sent her to Portsmouth, New Hampshire the week of August 5, 1781. They also captured an eight-gun sloop bound from New York to Québec with salt and tobacco, a brig bound from Barbados to Québec with sugar and rum, and a ship from Québec with lumber.[72]

The French and some Whig privateers took 22 transports bound to Québec with 5,000 British troops before September 16, 1782.[73]

Banks of Newfoundland

On Wednesday morning November 22, 1780, Captain Webster's British letter of marque *Nelly* arrived at Plymouth, England. She brought in with her a very large, rich French prize laden with sugar, coffee, cotton, and indigo which she took near the banks of Newfoundland on Wednesday, November 8.[74]

The convoy of the HMS *Egmont*, *Suffolk*, *Grafton*, *Bristol*, *Trident*, and *Endymion* captured an old French 64-gun ship, off the Banks of Newfoundland in May 1781. She was armed *en flute*, bound from France to Rhode Island with 80 pieces of brass cannon, clothing for 10 regiments, stores of all kinds for two ships of the line, and about 2,000,000 livres (about £80,000) in specie when the *Egmont* took her.[75]

Fort Prince of Wales, formerly called Fort Bonséjour, was a large masonry fort built by the Hudson's Bay Company between 1733 and 1771. Each wall measured about 300 feet from the tip of one bastion to the other. The fort surrendered to three French warships without firing a shot on August 8, 1782. The 39-man garrison was unprepared to defend the fort that was designed for about 400 men. Moreover, they were unaware that the war extended to their part of the world as no French ship had been there for more than 40 years. The French spent the next two days destroying as much as they could. They used explosives to destroy the 42 cannon and demolish the walls of the stone barracks. However, they did little damage to the outer walls, which measured up to 40 feet thick.[76]

CHAPTER 4

Naval Assistance

France had not yet declared war on Britain in 1776 but British vessels already preyed on French ships and the French often responded in kind. Spies kept the British informed of what was going on in France; the British knew that the French were supplying arms and munitions to the American colonies. They preyed on French ships both to harass them and to capture their cargoes. These actions usually involved privateers which were generally small vessels, such as schooners, sloops, and brigs, that were lightly armed but fast. These smaller vessels could travel faster and maneuver more quickly and easily than the large warships. In sufficient numbers and with great speed, they could successfully attack slower, lightly armed vessels.

Their intended victims were enemy merchantmen which were completely unarmed or only lightly so. The capture of a merchantman at sea by force of arms was an act of war. The capture of a privateer by a man-of-war was likewise an act of war. It was not unusual for the privateers to kill a few crewmen to convince the others to surrender. Privateers (also called letters of marque) were private vessels legally commissioned with a letter (letter of marque and retaliation) licensing or authorizing them to attack and seize vessels of a belligerent nation specifically mentioned in the terms of their commission.

Some people believe that privateers were not part of the navy and mitigate their contribution or ignore the thousands of fights at sea that occurred between privateers and enemy merchantmen, privateers, and naval vessels. Privateers engaged in a sort of guerilla warfare, or *petite guerre*, that weakened the enemies financially and militarily, eventually causing them to be unable to prosecute the war and to force them to withdraw. Even when privateers lost, a series of tactical losses could lead to strategic victories. Some historians even credit privateers with the eventual American victory at sea. Although privateers didn't engage in battles of the same scale and renown of the navy, they arguably inflicted more damage and greater economic and physical losses on the enemy.

In essence, privateers and pirates operated much the same way, except that the privateers had a legal commission to operate during wartime. When captured, the crew of a privateer were treated as prisoners of war, while a pirate crew were given a summary trial and executed, usually by hanging. Captured privateersmen were usually sentenced to a prison ship until freed. They were the last to be exchanged and usually spent a long time in captivity.

Another difference between privateers and pirates is in the partition of the booty. The owners of a vessel, officers, and crew all had shares based on their rank or financial interest in the vessel. These terms were specified in the "terms of sailing" which the crew would agree to when signing on for a cruise. The portion that would go to the owner of a pirate vessel would go to the government issuing the letter of marque and might be divided between the government and the ship owner.

When a privateer captured a vessel (the "prize" ship), the captain of the privateer replaced the crew with a prize crew which then sailed to a friendly port where the prize and her cargo would be libeled and tried in an admiralty court. If the court condemned her as a legitimate prize, the vessel and her contents were sold at auction and the captain, crew, and owners received a percentage of the total as agreed upon in the terms of sailing. The more prizes a vessel captured, the more profitable the voyage. Let's consider the actions at sea involving French vessels or mariners.

The West Indies

The West Indies were economically important in the 18th century because they were a principal market for the slave trade in the Americas and the primary source of sugar and rum consumed in Europe and America. The French allowed the American colonies to use their ports as trade centers and havens to bring captured vessels. The West Indies were also used as main ports for receiving supplies from France and transferring them to the American colonies. The island of Saint Domingue (Haiti) and the Dutch island of St. Eustatius became essential channels for gunpowder and military supplies provided by the French and the Dutch. American privateers, attempting to destroy Britain's lucrative trade with the Caribbean, needed nearby ports to bring their prizes. Not only did the privateers disrupt English commerce, but the sale of the captured cargoes helped fund the purchase of much-needed munitions. In addition, the merchantmen needed to travel in convoy under naval protection to ensure their safety. This diverted ships and troops that might have been used more effectively in combat.

The capture of British merchant vessels by privateers began as soon as Benjamin Franklin arrived in France. The *Reprisal*, aboard which Franklin crossed the Atlantic, captured two merchant vessels on her way to France. The Americans sold them in French ports by falsifying their papers. Vergennes complained, but the Americans continued with their privateering activities (see pp. 68–69).

France sent six army battalions to the West Indies in November 1775 and another five battalions in October 1777. When hostilities broke out between France and

Britain in the summer of 1778, France had stationed 19 infantry battalions in the West Indies, including eight at St. Domingue. She also had a sizable fleet in the area. As the island was not threatened in the 1770s, it served as a base for deploying troops and ships to the other islands and to the coast of North America. The colony also raised two battalions of local volunteers, one white, the other free blacks, and had a militia of several thousand men. The island was a major naval base and provider of troops for operations in the war. The British tried a naval blockade of Cape François at the end of 1778, but it failed as privateers got through easily.

1776

A fleet of 38 British men-of-war and transports headed from England to North Carolina and captured a large French ship with arms and ammunition on their passage. They arrived at Cape Fear about April 27, 1776. About the same time, the British sloop-of-war *Argos* chased a vessel among the Caribbean islands but was prevented from taking her by a French frigate which exchanged a few shots with the *Argos*, took the vessel under convoy, and brought her safely to a French island.[1] The official position of the French government at the time was to ignore these actions or verbally rebuke the perpetrators. Officially approving or condoning such actions would be an act of war, and France was not yet ready to go to war. (France would officially join the war two years later, on February 6, 1778, when it signed the Treaties of Amity and Commerce.)

In June 1776, a French guarda costa took Captain Samson's Savannah schooner *Bacchus's Delight*, Captain Thomas Webb's Long Island sloop *Lydia*, and Captain Thurston's sloop *Sango*. Captured vessels were tried in the Court of Admiralty; if condemned by the court, the captain of the capturing vessel or the state had the legal right to dispose of the vessel and its cargo, either dividing it among the captain, owners, and crew or selling it at auction, with the proceeds divided among the captain, owners, and crew. They were condemned by the Court of Admiralty in Hispaniola (Haiti) but the *Bacchus's Delight* and the *Lydia* were released by the governor.[2] A frigate from Halifax, Nova Scotia, joined the HM Frigate *Cerberus* at Block Island, Rhode Island, in June 1776. They took a French sloop and a ship before June 22. The ship was believed to be one of the transports previously taken by Captain Biddle's *Andrew Doria*.[3]

Sir Thomas Rich's HMS *Enterprize* met a French fleet of two ships of the line and several frigates commanded by the Duc de Chartres before July 17, 1776. The French bore down upon the *Enterprize*. The admiral hailed her and ordered Sir Thomas to come on board immediately. He replied that if the admiral had anything to communicate to him, he might come on board the *Enterprize*, as he would not leave his ship. The duc insisted that he board or he would sink him. The French ships accordingly pointed their guns at the *Enterprize*, but Sir Thomas declared that he only took orders from his own admiral and refused to go on board. The Duc de Chartres admired his spirited conduct and requested him to come on board as a favor as he wished to be better acquainted with him. So, Thomas Rich immediately went and was received with the utmost respect by all the officers.[4]

The Duc de Chartres and the French fleet were off Cape St. Vincent, Portugal, when they retook a Whig vessel from a British man-of-war before July 31, 1776.[5]

Captain Alan Gardiner's HM Frigate *Maidstone* fired to bring to (or bring alongside) Captain Talmash's schooner *Peggy*. She was boarded between Cape Nichola Môle (Môle Saint-Nicolas, Haiti) and Cape May, New Jersey, on Friday, September 6, 1776. A French frigate bore down on the *Peggy* at the same time. The French fired a shot to the leeward, hoisted out their pinnace, and sent their first lieutenant on board. He inquired if the vessel was from the United States of America and if he wanted protection. Being answered in the negative, he sheered off but continued at a small distance during the time Captain Gardiner was examining the *Peggy*'s papers. Captain Talmash informed Captain Gardiner of the French protection. The *Maidstone* dismissed the *Peggy*, which continued on her voyage to Jamaica and the two vessels steered the same course.[6]

A French schooner which sailed from Newburyport, Massachusetts, about mid-August 1776 was taken by a Crown vessel and retaken by the Newburyport privateer *Washington* before September 20.[7]

British Captain Chiene's transport *Malaga*, bound for Halifax, Nova Scotia, captured a Whig privateer in the Bay of Biscay before November 15, 1776. She was bound for the French West Indies with tobacco and flour to barter for stores. Captain Chiene brought the privateer to Halifax, Nova Scotia, but, as he did not have a letter of marque, his prize became the property of the king, who was graciously pleased to give her up to the captain and crew.[8]

Captain Lambert Wickes's 16-gun Continental ship *Reprisal*, with a crew of 128 men, was sent to France, with American Commissioner Benjamin Franklin aboard as a passenger. En route, she captured James Pratchell's brigantine *La Vigne* on Wednesday, November 27, about 16 leagues or about 50 miles southwest of Belleisle, France.

The *La Vigne* was owned in Hull, England, and was homeward-bound from Rochefort, France, with a cargo of flaxseed and brandy, owned by various French merchant firms. She had sailed on November 22. The *Reprisal* sent over a boarding party, examined the brig's papers, took Pratchell, and returned to the *Reprisal*. They removed the mate and four of the crew and put a prize crew aboard. The *La Vigne* accompanied the *Reprisal* to the Palais de Belleisle but the weather forced both vessels out to sea and the *Reprisal* anchored in Quiberon Bay. Some of the brandy from *La Vigne* was removed to the *Reprisal* here, and the brig was soon missing.

Both the brig and her cargo had been sold to private parties. The *Reprisal* was at the entrance to the Loire River, with one of the brigs in company, perhaps the

George, on December 3. She was captured about the same time as *La Vigne*, bound from Bordeaux, France, to Cork, Ireland, with a cargo of claret and staves.

Wickes reported to the Committee of Secret Correspondence on December 13, noting that the prizes were "both small Brigs," one bound from Bordeaux, France to Cork, Ireland, with a cargo of claret and staves; the other from Rochefort, France to Hull, England, with a cargo of flaxseed and brandy. Although Wickes wasn't sure he would be allowed to sell the prizes, he reported that no fewer than 10 different French merchants had been aboard seeking to purchase the brigs. The *Reprisal* got up to Paimboeuf, France, on December 18, where Pratchell was released.[9]

A British warship captured a French schooner exiting the Delaware Capes in early December. Lieutenant John Baldwin's Continental Navy schooner *Wasp* recaptured her off the Delaware Capes and was escorting her to Egg Harbor, New Jersey, on Wednesday, December 18, when a fleet of 15 vessels, including two two-deck ships and two frigates, came in sight. An armed brigantine pursued the *Wasp* so closely that Baldwin abandoned his prize and scooted into the inlet "fast as he cou'd."[10]

1777

The HMS *Flora* captured a French snow laden with salt and dry goods off Fisher's Island. The British sent her to Newport, Rhode Island, where she arrived about January 12, 1777.[11]

Captain Lambert Wickes's *Reprisal*, with Dr. Benjamin Franklin as a passenger, took two prizes off the coast of France in February 1777. One was a 16-gun, 50-man Lisbon packet bound from London with three vessels under her convoy. Captain Wickes had one man killed and two wounded in the obstinate 2½-hour engagement. He brought his prizes safely into a French port by February 27.[12]

Captain Robert Cochran's South Carolina brigantine, *Notre Dame*, was sent to France for supplies. A large portion of her crew consisted of French sailors taken on at Nantes. As the *Notre Dame* approached her destination—Charleston, South Carolina—on Friday, February 7, 1777, after a passage of seven weeks, Captain Cochran spotted Captain Coombes's Royal Navy victualler *Mackerel*, bound for New York from Cork, Ireland. The *Notre Dame* captured the *Mackerel* easily after exchanging a few shots. Captain Cochran placed a prize crew on her to sail her to Charleston. The HM frigate *Camilla* spotted the *Mackerel*'s sails at 7 AM the following morning and gave chase. By 9 PM, the *Camilla* lit a signal fire and fired a 9-pounder to alert the HM frigate *Perseus* nearby. Both frigates pursued the *Mackerel*, closing in on her by 10 PM. They recaptured her and Captain George Keith Elphinstone, viscount Keith, of the *Perseus,* put a petty officer and seven men on board as a prize crew, noting that all but one of the *Mackerel*'s crew were French.[13]

The HM Frigate *Pearl* captured Jean Tennet's French schooner *La Marie* on Sunday, April 6. She was bound from Cap François (Cap Haitien), Saint-Domingue

(Haiti) to Philadelphia, Pennsylvania, with a cargo of rum, sugar, and molasses. Some sources indicate she was captured on April 11. The prize appears in all lists as the *Mary*. She was sent to New York where she arrived by April 21. She was tried in the Vice-Admiralty court and condemned in 1777. The court records note that she was an American merchant vessel with a "congé" (pass).[14]

Captain Archibald Dickson's HM Frigate *Greyhound* and Captain Charles Fielding's HM Frigate *Diamond* were 48 miles southeast of Cape Ann, on the southern part of Massachusetts Bay, when they sighted a vessel to the northeast at 4 AM on Saturday, April 12. They sailed after her. The *Greyhound* started firing at the chase at 5 AM. After firing 11 9-pounders, the vessel surrendered at 5:30 AM. She was Joseph Blaid's brig *Timoleon* bound from Bordeaux, France, with a cargo of lead, gunpowder, and bale goods. The British discovered that the *Timoleon* had an all-French crew with a Whig pilot.

The HMS *Diamond* came down and joined her consort at 7 AM. Captain Dickson sent a mate and a midshipman on the prize in the afternoon and the *Diamond* furnished six men to make up the prize crew. Six prisoners were taken aboard the *Greyhound*, and six others were sent to the *Diamond*. The prize parted company at 5 PM.[15]

Captain Moor's HMS *Exeter* fell in with a 74-gun French ship before April 25. The *Exeter* hailed her and requested a boat be sent on board. When the French answered they had none, one of the lieutenants of the *Exeter* went on board the French vessel to inquire the reasons for their behavior, as their guns were pointed and men were in the tops with small arms. The French showed them their orders from the French court, which ordered them to protect any Whig ships in their seas.[16]

Captain John Jervis, of the *Foudroyant*, saw two brigs heading for Nantes, France, at daybreak on Monday, April 28. When the brigs recognized the *Foudroyant* as a British vessel, the first one kept her course for land while the other headed out to sea. There was little wind and the *Foudroyant* had little hope of making the short run to the land and catching up with the first brig, so she chased the second, coming up to her at noon. She proved to be the *Barbara* bound from Bordeaux, France, to Dublin, Ireland. She had been taken the previous day by the other brig, Master John Clouston's *Freedom*. She had been out seven weeks from Boston and had captured 12 prizes, seven of which were sent to Boston.[17]

The *Foudroyant* intercepted Commander John Porter's South Carolina privateer sloop, the Bermuda-built *Alice* (*Ellis*), on Wednesday afternoon, April 30. The *Alice* sailed from Charleston on March 1 headed to Nantes, Bordeaux, or the first port in France she could reach, to deliver her cargo of rice and indigo. She would then load clothing and implements of husbandry to return to Charleston. Captain Porter was 24 miles from the mouth of the Loire, off Belle-Île, when he encountered the *Foudroyant*. He threw his papers, commission, and guns overboard in an effort to escape. The British captured the *Alice*, but treated Porter as a merchant skipper.

He was taken to Plymouth, England, where he arrived on May 4 and underwent a very long examination. The *Alice* was tried and condemned in the High Court of Admiralty. Porter soon escaped and was at St. Malo on June 6. From there he worked himself back to Charleston by the fall of 1777.[18]

Captain Gustavus Conyngham returned to Dunkirk, France, with two prizes before May 22. He and his crew were arrested at the request of the court of England and put in prison on pretense of piracy. As they had a commission from Congress, they were discharged. The prizes were reclaimed.[19]

Captain Andrew Snape Hamond's HM Frigate *Roebuck* sighted Beruaa (Boruau, Bernard) Durcourdroy's (Durcauday) French brig the *Empereur* east-northeast of Cape Henlopen, Delaware, at 5 AM on Monday, June 2, 1777. The *Empereur*, owned by one Bassacre, was bound from Guadeloupe in the French West Indies to Miquelon Island with a cargo of molasses, sugar, coffee, rum, wine, and dry goods. She had an official pass to proceed to Miquelon.

Captain Hamond sent his tender, the *Ballahoo*, under Lieutenant Richard Brewer, to chase the *Empereur*. He dispatched a second tender, the *General Washington*, under Midshipman Rogers, to assist the *Ballahoo* at 7 AM. The *Roebuck* saw her tenders and the brig to the northeast at 4 PM. They spoke to the *Ballahoo* at 8 PM and Brewer informed Hamond that he captured the prize. The *Empereur* was sent to New York, where she arrived on June 14 and was tried and condemned in the Vice-Admiralty Court.[20]

Captain Samuel Barrington's HMS *Prince of Wales* captured John Roberts's (Robards) schooner *Mary* at Nantes, France, about Tuesday, June 10. She had arrived from Charleston, South Carolina, with a cargo of salt, brandy, and dry goods and was ordered to Plymouth, England. A French officer who was a passenger aboard the *Mary* was ordered to be confined as a prisoner of war on June 20, 1777.[21]

Robert Sawyer's HMS *Boyne* captured Benjamin Evans's brig *Constant Friend* off the French coast on Thursday, June 12. She was bound from Charleston to Bordeaux, France, with a cargo of rice and indigo. She was escorted to Plymouth, England, where she arrived on June 16. The master was a native of England and there was some question as to whether he should be liberated. He was ordered freed on June 20. The crew, all French except for the mate and a black sailor, were distributed to various British warships as prisoners and ordered to serve in their crews.[22]

The HMS *Seaford* took a large 400-ton French ship, mounting 14 guns, on Thursday, June 26. She was loaded at Le Havre and destined for Martinique, French West Indies, and North America with 10,000 stands of arms; 170 bales of tents; two bronze mortars with 300 shells; 17 pieces of cannon, 18-pounders; a quantity of ball, powder, etc.[23]

Captain Benjamin Caldwell's HM Frigate *Emerald* and the HM Brig *Raleigh* were anchored at the entrance to the Chesapeake Bay when they sighted a strange vessel off Cape Henry on Monday, June 30. Captain Caldwell sent off the *Raleigh* and his boats to investigate. They drove the stranger ashore a little south of Cape Henry, Virginia. She was a French brig bound to Virginia with sails, cordage, rum, and bale goods. The British burned her.[24]

Captain Gustavus Conyngham's Continental Navy cutter *Revenge* sailed from Dunkirk, France, on July 8. She captured several prizes in the German Ocean, the North Sea, the Irish Channel, and the Western Ocean and destroyed several other vessels. The prizes were sent to America, the West Indies, and other places that would benefit from their cargoes. Few of them arrived safely. Some of the prize masters took the cargoes for their own use.

The *Revenge* fell in with the French brig *Grasiosa* off Cape Ortinzal on Thursday, July 10. She was bound from London to La Coruña, Spain, with a cargo invoiced at £75,000. A prize crew was put on board and she was sent to Bilbao, Spain.[25]

Captain Squires's letter of marque *Favourite Betsey* ran into Ocracoke Harbor on Thursday, July 17. The 16-gun, 93-man privateer *Sturdy Beggar*, a 10-gun sloop, and seven vessels were anchored there destined for Hispaniola (Haiti). When the *Favourite Betsey* showed her colors and fired a gun, the other vessels immediately hoisted sail, ran over the bar up the river, and got clear, except the sloop *Lovely Lass* belonging to Bermuda and bound to Edenton, North Carolina, with 1,000 bushels of salt. The *Lovely Lass* was destroyed along with a French brig pierced for 16 guns but carrying only four 4-pounders. Captain Squires also took, during his cruise, Master Elliott's Boston, Massachusetts schooner *Hannah* bound to North Carolina for provisions and the schooner *Little Polly* laden with mahogany and logwood.[26]

Commander John Lee's Massachusetts privateer brigantine *Fancy* captured Mr. Le Fevre's (Le Fabre) 180-ton brig or brigantine *Dillon* in European waters on Thursday, July 24. The French vessel, owned in Dunkirk, France, was bound from North Yarmouth, England, to Genoa and Livorno, Italy, with a cargo of 247 bales of the first and second cloths and a great quantity of other valuable articles and bale goods. She arrived at Newburyport, Massachusetts, on September 4, 1777, where she was said to be the richest prize of the war. The *Dillon* was libeled on September 18 and her trial was set for October 7.[27]

Three armed vessels from Dunkirk, France, under Continental commissions as privateers, took several British vessels before July 30, 1777, including two packet boats headed to Germany with £66,000 in specie.[28]

Paul Berthelot's brigantine the *Aimable Reine*, owned by Ruste de Rezeville Frères of St. Pierre, Martinique, French West Indies, sailed from Dunkirk in October 1776 to St. Pierre, Martinique. She then sailed from St. Pierre for Dunkirk with a cargo of sugar, coffee, rum, indigo, and tobacco on July 16, 1777. She encountered a "convoy" of 11 British transports along the way. They were en route to New York with supplies for the British Army. William Medows's British privateer ship *Swan* stopped the *Aimable Reine* and searched her. Medows informed Berthelot that the indigo and tobacco were contraband. He seized the French vessel and took her to New York as a prize. The "convoy" and the prize arrived on October 1, 1777. Berthelot received "very rough treatment in that country." The Admiralty Court condemned the tobacco and indigo but restored his brigantine. Berthelot filed a formal protest and then sailed from New York on December 19. The *Aimable Reine* arrived at Dunkirk on January 20, 1778. The owners of the cargo protested to the French Minister of the Navy, who forwarded the protest to the Comte de Vergennes, the French Foreign Minister. The owners of the brigantine sent a formal protest to Vergennes on or before February 6, 1778. The matter had been presented to Lord Weymouth, the British Foreign Minister, by February 6.[29]

Thomas Venture's British privateer ship *True Briton* encountered Andrew Laffont's French brig *Assumption* about the end of August or the beginning of September 1777. The *Assumption* was going from Martinique, French West Indies to Charleston, South Carolina, with salt. The *True Briton* presumably detained the *Assumption*. When the *True Briton* fought Captain Nicholas Biddle's Continental Navy ship *Randolph* on Thursday, September 4, the *Assumption* was also captured, taken to Charleston on September 7, and released.[30]

Two British brigs, one a very large one, the other mounting 10 or 12 guns, arrived at New Bern, North Carolina, in early September and took several vessels anchored there, particularly a large French brig. There were many vessels ready to go out, but most of them escaped by running up into the rivers again. The 14-gun, 100-man privateer *Sturdy Beggar*, Captain Farmer's 16-gun and 80-man state brig *Pennsylvania*, and the 10-gun, 80-man New Bern sloop *Heart of Oak* prepared to sail in quest of the raiders.[31]

John Tyrie's London-owned sloop *Amelia* was en route from Senegal, West Africa, to Jamaica, British West Indies with a cargo of 68 slaves on Monday, September 8. Mr. Davie's Whig privateer *Tyger*, mounting 12 guns and 12 swivels, caught up with her off Alto Velo Island near Santo Domingo, Spanish West Indies (Dominican Republic today). Davie was a Frenchman as were most of his crew of 90 men. He had only one Whig aboard, a common sailor. The French crew boarded the *Amelia* and one Thomas Freeman informed the British he had an American commission, "although, at the same Time, he confessed it, to be, a mere Forgery..." No commission was shown to the British.

The sloop was taken into the Baye des Flamands, Saint-Domingue, French West Indies (Haiti). Two of the British escaped and the remaining eight were robbed of their "Cash, papers, Clothes &c..." before they were put aboard a French merchant vessel on September 20. The trader landed them at Fisher's Bay, Jamaica, on September 23. The slaves had been taken ashore, along with two free black crew members, and the *Amelia* was at anchor in the bay when the British crew left. Vice Admiral Clark Gayton forwarded copies of the master's, and the crew's, depositions to the Comte d'Argout, the French governor of Saint-Domingue, on October 10 with a demand for restitution. Gayton wrote to d'Argout on February 2, 1778, thanking the governor for taking up the "Pirate" and hoping the property illegally seized would soon be restored.[32]

The Continental Navy frigate *Randolph*, which had recently been refitted at Charleston, South Carolina, captured four vessels near Wilmington, Delaware, a few days before September 19, probably on Saturday, the 13th. As there were no seamen available there, a number of volunteers and a Mr. John McQueen, with several of his slaves, went on board the *Randolph* and proceeded to sea. The *Randolph* took a large three-deck ship of 20 guns and two other vessels of eight guns each bound from Jamaica to New York. Their cargoes consisted of 600 hogsheads of rum, 800 hogsheads of sugar, and a chest of johannesses (Portuguese gold currency) believed to belong to the commissary who was also taken aboard the ship. The *Randolph* also retook a French vessel laden with salt.[33]

Captain Thomas Thompson's Continental Navy ship *Raleigh* and Captain Elisha Hinman's Continental Navy ship *Alfred* were en route to France in late September 1777 when they encountered two stragglers from the Jamaica convoy at 49°13′N, 10°56′W, at the mouth of the English Channel, on Tuesday, September 30. The *Raleigh* captured David Watt's (Watts) 800-ton ship *Jamaica* (or *Jamaican*), owned in London and bound from Jamaica, British West Indies to London, England. The *Jamaica* was a big three-decker, mounting 14 (or 16) guns to protect her cargo of rum, sugar, cotton, and coffee valued at £60,000, but she made no resistance. She was two months out from Jamaica and had parted from the convoy only a few days before.

The *Alfred* took John Taylor's (Johnson) 500-ton ship *Anna Susannah* (or *Anna and Susannah*), also owned in London and bound there with a similar cargo. She had also left the convoy a few days before. Both prizes were manned and kept in company with the Continental ships.

Hinman and Thompson resumed their course for France with the prize ships. The prizes parted company during the night of October 4 and were off Belle-Île, France, the following morning and in sight of Île de Groix by the afternoon. A calm came up and night came down, so the Continental ships stood off and on until morning. Both prizes were nearby on the morning of October 6. Pilots came out and the *Alfred* and *Raleigh* were soon riding at anchor in Port Louis. The prizes anchored under the Île de Groix.

Thompson went ashore immediately and contacted Gourlade, Bérard frères, & Montplaisir, the Continental agents at Lorient. A letter to the American Commissioners in France announced their arrival, with the news that Thompson had no dispatches and had just missed the post. He would write the following day. Gourlade, Bérard frères, & Montplaisir noted that the frigates had several "wants of Cables Ankers Sails Ballastg. Of Iron, Guns, and several other things which we will provide having declared them in such a manner as to avoid trouble…" The Frenchman meant he had entered the ships as distressed, to avoid any inconveniences caused by British protests. The vessels needed to be cleaned, and the French agents suggested that the American Commissioners get the "approbation of the Minister that difficulties may not be Started." As to the prizes, "we will do our best ... and dispose of them as soon as possible as they stand before the answer of the court, or any aplication can be made from ye Court of England or the owners..."

Thompson reported from Lorient on October 10. He acknowledged that he was following orders four months old when he sailed, and that the American commissioners would be surprised to find two frigates had arrived with no dispatches. Thompson had come to complete the *Raleigh* and refurbish the *Alfred*. They had obtained permission to refit "after various pretences, not consistant with the Honour of the United States, nor the Respect due to a Man of War belonging to a free and Independant Empire—But small Folks must sing small, & for the sake of Convenience must abate their Dignity..." Thompson and Hinman had met with every "personal Respect" at Lorient and were well received by the population. Thompson requested orders from the American commissioners, and suggestions as to a "Line for my Conduct during my stay here..." Thompson sent a copy of his battle report, and his journal, noting that he had come into Port Louis "in Distress." The prizes were left under the Île de Groix until he saw what kind of reception he obtained. They were still there, but had already been sold, for about half their value; but there seems a "necessity for secresy & Dispatch..." The *Alfred* and *Raleigh* were preparing to heave down, and the work would be forwarded as fast as possible. Thompson passed along the news he had, which wasn't much.

The French line of conduct was laid down by the Minister of the Navy, Gabriel de Sartine, on October 11. The Commissary of the Port, Jean-François-Timoleon Viger, was to verify the repairs to the *Alfred* and *Raleigh* and furnish necessaries for payment. No warlike supplies or munitions were to be embarked. They were only to remain until they were ready for sea, and Viger was to expedite their departure. The prizes, which had been reported as American merchant vessels being escorted by the warships, were allowed to trade freely.

The American commissioners wrote to Gourlade, Bérard frères, & Montplaisir on October 13, asking them to assist the two ships and to deliver a letter to Thompson requesting him to forward any letters by way of Gourlade and company, which was much safer than other routes. To help smooth the way for the two Continental captains, Jonathan Williams, the Continental Agent at Nantes, sent Captain Samuel Nicholson to Lorient. Nicholson had long been in France and was familiar with the tricks necessary to avoid delay and detection by the English.

By October 13, Sartine had been informed that the two merchant vessels were prizes, and had been sold. Viger had ordered them out of port at once, but Sartine had learned from another source that the "entirety of the two cargoes was sold to foreigners. I could hardly believe it after the positive orders I gave to you and the king's wish which is well known to you." Sartine demanded a special report by courier of this transaction. Two days later, Sartine was answering an inquiry by Lord Stormont, through the Comte de Vergennes, about the two ships and the prizes. Sartine noted that they had been allowed to repair only after an inspection and that the prizes had not been allowed to enter port. He did not state that he knew that the prizes had already been sold.

On October 15, in a report to his British spy masters, George Lupton (James Van Zandt) mentioned that the prizes had been sold for £9,600. The same day, Lord Stormont protested to the Comte de Vergennes concerning the two ships. He requested they be ordered out to sea and that the prize vessels not be sold. Vergennes seemed surprised, said Stormont later; however Maurepas, the French Prime Minister, knew of the arrival. Maurepas claimed they were admitted in distress and were leaky. Maurepas thought the prizes had left. Stormont countered that "Vessels would always appear Leaky to those who had a Mind to think them so, and that in a Word the whole was a mere jest, and was considered as such by the Americans themselves…"

Jonathan Williams had learned the details of the sale of the prizes by October 18 and was stunned. The property had been sold for £9,600, which Williams thought was about one-third of its value; and about one half of what it should have sold for in "their circumstances." Williams disapproved and had written to Lorient offering £2,000 more, on the American commissioner's account, if the deal was not yet completed. If he got the goods they would be sent to Holland as French property and sold there. Williams had a good opinion of Gourlade but thought that advantage had been taken by others in the haste of disposal of the property. Answering the letters of the American commissioners in France on October 20, Thompson also regretted the prizes had sold so low. He thought the two would be worth £21,000 in England. A British spy in the American headquarters reported that there was much to-do about this sale. Chaumont begged the purchasers to make up the price to £13,000 for the "Honor & Interest of France…"

These prizes attracted the attention of troublemaker Thomas Morris who was, in theory, the Continental Agent for France. Morris deputized a "Mr. Pinet" and recommended him to the two Continental captains. Penet picked out a third person who went to Lorient express to attend to the prizes. All these men urged "Secrecy & Dispatch" and asked for permission to sell the prizes, even though Morris and Penet were no closer than Nantes. Thompson informed the American commissioners of this unusual request on October 20, saying he had told Morris that others, recommended by the American commissioners, had handled the matter.

Meanwhile the British prisoners aboard the *Raleigh* and the *Alfred* had to be disposed of in some way. About 70 prisoners were put in a French brig and sent to England, sailing on October 11. As the brig got under way, so did the two prize ships. Although there was some talk of attempting to recapture the ships, cooler heads prevailed. They arrived at Christchurch on October 20. Among the prisoners thus released were Watt (*Jamaica*), Hooper (*Nanny*), Marshall (*Sally*), and *Athens* (the schooner from New York). These landed at Portsmouth, England, and, in passing through customs, revealed that the two prizes were unloading, their cargoes having been sold. The two Continental frigates were discharging their guns, preparing to clean, and a third frigate, built in France, was about to be launched at Lorient. The three together, when ready, were to escort a convoy of 20 vessels to America. The customs officials passed this information to London.

Sartine wrote to Charles Pierre Gonet, Commissary at Lorient, on November 7, concerning the *Alfred* and *Raleigh*. He was to impress on the captains the urgency of their completion of the refit of the ships, and of their departure. As to the prizes, Bérard "surely would merit being punished" if it were proven he was behind the movement of the ships and their sale. He had already paid a fine for breaking other regulations. Sartine emphasized the point: "Enjoin him to be more circumspect in the future…" As to the French sailors who had moved the prizes: "… come to an understanding with the Admiralty officers of Vannes…" to remove the sailors and get the prizes away from French shores.

Against all odds, it would seem, Lord Stormont had now located one of the *Raleigh*'s and *Alfred*'s prizes, the *Anne Susannah*. She was at Pelerin, 9 miles from Nantes, on November 26. There, she was being altered, her name erased, and her appearance changed. She had been renamed *La Mignone*. Stormont demanded the return of this vessel and her cargo in a memorandum dated December 2. Sartine investigated and reported, on December 28, that the ship in question was not the *Anne Susannah*, although it was the *La Mignone*. There was no known evidence to connect the two, said Sartine.[34]

The large French brig *Lyon* was loaded at Yarmouth, England, and bound to Livorno, Italy. She was taken and carried to Newburyport, Massachusetts. The British cargo was condemned at Salem on November 11. The cargo consisted of 60 tons of lead, 243 large bales of Yorkshire woolens, and Norwich stuff valued at £30,000. Several tons of lead and a few bales of goods which were the property of some Italians were not condemned but returned to the captain with the vessel.[35]

On December 19, 1777, one observer noted that the French agents had "abused the confidence" of the Americans: they had gained 60,000 livres on one prize alone, made advance charges on all goods furnished for refit and cargo, "besides the impudent advantages they have taken in becoming purchasers of prize-goods at an under-value."[36] In other words, the captain of the *Lyon* purchased the condemned cargo at auction at a greatly reduced price, only to turn it around and sell it at a great profit.

Sir Thomas Rich's HMS *Enterprize* captured the *Venus*, a large ship bound from Philadelphia to Nantes with 1,100 barrels of rice and indigo. The *Enterprize* also captured a French brig bound from Nantes to South Carolina with arms, bale goods, and salt, along with another very valuable prize.[37]

1778

Captain John Lewis Gidoin's HM Frigate *Richmond* was in the York River, Virginia, on Saturday afternoon January 3, 1778. Her consort, Captain Benjamin Caldwell's HM Frigate *Emerald*, signaled that he sighted a strange vessel at 2 PM. The two frigates and a tender began to chase her at 3 PM. The *Richmond* saw several gun flashes at 5 PM as the tender fired at the chase which then surrendered. The *Richmond* closed enough to speak to the tender's prize at 6 PM, whereupon the chase hove to. She was Jean François Forand's French brig *Alexandrine*, bound from Baltimore (or the Rappahannock River, Virginia) to Dunkirk, France, by way of Martinique, French West Indies, with a cargo of tobacco and 12 hands. The *Alexandrine* was captured in the Rappahannock River and sent to New York for trial. She arrived there on January 16. Howe attributed her capture to the *Richmond* in his prize list, but she was condemned to the *Emerald* at her trial on February 20.[38]

Peter Collas's brig (or ship) sailed from Boston, Massachusetts, on January 14 bound for France. Collas carried a packet of letters for the American commissioners in France, as well as several private letters. He was off Belle-Île and had taken a French pilot for Bordeaux aboard on Saturday, February 14. Although Collas had taken the precaution of avoiding all vessels sighted, there was a small schooner near Belle-Île. The French pilot assured Collas that the schooner was a Whig privateer, stating he had been aboard her a few days before. The privateer was actually Peter Agnew's Crown privateer schooner *Active*. She approached and soon captured Collas's brig as well as his dispatches. The brig was taken to Guernsey, Channel Isles, and Collas was sent to Plymouth, England, after being guarded for eight days. He informed Jonathan Williams of the loss from Plymouth on March 22.[39]

British vessels patrolled the coast of North America, attempting to impede shipping and to prevent military supplies coming from Europe from reaching their destination. Bertrand Olivier's (Edenton, North Carolina) French ship *La Felicité* was en route from Beverly, Massachusetts, to Saint-Domingue on Sunday, February 15. She was sailing in ballast but with some cordage and a little wine. Captain Philemon Pownoll's HM Frigate *Apollo* sighted her near St. George's Bank at 9 AM and gave chase in windy and dirty weather. The *Apollo* overtook *La Felicité* at 1 PM, fired a shot, and brought her to. The captain, mates, and part of the crew were removed, and a petty officer and a few men were sent aboard *La Felicité*. Most of the prisoners were put on the schooner *Polly* and sent to Salem, Massachusetts. The prize was kept with the *Apollo* for a few days.

Captain Samuel Tucker's Continental Navy ship *Boston* came in sight on February 19 and the British frigates chased her in company with *La Felicité*. The *Boston* escaped, and *La Felicité* parted company on February 20, went to Newport, Rhode Island, and eventually to New York where she arrived on March 7. The prize was libeled on March 11 and tried on April 8. This vessel was claimed by Walter Franklin for Peter and John Berthon, but her cargo was condemned.[40]

Captain Symonds's HMS *Solebay* captured Pierre Marie Donnat's ship *Vicomte de Vaux* off the Virginia Capes on Monday, February 23. She was bound from Lorient, France, with a cargo of woolens and other goods for the Continental Army. The *Vicomte de Vaux* was a 600-ton ship mounting 24 carriage guns. She arrived in New York on Tuesday March 17.[41]

The HMS *Solebay* captured a 600-ton 24-gun French frigate with a crew of 100 off the Virginia Capes as she came into the capes on Sunday, March 1. The *Solebay* chased her all day, but she escaped during the night along with a richly laden 40-gun French ship which was a consort to the *Solebay*'s prize. She was captured by the *St. Albans* and the *Solebay* on February 23.[42]

The HMS *Emerald* and the HM Frigate *Richmond* sailed up the Rappahannock River in pursuit of three French tobacco vessels, viz. a ship, a brig, and a snow before March 6. They captured all three the same day along with 800 hogsheads of tobacco valued at £25,000 minimum.[43]

The guns of the HMS *St. Albans* sank a fine French ship with clothing and other supplies for the Continental Army as she tried to pass the *St. Albans* during the night before March 6.[44]

The Indiaman *Nottingham* took the French brig *Sea Nymph* on Friday, March 6, and sent her to New York. The captain and part of the crew were taken to Philadelphia.[45]

The HM Frigate *Unicorn* captured a French ship that sailed from France in company with another ship that arrived safely at New London, Connecticut.[46]

The French frigate *Olsea* captured the privateer *Hawke*, cruising near the French coast, and took her to Lorient before March 9, 1778.[47]

Captain Molloy's HMS *Senegal* captured the French ship *Hector* on Wednesday, March 11. She was bound from St.-Malo to Virginia with a cargo of salt and dry goods and sent to New York.[48]

Captain Carey's Crown privateer sloop *General Howe* captured the 500-ton French ship *St. Jago* headed from South Carolina to Nantes with 1,000 tierces of rice on Thursday, March 12. The *St. Jago*, sailing under Spanish colors but believed to have a commission from Congress, mounted six 6-pounders and had a crew of 20 men. She had previously been captured by a Whig privateer and taken to Martinique with slaves.[49]

Captain Fanshaw's HMS *Carysfort* captured a valuable French snow from St. Eustatius, Netherlands West Indies, and sent her to New York where she arrived on March 19.[50]

Commander Richard Onslow's HMS *St. Albans* captured Mr. André's ship *Jean* bound from Bordeaux, France, to Virginia with a cargo of salt, cordage, and dry goods on Friday, March 13. She was sent to New York where she arrived on March 19.[51]

British cruisers patrolled off the coasts of Carolina and Florida in early 1778. Captain George Keith Elphinstone's HMS *Perseus*, Captain Faushawe's HMS *Carysfort*, and Captain McKenzie's *Lizard* took or destroyed 35 prizes before April 4. They included:

- the brig *Reine Blanche* from Rochelle, France, to Charleston with salt, dry goods, wine, and brandy;
- the 10-gun ship *Marquis de Pesey* from Bordeaux with clothing, salt, wine, brandy, soap, and dry goods;
- a schooner bound from Charleston to Virginia with arms, clothing, and 17 French officers for a French corps;
- the 10-gun ship *Bourbon* from Bordeaux with rum, sugar, coffee, and salt;
- the brig *Flambeaux* from Hispaniola (Haiti) with rum, sugar, and coffee;
- the brig *Reflection* from Nantes;
- the 20-gun ship *André* with clothing, cordage, canvas, wines, brandy, and salt;
- the ship *Glaneur* from Rochelle with clothing, cordage, canvas, wines, brandy, and salt;
- the armed snow *Le Noir* from Bordeaux with naval stores, clothing, and wines;
- master Pierce's sloop bound to France with rice and indigo;
- the schooner *Marianne*.[52]

The HM Frigate *Ariel* was the only British warship stationed off the coast of North Carolina in the spring of 1778. She patrolled between Cape Hatteras and Cape Lookout and captured six vessels in two months. Her captain demanded that the pilots help carry the ship over the bar to attack a French merchant ship and a brig or be put to death. They complied. The privateers boarded the ship and the brig, hoisted 100 hogsheads of tobacco from the ship onto the brig, and took her with them along with a sloop from Bermuda loaded with salt on Saturday, April 4.[53]

Captain Duncan's letter of marque ship *Rose* drove two vessels on shore, captured two sloops—one with French merchandise—and a brig with 126 hogsheads of Roanoke tobacco and a large quantity of staves before April 6. The French sloop was bound from Cape François to Virginia with a cargo of rum, sugar, molasses, duck, calico, chintzes, and medicines. She was sent to New York where she arrived on Friday, April 17. The *Rose* arrived in St. Augustine, Florida, on Monday, April 6, along with the other sloop and the brigantine.[54]

A boat with six men captured a British schooner fitted out as a tender to Captain Mowatt's HMS *Albany*. The schooner, commanded by a Mr. Browne, midshipman of the *Albany*, and eight hands, pursued a French vessel in one of the eastern ports before April 7. The men boarded and captured the French vessel and took her to Salem, Massachusetts, on Tuesday, April 7.[55]

Lieutenant Wright's brig *Dunmore*, tender to the HM Sloop *Otter*, captured the French snow *Le François* laden with dry goods, wine, and brandy before April 21.

He also captured the schooner *Le Loup* bound from Rochelle with salt from St. Domingue. The prizes arrived in Philadelphia on Tuesday, April 21.[56]

British Captain McKenzie's frigate *Lizard* captured a fine Swedish snow, two French ships of 16 guns each, and a brig.[57] The HM Frigate *Maidstone* captured a brigantine with molasses, a snow with a number of French and English on board, and a 12-gun privateer sloop. All the prizes were brought to Sandy Hook, New Jersey, before April 23.[58]

Five Whig soldiers from the fort at Savannah, Georgia, boarded a French schooner anchored there about Friday, April 24. She was laden with rice for Martinique, French West Indies. The French schooner was weakly manned. The captain thought the soldiers were coming to his assistance and permitted them to weigh his anchor, after which they took command of the vessel and brought her to St. Augustine, Florida.[59]

The HMS *Ariel* chased a French polacre ashore in North Carolina in April or May 1778. The crew scuttled her after taking out three boats full of her lading but the *Ariel*'s crew got some of the goods before the polacre was totally destroyed.[60]

A tender belonging to Sir James Wallace's HMS *Experiment* took the French ship *Citizen* in latitude 38.38, longitude 72 on Tuesday, May 12, 1778 and sent her to New York. She was bound from Boston to Virginia with salt.[61]

Captain Scott captured two prizes laden with 260 hogsheads of tobacco and brought them to the Isle of Guernsey about May 12, 1778. One was a French snow bound from Bordeaux to Boston with salt and bale goods captured by Captain Cabot's letter of marque *Macaroni*.[62]

Meanwhile, Captain Kirby's privateer captured three French vessels bound for America and brought them to Jersey. One of the vessels mounted 16 6-pounders. When Captain Kirby came alongside and asked where she came from, they responded with a broadside and fought for two hours. Captain Kirby had one man killed and 15 wounded. He captured the three vessels at the same time as they were in company.[63]

Captain Agnew captured a French snow in the English Channel about the same time. She was laden with 600 hogsheads of rice, 38 hogsheads of tobacco, 4 tons of indigo, 250 barrels of turpentine, logwood, fustic, and mahogany.[64]

The letter of marque brig *Juno* captured the French vessel *Luteil* bound from the York River, Virginia, to Nantes, France, with tobacco and took her to Waterford, Ireland, before May 14.[65]

Captain Sampson's brigantine *Hazard* captured a schooner and two brigs on his passage from Martinique, French West Indies. The schooner and one of the brigs were retaken. The other brig arrived in Boston, Massachusetts, with the *Hazard* on Saturday, May 16. On his return to Boston, Captain Sampson took a brig from France bound to Lord Howe with wine and brandy and a ship bound from Bristol, England, to New York with salt, cordage, nails, and glass.[66]

Commander Charles Phipps's HMS *Ariel* chased a French polacre on shore at North Carolina before May 25, 1778. The crew scuttled her after taking out three boats full of her cargo, but the *Ariel*'s crew got some of the goods before she was totally destroyed.[67] The *Ariel* then chased a 22-gun, 240-man French frigate which boarded a schooner off Cape Henry, Virginia. The Frenchman had been at sea for three months and knew nothing of his king's preparations for war.[68]

A party of Loyalists from New York, in a pilot boat, captured a French sloop laden with molasses off Sandy Hook, New Jersey, on Monday afternoon, May 25.[69]

Captain Sibbles's New York letter of marque brig *Tryon* captured a 150-ton French polacre bound to Virginia in June 1778. A few days later, she captured Alexander Kennedy's Whig brig *Esther* off the Virginia Capes. She was bound from the James River, Virginia, to Boston, Massachusetts, with a cargo of 1,000 barrels of flour, 50 barrels of bread, and seven hogsheads of tobacco.[70]

A French sloop fitted out at Charleston, South Carolina, and the 16-gun Connecticut brig *Defence* captured two small armed sloops from St. Augustine, Florida, commanded by captains Osborn and Beckup about June.[71]

Captain Bentley's privateer schooner, belonging to Newbury, Massachusetts, fell in with and captured a French snow off Montauk Point, Long Island, on Wednesday, June 10. She was headed to Newport, Rhode Island with a cargo of salt and a large quantity of calicoes. The most valuable articles were taken on board the privateer and brought to New London, Connecticut. The snow was ordered to Newbury.[72]

Captain Michel's French ship *Lyon* fell in with an English frigate south of Long Island, New York, on Friday, June 12. The two vessels parted after an engagement which lasted four hours.[73]

The HM Frigate *Arethusa* attacked the French frigate *Belle Poule* and captured the frigates *Licorne* and *Pallas* and the sloop *Coureur* before Sunday, June 28.[74]

When France entered the war on February 6, 1778, King Louis XVI sent Admiral Jean Baptiste Charles Henri Hector, Comte d'Estaing, to America with a fleet of 12 ships-of-the-line and three frigates. They captured a 26-gun New York privateer cruising along the Virginia coast in late June 1778 and a ship from New Providence (Nassau, Bahamas) bound to London. They also recaptured a French snow laden with dry goods and drove ashore and destroyed the 32-gun HM Frigate *Mermaid*.[75]

The French also captured the following prizes in the Atlantic Ocean in July:

- the Liverpool, England, ship *Peggy*, mounting 14 guns and 57 men, bound from Barbados, British West Indies, to New York;
- a Liverpool ship, mounting 14 guns and 43 men, bound from Rhode Island to New York;
- a ship from the West Indies mounting four guns;

- a snow from New York bound to Lord Howe's fleet with 13$^{1}/_{2}$ tons of gunpowder. She was driven by a violent squall near the Long Island shore and taken by the boats of the French fleet.
- a snow from Barbados mounting six guns;
- a sloop from St. Kitts, British West Indies, mounting six guns;
- a sloop from Antigua, British West Indies;
- a brig from Barbados;
- a sloop from the West Indies;
- a sloop from the West Indies mounting six guns. All these vessels were bound to New York or to the British headquarters.
- the sloop *York*, a tender mounting 12 guns and 54 men commanded by a lieutenant;
- a schooner;
- a tender of four carriage guns, 12 swivels, and two cohorns, recaptured;
- the ship *Peggy*;
- a brigantine belonging to Mr. Marmajou.[76]

The French fleet anchored 5 miles off Sandy Hook and captured 14–17 prizes. On Saturday, July 18, the Allied forces exchanged cannonades with the British fleet off Sandy Hook.[77]

A vessel from the French fleet drove Captain James Hawker's 32-gun HM Frigate *Mermaid* ashore near Chincoteague, Maryland, or Cape Henlopen, Delaware, in early July 1778.[78]

A French frigate came near St. Helen's on Thursday, July 2. A signal was made for the HM Frigate *Milford* to give her chase but she was too far away to overtake her.[79]

As Admiral d'Estaing's fleet approached the North American coast, he ordered the Chevalier de Gras Préville's 32-gun frigate *Engageante*, with 300–400 men, to precede the main squadron and to take soundings at the entrance of the Delaware Bay. The *Engageante* encountered James Duncan's 24- or 26-gun privateer *Rose* there. The *Rose* was forced to surrender after a five- or six-and-a-quarter-hour battle that occurred in the presence of 12 French ships of the line and five frigates on July 4 or Monday, July 6. The French vessels were 4 miles away but could not get any closer on account of the calm wind.

When the attack began, the *Rose* had 60 men on board, eight of whom were sick and unfit for duty. When she surrendered, she had only 44 left. Duncan fought until the *Rose* sank. Several of her officers were killed. Her captain was wounded along with her first lieutenant who was mortally wounded.[80]

Captain David Squires's New York brig *Enterprize*, belonging to Messrs. Moore and Neil, captured an 18-gun French snow laden with salt and dry goods on Tuesday, July 14. She was bound from Bordeaux to North Carolina and was sent to St. Augustine, Florida.[81]

The Whig fleet captured the HM Frigate *Digby* and five privateers out of the port of Digby, Nova Scotia, off the coast of France before July 17, 1778. The French frigate *Iphigenia* took them to Brest.[82]

A French frigate chased Captain Sibbles's New York letter of marque *Tryon* outside of Sandy Hook, New Jersey, about Wednesday, July 22. He outsailed the frigate and escaped. That evening, he met the Halifax fleet under convoy of the *Hope* and alerted them of the presence of the French fleet. The Halifax fleet avoided a trap and sailed to Sandy Hook. Captain Sibbles helped convoy the fleet through Long Island Sound. A Whig privateer sloop dogged them in the sound but kept her distance to avoid capture.[83]

A privateer schooner, belonging to Messrs. Bartere and Co., merchants at Port-au-Prince (Haiti), and commanded by a Frenchman, a native of Dunkirk, with a commission from Congress on board, captured two vessels before July 25. One belonged to Mr. Flamingo, the other to Mr. Lindo, both of Kingston, Jamaica. Both were bound for Hispaniola. It was later discovered that the Frenchman had committed several acts of piracy on both French and Congressional vessels. He was seized at Port-au-Prince and placed in irons along with his officers and one of his owners.[84]

Admiral Comte d'Orvilliers left Brest with 32 ships of the line on July 8, but three were not fit for action. Admiral Augustus Keppel put to sea the next day with 33 ships. However, unfavorable winds prevented him from engaging the French forces until Sunday, July 26. He executed a series of maneuvers to bring his force within range of the French, but he decided not to arrange his ships in line of battle. He thought it best to engage the French as the opportunity presented itself rather than wait and possibly allow them to escape. The British engaged the French off the island of Ushant (Ouessant) as they were in the process of executing their own maneuvers and it was difficult for them to escape. The fourth ship of the French line fired the first broadside about 11 AM. The fighting continued in disorganized fashion until about 2 PM, when Admiral Keppel tried to reorganize his fleet and arrange them in line of battle. Unable to do so, by 4 PM, he had separate lines of vessels, two of which were directly west of the French.

Meanwhile, the French had also reformed into a single line, but they did not attack. Admiral Keppel did not summon his rear division, under Vice Admiral Hugh Palliser, until 7 PM, but then it was too late to renew the fighting. Most of the French escaped by dawn. Some of the ships at the back of the French fleet chased a British ship on Monday, July 27 but with no effect. The French captured a sloop-of-war, badly damaged many British ships, and killed many officers and men. The British fleet returned to Portsmouth. The French fleet returned to Brest on the 29th. Both sides had heavy losses. Keppel lost 133 killed and 373 wounded. The Comte d'Orvilliers lost 161 killed and 513 wounded.[85]

Admiral Keppel's fleet captured two French frigates, one of 32 guns the other of 36, and brought them to England in August. The French and English frigates also had a smart engagement after which the British frigate withdrew.[86]

About the same time, a French frigate captured a British one after a smart engagement and brought her to Cape François.[87]

The *Bellona* sailed to North Carolina as part of a convoy coming from St. Eustatius under the protection of the French frigate *Dilligente* in August 1778. She was outfitted as a privateer with 12 cannons in September. The merchants of New Bern further outfitted her with 16–18 guns for action against the British. They also outfitted the 18-gun privateer *Chatham*.

The *Bellona* sailed from New Bern in September and captured the St. Augustine brig *Elizabeth* with a cargo of indigo and lumber. She also captured the New York schooner *Actason*, a sloop, and the New York privateer *Harlecan*, which had been outfitted with six carriage guns, four bronze cannons, and eight swivel guns, but surrendered without a fight.[88]

A French privateer attacked the packet *Harwich* the first week in August 1778 shortly after she sailed from Helletvoetsluis, Netherlands. Several shots were exchanged and both vessels lost several men.[89]

When France entered the war, King Louis XVI sent Admiral d'Estaing to America with 12 ships of the line and three frigates and some 4,000 French soldiers. They arrived off the coast of Delaware in late June 1778 and proceeded to New York to try to capture Sir Richard Howe's fleet of nine ships in New York harbor. However, when he arrived off Sandy Hook on July 9, he discovered that the water was too shallow for his ships to get at the British fleet. General George Washington and d'Estaing decided instead to attack the British at Newport, Rhode Island, the second largest British seaport at the time. The British had held Newport since December 1776. General Sir Robert Pigot now defended it with only 3,000 men.

Major General John Sullivan commanded about 1,000 Continental soldiers. He called out about 6,000 militiamen. General Washington sent him 3,000 more Continentals under Major General Marie-Joseph Paul Yves Roch Gilbert du Motier, Marquis de Lafayette, bringing the total Congressional force in Rhode Island to 10,000 troops in July. In the first week of August, Sullivan's army was camped at Tiverton, Rhode Island.

Admiral d'Estaing's fleet arrived off Point Judith (less than 5 miles from Newport), on Wednesday, July 29, It captured seven prizes on Monday, August 3. One of them was the sloop-of-war *York*. The others were laden with sugar, rum, and coffee. The fleet also captured a sloop laden with pines, lemons, limes, and turtle (a delicacy of the time) and took 245 prisoners aboard these prizes.[91] Captain Law's sloop *Prince of Wales* recaptured the sloop *York* three days later and brought her to Sandy Hook.[92]

Two large French ships and a snow from Cape François attacked British Captain Wheatley's *Sovereign* and some other vessels of the Cork fleet on Friday,

August 7. A smart engagement ensued in which three men aboard the *Sovereign* were wounded, one of whom was Captain Boyd of the brig *Glasgow* who went to assist Captain Wheatley. His leg was shot off and he later died. The French captured two vessels from the Cork fleet, one of them a 500-ton ship, the other a large brig. They arrived at Bedford (New Bedford, Massachusetts) before August 7. The French snow was captured but the two ships escaped. Several privateers, one of them a brig, later attacked the captors off Egg Harbor, New Jersey. They captured the brig *Recovery*.[93]

The arrival of four ships from Vice Admiral John Byron's fleet greatly strengthened Admiral Richard Howe's fleet in New York. He now had 36 vessels ranging from the 74-gun HMS *Cornwall* to two little bomb ketches and four row galleys. Howe's fleet of 20 fighting vessels carried 1,064 guns compared with d'Estaing's fleet of 15 warships and 834 guns, but the French ships were larger and had more firing power than Howe's.

Howe set sail for Rhode Island on Thursday, August 6, and arrived on the 9th, to the delight of the British troops. The French troops that had been landed on Aquidneck Island re-embarked, as d'Estaing prepared for combat the following day.

The French enjoyed a favorable wind from the northeast as they sailed to meet the British on the 10th. The British fired the guns in the forts as the French passed. The French responded with "a prodigious fire" but neither side inflicted much damage. As soon as they passed the harbor, the French "crouded all the sail they could set, even to Studding Sails and Royals and stood directly at the British fleet."[94]

This did not please Lord Howe, who would have to sail against the wind. He refused to engage and remained to the southward, hoping for the wind to turn in his favor. The two fleets dogged each other for two days when, on Wednesday, August 12, a hurricane scattered both fleets and forced the ships to engage in combat individually. Admiral d'Estaing's flagship, the 84-gun *Languedoc*, engaged the 50-gun *Renown* in a brief but indecisive battle on the 13th. The 80-gun *Marseillais* fought the 50-gun *Preston* until darkness forced an inconclusive end to the battle. The 74-gun *César* was defeated by the 50-gun *Isis* but remained in action on the 16th. The storm badly damaged many of the ships, rendering them unseaworthy. The frigate HMS *Apollo* lost her mast, as did the 80-gun *Tonant*. Howe's fleet returned to New York to refit. The French returned to Rhode Island on the 20th and proceeded to Boston for repairs on the 21st, after which they sailed away to Martinique.[95]

Meanwhile, in Europe, the British frigates *Defiance* and *Fox* were ordered on a cruise on Friday, August 14. They fell in with the *Exeter*, *Pluto*, and a cutter Sunday night. Early Monday morning, August 17, they saw several vessels ahead, in sight of St. Paul de Leon. The *Exeter*, *Pluto*, and cutter kept in with the land while the *Defiance* pursued its own course with a French ensign and pendant hoisted. The

Exeter soon fired several guns and hoisted British colors, driving a French frigate ashore.

When the French saw the *Exeter* firing at them under her own colors and the *Defiance* flying French colors, they sought protection from the *Defiance*. To their great surprise, the *Defiance* began firing at them and hoisted her own colors and captured seven or eight of them. The *Exeter* also captured her share of prizes. They left the HM Frigate *Fox* at night in chase of two ships.[96]

British cruisers captured a French ship, three French brigs, a sloop, and a vessel bound from Hamburg to Brest with staves. They all anchored in Cawsand Bay, England, by Monday, August 17. The *Fox* brought five French vessels, one of them a fine ship, to Cat's Water, England.[97]

The French privateer frigate *Courageux*, in company with the *Terpsichore* and *Rossignol*, were convoying to France Captain John Kirby's Jersey privateer *Lively*, captured two weeks earlier, and a brig from Oporto, Portugal, in ballast. They captured Captain Dashwood's HM Packet Boat *Duke of York* about 250 miles southwest of the Lizard on Monday, August 17. The *Duke of York* was bound from Lisbon, Portugal, to England with the mail.[98]

The HM Armed Ship *Hawke* captured the 16-gun French privateer *Duc de Angouleme* and sent her into Sussex, England, before Saturday, August 22.[99] And Mr. de Vialis's frigate *Gracieux* captured Captain James Carnichef's HMS *Great Britain* off the Barbary coast on Monday, August 24. She was from Tetuan, Algiers, with a cargo of wood and 57 moors. The ship was seized but the cargo and the moors were given to the Moorish owners. The *Gracieux* also captured Sir Thomas West's 14-gun sloop *Zephyr*. The *Zephyr's* 100-man crew were quarantined at the Lazaret at Toulon, France.[100]

The Jersey privateer *Phoenix* captured many valuable French ships before September 3, 1778,[101] and Jonhen Cullen's privateer *Active* captured a small unknown French sloop and sent her to Dover, Delaware, before September 8. She was bound from Havre de Grace, Maryland, with butter.[102]

A ship from East Florida, formerly Captain Engs's *Franklin*, laden with naval stores, lumber, and indigo was seized by her crew, mostly Frenchmen, and brought to Georgia.[103]

The letter of marque schooner *Hammond* captured the ship *Constant* bound from St. Domingue to Nantes. However, as she was sailing under French colors, there was no legal authority to put her in possession of the *Hammond's* crew. She was taken to Halifax as a prize to the HM sloop *Hope*. She arrived before September 29.[104]

Captain Thomas Pickering's 20-gun (9- and 6-pounders) Portsmouth, New Hampshire, privateer ship *Hampden* captured four prizes on her cruise to Europe and sent them to France. One of these was the brig *Harmony*, with a cargo of great value. Another was the French vessel *La Constance*, and a third was the Danish vessel *Linderust*. The *Hampden* arrived at Brest on October 6, 1778.[105]

The HMS *Levant* and the HMS *Alarm* captured three French coasters from ports in the Bay of Biscay, bound up the Mediterranean, before September 4. They also captured a Whig vessel bound from Europe to Cadiz.[106]

A small privateer belonging to Mount's Bay, England, captured a French ship valued at £15,000 on Saturday, September 5 and brought her to Mount's Bay.[107]

Before September 9, a privateer captured the *St. Foin*, a French ship of about 350 tons, bound from St. Domingue to St.-Malo (a port in Normandy) and sent her to Falmouth, England. The letter of marque *Warspite* captured a 10-gun French privateer snow and sent her to Milford, England. She had three hostages on board.[108]

A French xebec captured a rich English merchant ship laden with all sorts of cloths, supposed to be destined for Leghorn, England. The xebec was carrying her prize to Marseilles when the prisoners retook the English ship and brought it to Port Mahon, Spain, before September 11.[109]

Two French frigates captured two 32-gun British frigates, the *Active* and the *Minerva*, and their tenders before September 12. The tenders were both schooners, one with 12 4-pounders, the other with 16 swivels.[110]

On Sunday evening, September 15, two British sloops of war, two tenders, and one galley came up the Hudson River to destroy the stores being transported from West Point to the army. Meanwhile, two sloops going down the river, laden with cannon and powder, turned about and headed for Tarrytown as soon as they discovered the enemy. They ran aground, and the British, having the advantage of a fair wind and tide, came up the river so fast that the infantry did not have time to arrive to unload or protect the stores. The only troops at Tarrytown were an outpost from the Soissonais Regiment under the command of a sergeant.

Colonel Elisha Sheldon's dragoons, who were stationed at Dobbs Ferry to guard several barges, set out for Tarrytown, dismounted, and helped to unload the stores. The British, anchored off Tarrytown, began a heavy cannonade to cover two gunboats and four barges sent to destroy the vessels. Captain George Hurlbut, of the 2nd Regiment Light Dragoons, was stationed on board one of the vessels with 12 dragoons armed only with pistols and sabres. He kept his men hidden until the British came alongside. The dragoons fired. The British returned fire, killing one of the dragoons. Surrounded, Captain Hurlbut ordered his men to jump overboard and swim to shore.

The British boarded and set fire to the vessels, one of which had cloaks and swords for Sheldon's dragoons and another had a number of French bakers and a large quantity of bread on board. But severe fire from the dragoons and the French guard forced them to retire. Captain Hurlbut and several others jumped in the river and swam to the sloops to extinguish the fire and save the vessels. While in the water, Captain Hurlbut received a musket ball through the thigh.

Major General Robert Howe arrived with a division of troops and some artillery about daybreak. They opened a battery on the enemy, forcing them to slip their cables and head down the river about 2 miles, where they remained until about noon on Tuesday, July 17. At that time, General Howe opened another battery on them, forcing them to sail up the river. They remained near Teller's Point until Thursday, when they sent their gunboats on shore, to burn the elegant house of Captain Roberts at Haverstraw.

A British privateer captured the 600-ton French ship *Victoria* before September 25. She was bound from St. Domingue to Bordeaux with 400 hogsheads of sugar, six barrels of coffee, 40 hogsheads of tobacco, and other goods. The *Victoria* was sent to Plymouth, England.[111]

A French 40-gun ship attacked Captain Thomas Windsor's 18-gun HM Frigate *Fox* and the two fought for 3½ hours before the *Fox* surrendered with all her masts destroyed. Captain Windsor lost his right hand during the action. His first lieutenant and 30 of his men were killed and two-thirds wounded. The *Fox* was taken to Brest.[112]

The sloop *Speedwell* bound from South Carolina for Dunkirk, France, with a cargo of indigo, tar, turpentine, and tobacco worth £30,000 brought a valuable ship to Brest before September 25.[113]

Admiral Augustus Keppel's British fleet headed toward England from the southwest with a 20-gun brig when they ran into some French West Indiamen which they captured in the Bay of Biscay. A British man-of-war also captured the French frigate *Iphigenie* before September 25. The number of French West Indiamen taken since the order for reprisals amounted to 36. As none of them were under 300 tons, they were valued at an average of £15,000. Some were worth between £30,000 and £40,000, bringing the amount to £450,000.[114]

A 12-gun cutter from Hastings, England, captured a small French privateer of 18 men and a boy, in the North Channel after a long chase on Sunday, September 27. The privateer had taken six or seven vessels, mostly colliers. The privateer was so much strained by carrying the sails that the British took out the crew and brought them as prisoners to Hastings and sank the privateer.[115]

The French East Indiaman *Duc de Fitz James* was captured off the Azores before Monday, September 28 and sent to Plymouth, England. She was valued at 2,000,000 livres tournois.[116] Captain Chillcott's Bristol, England, privateer *Tartar* captured a large Dutch ship about the same time. She was bound from Nantes to Cadiz with French goods and brought to Dartmouth or King Road, England. The Dutch ship was part of a fleet of 11 vessels under convoy of a French frigate and two armed ships and had become separated from the convoy in a gale.[117]

A Guernsey privateer captured the French vessel *La Constance* in European waters on Tuesday September 29. Captain Thomas Pickering's 20-gun (9- and 6-pounders) Portsmouth, New Hampshire privateer ship *Hampden* recaptured her on Friday,

October 2. Pickering reported on his cruise to the American commissioners in France in a letter dated January 28, 1779:

> This will Inform you that I arriv'd here on the 6th Octor. last from a Cruize from the Port of Pisscataqua in the State of New hamshire N. America. that in the Course of my Cruize I fell in with a French Ship called the L'Constant from St. Domingo bound to Bourdeaux. Which sd. Ship, had been taken four days before by a Guernsey Privateer. The Ship I retook again & sent in here. That when I came in I apply'd to Monsr. Peter Riou Kings Lingester. who Immediately told me the Ship was a Lawful Prize to the Ship Hampden, as wel as several other Gentlemn here which told me the same.
>
> Some few days after several Gent. apply'd to me to Purchase Ship & Cargoe. as being a Lawful Prize, (as they declar'd She Certainly was according to the Laws &c. of France) On this I agreed with sd. Gentl. & sold Ship & Cargoe for the sum of £12,600 Sterlg. On Condition that they should indemnify me from all Damages and Incumbrances whatsoever that should attend the Sale thereof; (if any should Arise,) and they to abide by the Consquence.—
>
> Also in regard of the Cargoe of the Ship, as she was Leaky when I retook her, in this also I was to be Clear & free from all Damages therein.—[118]

British frigates captured the following French ships and brought them to Gibraltar before September 30:

- the *Victoire* bound to Marseilles with a cargo of iron;
- the *Duchesse de Gramont* bound from Toulon to Rochefort;
- the *Triomphante* bound from Martinique to Marseilles;
- the *Lasso* bound from Marseilles to Martinique.[119]

Four French men-of-war chased Sir Chaloner William Bunbury's HM Frigate *Milford* for more than 52 hours at the end of September, but the *Milford* evaded them.[120]

There were a number of captures in the English Channel and off the coast of England in October 1778. A British vessel captured a French ship bound from Marseilles to Martinique, French West Indies, and brought her to Gibraltar before Thursday, October 1.[121]

Six French East Indiamen—the *Ferme, Modeste, Gaston, Aquilon, Pondicherry*, and *Trois Amis*—came around Cape François together. British privateers captured the first three. The Bristol, England, privateers *Tartar* and *Alexander* captured the small French East Indiaman *La Ferme*, worth less than £100,000 and brought her to King's Road before October 2.[122]

Captain Finch's 16-gun HM Sloop *Porcupine* captured the 1,300-ton French East India ship *Modeste* on her voyage from Lisbon to England. She was homeward-bound from China and taken to Plymouth on Friday, October 2. She had a cargo of tea valued at £300,000 and more than £40,000 in specie on board. Captain Finch also captured the large French ship *César* with an American cargo of 284,000 hogsheads of the best York and James River tobacco valued at about £300,000.[123]

One Jersey and two Guernsey privateers captured two homeward-bound French East Indiamen a few leagues off Lorient before Friday, October 2. Neither of the French vessels was aware that hostilities began between England and France and disposed of their guns in the East Indies to make room for additional cargo.[124]

The British schooner *Lord Howe* fell in with four French vessels about Saturday, October 3. The largest was a 16-gun polacre. The French vessels engaged the schooner but Mr. Colvill, who had the command, came alongside the schooner, gave three cheers, and surrendered his ship, the *Divine*, bound from Marseilles to Philadelphia with a cargo of brandy, olives, capers, and salt. The other vessels got away because Mr. Colvill could not man any prizes, if he caught any, because he had only 17 crewmen.[125]

Two Liverpool privateers captured the French homeward-bound East Indiaman *Gaston* valued at £500,000. She had a French general on board. They arrived at the Motherbank on Sunday morning, October 4.[126]

Four new privateers sailed from Glasgow on October 4. Two of them captured 36 French prizes with valuable cargoes on Thursday, October 8, and sent them to Glasgow.[127]

The Guernsey privateer *Beazely* captured three homeward-bound French West Indiamen in latitude 47 before October 10. The *Beazely* was formerly the Whig privateer *Lexington* captured by Captain Beazely's cutter *Alert* which he renamed after himself.[128]

Another Guernsey privateer captured a French ship of about 400 tons and sent her to Falmouth on Sunday, October 11. She was from St. Domingue with a cargo of coffee, sugar, and indigo and had about £20,000 in specie on board.[129]

The HMS *Romney* arrived at St. John's, Nova Scotia, on October 12 along with the HMS *Pallas*, a 400-ton French letter of marque, and a snow. Both were from Bordeaux loaded with provisions for St. Pierre and Miquelon. They both went into St. Pierre's Road after the place had surrendered.[130]

The privateer *Defiance*, from Poole, England, captured a French brig laden with wheat and mustard seed about mid-October. The brig was lost at the back of the island of Portland, England, and all hands perished.[131]

One of Admiral Augustus Keppel's cruisers captured the *Montpelier*, a large French ship, bound from Martinique to Bordeaux before Saturday, October 17. She was sent to Falmouth, England. About the same time, a British frigate captured Mr. St. Michael's French armed ship *Mount*. She was bound from Cadiz to Toulon and taken to Gibraltar after a half-hour engagement in which many Frenchmen were killed.[132]

Mr. Robinson's Bristol, England, privateer *Ranger* captured the 300-ton *Le Crigale* off Milford before Tuesday, October 20. She was bound from St. Domingue to Nantes with tobacco, indigo, and rice and was sent to Milford.[133] About the same time, Captain Tuck's privateer *Corbec* captured Mr. Bushead's *Theodore* bound from Cape François to Nantes and brought her to Plymouth, England, and the Guernsey privateer *Wasp* captured the French vessel *Louis le Grand* laden with tobacco from Virginia.[134]

The Comte de Ligoudez, captain of the 64-gun *Triton*, discovered two British ships at noon on Tuesday, October 20, and headed toward them, prepared for action. The action began at close range late in the evening, making it impossible for the Comte de Ligoudez to count the enemy's guns, but he discovered she was of superior force by the size of her balls.

As soon as they began to engage, the 30-gun frigate sailed across the *Triton*'s bow. Mr. de Ligoudez counteracted their action and the engagement continued within pistol range. After an hour and a half of combat, the Comte de Ligoudez had part of his right hand shot off and received a ball in his left arm, obliging him to leave command of the ship to Mr. de Rocan, his second in command. Half an hour later, the frigate took advantage of the night and disappeared. The British ship fought an hour longer and then crowded all sail, hid all her lights, and ran away. The *Triton* pursued the British ship but lost sight of her in a heavy gale of wind and rain. She was thought to be the *Cerberus*, a new 74-gun ship built at Portsmouth.[135]

The privateer *Brilliant* captured the *St. Meuchon*, a large French ship from Guadeloupe, laden with sugar and other goods, before Thursday, October 22. She was taken to Whitehaven. The Jersey privateers *Laroprier* or *Lampier* and *Vigna* captured another large French ship about the same time and brought her to Kinsale. She was bound from South Carolina to Nantes with 320 barrels of rice, 80 barrels of indigo, some hogsheads of tobacco, and a quantity of skins. Captain Agew's Guernsey privateer *Triumph* captured a large French West Indiaman bound from St. Domingue to Nantes loaded with sugar, cotton, indigo, and other goods and brought her to Guernsey.[136]

The Guernsey privateer *Shaftsbury* captured the *Deux Frères* and brought her into the Cove (in Guernsey, south of Georgetown) on Wednesday, October 21. She was from Bordeaux with a cargo of pitch. Captain Roper's Lancaster letter of marque *Betsy* and two other vessels captured four French prizes and sent them into the Cove the following evening. One was 400 tons, the other 600 tons, and both were bound from St. Domingo (Dominican Republic) with sugar and cotton. The other two, a brig and a schooner, were laden with tobacco.[137]

The French ship *Hazard* was brought to Guernsey and the *Ellis*, of Liverpool, captured the French brig *Eagle* and brought her to Kinsale before Saturday, October 24. The *Magdalene* and *Le Frère* were taken about the same time. The British privateer *Hunter* and the *Meriton*, of Liverpool, captured the *Magdalene* with fish and oil and took her to Cork. The *Swallow*, of Guernsey, captured *Le Frère*, bound from Marseilles to Brest.[138]

The HMS *Vigilant* captured the *Duc de Choiseul* during the week of October 25. She was bound from St. Domingo (Dominican Republic) and taken to Bristol. The British *Rover* captured a French vessel during the same week and sent her to Bristol. And the *Lord Cardiff* captured a polacre from Marseilles and sent her to Crookhaven, Ireland. The *Tartar* also captured a vessel from Bordeaux and sent her to Cork.[139]

Admiral Augustus Keppel's fleet captured several French vessels before the end of October. Captain Lockhart Ross's 74-gun *Duke* fired one broadside at a French ship-of-war which immediately surrendered. She was brought to Falmouth on Monday, October 26.[140] The 500-ton *Justicia* and four other ships from St. Domingue were taken. The *Justicia* was brought to Hoylake, England. The *Volante* bound to Bordeaux was brought to Spithead. The brig *Antigua* captured Captain Bellinger's *Ville de Lyons* bound from Bordeaux to St. Domingue with silk, lace, linens, and cordage.[141]

Captain Clarke's privateer *Hawke* captured a French brig laden with salt and brought her to Falmouth. The privateer *Wasp* sent a Swedish vessel loaded with wine and tobacco into Liverpool, England. She was bound from Cadiz, Spain, to France. A French man-of-war and a frigate fired at the *Wasp*, killing one man and wounding the captain and several crewmen. Captain Gardener's Bristol letter of marque *Albion* captured a French snow bound from Martinique to France and sent her to Cork, and the British captured the *Elspie* bound to Bordeaux before Saturday, October 27.[142]

The Guernsey privateer *Union* captured a French ship of about 300 tons bound from Guadeloupe to Bordeaux with sugars valued at more than £18,000 and brought her to Kinsale. Captain Roach's Dublin schooner *Rambler*, carrying four cannons, 12 swivels, 20 oars, and 50 men, captured the three-masted French tartan *St. Foreign Palanque* and brought her to Leghorn, England, on Wednesday, October 28. She was pierced for 16 guns but carried only 10 and was bound from Marseilles to Civita Vecchia, Naples, and Messina with sugar, molasses, tanned hides, alum, Campeche wood, and 70 bales of merchandise. She was valued at £15,000.[143]

The 12-gun, 280-man French frigate *Zephyr* captured two privateers, one of 20 and the other of 24 guns, before October 30. The first one made a very obstinate resistance. The *Zephyr* also captured the Bristol letter of marque galley *Ann*. She was bound to Jamaica and taken to Brest.[144]

The 10-gun, 80-man British privateer *Pitt* had a smart two-hour engagement with a French letter of marque in the Bay of Biscay before Friday, October 30. The *Pitt*'s crew tried to board the French vessel twice but the difference in their height from the water rendered both attempts fruitless. The *Pitt* lost three men killed and five wounded. She left the Frenchman to go to Penzance to repair her damage and to replenish her crew. She captured two prizes during her six-week cruise: an outward bound French ship and a neutral ship with French property on board.[145]

Mr. de Montazay, captain of the 26-gun privateer *Vengeance*, encountered a 36-gun British frigate near the Madeira Islands before November 2, 1778 and bore down on her, intending to engage. The French crew tried twice to board but were repulsed vigorously. The third time, they succeeded, sword and pistol in hand. Some think the prey was the 36-gun *Pallas*; others think it was the 28-gun *Pelican*. She was brought to Lisbon and put under the care of the *Belle Poule* which brought her to Brest. Captain de Montazay was wounded in the engagement. M. de Mandavit, his lieutenant, took command and also captured a British Guineaman valued at 50,000 livres near the Madeira islands.[146] The *Belle Poule* and another ship captured eight prizes, including five privateers, and brought them to Brest about the same time.[147]

Captain Gardner's HM Frigate *Maidstone* captured Captain Michel's 40-gun, 280-man French ship *Lion* off the Virginia Capes on Monday, November 2, after an engagement of seven hours. She was bound from the Chesapeake Bay to Lorient with a cargo of 1,400 hogsheads of tobacco and brought into a British port on Wednesday, December 2.[148]

A French privateer appeared off the coast of Aldeburgh, in Suffolk, on Friday, November 6. Two of the cutters anchored there weighed anchor and went in pursuit of her. They brought her in about eight hours later. She mounted 12 guns and had been out of Dunkirk only a short time.[149]

An armed ship captured the 360-ton French ship *Aiguillon* bound from St. Domingue to France with a cargo of sugar, indigo, and cotton valued at £20,000 and brought her to Milford. A French ship-of-war took two large British privateers or frigates and brought them to La Coruña before November 18.[150]

A French ship bound from France to Virginia with dry goods was chased ashore by one of Captain Goodrich's tenders south of Cape Henry and was captured the last week in November.[151]

Captain Fairweather's Liverpool privateer *Bellona*, of 24 guns and 150 men, blew up a 36-gun French frigate in an action 24 leagues from Ushant on Tuesday, November 24.[152]

Five homeward-bound French East Indiamen fell in with a British man-of-war off Cape Finisterre, Spain, before Wednesday, November 25. Three of them were taken and sent to Plymouth. A Liverpool privateer captured the fourth and another British ship-of-war pursued the fifth.[153]

The Jersey privateer *Valiant* captured Mr. Pied de Port's French ship *St. Jean* before November 28. She was bound from Martinique to Nantes and brought into King Road.[154]

A French frigate captured the British 20-gun ship *Glasgow* off the coast of Puerto Rico in December. The *Glasgow* lost her captain and several men killed.[155]

Captain Tweed's New York privateer sloop *Dolphin* captured a valuable French snow bound from Marseilles to St. Domingue with dry goods. Meanwhile, a French ship-of-the line captured the frigate *Terpsichore* off Saint Domingue in early December.[156]

The armed ship *Le Ruse* sailed from Le Havre on Tuesday morning, December 8. Before noon, she fell in with a British frigate from Madras, India, which she captured without much trouble, as the British captain was unaware that Britain and France were at war. That frigate, which ought to have carried 20 guns, only had six. She was laden with a cargo valued at 2,000,000 livres tournois.[157]

About 15 prizes were sent to Bermuda between November 2 and December 15. Captain Mackenzie's HMS *Ariel* captured the 20 carriage gun French letter of marque *Duchesse de Gramont* and sent her to Bermuda between December 8 and December 15. She was bound from Piscataqua, New Hampshire, to France with a load of lumber. She was blown off course going into York and was stranded on the rocks of Bermuda. Her cargo, 16 of the guns, and most of the materials were saved.[158]

Four ships were captured and taken to Brest before mid-December. They included a ship bound from London to Dublin; one from Newfoundland; one from New York with exchanged folders, and the *Friendship* taken by a Guernsey privateer and retaken by a French frigate.[159]

Captain Thomas Pickering's privateer ship *Hampden* sailed from Brest on December 1, in company with seven French frigates. His cruise was intended to last four months, after which he would proceed to North America, but he met with bad weather and contrary winds on the coast. He soon lost company with the French ships but continued his cruise.

Two frigates chased him in the English Channel on December 8. He thought they were English cruisers, but they were French frigates. He crowded so much sail to avoid being taken that he lost his fore-topmast and sprung his bowsprit. His ship sprung a leak and he was forced to return to Brest where he arrived about December 19.

Yet, he managed to capture two prizes on this short cruise. One was a brigantine from Newfoundland laden with codfish; the other was a Dutch dogger from Barcelona bound to London with nuts.[160]

A British cutter captured four French prizes and a privateer and brought them to Plymouth, England. A Liverpool, England privateer also captured two French privateers and brought them to Scilly. The Bristol, England privateer *Alexander* captured the *Coveillon* bound from Bordeaux, France to Martinique, French West Indies and brought her to Whitehaven, England before December 19. The French, in turn, captured Captain Gibson's *Fortitude* and brought her to Brest.[161]

The French fleet fell in with and captured 13 richly laden British vessels before December 21.[162] Comte d'Emblimon, captain of the *Revenge*, brought in five privateers and three merchantmen by December 25. He met with the 74-gun HMS *Berwick* on Tuesday, October 13, and gave chase in company with the *Belle Poule*, without being able to engage her. The British crowded all their sails and threw everything overboard to lighten the ship. The 26-gun frigate *Zephyr* captured a prize of 22 guns and 130 men, commanded by M. de Villeneuve Cillard after an engagement of ¾ of an hour and sent her to Brest. The *Zephyr* returned to port a few days later with another 24-gun privateer.[163]

The 28-gun *La Dedaigneuse* returned to port with two British armed vessels and the 28-gun HM Frigate *Active*. Captain de la Fouchtreville's 80-gun *Neptune* returned to Brest at the same time. He was chased a long time by seven British ships and brought in with him a 30-gun privateer, a 10-gun brig recaptured, and a French vessel valued at 700,000 or 800,000 livres. The French frigate *Belle Poule* also returned to port with five prizes. Three of them were privateers and two merchantmen.[164]

Two French frigates captured the Bristol privateer *Vigilant* on Wednesday, December 30. One of the frigates brought part of the crew to Lorient.[165]

The HMS *Culloden* brought about 60 French prisoners from Halifax to England, along with one Murphy, formerly captain of a Whig privateer. As Mr. Murphy had behaved well, he was allowed on the quarterdeck as a midshipman. He plotted with the French prisoners to seize the ship and throw the captain overboard, but the plan was found out just before they were to execute the plot. The Frenchmen were secured and Murphy was tied hands and feet and hung over the poop until he arrived in England, where he was tried for conspiracy and found guilty.[166]

Mr. de la Motte Piquet, commander of the *St. Esprit*, and two other French ships returned to Brest by the end of 1778 with 10 prizes, one of which had on board an English regiment. The prizes included two colliers which their masters endeavored to ransom, but, on examining their cargoes, 88 pieces of heavy artillery were found among the coals.[167]

A great number of French privateers, of 20 to 30 guns, from Bayonne, France, cruising in the Mediterranean Sea, captured many rich prizes in late 1778. The Jersey and Guernsey privateers did not leave their ports with confidence.[168]

1779

Two ships of the line, one of 64 guns, the other of 74 guns, were sent from France to the coast of Africa in early 1779 to destroy all the forts and factories belonging to the British. They performed their task but kept possession of only one fort, in which they left a garrison of 300 men. They took 1,800 Africans and a considerable quantity of ivory and gold dust which they brought to Goree, Senegal. The two ships then joined the Comte d'Estaing's fleet at Martinique.[169]

A 26-gun French privateer captured a 32-gun British frigate and brought her to Coruña after a bloody engagement in which the French captain, Mr. Despeaux de Montazeau, was killed in the first broadside. The lieutenant took command and captured the frigate.[170] The French also captured a large British privateer and a merchant ship off Brest before January 1, 1779. They anchored there in a heavy gale.[171]

The *Belle Poule* captured no fewer than 20 vessels which were sent to Brest. One of M. de Fabry's frigates captured a vessel carrying dispatches to Port Mahon, Spain. The vessel was sent to port and the dispatches sent to Versailles.[172]

Two small letters of marque belonging to Lancaster, England, captured a French packet from the island of Mauritius and took her to Cork about Friday, January 1. The captain of the packet knew nothing of any hostilities having commenced between Great Britain and France, making him an easy conquest.[173]

The HMS *Enterprize* captured a 160-ton French ship from Saint Domingue and brought her to Gibraltar, and the Folkstone privateer *Fame* captured two French privateers and sent them to Falmouth before January 5.[174] The *Ironside*, of Liverpool, captured the *Iris*, a homeward-bound French East Indiaman, before January 5. She was lost off Beaumaris, but her cargo and crew were saved. The privateer *Night*, also from Liverpool, captured the East Indiaman *Duc d'Arne* about the same time. The prize was lost off Point Air, between the rivers Dee and Mersey, England. Her cargo was saved.[175]

The Liverpool privateer *Bellona* captured a French frigate of 20 guns and 260 men and brought her to Faial.[176] Liverpool privateers also captured the *Loifer* bound from Bordeaux to Martinique and the *Belle de Paris* before January 7.[177]

The French men-of-war *Cato*, 64 guns and 600 men, and *Destin*, 74 guns and 700 men, sailed from Toulon on December 25, 1778 and arrived at Malaga by January 8, 1779. They captured three British prizes: two loaded with cod and the *Westmoreland* from Lisbon valued at 100,000 livres.[178]

A ship, probably Captain Hugh Porterfield's French-built *Jason*, fitted out at New York as a privateer and mounting 22 6-pounders, chased Captain Padock's ship with 75 men and boys in latitude 31.28 off Charleston bar, South Carolina, on Saturday, January 9.[179]

Before January 10, the Waterford, Ireland privateer *Smiling Sally* captured the French ship *Sanctimony* bound from Martinique to Bordeaux. She was valued at £20,000.[180]

A French frigate carried the 18-gun privateer ship *Marchioness of Granby* to Brest.[181]

Captain Fairweather's Liverpool privateer *Bellona*, of 24 guns and 180 men, captured two prizes off Finisterre before January 10. They were the *Bon Vivant* bound from France to Martinique with provisions and bale goods and a large ship bound from Boston to France with tobacco, lumber, and masts valued at £10,000.[182]

The cutter *Alarm* captured a French vessel bound from Cherbourg to St.-Malo before January 14, and the Falmouth cutter *Customhouse* captured a French privateer of 30 guns before January 16.[183]

Captain Alexander McPherson's privateer schooner *Experiment* captured the French snow *La Terrios* bound from Cape François to Virginia with rum, sugar, molasses, coffee, and cordials; Mr. Mallet's French brig *La Amiable Confiance* bound from Cadiz to Virginia with salt and dry goods; and several other vessels. He also chased a large French brigantine and a schooner ashore on Ocracoke bar before Monday, January 18.[184]

Captain Ridley's Crown sloop *George and Elizabeth* returned from a cruise in the West Indies on Saturday, January 23, 1779 and brought in a sloop with 110 hogsheads of tobacco, a French brig with wine and brandy, and a prize schooner from Virginia. She also brought two prizes bound to Providence, Rhode Island and two bound to Bermuda. She captured or burned no fewer than 18 vessels during this cruise.[185]

Captain Maclean's privateer *Rover* arrived at New York on Sunday, January 24, with a large French schooner loaded with sugars and dry goods for the Mississippi.[186]

Before January 28, Captain Villiers Fitzgerald's HMS *Royal Charlotte* captured an 18-gun French privateer in the north English Channel and sent her to London. Captain Baker's *Eclipse*, of Folkstone, captured the 16-gun *Comte Delon*, belonging to Dunkirk. The cutter *Swiftsure* captured the eight-gun French privateer *Morante* and brought her to Leith, Scotland. The *Tartar*, of Folkstone, captured a ship bound from Bordeaux to South Carolina with gunpowder and a brig bound from Bordeaux to La Rochelle. The Loyalist privateer *Sandwich* captured the 14-gun, 260-man French privateer *Terpsichore* in an afternoon engagement of three-quarters of an hour.[187]

The French, in turn, captured 40 British privateers and brought them to the ports of Brest, Lorient, Nantes, and La Rochelle in January and February 1779. They included:

- *Iphigenie*, a richly laden transport bound to Gibraltar, captured on November 5, 1778 and brought to Lorient;
- *Therpsicore*, captured and taken to Rochefort;
- the packet *Lisbon*, bound to London with a large quantity of gold and diamonds;
- *Juno* captured the *Fox*;
- *Iphigenie* captured the *Lively*;
- *St. Michel* brought two frigates to Coruña;
- *Vengeur* captured eight large prizes;
- frigates *Consolante* and *Engageante* captured 16 prizes in the Baltic Sea.[188]

A French vessel from Martinique was captured off the Charleston bar on Tuesday morning, February 2, 1779. Three of the seamen got ashore.[189]

Before February 10, 1779, Captain Tapley's letter of marque *Fama* captured the French West Indiaman *Bordelaise* worth about £80,000 and sent her to Dover. The letters of marque *Active* and *Unicorn*, both from Folkestone, captured a shallop with about £10,000 and sent her to Dover.[190] Captain Scott's Liverpool letter of marque *Charming Nancy* captured a French schooner. She was bound from Marseilles to St.-Malo with bale goods and brought to Kinsale. The Liverpool privateer *Draper* captured the *Bonfoy* bound from St. Domingue to France and brought her to

Ilfracombe, England. The Guernsey privateer *Surprize* captured the 250-ton *La Proberne* bound from Bordeaux to St. Domingue with bale goods, wine, and beer. She was brought to Weymouth.[191]

Mr. Legordeur de Tilly's French frigate *Concorde*, mounting 26 guns—20 12-pounders on her main deck and six 6-pounders on her quarter deck—lost her mainmast and sprung several leaks in a storm. Her crew threw overboard 12 guns from her main deck to lighten the ship. Even so, the frigate was taking on 15–24 inches of water an hour. In this condition, the *Concorde* took an English privateer of 14 guns before February 10.

The *Concorde* then met the HM Frigate *Congress*, which had been captured from the Whigs. The *Congress* mounted 26 9-pounders on her main deck and six 6-pounders on her quarter deck. The two frigates battled each other for 3½ hours, after which the British frigate broke off.[192]

Captain Favre's French privateer *Phoenix*, from Le Havre, mounting 12 6-pounders, left port on December 19, 1778 and captured a ship of 150 tons before February 10, 1779. Captain Favre soon found himself surrounded by five enemy vessels, each of six guns comprising 4- and 6-pounders. He fought both sides of his vessels for three hours when he saw two of them strike. At this moment, four other British cruisers came up, one of 12, one of 10, one of eight, and one of six guns. Captain Favre renewed the combat with 10 privateers. He fought from daylight until 10 PM. The *Phoenix* received 10 cannonballs in her hull and had her braces, stays, and rigging cut away. Captain Favre, lost seven men killed, 21 rendered unfit for action, and almost all his officers wounded. He was forced to strike.[193]

Mr. Royer's French privateer *Le Commandant, from Dunkirk,* sailed in company with three other privateers. Two of them had left him and the third was at a great distance when Royer came up with and engaged a cutter from Folkestone. The action lasted from 5 AM until 8 AM. Many of Mr. Royer's crew were driven from their guns, but he forced them back again. Finding them giving way a second time, he drew his purse from his pocket and offered it to them to drink the king's health if they would continue the fight. Soon afterward, the British cutter struck her colors.[194]

The HM Frigate *Apollo*, mounting 36 guns, 26 of which were 12-pounders, captured the French frigate *Oiseau* of 26 8-pounders before February 10. The *Oiseau* had her ensign staff shot away twice and lost her mast in the long and obstinate engagement.[195]

Before February 11, the armed ship *Spy* captured Mr. Lackie's French ship *Neptune* bound from Carolina to Bordeaux and sent to Cork. Mr. Cooper's 20-gun *Sturdy Beggar* captured a French privateer snow and brought her to Liverpool, England, where she went to refit, having lost her topmast in the engagement.[196]

A Mahon, Spain, privateer cut four vessels out of the quarantine road at Marseilles and brought them to Mahon. The Liverpool private ship-of-war *Mentor* also captured the privateer *Comtesse d'Artois* and sent her to Beerhaven. The *Marchioness of Granby* captured the *Labore* bound from Lorient to Boston with merchandise worth £35,000 and a snow laden with brandy. Captain Washington's *Ellis* captured the *Joseph* inbound from Saint Domingue to France. The prizes were all sent to Liverpool by February 11.[197]

The ship *Marquis de Brancas*, part of the French convoy under Mr. Legordeur de Tilly's frigate *Concorde* and mounting nine 6-pounders, met a British privateer of 18 guns before February 12. The two engaged for more than two hours when the privateer sailed away.[198]

The New York privateer *Spitfire*, carrying one gun and seven men, captured a French brig of eight guns and 20 men before February 15 but later had to abandon the prize.[199] Captain John Hilton, in the Crown vessel *Westmoreland*, captured a French ship from Hispaniola with 537 hogsheads of sugar, some tons of indigo and cotton and brought her to New York on Sunday, February 15.[200]

The British and French fleets had an engagement in the English Channel before February 15. The French captured four frigates and 70 privateers of all sizes and a great number of seamen. Some accounts put the total prisoners at 12,000, most of them taken in privateers, and about 3,000 sailors brought to England. The British captured four French East Indiamen and a number of rich trading vessels from the West Indies and other ports.[201]

The HM Frigate *Minerva*, captured by the French, captured two privateers of 10 or 12 guns from Jamaica before February 16. The *Minerva* also had a bloody engagement with a 22-gun transport ship that lasted the whole night. The transport surrendered; but, before the French could take possession of her, she blew up. Only 30 of her crew of 300 were saved. The *Minerva* had about 25 killed and wounded.[202]

Before February 20, the 12-gun 90-man Bayonne, France, privateer *Esprit* was captured and sent to King Road. A ship bound from Saint Domingue to Nantes was captured and sent to Guernsey. A British frigate captured the 24-gun *Esperance* and sent her to Penzance. She captured four prizes. The Bristol privateer *Gipsy* was taken and brought to St.-Malo. The privateer *Marquis of Rockingham*, belonging to Hull, England, captured a 12-gun French privateer and brought her to Torbay, England. The London privateers *Bellona* and *Enterprize* captured a 20-gun French frigate and sent her to Lisbon.[203]

The *Neptune*, a new ship of 80 guns, built at Rochefort, sailed from there to join the fleet at Brest. On her passage, she captured a 36-gun British privateer. After an engagement of three quarters of an hour with an English 64-gun ship, the *Neptune* forced her to strike her colors. The crew of the *Neptune* could not take possession of their prize because five British ships-of-the-line appeared and gave chase. After having sustained fire from those six ships, the *Neptune* arrived safely at Brest with her prizes.[204]

Before March 13, the 16-gun Southampton, England, privateer *Admiral Keppel*, the property of six ladies of that town, captured a large French West Indiaman valued at £30,000. The French frigate *La Courageuse* captured the 24-gun *Valiant* from Bristol and brought her to the Isle of Aix.[205]

The privateer *Knight* captured the French Indiaman *Deux Amis* after a six-hour engagement before March 20. She had two iron chests on board with £200,000 in gold. The prize met a schooner soon afterward with 24 British and 24 French on board. Only 10 British and five French were saved. When the schooner surrendered, the remainder of the Frenchmen jumped overboard. One of them, in the confusion, took with him a box of diamonds worth £16,000. Another took a wedge of gold weighing 12 pounds. Both articles were lost as well as the men.[206]

Mr. de Kerfin, lieutenant in the French Navy, captured two prizes during the last week in March. One was the copper-bottomed merchant cutter *Eliza*, of 28 12-pounders and 140 men. Her cargo consisted of wine and cloth valued at 25,000 livres. The other was an 18-gun, 86-man privateer. A French frigate also captured a 26-gun British frigate.[207] Four French ships-of-the-line captured Captain Reeks's *Concordia* bound from Cadiz, Spain to London. A letter of marque from Greenock, Scotland, later retook the prize and brought her to Greenock before April 1.[208]

The HM Sloop *Delight* fell in with the 20-gun, 100-man French privateer *Jean Burt* off Dunmore, Scotland, about 10 AM on Thursday, April 1, 1779. The two vessels were engaged for some time, during which Mr. Randall, the boatswain, was killed and two men badly wounded. The *Jean Burt* surrendered about 1 PM and was brought to Plymouth by the HMS *Jupiter*.[209]

The 20-gun cruiser *Prince de Montbarry* attacked the HMS *Montague* coming from Leghorn, England, with 40 men, 12 guns, and eight mortars on Monday, April 19. The *Montague* surrendered after an engagement of 2½ hours, totally disabled. The prize was brought to Grenville, France, on May 22. She was said to be worth £500,000 and her cargo valued at £180,000.[210]

Captain Harding's cutter *Dublin,* mounting 10 4-pounders, fell in with a large French snow of 18 guns in latitude 35.14 longitude 50 on Sunday, April 25. The two had a brisk engagement for some time so closely that their guns sometimes touched each other. The French snow outmanned and outgunned the *Dublin*, which broke off the engagement and sailed after Captain Harding had been killed and the cutter badly damaged.[211]

The Guernsey privateer *Defiance* captured the French ship *La Roche*, of about 350 tons, before April 27. She was bound from Martinique to Bordeaux with coffee, sugar, cotton, and indigo. She was brought to Guernsey and was one of the largest of the fleet's 30 vessels, 18 of which were captured by Crown privateers and men-of-war.[212]

Before April 27, Captain Allanson's Liverpool privateer *Vulture* captured the 400-ton *St. Cyprean*. She was bound from Martinique to France with sugar, coffee, cotton, and indigo valued at £20,000. Three British cutters and a frigate engaged two French privateers for some time on the coast of Holland. The French privateers surrendered and the British took possession of them.[213]

Before May 1, 1779, the Whitehaven privateer *Diamond* captured the French ship *St. Paul de Tricasten* bound from Saint-Domingue, French West Indies, to Bordeaux with coffee, cotton, and indigo. She was valued at £12,000 and brought to Waterford. The Jersey privateer *General Conway* captured the 300-ton *Judith* bound from Martinique to Bordeaux, and the privateer *Swiftsure* captured the French ship *Chalon sur Soanne* bound from Marseilles to Cadiz with bales of silk and other goods. The prize was leaky, so her cargo was taken aboard the privateer and the vessel was brought to Gibraltar and sold.[214]

Captain Wilson's privateer *Happy* captured the French ship *Pont l'Eveque* laden with sugar, coffee, indigo, and cotton and brought her to Waterford on May 4.[215]

A French fleet of three ships, a brig, and two sloops anchored at Coutances Bay, France, the night of May 10. The British fleet (the *Experiment, Pallas, Unicorn, Fortune, Richmond*, the sloop *Vulture*, and the brig *Cabot*) was anchored at Bouley Bay, Jersey. Sir James Wallace divided his force and proceeded around the west end of Jersey and headed for them the next morning at 3 AM. When the British got within three or four leagues of the French, the HMS *Experiment* gave the signal to weigh (hoist the topsail yards aloft with the sails furled). The British vessels immediately weighed and headed toward St.-Malo with all their sails set.

The British continued following the French until 10 o'clock that night when the wind was almost calm and the tide against them, forcing them to anchor. They were then in the narrow passage between Granville and the Chose Islands in the English Channel. There was very little wind and it was southerly, forcing the *Richmond* and the other ships to anchor in the forenoon as the tide was still against them. A smart cannonade began just before noon in which the shore batteries took part.

At dawn on the 13th, the British saw a frigate and five or six other vessels coming out of St.-Malo heading to Cancale Bay. The HMS *Experiment* gave chase to the frigate which got in under the batteries of St.-Malo. The *Experiment* then chased the other vessels (three frigates and an armed cutter) to the leeward. They went into Cancale Bay and ran ashore. The *Experiment* ran in directly among them and began an action. The French crews abandoned ship. The British boarded their boats and brought off the French vessels. The French brought some cannons and howitzers to the shore and kept up such a smart fire that the British burned two frigates and scuttled the cutter on shore. The British brought the third frigate with them, along with a brig and a sloop. These ships were to cooperate with 2,000 troops of the Prince of Nassau who were then encamped on a small island about two leagues from St.-Malo.

The *Experiment* was hulled in several places and her sails and rigging were badly damaged by the shot. She had two men killed and 13 wounded, two of them dangerously. The purser of the *Cabot* had his leg shot off and two of her men were wounded.

Other vessels captured included:

- The 34-gun, 250-man *Danae* was taken to Portsmouth or Plymouth under the command of Lieutenant Rothe of the *Experiment.*
- The *Dieppe*, a 16-gun, 80-man cutter, was scuttled and left on the shore.
- The 40-ton, four-man sloop *Fleur* was taken about 10 AM. She was bound for St.-Malo from the river Vivien with timber for building.
- The 26-gun, 260-man *Voleur* was burned by Captain Dod of the *Cabot.*
- A 50-ton brig and a 50-ton sloop were abandoned by their crews. One was loaded with linseed, the other with lead.
- Several fishing boats and other small craft were destroyed.[216]

Captain Bastone's British privateer *Olive* captured two French prizes and brought them to Leghorn, England, before May 15. One was from Smyrna, Turkey,, laden with cotton and other valuable merchandise and a quantity of silver on board. The other was laden with sugar, coffee and cocoa.[217]

Captain James Clarke's Glasgow letter of marque *Tartar* arrived in New York on Thursday, May 27. She brought with her two prizes: a French brig laden with indigo, tobacco, and rice and a schooner laden with naval supplies.[218]

The Bristol privateer *Terrible* had an action with the French 40-gun ship *Juno* about May 28. In the height of battle, the *Juno* blew up and only 17 hands were saved.[219]

French cruisers captured a number of prizes, particularly two ships from the Straits of Gibraltar with very rich cargoes. They were captured by two frigates and sent to Malaga before the end of May.[220]

The *Duke of Cumberland*, of 26 9-pounders, captured the Chevalier Bouquernois's *Rochelle*, of St.-Malo, with 30 12- and 6-pounders, after an engagement of two hours on June 5. She had 13 men killed and 33 wounded. The Chevalier Bouquernois lost his right leg, his second lieutenant and four men were wounded, and 11 killed.[221]

The Massachusetts frigate *Boston* captured Captain Templeman's brig *Boyd* bound from New York to Québec and recaptured the French ship *La Vern*, previously taken by Captain Mease's *Norfolk's Revenge*, and sent them to Boston before June 9.[222]

Captain Brewer's *Active* captured a French ship with 300 soldiers on board and brought her to Poole, England, before June 10.[223]

Captain John Hastie's privateer *Hawke*, belonging to Clyne, England, had an engagement with two French privateers, one a ship, the other a brigantine, for half an hour on Friday, June 11 when they sheered off. He fell in with them again the next afternoon for three hours before they set sail and put about. The *Hawke's* sails and rigging were damaged and she had several holes in the hull, all from 9-pound shot. Captain Hastie had three men wounded, so he did not think it proper to pursue the privateers. The brigantine mounted 24 9- and 6-pounders; the ship mounted 16 nines and sixes. The *Hawke* fired her 10- and 11-pound carronades through both sides of the brigantine.[224]

Two French privateers captured Captain Rogers's East Indiaman *Osterly* off the Cape of Good Hope before Monday, June 14, 1779. She was valued at £200,000.[225]

Captain de Latouche's galley *Rossignol* was sailing alone on Monday, June 15, when she sighted a cutter which appeared to be a merchant ship because her gun ports were masked by canvas of the same color as her sides. The *Rossignol* gave chase, gained on her quickly, and captured her after firing three cannon shots. She proved to be the *Morning Star*, carrying six guns and 36 men. Captain de Latouche took 17 prisoners and formed a prize crew. The sloop accompanied the *Rossignol* for several days.[226]

Captain Fisher's Liverpool letter of marque *Betsey* captured the French East Indiaman *La Favar* before June 16. She weighed about 250 tons, was valued at £50,000, and was brought to Liverpool.[227]

The HM Frigate *Alarm* captured the French 250-ton ship *La Marchionesse au Point* before Saturday, June 19. She was bound from Marseilles to Cadiz with bales of silk. She also had dispatches on board from the governor of Cadiz.[228]

Robert Scott's British privateer *Lapwing*, carrying 10 guns, two mortars, and 12 swivel guns, and a crew of 40, approached Captain de Latouche's galley *Rossignol* on June 20. Her battery was masked. Captain de Latouche hoisted his colors and fired a few cannon shots. The privateer displayed British colors. Latouche fired a few more cannons and the privateer struck her colors, making it appear she was ready to surrender. She continued to advance, raised her colors anew, and headed to board the *Rossignol*, which fired two volleys of grapeshot which completely disabled the privateer. Meanwhile, the French continued constant musket fire, which made the British abandon their plan of setting the *Rossignol* on fire with grenades, as two mortars were found loaded to the mouth. All the British threw themselves in the hold. They had no killed or wounded. The helmsman tried to board the *Rossignol* but gave up under a hail of musket fire. Only 28 of the crew of 40 remained aboard; the others were divided among the prizes.

On the way back to port on June 23, two prisoners from the *Morning Star* identified a British sloop which was briefly lured by the *Rossignol*. She approached but became suspicious and escaped.[229]

The HM Frigate *Ambuscade* captured the 16-gun, 120-man French privateer *Prince de Moulbeny* and sent her to Plymouth before July 1, 1779. The schooner *Anne*, bound from Morlaix to Virginia, and the *Prince of Hesse*, bound to Barcelona with dry goods, were also sent to Plymouth. The HM Frigate *Southampton*, one of Sir Charles Hardy's fleet, captured Captain Simon de la Torre's *Conception*, bound from Cadiz to Ostend with wine, barilla, oil, and $14,000, and sent her to Portsmouth on Thursday, July 1. When the prize left the fleet on June 27, they were in latitude

48.5 and had taken two privateers—one Whig and the other French—and three other prizes.[230]

The armed brig *Swallow* hoisted Continental colors as a feint and was chased by two cutters from Sir Charles Hardy's fleet before July 5. She came to under the fort of Brest and discovered several men-of-war in the harbor with their yards and topsails struck. The *Swallow* prepared to get away but was fired at from the fort and prevented from doing so until a 74-gun ship came to her assistance and fired three broadsides at the fort. The *Swallow* then managed to escape. The French transport *La Falaise* from St.-Malo was taken to Jersey about the same time.[231]

A number of privateers fitted out from St.-Malo and Nantes captured and plundered the island forts of Jersey and Guernsey before July 6. Captain Todd's HM Sloop-of-War *Cabot* drove some French ships on shore after they attacked Jersey.[232]

The privateer *Hope* fell in with the 28-gun French privateer *Monamis* of Bordeaux on Monday, July 7. The *Hope* sighted the privateer early in the morning in a thick haze. Most of the people on board thought she was about 600 or 700 tons and from Saint-Domingue or Martinique. They chased her for about two hours. As the *Hope* came alongside, the privateer hoisted French colors and fired a gun. The *Hope* hoisted English colors and poured a broadside into her, beginning a fierce engagement that continued for half an hour. The *Hope* soon found she was outgunned. The French vessel had 28 guns, firing mostly 12-pounders, and a crew of 150 men. The *Hope* had 20 6-pounders and a crew of 104.

The *Hope* was about ready to surrender when a large cloud of smoke rose from the French vessel followed by a loud report. Several men were seen swimming in the water toward the *Hope*, which took up two of them. They reported that a spark of fire had caught a barrel of gunpowder under the quarterdeck and had blown up a great part of the quarterdeck and several men that were on it and that they were on the quarterdeck along with them. The *Hope* lost three men killed and seven wounded. The French had six killed and 12 wounded and 20 6-pound shots in her mainmast before the accident.[233]

A privateer returned to Ireland from a cruise on Wednesday, July 28. Her captain reported that he fell in with two fleets of ships, all men-of-war and frigates, under French and Spanish colors. They fired several shots to bring him to, but the captain of the privateer sailed away immediately, assisted by a sudden gale of wind. He fell in with two small French vessels bound to the West Indies and loaded with ammunition on Monday, July 26. He captured one of them and brought it back to Ireland with him.[234]

The HMS *Galatea* fell in with the *Minerva*, a French frigate of 32 guns, off Boston Bay before Thursday, July 29. The *Minerva* gave the *Galatea* a severe drubbing, killing her lieutenant and several men.[235]

The HMS *Solebay* captured the French ship *Palatine*, which was cut out of the Chesapeake Bay on Friday, August 6. She was loaded with 180 hogsheads of tobacco and brought to New York on September 3.[236]

Before August 20, the French *Epevier* had five different engagements with British ships of superior force on her passage from the coast of Africa. The *Triton* and *Andromache* came to Brest Road with a convoy of 23 vessels from Saint-Domingue. En route, the *Andromache* captured a 24-gun British cruiser, which she sank after taking out the crew and cargo. The frigate *Denis* captured four valuable prizes with 400 prisoners and brought them to Lorient. M. de Cardaillac's frigate *Concorde* captured a 26-gun British cruiser off Cape Finisterre.[237]

A British frigate had an engagement with a large French ship near Madeira before August 21. A strong wind blew throughout the fierce engagement and the waves were high. The French ship, which was near the shore, drove on a ledge of rocks where she was totally destroyed. The captain, surgeon, and 195 crewmen perished on board. The others were saved by the frigate's crew with much difficulty.[238]

M. de Flotte's 24-gun *Aurora* put into Algiers in a storm. The French consul there informed him that he had learned from the British consul that four British cruisers were anchored off the port to intercept him if he went out. M. de Flotte slipped his cables and sailed immediately to meet the four British vessels about two leagues away. They ranged in order of battle and waited for him. M. de Flotte fired several broadsides, piercing the cruisers several times and forcing them to surrender. M. de Flotte returned to Algiers with his prizes before August 21. The prizes included the 20-gun *Saville*, the 20-gun *Salerno*, the 16-gun *Italian Merchant*, and the 10-gun *Favourite*.[239]

Three 74-gun ships and two frigates of the combined French and Spanish fleets attacked Captain Philip Boteler's 64-gun (26 24-pounders on her lower deck, 26 18-pounders on her upper deck, 12 9-pounders on the quarterdeck and forecastle, and 12 swivels) 523-man HMS *Ardent* as she attempted to join Admiral Hardy's fleet off Plymouth on Sunday, August 22. Captain Boteler discovered his error almost immediately and received a broadside from a 74-gun French ship which he fought and was trying to escape when two other ships of the same force bore down and engaged him. All these vessels engaged in a running fight for almost three hours. The *Ardent* was obliged to strike to this unequal force after her mainmast and every yard were shot away. She lost five men killed and eight wounded and sank soon after surrendering.[240]

The French frigate *La Gentille* captured the sloop *Emerald* on Monday, August 23 and sent her to Brest. She was bound from Portsmouth to Québec with provisions and brandy.[241]

Before August 24, the *Vigilant* and *Modeste*, two French East Indiamen, fell in with three Whig privateers who mistook them for British vessels and ran alongside them, firing broadsides into them. A regular engagement ensued and lasted a considerable amount of time. The French vessels lost a number of men and had the greatest part of their rigging shot away, obliging them to cease fire. The captains of the privateers, when they discovered their mistake, gave the French all the assistance they could. The HM Frigate *Stag* captured the 18-gun French privateer *Magnionette* and the privateers *Nonsuch*, *Fame*, and *Achilles* captured a number of Spanish and French prizes and brought them to Gibraltar.[242]

Some French privateers were seen chasing a British vessel off Rye on Wednesday, August 25. They continued chasing her for several hours and drove her on shore near Lydd in the evening. An express was immediately dispatched to the commanding officer at the camp at Pleyden, near Rye. He immediately sent 100 men and a piece of ordnance which arrived at Lydd in time to save the sloop and force the privateers to sheer off. The sloop was laden with deal plank and had cleared out of the port of Hastings the day before.[243]

Captain Doyle's letter of marque *Blossom*, bound from Liverpool to Africa, captured the French snow *Chamont*, bound from Beaufort, North Carolina to Nantes with a cargo of tobacco, naval stores, and indigo. The *Chamont* arrived at Liverpool on Thursday, August 26.[244]

Captain de Latouche's frigate *Hermione* sighted Captain Stocker's British cutter *Hawker* during the night of August 27, followed her, and surprised her at dawn. The *Hawker* tried to defend herself but surrendered after receiving 40 cannon shots and three men wounded. She left Weymouth on August 12 without taking any prizes, but her log indicated that she escaped from some 20 vessels which chased her. A prize crew was put aboard and she was taken to La Coruña.

Captain de Latouche gained Captain Stocker's confidence and obtained the permanent signals used by British privateers (not the ones used for day or night or times of fog). The Ministry of the Navy sent the signals to all French warships in a letter dated September 27, 1779. Captain de Latouche also obtained other interesting information about the practices of the British privateers. In exchange, he promised to land Captain Stocker and his officers in Spain.[245]

The New York privateer brig *Dunmore* captured Captain Fairchild's Philadelphia brig *Chance* on Thursday, August 26 or on Monday, August 30, 1779. Two French frigates recaptured her west of Bermuda on Wednesday, September 1 or Monday, September 6 and sent her to Philadelphia. She fell in with Commander John Collins's HMS *Camilla* about 70 leagues east of Sandy Hook on Tuesday, September 7 and was ordered to New York. She arrived Saturday noon, September 11, with a cargo of salt.[246]

The Hull, England, privateer *Palliser* captured the Dunkirk privateer *Maréchal de France* on the north coast of England on Tuesday, August 31. The *Maréchal de France* had captured more than 18 vessels in less than six weeks.[247]

Sir Charles Hardy had an engagement with the combined fleets of France and Spain off Cape Clear, Ireland on September 2, 1779. The British fleet captured five ships of the line and sank 10. The *Spanish Admiral* went down alongside the *Britannia*. The same day, the French ship *Monsieur* took Captain P. Tremblet's 250-ton ship *Villanova*. She was bound from Porto, Portugal, to London with wine.[248]

The British sent out patrols to determine the location of Admiral d'Estaing's fleet as it approached Georgia. The HMS *Rose* went out of Savannah on Friday, September 3 to investigate a report of several large ships. She returned with news that the French ships were near the coast.

The 74-gun ship-of-the-line *Magnifique* captured the sloop *Polly* and her crew on Monday, September 6. Five French sailors boarded the *Polly*, but that night, a gale blew her away from the French fleet toward Tybee. The French sailors, unaware of their location, sailed the *Polly* up the Georgia coast. The English prisoners on board added to the confusion by telling their captors that the Savannah River was the entrance to Charleston.

The crew sailed the *Polly* in the mouth of the river and anchored, whereupon she was captured. The sailors informed their captors that the French fleet consisted of the 74-gun *Magnifique*, the 64-gun *Sphinx*, two frigates, a schooner, and a cutter, all bound to Boston for masts and spars.[249]

The French ship *Monsieur* took Captain A. Brodet's ship *Sweet* on Tuesday, September 7. She was taken to Brest with her cargo of Madeira wine.[250]

Three French ships of 74 guns surrounded Admiral Barrington's ship on Wednesday, September 8. Admiral Barrington was wounded severely. He had many men killed and his ship received 22 shots.[251]

The Comte de La Perouse's French frigate *Amazone*, mounting 30 18-pounders and 10 6-pounders, was chasing a ship off the Charleston bar, as she came in on September 10 and soon came up with her. She was Captain Mackenzie's 20-gun (9- and 6-pounders) HM Frigate *Ariel*, which was captured after an engagement of 1¼ hours. All the masts and most of the rigging were shot away and the *Ariel* was almost a wreck. The French loaned the *Ariel* to the Americans until 1781.[252]

Captain Brownson's letter of marque *Druid* captured the French privateer *Perdrix*, from Calais, after a desperate engagement of 1½ hours about September 10. The *Perdrix* was sent to Harwich with five hostages on board.[253]

A French cutter, thought to be Captain Stephen Merchant's New York privateer ship *Black Prince*, captured 10 sloops in the Irish Channel on Tuesday, September 14. The *Black Prince*, mounting 16 carriage guns and 32 swivels, was fitted out at Dunkirk under a Continental commission. She sailed from Dunkirk on June 12. Her crew consisted mostly of Irish and English smugglers and a few Americans. She brought the prize sloops to Fishguard, England about 12 miles from Pembroke. One of them was Mr. Bowen Longwair's *Old George* bound from Bristol to Belfast which was ransomed for £700. Some of the sloops were stripped. They were ransomed for 100 guineas each. The cutter fired about 100 shots at the town with little effect. She was so near the town that several 6-pound shots were picked up in the streets and two hand grenades had been flung into the town. The *Black Prince* weighed anchor and put to sea about 8 o'clock the next morning.[254]

A French-built frigate of about 40 or 50 guns appeared about 7 or 8 miles off the coast of Dunbar, Scotland, around Tuesday, September 14. She captured a three-masted vessel which had come out of the Firth of Forth and brought her to the south.[255]

Captain Sibbles's privateer brig *Tryon* returned to New York on Wednesday, September 15, with the French letter of marque snow *Sea-horse*. The *Sea-horse*, mounting 10 carriage guns and six swivels, was bound from Marseilles to Fredericksburg with a cargo intended for the Continental Army. This was the sixth prize the *Tryon* captured on her cruise.[256]

The commander-in-chief, the customhouse, and the Lord Provost at Edinburgh received expresses early Wednesday morning, September 22, acquainting them that four French privateers captured two prizes in the mouth of the Firth, off the coast of Eyemouth, on Tuesday afternoon, September 14. The largest was a frigate thought to carry 40 or 50 guns.

Two men skilled in maritime affairs were sent to reconnoiter those ships on Wednesday. They returned to Edinburgh on Thursday and reported that they found the ships lying off Dunbar. They sailed within 3 miles of them and saw them to be four French ships, one of 50 guns, two frigates of 20, and one of 14. They had two prizes with them.

The fleet was opposite Leith, near the island of Inchkeith, on the north side, about 4 miles from Leith, on Friday morning. A swift sailing cutter was sent to reconnoiter. She fell in with a prize they had taken in the mouth of the Firth and recaptured her, but the cutter was obliged to abandon the prize by a 24-gun French frigate which approached her. A boy jumped from the prize on board the cutter and was brought to Leith.

Lord Provost, Captain Napier, and others examined the boy who said that the French put four British soldiers, four men, and two officers aboard the prize, all of whom spoke English. He also said that the squadron consisted of a 50-gun ship, a 24-gun frigate and a 10-gun brig whose crews intended to come up the Leith Road, but they didn't sail well.

The wind blew violently from the southwest on Friday, driving them down the Firth, a good way below the island of Inchkeith. The commander of the 50-gun ship was thought to be a Scot who knew the coast. Seven vessels had originally left Dunkirk, but these three parted from the rest in a gale in the North Sea.

Another account says that the French captured 10 prizes within a few days. Seven of the cutter's crew were on board one of the prizes belonging to Mr. Wemiss Fife.[257]

Several large French privateers appeared on the coast of England, off Shields on the northeast coast, on Sunday, September 19. There were at least six, two of which did not carry fewer than 40 guns each. They captured a brig belonging to Saltcoats and two sloops belonging to Greenock and one to Liverpool, all loaded with kelp. They were taken in view of the shore. The privateers chased a fleet of loaded colliers which escaped by running into Stockton. They came so close to the harbor that the British thought they were going to land. The farmers drove the cattle off the coast and several people fled from their houses.[258]

The same day, the Dunkirk privateer *Black Prince*, mounting 16 6-pounders and a crew of 71 men, captured the *Three Friends* in Lalliman's Bay, in the island of Jura, Scotland. The *Three Friends* was a letter of marque ship bound from Liverpool to New York with a valuable cargo of West India goods. The *Black Prince* also captured Captain Maziol's *Francisco de Paola* in Lalliman's Bay (in the island of Jura). She had previously been taken by Captain Thompson's *Defiance* and was laden with hat wool, hides, and $17,000. The dollars were landed before the *Black Prince* captured her. Both vessels were worth more than £16,000.

The *Black Prince* sailed around the coast of Britain and Ireland and captured 37 prizes in less than three months. They include:

- the brig *Blossom*, the brig *Liberty*, and the sloop *Sally* (June 20);
- the brig *Hampton*, the brig *Three Sisters*, the sloop *Elizabeth*, the brig *Orange*, and the brig *Goodwill* (June 21);
- the brig *Ann* (July 17);
- the brig *Lucy*, the sloop *John*, the sloop *Rebecca*, and two sloops, both called the *Two Brothers* (July 18);
- the brigs *Union* and *Sea Nymph* (July 19);
- the brig *Dublin Trader*, the sloop *Charlotte*, and retook the Spanish snow *Saint Joseph* (July 20);
- the brig *Monmouth* (July 22);
- a whaleboat, the brig *Diligence*, and the sloop *Friends' Adventure* (August 18);
- the *Matthew and Sally*, the sloops *Betsey* and *Resolution* (August 19);
- the ship *Southam* (August 20).

The snow *Hopewell* fought a privateer schooner, took and burned a sloop (September 9); took a sloop and captured and burned the *Peggy* (September 10); burned two brigs and fired on the town (September 15); and recaptured the *Hopewell* (before September 16), the *Three Friends*, and recaptured the *Francisco de Paola* (September

19). Three of them were retaken, four burned after taking out what was valuable, and the rest were either ransomed or arrived safely in port before March 9, 1780.[259]

Before September 20, 1779, the HM Frigate *Milford* fell in with and captured the *Lilly of France* after an engagement of four hours. The French frigate, which mounted 38 guns and had a crew of 300 picked seamen, lost a great part of her crew in the conflict. The *Milford* suffered minor damage. The French privateer *Le Commandant* from Dunkirk also captured Mr. Thomas's *Nancy*, Mr. Gilbert's *Prince of Wales*, and several other vessels. The *Nancy*, bound from Bristol to Belfast, was ransomed for £350, the *Prince of Wales* for 100 guineas, and the other vessels for £200. Mr. Mahon's letter of marque *Queen Caroline* also took a French Turkeyman which he cut away from under the Castle of Estapona, a Spanish fort between Gibraltar and Malaga, and brought her to Minorca.[260]

A large French privateer cutter, supposed from Dunkirk, sailed through the Downs in sight of all the ships anchored there on Monday morning, September 20. As soon as she was determined to be an enemy vessel, two cutters and a sloop-of-war slipped their cables and went after her. They returned the following morning with no prize. A French privateer did the same thing about three months earlier and escaped, even though she was closely pursued.[261]

The same day, a frigate, a sloop, and a cutter, believed to be French, appeared about a mile off the Scarborough pier. They fired at several ships, captured two, and forced two others to run into the harbor with damaged rigging and sails from continual fire. The frigate, sloop, and cutter then headed northward.[262]

Commander Charles Thompson's HM Frigate *Boreas* captured the 20-carriage gun, 150-man French letter of marque *La Cumfas* and sent her to Barbados on Tuesday September 21. The French ship had 20 men killed in the 1¼-hour engagement. The *Boreas* had four men killed and some wounded. She was bound from Martinique to France.[263]

The Guernsey privateer *Fortune* captured Captain La Seyenis Widamora's French ship *Alquiperes* on Tuesday, September 21 and brought her to Guernsey. She was bound from Marseilles to St.-Malo with bales of silk. The same day, Captain Farmer's frigate *Québec* captured the six-gun, 36-man privateer *Espervier* and brought her to Portsmouth.[264]

The French ship *Monsieur* took Captain I. Peel's *Joseph* on Wednesday, September 22. She was bound to Madeira in ballast. The following day, *Monsieur* retook the Spanish ship *St. Antoine*, previously taken by an English letter of marque. She was bound from Havana and sent to St.-Malo.[265]

John Montagu, 4th Earl of Sandwich, First Lord of the Admiralty, and the English people feared a French assault upon England. When Spain declared war on Great Britain on Wednesday, June 16, 1779, the danger of foreign invasion became more real than ever. A combined French and Spanish fleet of 66 ships entered the English Channel in July 1779, bringing that fear to a new height. The fleet remained in the Channel for several weeks and captured only one British ship-of-the-line. They anchored off Plymouth on Monday, August 16 and prepared to defeat the British fleet of 35 ships. The general in command of the port of Plymouth admitted that the fleet could have taken the dockyard in a few hours. But the battle never occurred. The French were low on provisions and returned to Brest in September. The Spanish fleet returned to attack Gibraltar.

Captain John Paul Jones

Whig privateers were also destroying British commerce and making the American war increasingly more repugnant to the British public. John Paul Jones, in command of the 18-gun *Ranger*, landed at Whitehaven Bay, spiked the guns of the fort, and burned some coastal shipping. He later captured the 20-gun HMS *Drake* in the Irish Sea.

During this period, Benjamin Franklin, who was in Paris, obtained from the French government a slow, 14-year-old French cargo ship, the 900-ton East Indiaman *Duc de Duras*, in February and gave it to Captain Jones. Jones refitted it, mounted guns, and renamed it the *Bonhomme Richard* to honor Franklin, the author of *Poor Richard's Almanac*. Jones set sail for England with a French frigate and four smaller vessels.

The Gazetteer and New Daily Advertiser for July 7 printed a letter dated June 15 from a British officer in prison in Brest:

> Captain Paul Jones, who some time since landed in Scotland and other places, has fitted out an Old East Indiaman, to mount 50 guns, and has had her full manned except about 40. She is to carry 300; most of them are English prisoners, who are allowed to enter on board the American vessels. Numbers of them, I am sure, would never have gone on board, but for the bad treatment they experience in prison. The above ship is to sail in consort with an American frigate called the *Alliance*.

Captain Jones intended to have 28 18-pounders on the gun deck, 28 8-pounders on the upper deck, and six 8-pounders on the forecastle and quarterdeck. Although arrangements had been made for the ship to carry 16 18-pounders on the gun deck, it went to sea with only six old guns of this caliber. The ship's main strength was in the 28 12-pounders on the upper deck and the six 8-pounders (two in the forecastle and four on the quarterdeck). She had just 40 guns and a crew of 322 men.

Jones put to sea on August 14 with Captain Denis Cotteneau's 32-gun *Pallas*, Captain Ricot's 12-gun *Vengeance*, Captain Landais's 36-gun privateer *Alliance*, and the *Bonhomme Richard*. The squadron passed the north of Scotland and proceeded southward down the east coast of England. Jones planned to raid Leith, to capture ships and hold them for ransom, but a storm prevented this. He then proceeded to the North Sea, where he found a fleet of 41 merchantmen returning from the Baltic laden with naval stores. The merchant fleet hurried to port while Jones prepared to do battle with Captain Richard Pearson's 44-gun *Serapis* off Flamborough Head at 2 PM on Thursday, September 23, 1779. The French frigate *Pallas* engaged the other escort, Captain Thomas Piercy's 20-gun *Countess of Scarborough*.

Jones's squadron closed in from the south, while Captain Pearson's two ships were between him and the land to allow the merchantmen to escape. The battle began about 7:15 PM at a range of about 100 yards and continued well into the night. The *Serapis* fired the first shot. Each ship hulled the other in the first volley. The *Serapis* fired a second broadside at only 20 yards.

When the *Bonhomme Richard* returned fire, one, and possibly two, of her old 18-pounders blew up, probably from the strain of being double shotted. Many of the crew were killed or wounded and part of the ship side was blown out. Jones ordered his crew to abandon the other 18-pounders. The *Serapis* sailed around the *Bonhomme Richard* at will, in the savage four-hour battle, and poured several broadsides into her. Captain Jones planned to close with the enemy and board. Lieutenant Richard Dale, who commanded a battery of 12-pounders on the *Bonhomme Richard*, recalls:

At about eight, being within hail, the Serapis demanded, "What ship is that?"

He was answered, "I can't hear what you say."

Immediately after, the *Serapis* hailed again, "What ship is that? Answer immediately, or I shall be under the necessity of firing into you."

At this moment I received orders from Commodore Jones to commence the action with a broadside, which indeed appeared to be simultaneous on board both ships. Our position being to windward of the *Serapis* we passed ahead of her, and the *Serapis* coming up on our larboard quarter, the action commenced abreast of each other. The *Serapis* soon passed ahead of the *Bonhomme Richard*, and when he thought he had gained a distance sufficient to go down athwart the fore foot, to rake us, found he had not enough distance, and that the *Bonhomme Richard* would be aboard him, put his helm at lee, which brought the two ships on a line, and the *Bonhomme Richard*, having head way, ran her bows into the stern of the *Serapis*.

We had remained in this situation but a few minutes when we were again hailed by the *Serapis*, "Has your ship struck?"

To which Captain Jones answered, "I have not yet begun to fight!"[266]

As we were unable to bring a single gun to bear upon the *Serapis* our top sails were backed, while those of the *Serapis* being filled, the ships separated. The *Serapis* bore short round upon her heel, and her jibboom ran into the mizen rigging of the *Bonhomme Richard*. In this situation the ships were made fast together with a hawser, the bowsprit of the *Serapis* to the mizen mast of the *Bonhomme Richard*, and the action recommenced from the starboard sides of the two ships. With a view of separating the ships, the *Serapis* let go her anchor, which manoeuver brought her head and the stern of the *Bonhomme Richard* to the wind, while the ships lay closely pressed against each other.

A novelty in naval combats was now presented to many witnesses, but to few admirers. The rammers were run into the respective ships to enable the men to load after the lower ports of the *Serapis* had been blown away, to make room for running out their guns, and in this situation the ships remained until between 10 and 11 o'clock PM, when the engagement terminated by the surrender of the *Serapis*.

From the commencement to the termination of the action there was not a man on board the *Bonhomme Richard* ignorant of the superiority of the *Serapis*, both in weight of metal and in the qualities of the crews. The crew of that ship was picked seamen, and the ship itself had been only a few months off the stocks, whereas the crew of the *Bonhomme Richard* consisted of part Americans, English and French, and a part of Maltese, Portuguese and Malays, these latter contributing by their want of naval skill and knowledge of the English language to depress rather than to elevate a just hope of success in a combat under such circumstances. Neither the consideration of the relative force of the ships, the fact of the blowing up of the gundeck above them by the bursting of two of the 18-pounders, nor the alarm that the ship was sinking, could depress the ardor or change the determination of the brave Captain Jones, his officers and men. Neither the repeated broadsides of the *Alliance*, given with the view of sinking or disabling the *Bonhomme Richard*, the frequent necessity of suspending the combat to extinguish the flames, which several times were within a few inches of the magazine, nor the liberation by the master at arms of nearly 500 prisoners, could change or weaken the purpose of the American commander. At the moment of the liberation of the prisoners, one of them, a commander of a 20-gun ship taken a few days before, passed through the ports on board the *Serapis* and informed Captain Pearson that if he would hold out only a little while longer, the ship alongside would either strike or sink, and that all the prisoners had been released to save their lives. The combat was accordingly continued with renewed ardor by the *Serapis*.

The fire from the tops of the *Bonhomme Richard* was conducted with so much skill and effect as to destroy ultimately every man who appeared upon the quarter deck of the *Serapis*, and induced her commander to order the survivors to go below. Not even under the shelter of the decks were they more secure. The powder monkies of the *Serapis*, finding no officer to receive the 18 pound cartridges brought from the magazines, threw them on the main deck and went for more. These cartridges being scattered along the deck and numbers of them broken, it so happened that some of the hand grenades thrown from the main yard of the *Bonhomme Richard*, which was directly over the main hatch of the *Serapis*, fell upon this powder and produced a most awful explosion. The effect was tremendous; more than twenty of the enemy were blown to pieces, and many stood with only the collars of their shirts upon their bodies. In less than an hour afterwards, the flag of England, which had been nailed to the mast of the *Serapis*, was struck by Captain Pearson's own hand, as none of his people would venture aloft on this duty; and this too when more than 1500 persons were witnessing the conflict, and the humiliating termination of it, from Scarborough and Flamborough Head.[267]

Midshipman Nathaniel Fanning, perched in the maintop of the same ship, elaborates:

It was, however, some time before the enemy's colours were struck. The captain of the *Serapis* gave repeated orders for one of his crew to ascend the quarterdeck and haul down the English flag, but no one would stir to do it. They told the captain they were afraid of our riflemen, believing that all our men who were seen with muskets were of that description. The captain of the *Serapis* therefore ascended the quarter deck and hauled down the very flag which he had nailed to the flag staff a little before the commencement of the battle, and which flag he had at that time, in the presence of his principal officers, swore he never would strike to that infamous pirate J. P. Jones.

The enemy's flag being struck, Captain Jones ordered Richard Dale, his first lieutenant, to select out of our crew a number of men and take possession of the prize, which was immediately put into execution. Several of our men (I believe three) were killed by the English on board of the *Serapis* after she had struck her colours. Thus ended this ever memorable battle, after a continuance of a few minutes.[268]

Captain Pearson struck his flag at 10:30 PM, as his mainmast was in danger of falling. Captain Jones began to transfer his crew—half of whom were casualties (150 of a crew of 322)—from his blazing ship to the captured *Serapis*. The *Serapis* lost 49 killed, 68 wounded, and 203 captured of her crew of 284. The *Countess of Scarborough* had four killed, 20 wounded, and 126 captured. The *Bonhomme Richard* sank the next day. This victory, within sight of the English coast, had an immense moral effect. It showed that American vessels could defeat British men-of-war—the largest and most powerful navy in the world at the time—off their own coast. Captain Jones brought his ships back to the Texel Road in Holland.[269]

A French lugsail privateer got among the fleet from St. Kitts, British West Indies, bound to Dover, England and might have captured some of them. The cutter *Kite* came up at that moment and took the privateer and brought her to Dover on Thursday, September 23.[270]

Captain Thomas Crowell, Jr.'s New York sloop *Olive Branch* captured and sent to Bermuda two French ships bound from Cape François to France on Thursday and Friday, September 23 and 24. One was a polacre loaded with 180 hogsheads, 72 tierces, and 47 barrels of white sugar; 37 tierces, 27 barrels, and 140 bags of coffee; 160 bags of cocoa, and 60 hogsheads of codfish. The other was a large ship with 480 hogsheads, 40 tierces, and four barrels of white sugar; 60 bales of cotton; 40 hogsheads and 60 tierces of codfish. These vessels sailed from Cape François in company with the grand fleet but were both obliged to throw their guns overboard and were dismasted, as were several other vessels of the fleet. The *Olive Branch* brought her prizes in on the 26th and went out again in search of other prizes.[271]

Sir James Wallace's 50-gun copper-bottomed HMS *Experiment* was on her way from New York to Savannah with Major General George Garth and 20 British officers and £30,000 in silver to pay the Crown troops in Georgia when she lost her masts and bowsprit in a gale. General Garth was supposed to replace Major General Augustine Prevost as commander in Savannah.

The *Experiment* rendezvoused with a British store ship and a navy victualler from New Providence (Nassau, Bahamas) near Hilton Head on Thursday, September 24. The captain of the store ship, which had 65 prisoners aboard, warned Sir James Wallace that he had seen 20 large ships south of Hilton Head.

The *Experiment* spotted three large ships in the distance at 3:45 PM and tried to outrun them. About 45 minutes later, Captain Wallace saw two more ships heading toward him from the west. The unknown ships hoisted the French colors at 8 PM and closed with the *Experiment*. The 50-gun French man-of-war *Sagittair* gave the *Experiment* two broadsides, but only a few shots reached the *Experiment* due to the distance between them. Captain Wallace hoisted more sail to get farther away from the *Sagittair*. He hoisted his colors at 8:30 and prepared to fight. All the French ships, two ships-of-the-line, and two frigates soon came within the *Experiment*'s range. They dismasted the *Experiment* and Captain Wallace struck his colors by 9 AM the next day.

The HM Frigate *Lively* was cruising in the same area and captured two vessels loaded with provisions. When the *Lively*'s captain learned that the vessels became separated from the *Experiment* in the storm, three ships were dispatched to find the *Experiment* off Port Royal.[272]

Sometime in October 1779, a 12-gun French privateer belonging to Cherbourg was taken and brought to Weymouth. The British cutter *Terror* also captured the 10-gun, 75-man *Aimable Princesse* of Dunkirk.[273]

Captain Babcock's privateer ship *General Mifflin* arrived at Hartford, Connecticut, on Saturday morning October 23. In his 10-week passage from France, he captured three prizes. One of them was a snow belonging to the Comte d'Estaing's fleet, which became separated from the fleet in a windstorm and captured by a New York privateer. She was retaken by the *General Mifflin* off Sandy Hook about Friday, October 15.[274]

There was a bloody engagement between the French frigate *La Surveillante* and the HM Frigate *Québec*, both of equal force, about 8 leagues from Ushant before October 20. Both vessels lost all of their masts. The French frigate only saved her bowsprit. She used her oars to board the *Québec* after throwing a shower of hand grenades on the deck. The remaining part of the exhausted crew were on the point of jumping on board when they saw a flame fore and aft. They immediately disengaged by cutting away the remains of the bowsprit. They saved 43 British sailors and two officers and rowed a distance when the *Québec* blew up. The *Surveillante* had 33 men killed and 85 wounded. Captain de Coedic received three shots, two in the head, which were not serious, and one in the body. His second-in-command was killed, and the sixth officer on board was the only one capable of bringing her into the port of Brest. All the other officers were either killed or wounded.[275]

Captain Falaise's privateer *Surprize* captured the *Saint Joseph* bound from Martinique to Marseilles and the *Comte de Noyon* bound from Martinique to Bordeaux about October 22. The privateer *Revenge* belonging to Penryn, England, fell in with a French privateer on the English coast on the same day. A smart and bloody engagement ensued which lasted 1½ hours, when a 9-pound ball from the *Revenge* entered the French privateer near the water line. She immediately filled with water and sank 10 minutes later with all her crew. Several men were wounded on board the *Revenge* but none were killed and her rigging was badly shattered.[276]

The *Hermione* sighted a large English privateer at dawn on October 27. She abandoned her two prizes and attempted to take the privateer by the stern. A chase of 36 hours ensued to capture the vessel of 36 guns, 20 of them 9-pounders. Captain de Latouche brought some cannons forward, but the change in weight decreased his speed. Two British frigates and a cutter came to the privateer's assistance. Captain de Latouche fired three broadsides which dismasted the cutter's mainmast and hulled her several times, but he thought it wiser to break off the engagement rather than to do battle alone against four vessels.[277]

The 12-gun Dunkirk privateer *Duc de Brissac* captured 15 prizes richly laden with hemp, linens, iron, and tallow before November 6, 1779 and sent them to Kristiansand, Norway. They included a British brig and the ship *Norfolk* taken off the Dutch coast before November 1, 1779.[278]

A French privateer captured Captain Richard Wood's *Beaver* on his passage from Poole to Québec before November 3. The crew, who were New Englanders, took the command of the ship from him. Captain Wood seized the Master of Arms while asleep and called one man, an Englishman, to his assistance. He reassumed the command of the ship and brought her safely to Québec.[279]

Before November 4, the 20-gun Weymouth privateer *Queen Charlotte* captured three French ordnance ships between Lorient and Brest. The prizes were M. Chateau's the *Amerique*, M. Monquois's the *Lovorette*, and M. Amenual's the *Favorite*. In addition, the 14-gun, 100-man privateer *Duc de Choiseul* from Dunkirk captured the six-gun, 24-man cutter *Fortune*, of Weymouth, after an action of nearly an hour and brought her to St.-Malo.[280]

A French vessel captured a Danish vessel commanded by an Englishman named Stevenson near the island of Ceylon (Sri Lanka) before November 9. Mr. Stevenson was brought to Mauritius. From there, he was sent home to France in a French East Indiaman. A Guernsey privateer captured the vessel in which he was a passenger along with another that sailed with her off Cape Finisterre. The prizes were sent to Ireland where Stevenson was set at liberty.[281]

The 36-gun French frigate *Iphigenie* fell in with Captain Braithwaite's *Centurion* before November 10. The *Iphigenie* mistook the *Centurion* for a storeship and fired at her. When the *Centurion* showed her guns, the *Iphigenie* surrendered immediately.[282]

The Guernsey cutter *Surprize* captured Captain De Spo's *Comte Denson* about November 12 and sent her to Portsmouth. She was bound from Cape François to Bordeaux with sugar, coffee, cotton, etc. valued at £10,000.[283] About November 16, the Jersey privateer *Liberty* captured a vessel from Saint-Domingue and the privateer *Eagle* captured a French West Indiaman. The former was brought to Jersey and the latter sent to Liverpool. The HMS *Jupiter* captured a French cutter and sent her to Portsmouth.[284]

The HMS *Ruby* captured the 36-gun French frigate *Providence* on Thursday, November 18 and brought her to Woolwich. Two days later, the privateer *Atlantic* captured the French ship *Royal Lewis* from Martinique with sugar, coffee, and other provisions. She was brought to Poole.[285]

A privateer from Marseilles met four British ships under convoy of a frigate before November 27. They fought for some time. The privateer was about to retire when the French frigate *Flora* came up and assisted in capturing the four ships which were valued at £5,000,000.[286]

Two large French ships, one of 74 guns, the other of 50, cruised off the coast of the Shetland Islands in December. They were probably cruising for the eight East India ships which had arrived at Limerick. They went to Ireland on account of the bad health of the crews.[287]

The French frigate *Aigrette* captured the Southampton privateer cutter *Duke of Cumberland* on Tuesday, December 7 and brought her to Brest. The following day, Captain Perouse captured the British privateer *Tiger*. The *Tiger* was originally a French privateer commanded by Captain Jacques Baby (dit Duperon) and captured by the HMS *Ceres* off the coast of South America in October 1778. Both ships joined the French fleet departing Savannah.[288]

The letter of marque *Polly* captured the French privateer *Landore* on Thursday, December 9. She was from Dunkirk and sent to Lisbon. The HMS *Portland* captured the French ship *Triumphante* from Saint-Domingue with indigo and coffee. She arrived at Spithead on Friday, December 10.[289]

The Crown privateers *Rambler* and *Lion* captured a large French snow and a brig with provisions for Hispaniola (Haiti) as well as a sloop from St. Eustatius and brought them to New Providence before December 11.[290]

The *New Charlotte* of Weymouth was chasing a French privateer about 4 PM on Sunday, December 12 when she ran on the rocks between Guernsey and Jersey. She was soon beaten to pieces and only the captain and three crewmen were saved out of the 35 on board. The following day, a French letter of marque captured a ship mounting 18 6-pounders after a smart conflict and sent her into the Delaware River. She was owned by Jack Butler and commanded by one Woodberry of Salem, Massachusetts.[291]

The Dublin privateer *Fame* captured a French homeward-bound Turkey ship and brought her to Messina, Sicily, before December 15. She was estimated to be worth between £30,000 and £40,000.[292]

Captain Gosselin's Guernsey privateer captured two French East India ships laden with tea, silks, china, coffee, indigo, chintz, muslin, seven chests of gold dust, and $600,000 valued at £250,000. With the assistance of the London privateer *Hannah*, Captain Gosselin brought his prizes to Limerick before December 23. The value of these prizes and 12 English East Indiamen, which a strong squadron had been sent to convoy to England, amounted to more than £4,500,000.

Also, the HMS *Grasshopper* captured a French transport bound from France to the West Indies with 300 officers and soldiers and took her to Waterford.[293]

The French privateers *Black Prince* and the *Black Princess* captured an unidentified brig off Cape Cornwall on December 29 and brought her to Milford, where she was ransomed for 300 guineas. Two masters who were taken prisoner reported that the privateers had taken 16 vessels, 10 of which they sent to France.[294]

1780

A French frigate captured the 250-ton British letter of marque *Foxhunter* in the Bay of Biscay at latitude 46 longitude 11 and sent her to Groyne, Ireland. The precise date is unknown. She mounted 18 9-pounders and was bound from London to New York with a cargo worth £15,000. The *Foxhunter* fought bravely for some time but her captain thought proper to surrender when his mainmast was shot away.[295]

Captain Cottin's French privateer *Marquis de Seignelay*, from Le Havre, carrying 20 8-pounders and 160 men, captured the HMS *London*. She sailed again on January 3, 1780 and got on the English coast. She met a three-masted ship between 8 and 9 AM and chased her until noon when she came within cannon shot. The English ship then hoisted her colors and fired a gun which the *Marquis de Seignelay* answered. When the two ships got within pistol range, the English fired a broadside.

Captain Cottin, finding the enemy had 20 12-pounders and 12 4-pound bronze howitzers, considered himself outgunned and surrendered. The English ship proved to be Captain Lionel Hill's privateer going from London to Plymouth to complete her complement of men, as she only had 58. She lost 10 men killed and 15 dangerously wounded, including the captain. The *Marquis de Seignelay* had two men killed and several wounded. She lost her bowsprit with its sails and rigging.

Unable to keep the sea, she was obliged to steer for France. On her way, she captured the 12-ton British merchant ship *Anne* going from London to Chester with eight men and laden with sundry goods. She was brought to Cherbourg with 56 prisoners. The *Marquis de Seignelay* then sailed for Le Havre with her prize, arriving on January 11.[296]

Before January 5, 1780, the letter of marque *Active* captured Captain Le Pignerol's *Le Don le Roy*, a 16-gun privateer, within a league of Scilly, England. The *Dreadnought* captured Captain Leviviers's *Le Joinville* and brought her to Guernsey, Channel Isles. She was bound from Marseilles to Le Havre with bale goods.[297]

Admirals Rodney, Digby, and Ross sailed from Portsmouth for Gibraltar and the West Indies on December 26, 1779. Their seven warships convoyed 15 merchant vessels. The warships consisted of a 64-gun ship, two three-gun frigates, two 28-gun frigates, one 16-gun frigate and a 10-gun frigate. The merchant and supply ships separated from Admiral Rodney's force on January 7, 1780 and fell in with a fleet of 20 unarmed vessels off Cape Finisterre, Spain, the following day. Admiral Rodney captured seven French warships and 13 merchant vessels carrying naval matériel and provisions valued at more than $5,000,000 for the Spanish fleet at Cadiz, Spain. Rodney sent the merchantmen to Gibraltar immediately to provide some supplies to the beleaguered garrison there.[298]

The British captured the French ship *Isabella* on her passage from the French sugar islands. Captain McNeal retook her and brought her to France before January 20.[299]

A British cutter captured a French privateer and two of her prizes and brought them to Carrickfergus, Ireland before January 29, 1780.[300]

The French fleet captured Captain Potter's *Hope* which sailed in February 1780 bound from Liverpool to Africa. She was sent to Martinique.[301]

The 74-gun HMS *Intrepid* fell in with and captured a French ship which was part of a fleet of about 100 vessels bound to the West Indies.[302]

Captain John Outtan's brig *Tiger* captured a French galiot bound from Marseilles to Boston with wines, small arms, bales of dry goods, and jewelry and brought her to New Providence on February 15. The French captain had several of his men killed and fought the brig for an hour to an hour and a half.[303]

Admiral Digby's fleet fell in with a French convoy of two 64-gun ships, two large store ships, a frigate, and about 13 vessels bound to Mauritius about 1 PM on Wednesday, February 23 and chased them. The HMS *Resolution* caught up with Captain Chilot's 64-gun, 700-man *Prothée* about 1 AM and took her without losing a man. The entire convoy was loaded with military supplies and troops. The *Prothée* and the *Ajax*, both of 64 guns, had about £120,000 in specie on board. The *Marlborough* and the *Apollo* each took a snow loaded with military supplies.[304]

Before February 25, a French cruiser captured the *Ann* and the *John*, both from Newfoundland, and ransomed them. A French frigate retook the South Carolina ship *Lucy* from Barbados with 280 puncheons of rum. She had been captured by the New York privateer sloop *Mars* before February 12, 1779.[305] The British fought a French privateer in a four-hour engagement off the coast of Portugal. The French privateer blew up and everybody on board perished except one.[306]

On February 25, Admiral Rodney's fleet captured the 32-gun French frigate *Bellisle* near Gibraltar. She was charged with dispatches for Cadiz and was brought to London. A French frigate captured Captain Gilbert's letter of marque *Betsey*, from Antigua, and a Whig prize she was bringing to England. Another French frigate captured the privateer *Prosperous* from London and brought her to Nantes. Captain Gigon's Dunkirk privateer *American Union* captured two English prizes well-laden and bound to London.[307]

During the month of March 1780, the French privateers *Black Prince* and *Black Princess* captured eight British prizes, the *Dunkerquoise* three, the *Prince de Soubise* one, and the *Revanche* one in ballast.[308]

Captain Yeoman's privateer *Dart* captured Captain Pience's ship *Age d'Or* in latitude 35.6 longitude 10.30 W. on Saturday, March 4 and brought her to Dartmouth, England, on Monday, March 20. She was bound from Martinique to Marseilles along with four other ships without convoy, laden with sugar and coffee valued at £15,000. The engagement lasted 1½ hours. The *Dart* had two men killed and three wounded. The *Age d'Or* had three men killed and six wounded.[309]

The British man-of-war *Alexander* and the *Courageux* captured the 40-gun French privateer *Monsieur* about March 5. Upon examining her cargo, several casks were discovered in the hold, each containing several hundred pounds of dollars.[310]

Admiral Digby, on his passage home from Gibraltar, captured a French 64-gun ship with four East India ships and arrived with them off the Lizard on March 7.[311] Admiral Digby also captured Captain La Barleduc's 20-gun French privateer *Saint Laurent* and sent her to Plymouth, England, about March 9.[312]

Commander John Gibson's privateer *New Tartar* captured the French sloop the *Reine des Anges* and six other vessels on the coast of France and sent them to Falmouth on Monday, March 20. Four of the vessels were sunk, being of little value. One of them was stranded but her cargo of sailcloth and other goods was saved.[313]

The British privateer *Swift* captured Captain La Armanian's 300-ton French ship *La Morcalquier* Thursday afternoon, March 23. She was bound from Martinique to Bordeaux with sugar, indigo, cotton, and other goods.[314]

Before March 27, 1780, the New York privateer *Queen* captured a large French ship, while the privateers *Union* and *Sir George Collier* captured two French prizes. All the prizes were sent to Bermuda. One of them was from Martinique with sugar and coffee. Another was bound from France to Martinique.[315]

The privateer *Neptune* captured Captain Le Courtray's *La Franche Compté* and brought her into King Road before April 1, 1780. She was bound from Guadeloupe to Bordeaux with sugars, coffee, and cotton.[316]

A Guernsey privateer captured a French vessel after a 10-hour chase and brought her into Mount's Bay on Saturday, April 1. She was a packet bound to the West Indies with dispatches for M. de la Motte Picquet. Just as the privateer was about to board her, the mail was thrown overboard, but, not having sufficient weight, one of the sailors on board the privateer retrieved it.[317]

Master Luke Ryan's Dunkirk privateer cutter *Fearnot* captured two British ships and a vessel of 700 tons on Sunday, April 2. One of these vessels was most likely Captain Robert's *Noble Anne*, bound from Newcastle to Greenland. The *Fearnot*, with 16 4-pounders, 12 6-pounders, and 12 swivels, had been out 10 days and the *Noble Anne* was her first prize. Her crew of 96 men consisted of 45 Irish and Americans. The others were French, Spaniards, Italians, and Portuguese. The ships and two other prizes were ransomed for more than 33,000 guineas. The *Noble Anne* was sent to North Bergen.

Three days later, on Saturday, April 8, the *Fearnot* captured Captain Sinclair's *Friends* 22 leagues off Torr, Ireland. The *Friends* was bound from Clyde, Scotland, to Québec and surrendered after an engagement of 25 minutes. Ryan took out the master and crew, except two passengers, the mate, and cabin boy. He put 21 Frenchmen on board to bring her to France. The *Friends* was hulled by two shots at the water edge and parted from the *Fearnot* and *Jean* at 1 AM on Sunday, in a heavy gale and dark weather, with 6 feet of water in her hold.

The *Fearnot* also took Captain Brown's *Jean*, of Maryport, off Barrhead, on Tuesday, April 11, 1780. She was bound from Liverpool with salt. Ryan offered to ransom the *Jean* but at a higher rate than Captain Brown would give, so he put her up for sale. Captain Sinclair purchased her and brought her to Glasgow on April 15. The 51 prisoners who were put on board the *Jean* were released.[318]

M. du Manuir de Pelly's St.-Malo privateer *Duc de Mortimer* captured Master John O'Brian's brig *King George*, of Waterford, on Wednesday, April 5. The master and crew of the brig were brought to St.-Malo.[319]

The privateer *Tamer* captured the *Henriade*, a large French ship bound to the Isle of France with anchors, cables, provisions, and 137 soldiers, on Tuesday, April 18. The *Henriade* was taken to Lisbon. The same day, the Folkestone privateer *Unicorn* captured the *Louisa* and sent her to Falmouth. She was bound from Bayonne, France to Brest.[320]

The *Americaine*, a corsair from Grandville, captured the 100-ton English brigantine *Betsey* on Thursday, April 20. The *Betsey* was bound from London to Halifax with provisions and taken to Morlaix.[321]

Captain Pigot's 32-gun HMS *Jason* was convoying nine transports bound to the River Elbe for troops. She fell in with three French frigate-built privateers, each mounting from 18 to 30 guns, on Thursday, April 20. The *Lowestoffe* was 10 or 12 leagues away west-southwest at 8 AM. Captain Pigot made a signal for the transports to steer different courses, then to bear down on the French ships. He received their fire and returned it. Two of the French privateers veered off, intending to take the transports. Captain Pigot noticed this and headed after them.

Four of the transports arrived at Yarmouth Road Friday morning, April 28. The *Jason* arrived that evening with another. The following morning, Captain Pigot saw the French ships with one of the transports. He headed after them and attacked, but, having his fore-topmast shot away, he could not catch up with them and bore away for the roads. The other three transports were thought to be headed to the River Elbe. Captain Pigot had one man killed and three wounded.[322]

The HM frigates *Emerald* and *Champion* captured two Dutch ships on the coast of France on April 20. They contained military stores for the use of the French Navy, about 200 barrels of gunpowder, and a great quantity of copper for sheathing.[323]

The four-gun, 39-man French privateer *Printemps* was anchored at Hellevoetsluis, Netherlands, for several days, watching the motions of some colliers which sailed from there. She followed them, intending to board and capture them. Some armed Scottish colliers got below the limits of the port, tacked and engaged the *Printemps* under the lighthouse on Friday, April 21. They forced her to run ashore on Goree Island, Senegal, where most of the crew escaped. On boarding the privateer, the Scots found several men dead and about four or five others who did not have enough time to run away. They were brought to Sunderland along with the vessel.[324]

The *Maria*, from Tinmouth, arrived at Waterford, was captured by the French privateer *Dunkerquoise*, of Land's End, and ransomed for 250 guineas before April 23. Captain Marshall's HM Frigate *Emerald* captured the *Dunkerquoise*, of 22 9-pounders and 170 men, about April 24. She was fitted out by the ladies of Dunkirk about June 1779 and brought to St. Helen's. She was purchased by the British Postmaster General for a West India packet.[325]

The British privateer cutter *Folkestone* captured a French privateer snow of 10 guns and 86 men early Monday morning, April 24. The snow had been out of Dunkirk only a few hours and was on her first cruise. She was chasing a coasting vessel when the *Folkestone* fell in with her and took her to Dover.[326]

The British privateer *Greyhound* captured M. la Garonde's French privateer *Mothe*, of 6- and 9-pounders, in the Bay of Biscay after an engagement of half an hour before April 29. The French privateer had 10 men killed and eight wounded and was taken to Lisbon. The *Greyhound* had only four men wounded.[327]

The privateer *Wasp* captured Captain Gostenois's 350-ton ship *Nemours* and brought her to Jersey before April 29. She was bound from Saint-Domingue to Bordeaux with sugar, indigo, and cotton.[328]

Captain Nicholas Jesperson's London privateer cutter *Hector* engaged two 60-gun French men-of-war at 7 PM on Saturday, April 29. The *Hector* had two men killed and nine badly wounded in the very severe action. She also had great damage to her mast and rigging. She bore away from the French vessel which, despite her superior force, appeared badly shattered by the repeated broadsides.[329]

A French privateer of 10 9-pounders ransomed a small collier from Sunderland for 200 guineas. The collier arrived at Yarmouth Saturday evening, April 29. Her captain reported he captured 30 vessels and had chased several into Scarborough and Whitby.[330]

The French fleet that arrived at Martinique captured an 18-gun British packet on their passage before May 1, 1780. She was bound to the East Indies with dispatches from Lord George Germain but parted with four British ships-of-the-line and two East Indiamen the day before she was captured. Captain Colling's 24-gun, 210-man French privateer *Jean Bart* also captured two British ships. They were headed to the Greenland fishery and were taken into the Texel, an island in northern Holland.[331]

The French privateer *Duc de Coigny* captured 13 British prizes and brought them to Morlaix before May 4. Other French cruisers took 22 British vessels in the English Channel and brought them to Morlaix since March 24.[332]

A 44-gun French frigate captured Captain Werry's *King George* on Tuesday, May 9. A 64-gun Spanish ship arrived and received Captain Werry and some of his officers and crew as prisoners and took them to La Coruña.[333]

Captain William Burnaby's HMS *Milford* captured the 400-ton Granville privateer ship *Duc de Coigny*, carrying 28 guns, six swivels, and 191 men, about 30 leagues off Ushant on Wednesday, May 10 and sent her to Plymouth, where she arrived on Sunday morning, May 14. The *Milford* had four men killed and six wounded in the hour-long engagement. The privateer had 18 killed, including her captain, and 14 wounded, including her first lieutenant. The *Duc de Coigny* had been cruising between Scilly, England, and the coast of Ireland and had captured one brig.[334]

The HM Frigate *Milford* captured a French privateer after a smart engagement before Wednesday, May 17. The captain of the privateer and a great number of his crew were killed. The *Milford* also had many men killed.[335]

Captain de Latouche's French frigate *Hermione* captured a brig bound from Ireland to New York with 780 firkins of butter, a quantity of soap and candles, and sent her to a neighboring port. The frigate arrived at Newport, Rhode Island, on Thursday May 25. A few days earlier, she had a sharp conflict of an hour with a 44-gun British ship which sheered off. The *Hermione* had 14 men killed and a few wounded. She took and brought in with her the British ship's tender.

The *Hermione* had captured six British privateers and five merchantmen since the beginning of the war. Two of the privateers were taken together, each of more than 20 guns. One of them mounted 22 guns and was fitted out by some ladies in England and named the *Ladies Resolution*.[336]

A French rowboat captured the *Vigilant* off Durlestone Bay, England, in June 1780. She was bound from Milford, England, and arrived at Poole, England, where she was ransomed for £450.[337]

Eight British warships closely pursued a French fleet of 40 transports which sailed from the Isle of Aix for America on June 9, forcing them into the port of La Coruña. The French man-of-war *Guerrier*, which convoyed them, prevented any of the transports from being captured, but two of them were driven upon the coast and damaged.[338]

The Chevalier de Latouche's French frigate *Hermione* sighted a brig in the north at 5 AM on June 2. He gave chase and captured her at 4 PM. She was John Nairn's 100-ton *Thomas of Irvine* bound from Cork to the West Indies with 1,760 firkins of butter, 150 boxes of candles, and 150 boxes of soap. She left Cork on April 18 with a fleet of 100 vessels escorted by two frigates. Captain de Latouche replaced her crew of eight with a prize crew of four and sent her to Dartmouth, Massachusetts, where she arrived on Monday, June 5.[339]

The French privateer *Black Princess* captured Captain Ramsey's *William and John* 4 leagues west of Tuscar (Tuskar Rock, Ireland?) on Sunday, June 4. She was from Whitehaven and arrived at Waterford on Wednesday, June 7 where she was ransomed for 500 guineas. The privateer travelled in company with a lugger of four carriage guns and 16 swivels.[340]

The British privateer *Wasp* arrived at Livorno on Monday, June 5, with a ship from Bastia, Corsica, under French colors. The captured vessel had seven French officers, including a colonel, on board. She also had 776 French silver crowns which the captain of the privateer generously restored to the commander of the ship. He also returned to the officers everything belonging to them.[341]

Captain de Latouche's French frigate *Hermione* sighted a vessel to the northeast along the coast of Long Island at 4 AM on Tuesday, June 6. The *Hermione* caught up with her at 8 AM and captured her. She was Captain Georges Eavans's *Recovery*, which set sail from Bermuda on May 25 for New York with 500 bushels of salt. She had a crew of five men and two Negroes, all of whom were taken aboard the *Hermione*. They were replaced with the prize crew of two men under the command of Sieur Noel, ship's captain, with orders to sail immediately for Providence, Rhode Island.[342]

The *Hermione* fell in with a 40-gun British ship, an armed snow, a brig, and a schooner the following day. The HMS *Iris* chased a privateer brig to the south of Long Island at 4:30 AM but broke off at 6 AM to chase a privateer sloop and a schooner to the northward. Captain Hawker saw a large vessel 5 leagues to the south-southeast of Montauk Point, off the east end of Long Island, on the lee bow, heading westward at 7:30, and chased her. The vessel tacked at 8 AM, hoisted French colors, and headed toward the *Iris*. She was the 36-gun frigate *Hermione*. The two vessels crossed each other at 8:40 and exchanged broadsides. The action continued at close range for an hour and 20 minutes before the *Iris* made all the sail she could and departed. The *Hermione*'s braces were so badly damaged that she could not catch up with the *Iris*.

She chased the schooner into 4-fathom water on the back of Long Island, all the time in sight of the *Iris*. She gave up the pursuit in fear of running ashore. Captain de Latouche and his second-in-command were both slightly wounded in the left arm. Ten privates were killed and 37 wounded, three of them mortally. The British were thought to have suffered considerably more, as the *Hermione*'s fire was directed mainly at the hull while the British fired more at the rigging, The *Hermione* retired about 10 AM. The crippled *Iris* pursued in vain despite having all her running rigging shot away.

Captain Hawker saw another large vessel ahead at 10:40 AM and thought she was the *Hermione*'s consort. When she fired a signal gun, he thought it prudent to head south, at which time the *Iris*'s fore-topsail yard broke. The *Iris* had seven men killed and nine wounded, one mortally.[343]

Two French frigates and a privateer cruised off Aberdeen before June 10. The crews landed at several places, plundered the inhabitants, and carried off some live cattle. The residents armed two vessels which, with the assistance of two privateers anchored there, retook the vessels containing the cattle and the French privateer and brought them to Aberdeen. The privateers and armed vessels then went in search of the French frigates.[344]

The *Duc de Biron*, a new privateer cutter, captured two vessels laden with coal and brought them to Calais on June 12. She also brought in three ransomers whose hulls and cargoes were valued at £1,000, and the ransomers' bills amounted to £700.[345]

The 40-gun French frigate *Nymphe*, coming from Cape François, captured Captain Webber's *Diana*, bound from London to Newfoundland, before June 13. The French burned the *Diana* and brought the captain and his crew to Brest.[346]

Captain Cameron's New York cutter *Retaliation* fell in with a fleet of 25 vessels in the Chesapeake Bay on Thursday, June 15. They were bound from Virginia to France under convoy of a 54-gun French ship. He followed them for four days but to no purpose. The weather was very moderate and they kept close to their convoy.[347]

Admiral de Ternay learned, on June 14, of the surrender of Charleston, eliminating that port as an option for the arrival of the *expédition particulière*. A few days later, the French frigate *Surveillante* captured the brigantine *Botetourt* sailing from Charleston to the West Indies with some artillery pieces and five British soldiers who were trying to rejoin their regiments.[348]

Before June 16, two English privateers captured two French prizes in the Bay of Biscay. One was bound from Lorient to North America; the other from Bordeaux to Brest. *La Fortune* was bound from Cape François to Bordeaux with sugar, coffee, and indigo.[349]

A French privateer of 30 guns captured the English brigantine *Juliana* off the coast of Ireland and sent her to Brest. She was bound from London to Galway. On her way there, in latitude 49.56 W, commander Patrick Murray's privateer ship-of-war retook her and brought her to Folkestone on Saturday, June 17.[350]

A French frigate sighted a ship at 9 AM on June 18 and chased her with the frigate *Surveillante*. They captured it an hour later. It was a British cutter with 40 men and three officers bound from Charleston to Antibes. The cutter mistook the French for the British convoy it was awaiting. The command of the cutter was given to a subordinate officer of *Surveillante*.[351]

The French frigate *Amazon* sighted a ship at 10:30 AM on Wednesday, June 21. The frigate *Surveillante* and a cutter chased her and captured her. She was loaded with masts and had recently been badly treated by a Bermudian privateer.[352]

A 64-gun French man-of-war captured Captain Murdock's *Catherine* and Captain McDonald's *Venus* and two brigs off Cape Clear on Friday, June 23. The 20-gun *Catherine* was bound from Glasgow to Jamaica with a crew of 48. The 12-gun *Venus* was bound from Glasgow to Georgia with a crew of 25. The New York bound *Hurrier* was traveling with these brigs but escaped and arrived at Cork on the 27th.[353]

The Folkestone privateer *Tartar* captured a vessel bound from Bordeaux to Dunkirk with claret and sent her to Folkestone on June 25.[354]

Two Guernsey privateers fell in with a French convoy going from Le Havre to Brest, convoyed by a small French frigate. The privateers captured three of the merchantmen in July 1780 and put some hands on board. The rest of the fleet ran to shore during a wind storm to seek shelter under a small fort.[355]

Commodore Johnson or Johnstone sent Captain Atkins's *Aeolus* on a cruise in which he captured the 28-gun French letter of marque *Eulalia* after a short engagement and brought her to Lisbon on Sunday, July 2. A privateer had engaged her the day before but was beaten off.[356]

Captain Marden's or Martin's Dartmouth, England, privateer *Admiral Edwards* or *Admiral* captured a French schooner bound from Bordeaux to America with salt, wine, and bale goods before July 4. Captain Cunningham was on board the privateer.[357]

French frigates chased a ship at 11 AM on July 4. The *Duc de Bourgogne* also joined the chase at 1:30 PM and captured the ship at 2 PM after firing her cannons to stop her. She was a small English vessel, loaded with people and foreign wine, bound from New York to Charleston. Two enemy frigates approached very close to the French vessels during the night and fired some cannons at the *Duc de Bourgogne*, which chased them away toward morning.[358]

The British frigates *Prudent* and *Unicorn* fell in with Mr. de Cherval's 1,100-ton French ship *Capricieuse* on Wednesday, July 5. She was a new ship pierced for 44 guns but only mounted 32 and had a crew of 308 men. She was only eight days out of Lorient and was to return on July 12 to have her hull coppered. The two frigates chased the *Capricieuse* and gained on her fast, but it was 11:30 PM before Captain William Waldegrave's *Prudent* came within pistol range. She ran alongside the *Capricieuse* and engaged her alone until 5 AM, at which time her rigging was cut to pieces and she was obliged to drop a little to the leeward in order to repair the damage. The *Unicorn* then came up and gave the French frigate a broadside. She struck her colors after she had 5 feet of water in her hold. Her first captain, Mr. de Ransanne, and second captain, Mr. de Fontaine, and 50 men were killed and 30 wounded. The *Capricieuse* was badly damaged. The *Unicorn* had three men killed and seven wounded; the *Prudent* had 17 men killed and 31 wounded, three of them mortally. The British burned the prize, which was a wreck, after taking out the prisoners. The *Prudent* was also so badly disabled that she might have been considered a wreck.[359]

Commodore Johnson's 50-gun *Romney* captured the 42-gun, 470-man French frigate *Artois* and sent her to Lisbon before July 6. When the *Artois* left the *Romney*, the *Romney* was firing at a Spanish frigate she was chasing. The *Artois*, a gift to the French king from a subscription of ladies, had nine men killed and 18 wounded in the engagement. The *Romney* had only three wounded.[360]

Seven British ships fell in with two privateers, one of 22 guns under French colors, the other of 18 guns under Continental colors, on Thursday, July 6. They engaged the privateers and beat them off. The *Jenny* and the *Blacket* suffered a good deal of damage to their masts and rigging and had three men wounded.[361]

Two French privateers—one a ship, the other a cutter—chased a brig from Waterford off Comfort Point, England, on Sunday, July 9. The master of the brig immediately headed toward shore and would have run his vessel aground as the French privateers followed him. However, as night approached and the breeze blew strongly, they chose not to come too close to the land. The privateers had two vessels in company, thought to be prizes.[362]

Captain Robinson's ship had an engagement with the privateer *Black Princess* off Belfast for two or three hours before July 10 and beat her off.[363]

Nine British vessels were in the harbor at Lisbon on Saturday, July 15. They were with their 12 prizes, consisting of French, Spanish, and Congressional vessels. The British men-of-war had seven prizes in the Tagus, two of them king's frigates, one Spanish and one French.[364]

Several British frigates were seen a little to the east and north of Block Island almost every day during the week of July 9. About 20 vessels were sighted on Friday, July 21. They were thought to be Admiral Graves's fleet with eight or nine ships-of-the-line, some frigates, and some New York privateers attempting to intercept the second division of the French fleet. Three of the frigates tried to cut off a small sloop coming around Point Judith from Connecticut.[365]

The HMS *Nonsuch* drove a French frigate ashore and burned her near Belle-Île before July 22. She then captured *Le François* and five other French vessels, three of which escaped. *Le François* was laden with canvas, sails, cordage, and other naval supplies taken out of a French frigate which the *Nonsuch* drove ashore and burned.[366]

Captain John McBride's 64-gun HMS *Bienfaisant* returned, on Sunday, July 23, from convoying the fleet to the west. She brought in with her the 18-gun *Margarita* or *Jeune Margaretta*, bound from Saint-Domingue to Bordeaux. She was first taken by Admiral Geary's fleet, then retaken by the French 64-gun ship *Duc d'Artois* and taken a third time by Captain McBride.[367]

Admiral Geary's fleet sailed from New London on June 29, 1780 and arrived at Spithead on August 18. En route, they captured the 350-ton letter of marque ship *Le Comte de Hallwel*, carrying 24 guns and 80 men. She was bound from Cape François to Bordeaux with sugar, coffee, and indigo. They also took an English brig and her prize bound from Newfoundland to Lisbon and captured the privateer lugger *La Sauterelle*, carrying 18 guns and 26 men, off Paterall Point (near Ushant) on Thursday, August 17.[368]

M. de Beaumarchais's ship *Le Fier Rodrigue* captured several prizes before August 1. She arrived at the Isle of Rhe (Île de Ré), from New England with 11 Whig ships and four French ships under convoy. Their cargoes consisted of 4,600 hogsheads of tobacco. *Le Fier Rodrigue* also brought into port two Jamaica prizes. The rest of the convoy of 17 vessels arrived at Bordeaux and La Rochelle.[369]

Captain Pole's HM Frigate *Hussar* sailed from Spithead on July 23 with a convoy. She fell in with three French lugger privateers and took two of them before August

2—*Le Jeune Lion* and *Le Renard*. Each mounted 12 carriage guns and eight swivels and carried 44 men. They had been out of Dunkirk only three days.[370]

Admiral Cordova's fleet of 22 Spanish and 14 French ships-of-the-line and some frigates were cruising 70 leagues northwest of Cape St. Vincent (Cabo de São Vicente, Portugal) at 3 AM on Wednesday, August 9, when they fell in with a fleet of between 50 and 70 British merchantmen and transports under convoy of the HMS *Ramillies* and two frigates. They were headed to Madeira and Jamaica with a large quantity of military stores, provisions, and dry goods and 1,000 Highland troops. Most of the British fleet surrendered.[371]

The *Laly*, a little French privateer, sailed from Bordeaux to seek her fortune before August 10. She fell in with two 24-gun English privateers off the Cordouan lighthouse (Phare de Cordouan). As the 16-gun *Laly* was too closely pressed to escape, she tried to defend herself by running between the two English vessels. They were unable to make her surrender before nightfall, and the *Laly* could not escape during the night as the wind was calm. The battle resumed at daybreak. The two English privateers were about to leave when a British frigate came up. Overwhelmed by the fire of the frigate, the *Laly*'s master attempted to board the frigate when a large splinter of wood took him by the middle and drove him 20 paces from where he stood to command her. The crew, no longer able to resist, struck the colors. At that moment, the captain, recovering from the fall, threatened to shoot the first man who refused to hoist the colors again. But it was too late. It was impossible to reason with the crew and he gave up, swearing that it was treason.[372]

Captain William Peere Williams's 36-gun, 259-man HMS *Flora* saw a square rigged vessel and a cutter about 4 miles away near Ushant at 4:30 PM on Thursday, August 10. The *Flora* sailed toward them and got abreast of the ship, Chevalier du Remain's *Nymphe*, at 5:10 PM. When the *Flora* hoisted her colors, the ship fired at her. The *Flora* returned fire and continued the action for about an hour. When her wheel was shot away, her shrouds, back stays and running rigging cut to pieces, she dropped on board the ship and continued the engagement for another 15 minutes. The ship's crew deserted their great guns and attempted to board the *Flora* but were repulsed with loss. The crew boarded the ship, sword in hand. The *Nymphe* struck her colors, and the *Flora*'s crew soon took possession of her. Chevalier du Remain died that evening of the wounds he received in the action. The *Flora* had one midshipman, six seamen, and two marines killed and one master, 13 seamen, and four marines wounded, one seaman and two marines mortally. The *Nymphe* had her first and second captains and first lieutenant killed and 57 officers, seamen, and marines wounded.

The *Nymphe* was four years old, copper-bottomed and mounted 32 guns, though pierced for 40, and had a crew of 291 men. She had been out of Brest only four days and was reconnoitering off that port.[373]

Four French privateers from Dunkirk attacked a fleet of 52 English merchantmen escorted by a frigate in the North Sea before August 11. The privateers captured several of the merchantmen and brought them to ports in Denmark.[374]

The Cork fleet of 99 vessels set sail on Saturday, August 12, in company with the HMS *Bienfaisant, Charon, Licorne*, and *Hussar*. Captain John McBride's HMS *Bienfaisant* drove down as far as the Old Head of Kinsale when he observed a large vessel in the southeast chasing some vessels of the Cork fleet at daylight the following day. The *Bienfaisant* and the HMS *Charon* pursued the vessel and caught up with her at 7:30 AM. Two other British frigates were out of sight, off Cork. The action on both sides began with musketry. The French vessel, which proved to be the 64-gun ship *Duc d'Artois*, commanded by the Chevalier Clonard, hoisted British colors and kept firing. Captain McBride did the same until he came within pistol range.

Neither the French ship's bow guns nor the British ship's quarter guns could be brought to bear, so both sides continued the action with small arms. The *Duc d'Artois* hoisted her proper colors and attempted to board the *Bienfaisant*. It was a daring but unsuccessful attempt. After a smart action of an hour and 10 minutes, the *Duc d'Artois*, her rigging and sails cut to pieces, struck her colors. She had 21 men killed and 25 wounded from her crew of more than 644 men. Chevalier Clonard, a Lieutenant de Vaisseaux, was slightly wounded in the action. His brothers, one a colonel the other a colonel en second in the Irish Legion, were on board along with Lieutenant Perry of the *Monarch* and the crew of the prize *Margarita* or *Jeune Margaretta*. The *Bienfaisant* had three men killed and 22 wounded. The *Charon* had one man slightly wounded. The fleet continued on course in company with the HMS *Licorne*. The *Duc d'Artois* sold for £7,530 at Plymouth. She was bought for government service along with her prize the *Jeune Margaretta*.[375]

Captain Gilchrist's *Greyhound* captured a French transport snow, mounting 16 6- and 9-pounders and a crew of 48 men after a three-hour engagement and brought her to Philadelphia in mid-August. She was part of the French fleet with troops destined for Jamaica.[376]

Three of Admiral Geary's squadron saw a French ship-of-the-line departing Brest before August 16 and chased her. They came so close to her in a few hours that she threw all her guns and boats overboard to lighten her and escape. She was the new first rate *Magnanime*, mounting 110 bronze guns and 50-pounders on her lower deck. She sailed into the port of La Coruña.[377]

Two British privateers captured the 60-gun, 400-man French ship *Comte de St. Florentin* on her passage from Cape François to Rochefort. The *Comte de St. Florentin* lost her masts and had 90 men killed and wounded in the three-hour obstinate engagement.[378]

Captain Boteler of the British man-of-war *Ardent* gallantly defended his ship against the 74-gun *Soleil*, the 64-gun *Intrépide*, the 74-gun *La Magnanime*, and the frigates *Vainqueur* and *Invincible*, each of 36 guns, before August 28. Most of the French ships received some damage.[379]

Commodore Johnstone captured many prizes with the French frigate *Le Credule* and sent them to Lisbon before September 2, 1780.[380]

The Jersey privateer *Stag* captured three brigs before September 19 and sent them to Jersey. They were the 70-ton *St. Joseph*, Captain Hiloury's 100-ton *La Félicité*, and the *Darcheese*. They were all laden with pitch and tar. *La Félicité* was bound from Bordeaux to Lorient with flour and wine. The *Stag*, in company with the Liverpool privateer *Enterprise*, also captured the *Valiant*, laden with wine and flour, and a French dogger which was sent to Liverpool. The *Valiant* sank coming into Liverpool and all but one man drowned.[381]

Captain Montague's HMS *Pearl* fell in with the French frigate *Esperance*, of 28 12-pounders, off Bermuda on Saturday, September 30. The French frigate struck her colors after an action of two hours and arrived at New York on October 15.[382]

Before October 1780, a French and Spanish outward-bound fleet of 17 ships-of-the-line captured, off Madeira, 40 vessels bound to Jamaica, 15 bound up the Straits, and five headed to the East Indies.[383]

The French frigate *Aigrette* engaged three English privateers and captured an Imperial ship bound from Ostend with a cargo for a French port before October 1.[384]

Two letters of marque belonging to Liverpool sank the French privateer *Duc de Bourgogne* off Madeira on Sunday, October 1. She was from Bayonne with 18 12-pounders bound to the West Indies. Very few men were saved.[385]

The French frigate *Landremarque* (*Andromaque*) captured the British frigate *Unicorn* and brought her to Cape François about Monday, October 9.[386]

Before October 10, the Chevalier de Suzannet's frigate *Aimable* and the Viscount de Mortimar's *Diligente* captured three English privateers: the 22-gun, 82-man *Alert*; the 12-gun, 36-men *Tartar*, and the 12-gun, 43-man Jersey privateer *Eagle*. The prizes were brought to the Isle d'Aix. They also captured a ship from Hambrough laden with tobacco from Ostend. She was headed to Bordeaux and had been taken by the privateer *Tartar*.[387]

A French privateer arrived at the port of Kristiansand with nine British prizes captured in different obstinate engagements before October 10. The captain of the privateer lost both legs in one of the engagements.[388]

Two English privateers, each mounting more than 20 guns, captured two French letters of marque, one of 18 guns the other of 20, and brought them to Leghorn before October 10. They were captured up the Levant on their homeward-bound journey. The smallest ship had goods on board valued at £25,000. The cargo of the larger ship was near £30,000. They were bound to Marseilles and fought the privateers for more than an hour when they struck to their superior force. Each of the French ships had several men killed and wounded, but the British had only one man killed and four wounded in both ships.[389]

The French sloop *Cutter*, mounting 18 6-pounders, captured two brigs from Jamaica, British West Indies, about Thursday, October 12. One mounted 14 guns, the other 16.[390]

A British man-of-war captured four French ships in the Mediterranean Sea before October 14. They were bound from Marseilles to America without a convoy.[391]

Before October 16, the 64-gun HMS *Bienfaisant* captured a French 74-gun ship in the Irish Channel after a severe engagement. The British also captured the 16-gun Dunkirk privateer *Toise* and brought her to Milford as well as the *St. Atalanta* bound from Cape François to Bordeaux with sugar, coffee, and indigo and brought her to Penzance. In addition, the privateer *Priestly* captured the *Atmanara* bound from Saint-Domingue to Nantes and brought her to Jersey.[392]

A British fleet of 57 vessels, bound to different ports, fell in with 17 French and Spanish ships-of-the-line off Madeira before October 18. The French and Spanish captured the entire British fleet except for four vessels.[393]

The French privateer *St. Papeul* captured Captain McMurray's *Derwentwater* and brought her to Le Havre before October 20. She was bound from Oporto and Lisbon to Dundee with wine and fruit.[394]

The 18-gun Guernsey privateer *Mahon* captured a large French ship bound to La Rochelle and brought her to Mahon before October 20.[395]

The Liverpool privateer *Shark* captured a French privateer of 14 guns, 6- and 9-pounders, after an hour's engagement, and brought her to Weymouth on Friday morning, October 20. The French privateer was a new vessel belonging to Cherbourg and had not been out of port more than 48 hours.[396]

A French privateer captured two British ships laden with coals. A British packet boat then retook them and brought them to Hellevoetsluis on October 24.[397]

Admiral Arbuthnot's squadron of eight ships-of-the-line, a 40-gun ship, and two frigates captured Commander Silas Talbot's Providence privateer ship *General Washington* off Sandy Hook on Monday, October 16. Captain Talbot and about 20 of his crew were sent to New York; the remainder arrived at Newport in a flag of truce on Friday, October 20. The vessel was purchased by a number of Loyalists and sent out on a cruise. A few days later, she fell in with two frigates of Admiral de Ternay's squadron, was captured and sent to Rhode Island.[398]

Two frigates belonging to the British grand fleet captured two new French privateers, of 16 guns each, and sent them to Falmouth on Monday, October 30.[399]

The HM Frigate *Stag* captured the privateer *Sartine* before October 31. She was ordered to be purchased immediately and equipped as a sloop-of-war for the king's service. The *Stag*'s first lieutenant received command of the vessel.[400]

Lieutenant Inglis, commanding the HM sloop *Zephyr*, saw four vessels anchored off Barra Point, near the entrance to the Allt Heacair River, Scotland, at 11 AM on Thursday, November 2, 1780. They were two sloops, a French frigate, and a transport mounting 16 guns and manned with Frenchmen and blacks belonging to

Albedra, the banks of Gambia, and allied with the French. The transport and two sloops were set on fire at noon. The other transport was burned the preceding day.

The French frigate weighed anchor at 1 PM. The *Zephyr* came within pistol range and a warm action ensued which lasted until 4 PM when both vessels ran aground close to each other near low tide. The action renewed with redoubled violence and resembled more two batteries on shore than a sea fight. A letter of marque was anchored three quarters of a mile astern during most of the action. The *Zephyr* and the French frigate maintained a continual fire until 6 PM, when the French frigate struck her colors. She lost 12 men killed and 28 wounded. The *Zephyr* had two killed and four wounded. Her bowsprit, main topmast, and main yards were shot away. Her hull, mast, yards, sails, and rigging were badly shattered. Fire rafts, both under her bow and stern, threatened the *Zephyr* throughout the action but were unsuccessful.

After boarding the French frigate, they found her to be Lieutenant Commandant Allery's *Senegal*, carrying 18 6-pounders and 126 men. She was formerly the *Racehorse*, commanded by Lord Mulgrave.[401]

The privateer *City of Cork* captured Captain le Carektan's 500-ton French ship *Carcassone* about November 3. She was bound from Cape François to Bordeaux with sugars, coffee, and indigo and was brought to Kinsale. She was part of a fleet of 20 vessels but was separated from them in a gale.[402]

An English privateer arrived in New York on Monday, November 6, with two French merchant ships and a polacre. The following day, the Dunkirk privateer *Comtesse d'Artois*, carrying 17 guns and 110 men, took a brig loaded with herrings and sent her to France.[403] Captain McBride's HMS *Bienfaisant* fell in with and captured the *Comtesse d'Artois* on Wednesday, November 8. She had been out only seven days from Dunkirk and captured only one brig the day before.[404]

The *Harlequin* and another privateer captured M. Le Navarre's 36-gun French frigate *St. Jean Pied de Port* off the mouth of the harbor of Brest after an engagement of about half an hour on Thursday, November 9. The prize was sent to Penzance.[405]

The second day after the Cork fleet sailed, they fell in with a French man-of-war and engaged her. The convoy captured her before November 11 and sent her to Kinsale.[406]

Captain Watt's HMS *Pegasus* and Captain Murray's HMS *Cleopatra* fell in with and took the *Comtesse de Provence* on Saturday, November 11. She was a fast sailing privateer of 10 guns and 110 men. She had been out of Dunkirk almost two months, during which time she captured and ransomed a brig and a sloop.[407]

Captain Shaw's Crown privateer *Tiger* captured the snows *Modeste* and *Alliance* on Monday, November 13. They sailed from Saint-Domingue, but parted company with M. Guichen's French fleet in a gale off Cape Finisterre. The snows were valued at £20,000 each.[408]

The English privateer *Seahorse* took the 300-ton French ship *Granville* and brought her to Guernsey before November 21. She was bound from Marseilles to Bordeaux with bales of silk.[409]

The French frigates *Hermione* and *Surveillante* captured a large British ship off the Rhode Island coast before November 23. She had a cargo of more than 300 butts of wine and a quantity of fruit.[410]

The Jersey privateer *Stag* also captured the following prizes before November 30: *La Chaste Susanne*, *Notre Dame de Bon Secours*, and *St. Jean Baptiste*, which were bound from Bordeaux to Brest with wine, and Captain Nolet's The *Espoir en Dieu* bound from Brest to Martinique with flour, wine, and other provisions.[411]

Captain Dacres's *Perseus*, in company with the schooner *Racehorse* and the cutter *Expedition*, sighted a privateer brig at 7 AM on December 1, 1780 and gave chase. The *Perseus* fired a gun at the privateer at 11 AM. The privateer responded with two broadsides. The *Perseus* then discharged a broadside and the privateer struck. Lieutenant Baker, commander of the *Racehorse*, hoisted out his boat and went on board the privateer where he remained while his boat went to acquaint Captain Dacres of the situation.

The privateer sank at 11:15. The *Expedition* hoisted out her boat to save as many people as possible. They were swimming on oars and anything that floated. They retrieved three Frenchmen alive and Lieutenant Baker, who was found drowned with two Frenchmen, floating on the water in the heavy swells. The privateer's name was the *Comte du Bois*, commanded by Pierre Sivettel and carrying 12 6-pounders and 90 men. She was a new vessel pierced for 18 guns and had been out of Bordeaux only two days.[412]

The HMS *Romney* captured the 32-gun French privateer *Orphée* and sent her to Lisbon before December 2. She was a new ship owned by a banking house at Paris and cost more than £20,000. She was fitted out for a six-month cruise.[413]

Captain Charles Holmes Everitt's HMS *Solebay* fell in with two French privateers south of the western part of the Isle of Wight about 6 PM on Friday, December 9. The privateers immediately engaged the *Solebay* but broke off and tried to escape when Captain Lloyd's HMS *Portland* headed toward them. The *Portland* fired several broadsides into the forward privateer while the *Solebay* pursued the other. They maintained a running fight for three hours when the privateer struck. She was *La Comtesse Besançois* (*Comtesse de Buzançois*), of 20 12-pounders and 143 men. She lost 12 men killed and 15 wounded and her sails and rigging were much disabled. The *Solebay* had only one man badly wounded and two others slightly wounded and her masts and rigging suffered some damage.

The *Portland* pursued the chase during the night and captured François Cotton's privateer *La Marquise de Seignelay*, of 20 9-pounders and 150 men. She had two men killed and two wounded. The *Portland* had two men killed and seven wounded. She rejoined the company again the following morning.[414]

A French privateer captured Captain Elliott's *Two Friends* from Bristol, but the vessel was retaken by the Guernsey privateer *Hero* and sent to Plymouth on Sunday, December 10.[415]

The sloop *Lively* and the *Termagant* went in search of a French privateer which took a custom house lugger off the coast of Plymouth. The *Lively* returned to Plymouth on Sunday night, December 10. The *Termagant* returned on Tuesday night, December 12, with the privateer.[416]

Captain Charles Holmes Everitt's HMS *Solebay* chased the two cutters *Griffin* and *Rambler* and the brig *Eagle*, which they recaptured on Tuesday, December 12. The *Solebay* and the *Portland* brought *La Comtesse Bessançois, La Marquise de Seignelay*, the *Griffin*, *Rambler*, and *Eagle* to Spithead on December 13.[417]

Captain Delatre le Graud's 16-gun, 50-man French privateer *Le Furet*, from Dunkirk, captured Master John Adam's sloop *Jane*, from Greenock, near the entrance to Waterford harbor on Wednesday, December 13. She was laden with tobacco and ransomed for 1,600 guineas.[418]

A British privateer captured two prizes in the latitude of Cadiz and sent them to Faro on December 16. One of them was bound from Hispaniola to Cadiz with sugar, coffee, cotton, and some gold and silver. The other was a Whig ship from Boston with a cargo of sundries, pitch, tar, hemp, cordage, masts, yards, bowsprits, and many other articles. She was also bound to Cadiz. The privateer captured 10 other vessels, some French, some Spanish, some valuable, some worth very little.[419]

The private ship-of-war *Arc-en-Ciel* was captured and sent to Penzance before December 29. She was bound from Rhode Island to Brest with dispatches which were thrown overboard.[420]

The man-of-war *Canada* took the French privateer *Duc de Valois*, of eight guns and 76 men, and sent her to Plymouth, where she arrived on Sunday, December 31.[421]

1781

The British captured Claude Berard's *Activité* and Joseph Chabon's *Alert* in 1781. The *Activité* was tried and condemned in the High Court of Admiralty, where she is described as a French merchant vessel with a letter of marque. The *Alert* was sent to New York, where she was described as a French privateer, tried, and condemned.[422]

Lord Mulgrave's 74-gun *Courageux*, in company with the *Valiant*, captured Chevalier de Grimouard's 32-gun, 316-man French frigate *Minerve* about 14 leagues west of Ushant about 3 PM on Thursday, January 4. She sailed from Brest on January 3 with the *Fine*, the *Aigre*, and the *Diligence* to cruise off Scilly for two weeks. The Chevalier de Grimouard did not strike until the *Minerve* had been under fire from the *Courageux*'s broadsides within pistol range for about an hour. The *Courageux* had 10 men killed and seven wounded. Her foremasts, mizzenmasts, and bowsprit were damaged. The French lost a lieutenant and 49 men killed and 23 wounded.

Chevalier de Grimouard and his nephew were seriously wounded. The *Minerve*'s masts were rendered unserviceable and her hull was badly damaged, requiring her to be towed to port. The *Valiant* parted from the *Courageux* to chase one of the other frigates.[423]

Before January 10, the Crown cutters *Griffin* and *Rambler* captured the French privateer *Le General Ville Patoux*, carrying 12 guns and 56 men, and Lieutenant Furnival's cutter *Nimble* captured the French 14-gun and 41-man privateer the *Subtile*.[424]

The HMS *Alexander* captured the French privateer *le Dagesseau* on Saturday, January 13. She was a new ship of 30 guns and 205 men and was out from St.-Malo only three days. She was sent to Portsmouth.[425]

Captain Bennett's 16-gun French privateer cutter *Civilité* created great havoc among the convoys along the British coast during the week of January 14. She captured about 35 prizes. She also captured a British transport with troops on board and brought them to France before Thursday, January 25.[426]

Captain Edward Moore's 22-gun, 110-man Dublin privateer *Fame* fell in with five French merchantmen between Cape de Pallas and Cape de Gatt before January 17. The heavily laden merchantmen were bound from Marseilles to Cape François. The *Fame* captured four of them after a smart engagement of about an hour and brought them to Algiers. They were Captain Coucowrell's 300-ton *Deux Frères*, mounting 14 6-pounders and 55 men; Captain Compte's 300-ton l'*Univers*, of 12 4-pounders and 41 men; Captain Brican's *Zophir*, carrying 10 3-pounders and 32 men, and Captain Barard's *Nancy*, carrying four 6-pounders and 18 men.[427]

The French landed at Jersey at 2 AM on January 18. By 9 AM, they were all either killed, taken prisoner or put to flight.[428]

Before January 31, the privateer *Swiftsure* captured Captain L'Armancon's French privateer *St. Florentine* after a half-hour. She was brought to Guernsey. The Bristol privateers *Caesar* and *Greyhound* also captured l'*Amazone*, carrying 14 6-pounders and 47 men. She was bound from Rhode Island to Brest and was sent to Plymouth. The *Caesar* had two men killed and three wounded.[429]

A squadron of French ships which made an excursion to Virginia captured the 50-gun *Romney* and nine privateers, four of which were burned in February 1781. Five of the vessels were sent to Yorktown, Virginia and the *Romney* to Rhode Island.[430]

Two French privateers captured several vessels and two British cutters in the English Channel prior to February 3. Captain Hall's French privateer *Sans Peur* captured a number of English colliers and coasters north of the Yarmouth, England coast on Thursday, February 1. The prizes include Captain Pearson's *John*, of Shields, ransommed for 700 guineas; Captain Coxon's *Smelt*, also from Shields, ransomed for 400 guineas; Captain Porter's *Fanny*, from Yarmouth, ransomed for 300 guineas; and a snow from Shields, ransomed for 400 guineas. The snow engaged Captain Fall for almost three hours. Her mate was killed and the captain and two men wounded in the action.[431]

The *Sans Peur* fell in with the 16-gun, 160-man privateer *Eagle* on February 3. The *Sans Peur* sank the *Eagle* after an obstinate engagement of 3½ hours. She arrived at Hellevoetsluis with 100 British prisoners and 14 hostages whose ransom bills amounted to £5,400.[432]

The HMS *Ramilies*, *Albion*, and *Southampton* returned to London on Thursday, February 8, with the French ship *Franklin*, the Bordeaux snow the *Emeraude*, and a Whig sloop loaded with lumber. The two French ships left Bordeaux on November 4, 1780 with a large fleet bound to different parts of the world. They sailed with a convoy of 20 ships-of-the-line and several frigates commanded by the Comte d'Estaing and M. de Latouche Tréville. A strong gale dispersed the fleet about November 22.[433]

On February 9, Captain Waldegrave's frigate the *Prudente* captured the French privateer the *Américaine*, mounting 24 9-pounders on the main deck and eight 3-pounders on the quarterdeck, and brought her to Plymouth. About the same time, the Glasgow privateer *Stag* captured a Dunkirk privateer of 14 guns and 120 men and sent her to Falmouth.[434]

Captain Hall's French privateer *Sans Peur* took Captain Magnus Brightwell's privateer *Ranger*, of 12 guns and 45 men, off Goree Island, Senegal, and brought them to Hellevoetsluis before February 12.[435]

M. de Gardeur de Tilly's 64-gun French ship the *Eveille*, Captain de Villeneuve Cillard's frigate the *Gentille*, Captain de la Villebrune's frigate the *Surveillante*, and a Newport cutter sailed from Newport to the Chesapeake Bay on the evening of February 9. They arrived on the 13th and drove Benedict Arnold's fleet up the Elizabeth River. That fleet consisted of the 44-gun *Charon*, the 36-gun *Thames*, the 26-gun *Amphitrite*, the 18-gun *Hope*, the 16-gun *Loyalist*, the 16-gun *Bonette*, the 16-gun *General Monk*, the fireship *Vulcan*, and the galleys *Comet* and *Hussar*, carrying two 18-pounders each.

The French fleet also took a sloop with 100 barrels of flour, the 16-gun and 50-man privateer *Earl Cornwallis*, and the privateer *Revenge*, of 12 guns and 20 men. They also captured three of their prizes and another privateer of eight guns and 25 men.

Ten days later, the French fleet chased two vessels in the Chesapeake Bay on Monday, February 19. They proved to be Captain Gayton's HMS *Romulus*, of 44 guns and 260 men, and a large brig with 159 Virginia Loyalists and their effects on board. They were bound from Charleston to Virginia to reestablish themselves at their former homes. These two vessels struck after only one gun was fired. The *Romulus* had £10,000 on board to pay Benedict Arnold's troops and a quantity of clothing. The French also captured 600 prisoners and a number of officers. The brig had four men killed. The others were taken out and the vessel burned. The French destroyed six large privateers and left four large transports with 100 prisoners in the hands of the Whigs in the South.

As the fleet was returning to Newport on Sunday, February 25, Mr. de Tilly's 64-gun *Eveille* and a frigate captured nine small vessels in Gardiner's Bay. They were headed to join Benedict Arnold's squadron in the Chesapeake.[436]

The privateer *Rambler* captured a French privateer of eight guns and the French captured the Liverpool privateer *Lady Strahan* and brought her to Dunkirk about February 13.[437]

Before February 17, the letter of marque *Prince William* captured the 500-ton French ship *Le Saint Tarasion*. She was bound from Martinique to Bordeaux with coffee, indigo, and cotton and taken to Kinsale. Captain Moore's Dublin privateer *Fame* captured a French Turkeyman bound from Smyrna to Marseilles and brought her to Leghorn. She was valued at £10,000.[438]

Some French men-of-war captured three British ships from India and brought them to the Cape of Good Hope before February 22.[439]

Before February 27, the British vessel *Alarm*, of 10 swivel guns, was captured and taken to Brest. A 16-gun French privateer captured the London privateer *Dove* and brought her to Havre de Grace (Le Havre, France). And Captain Sloper's privateer *Mercury* captured Captain La Saintoigne's French ship *St. Royan*, bound from Nantes to the West Indies with wine and brandy, and took her to Jersey.[440]

The French frigate *Hermione* captured a ship bound from Bermuda to New York in March 1781 and sent her to Newport, where she arrived on Tuesday, March 27.[441]

The Jersey privateer *Mars* captured the 16-gun French privateer *Allemand* and sent her to Falmouth, England, on Thursday, March 1. The following day, the Dunkirk privateer *Victory* took Captain James's *Enterprize* bound from Swansea, England, to Portsmouth. After her guns and other fittings were removed, she was sunk. Her captain and crew were taken to Brest.[442]

Two 50-gun ships—one French the other English—engaged in an indecisive action in the English Channel about March 4. Both vessels left the scene of the action at the same time.[443]

The HM Sloop-of-War *Wasp* and the privateer *Dragon* captured M. Scaliger's 36-gun French frigate *St. Angoumois* after a hot engagement of one hour and sent her to Milford before March 13. The *St. Angoumois* lost her captain and 20 crewmen killed and many wounded. The privateer and the sloop had only four men killed and five wounded.[444]

Captain Trelane's schooner *Success* fell in with and retook Captain Sutter's New York brig *Fortune*, bound to Newfoundland, on Tuesday, March 13. Captain Peter Richards's 16-gun, 90-man Whig privateer brig *Marquis de Lafayette*, belonging to New London, had taken the *Fortune* three days earlier and sent her to Halifax. She was part of a convoy of 14 vessels that left Newport on Thursday, March 8, in company with the French fleet. Captain Richards left the fleet the night after they sailed.[445]

The French ship *Marquis Fayette* was headed from France to America with a cargo of clothing and other supplies when she encountered a 40-gun ship off Cape Clear, Ireland, about March 13. After an engagement of three hours, two 74-gun ships came up and joined the fight and captured the *Marquis Fayette*.[446]

A French privateer, carrying 20 guns and 140 men, captured two vessels from Yarmouth off Land's End on Thursday, March 15. The vessels, laden with malt, arrived in the bay at Yarmouth on Monday, March 19, and were ransomed.[447]

Admiral Charles René Dominique Sochet Destouches's French squadron of seven ships-of-the-line (Destouches's 80-gun *Le Duc de Bourgogne*, La Grandière's 74-gun *Le Conquérant*, Mr. Medine's 74-gun *Le Neptune*, Mr. Laclocheterie's 64-gun *Le Jason*, Mr. Tilly's 64-gun *Eveille*, Mr. Marigny's 64-gun *Ardent*, and Mr. Lombard's 64-gun *Provence*) and three frigates (the 44-gun *Romulus*, the 77-gun *Hermione*, and the 18-gun *Fantasque*), carrying a total of 583 guns, met Admiral Arbuthnot's slightly larger British fleet of seven ships of the line (the 90-gun *London*, the 74-gun *Bedford*, the 74-gun *Robust*, the 64-gun *Prudent*, the 64-gun *America*, the 64-gun *Europe*, and the 50-gun *Adamant*) and three frigates, including one of 90 guns, carrying a total of 660 guns, at 8:15 AM on Friday, March 16. They were 11 leagues east-southeast of the Virginia Capes. Both fleets were sailing in line of battle in opposite directions. The west wind, fog, rain, and rough seas prevented both fleets from sailing directly into the bay.

It took both fleets a while to tack to get into position. The British attempted to attack the French from the leeward but Destouches moved to the leeward at 9:15 AM, making a large curving column movement that brought the French line around on the opposite course from Arbuthnot's line. The British squadron tacked to parallel the French and was approaching the rear about 11 AM.

The *Robust* fired on the ships in the French van, beginning the battle at noon. The lead ships of both lines engaged each other. *Le Conquérant*, the lead French ship, returned the *London*'s fire and fought her for at least a quarter-hour within musket range. The *Jason* and the *Ardent* fired broadsides at the other two British ships. *Le Neptune* fired two broadsides at the *Robust*'s stern, putting her out of commission. She signaled a frigate for help and the British ships were in confusion for a while.

When the British turned downwind, the French followed and kept firing broadsides. The ensuing exchange of fire inflicted much damage on both vans and broke the French line. Unable to accomplish his original mission and unable to debark his troops under fire, Destouches moved his squadron in front of Arbuthnot's at 1 PM.

The British turned away as the fifth French ship brought her guns to bear on Arbuthnot's lead ships. The rear of both squadrons continued to exchange fire with little effect. Both sides ceased firing at 2 PM. Instead of taking advantage of the wind which had now "settled down to the northeast" and was favorable to enter the bay, Destouches led the rest of his squadron out to sea about 3 PM, firing broadsides at the British ships along the way.

Admiral Arbuthnot pursued in the *Royal Oak*, but soon lost sight of the French ships which disappeared in the haze. The French ships threw their top sails to the masts and remained in that situation for 15 hours with lights in the tops during the night, expecting the action to be renewed. However, by daybreak, the British fleet had disappeared. Admiral Arbuthnot abandoned the chase and entered the Chesapeake Bay because the *Robust, Prudent, Europe*, and *London* were disabled by the heavy enemy fire. The squadron anchored in Lynnhaven Bay.

The *Conquérant*, which had led the French battle line and engaged Arbuthnot's flagship *London*, sustained the most damage and the most casualties: 43 killed and 50 wounded. The entire squadron had a total of 72 killed and 112 wounded, including two naval officers killed (commandant en second Cheffontaine Trévient of the *Conquérant* and ensign Kergus). The *Conquérant* also lost her rudder, and her wheel was so badly damaged that she had to be towed. The *Ardent* and *Neptune* were also damaged.

The British had 30 men killed and 73 wounded. Although they suffered the most damage in the engagement, they succeeded in getting control of the entrance to the Chesapeake Bay, allowing Major General William Phillips to sail to Portsmouth, Virginia, with reinforcements for General Benedict Arnold.

A French frigate was sent to shore and her captain reported that he learned the British fleet sailed to the Virginia Capes. One of their main ships was being towed by two others, and another large ship had lost her topmasts. The French fleet remained in formation off the capes nearly the whole of the next day. Destouches convened his captains the following morning and decided that the *Conquérant*'s condition made it impossible to continue the battle. Finding that the British were not inclined to renew the action and, with the wind blowing from the westward, Destouches decided to return to Newport to refit. The squadron arrived on March 26.[448]

A French privateer mounting 20 guns and 140 men captured Captain Sinnot's *Lark*, of Dublin, off Scilly, about 6 PM Friday, March 16, and ransomed her for 4,000 guineas. She was bound from London to Dublin.[449]

Captain Izatt's *Mullet Hall* sailed from Portsmouth for Jamaica on Thursday, March 15. He intended to join the West India fleet but was taken two days later by a French privateer of 26 guns and taken to St.-Malo. She was a very valuable ship and heavily laden. The privateer that captured her was part of the French fleet of 11 vessels of equal force, that sailed from Concale Bay on February 14.[450]

As the French squadron was heading back to Newport from the Chesapeake Capes after the engagement of March 16, Captain Latouche-Tréville's frigate *Hermione* captured the 200-ton English merchantman *Union* or *Unity* at 3 PM on Monday, March 19. She was en route from the West Indies to New York with six officers returning from leave, a few crewmen, and a cargo of molasses and sugar with an estimated value of 40,000 to 50,000 livres.[451]

The Waterford privateer *Star and Garter* arrived at Kinsale on Tuesday, March 20. She brought in with her a large French sloop, of 16 guns and 120 men, which captured many coasting vessels along the Irish coast. Some of those prizes were ransomed and the others sent to France.[452]

The British letter of marque *Fanny* had an engagement with a French frigate which was just going to strike her colors when two other vessels came up, forcing the *Fanny* to run. They chased her for two hours but could not catch her. The *Fanny* arrived at Plymouth on Wednesday morning, March 28, having lost her fore-mast and her rigging badly damaged.[453]

Before March 28, the privateer *Antelope* captured the French ship *Marshall Belleisle*. She was bound from Guadeloupe to Havre de Grace (Le Havre) with sugars, indigo, and cotton. She was taken to Jersey. Captain Ridgly's Dartmouth privateer *Phoenix* captured a French packet with dispatches from India and brought her to Penzance. They had thrown their packet overboard.[454]

The Liverpool privateer *Good Look Out* and the Guernsey privateer *Prince of Orange* retook a vessel bound from Cork to Barbados with provisions before Thursday, March 29. The vessel had previously been captured by a French privateer off Cork.[455]

The French fleet, returning to Newport after an encounter with the British fleet, captured two vessels between March 16 and 31. One of them was a large ship from Jamaica with sugar.[456] The French frigate *Surveillante* also captured a large brig, which she sank before March 31.[457]

Admiral Darby's fleet was joined by the Gibraltar and New York fleets and departed from the Cove of Cork, past the Galley Head, Ireland, on March 27. Some vessels from the fleet captured two French privateers before April 3. One of them mounted 32 guns, the other 28 guns.[458]

The French privateer *La Josephine*, from Havre de Grace (Le Havre), captured a British packet bound from Falmouth to New York before April 3. The dispatches from the British ministry for General Clinton and Vice Admiral Arbuthnot were immediately sent to Versailles.[459]

Three privateers from the Île-de-France (Réunion and Mauritius) captured seven English merchantmen before April 6. They were richly laden. One had $600,000 in specie on board.[460]

Captain Patten's HMS *Belle Poule* and the HMS *Berwick* captured Commander Luke Ryan's 32-gun, 240-man privateer *Callonne* (formerly the *Tartar*) from Dunkirk. She was taken 4 miles off St. Abb's Head, near the entrance of the Firth of Edinburgh, after a short action at daybreak on Friday, April 7. The privateer mistook the *Berwick* for a Greenland ship and ordered her to come to. They fired several broadsides before discovering their mistake. When the *Berwick*'s lower ports were opened, they tried to make off at the same time by crowding their sails and cutting adrift a boat with a lieutenant and 13 men, which was lying at the stern, for the purpose of boarding the supposed Greenlandman. The *Belle Poule* shot ahead of the *Berwick*, chased the privateer, and engaged her for 45 minutes until the *Berwick* came up. The privateer struck her colors at 8:30 AM. She had one man killed and two wounded. The *Berwick* had one man wounded and the *Belle Poule* had no casualties.

Captain Ryan had been out from Dunkirk only five days and had captured Captain Ramsay's *Nancy* bound from Aberdeen to Newcastle, which he ransomed for 300 guineas.[461]

The packets *Anna Teresa* and *Antelope* sailed from Falmouth on March 15. The *Anna Teresa* was bound for New York and the *Antelope* for Jamaica. A French frigate of 38 guns intercepted them 20 leagues to the westward of Scilly. The *Anna Teresa* was taken after a chase of six hours and brought to Lorient. The *Antelope* escaped.[462]

The French lost 24 privateers before April 11, 1781. They include:

- one of 44 guns, two of 36 guns, four of 30 guns, all from St.-Malo;
- four of 36 guns, three of 32 guns, and three of 28 guns from Havre de Grace (Le Havre);
- two of 36 guns from Brest;
- one of 32 guns and two of 28 guns from Bayonne, France;
- one of 30 guns and one of 28 guns from Dunkirk.[463]

The Liverpool privateer *Sisters* also captured the French snow *Ferret*. She was bound from Nantes to Martinique with dispatches. However, the letters were thrown overboard and sunk.

Captain Gorham's Whig sloop *Nancy* sailed in company with a fleet of 80 vessels, 40 of which were convoyed by three French frigates. They parted from the convoy and headed south on the fourth day of the cruise. The other vessels—under convoy of the Whig frigates *Confederacy*, *Deane*, and *Saratoga*—headed to the Delaware River. A British ship captured the *Nancy* in latitude 38.30 and sent her to New York on Sunday, April 15, with her cargo of sugar and coffee.[464]

When Holland entered the war in 1781, the British government decided to send an expeditionary force to southern Africa to capture the Dutch colony of the Cape of Good Hope. Commodore George Johnstone commanded the squadron, which consisted of the 74-gun *Hero* and the 74-gun *Monmouth*; the *Romney*, the *Jupiter*, and the *Isis* (all 50 guns); the *Diana*, the *Jason*, and the *Active* (all 32 guns); eight smaller Navy vessels and 10 East Indiamen (all 26 guns). They departed on Tuesday, March 13, with a large number of troops and accompanied by Vice Admiral George Darby's Channel Fleet en route to Gibraltar.

The French sent Admiral Comte Pierre André de Suffren de Saint Tropez, Bailli de Suffren, to thwart this plan. He commanded a squadron of five vessels: the *Héros* and the *Annibal* (both 74 guns); and the *Artésien*, *Sphinx*, and *Vengeur* (all 64 guns). They left Brest on March 22 with the Comte François de Grasse's fleet. They also transported troops.

Commodore Johnstone arrived at Porto Praya in the Cape Verde Islands on April 11 and anchored. His flagship, the *Romney*, was in a cluster of other vessels, severely restricting its field of fire. The *Isis* sighted a squadron to the northeast at 9:30 AM on Monday, April 16, and signaled its approach. Johnstone was caught completely by surprise. He had 1,500 men on shore relaxing and collecting food, livestock, and water.

Suffren arrived at Porto Praya to collect water, not expecting to find the British squadron there. He immediately decided to engage Johnstone's squadron. He maneuvered around the east point of the bay in a column with his own ship, the *Héros*, in the lead, flying the signal for attack. Suffren anchored about 500 feet to the starboard of Commodore Johnstone's flagship *Hero* and opened fire. The *Annibal*, astern of the *Héros*, failed to clear for action and consequently contributed little to the fight. The *Artésien* was third in line and got entangled with one of the East Indiamen when her captain got killed and the second-in-command failed to anchor. The wind pulled the two vessels out to sea. The last two vessels, the *Sphinx* and the *Vengeur*, fired a broadside as they sailed past the mouth of the bay.

Suffren realized that nothing more could be achieved after the four-hour engagement and headed for the open sea. Commodore Johnstone ordered his ships to pursue. All but the *Isis* could do so. Captain Evelyn Sutton reported that his spars and rigging were so badly damaged that they would not bear up under the wind. Johnstone insisted that they do so. Shortly afterward, the fore-topmast of the *Isis* tumbled overboard, leaving Johnstone unable to keep pace with Suffren. The *Isis* and the *Monmouth* were at least 2 miles behind as night approached and the sea was growing heavier. Johnstone decided not to attempt a night engagement, allowing Suffren to escape. He abandoned the pursuit and returned to Porto Praya, where he remained for another two weeks. He ordered Captain Sutton arrested but he was later acquitted.

The British lost nine men killed and 47 wounded in the convoy by stray fire. Total losses were 36 killed and 130 wounded. French losses were 105 killed and 204 wounded, almost all of them aboard the *Héros* and the *Annibal*.[465]

The British privateer *Carlisle* captured Captain de la Feuillade's Spanish ship *N. S. Valenze de Alcantara* and brought her to Waterford on Monday, April 16. She was bound from Bayonne to Cadiz with military supplies. The *Carlisle*, having received some damage to her rigging in an engagement with a French privateer, put into Cork for repairs.[466]

Captain de Latouche's French frigate *Hermione* captured a vessel at 5:15 AM on Thursday, April 19. She was an American vessel captured in Long Island Sound the previous day by a privateer bound to New York carrying two cannons and three men. As she had nothing of value on board, Captain de Latouche had her burned.[467]

The French privateer brigantine *Le Cerf*, carrying 18 9-pounders and 170 men, took the Kingston privateer *Hercules* and a ship from Liverpool and sent them to Hispaniola before April 21.[468]

Captain Collins's HMS *Aurora* fell in with the St.-Malo privateer *Esperance* on Monday, April 23, between Scilly and Land's End. *Esperance* carried 10 6-pounders, six swivels, and 70 men. She was captured after a short chase and taken to Mounts Bay in the evening.[469]

The same day, Captain Pelley's 16-gun Glasgow privateer *Rusden* captured the Dunkirk privateer *Filander*, with six guns and 20 men. She was on her first cruise and had taken no prizes. Captain Chandler's English privateer *Salisbury*, of 20 6-pounders, also engaged a French privateer, of 26 12-pounders. They fired at each other for almost two hours. Captain Chandler and nine of his men were killed and 10 wounded.[470]

Before April 24, the British letter of marque *Mars* captured the French privateer *St. Quentin*, of 16 6- and 9-pounders, and sent her to Kinsale. And the HMS *Cerberus* captured the French privateer *Duc de Brissac*, carrying 20 6-pounders and 110 men, and sent her to Plymouth.[471]

The Guernsey privateer *Medway* engaged a French frigate off Scilly on Wednesday, April 25. She had all her rigging shot away and arrived at Plymouth a wreck. The French frigate had 10 men killed and seven wounded and left the *Medway* to pursue two vessels under English colors that came into sight.[472]

Captain John Barry's Continental frigate *Alliance*, in company with a 40-gun French frigate, captured a 36-gun, 120-man Guernsey privateer brig and sent her to Boston about April 25. The privateer made some resistance, but, on receiving a broadside from the *Alliance*, she struck her colors. She had 15 tons of gunpowder on board and mounted 20 iron 12-pounders and 16 bronze 4-pounders and had a crew of 112 men. Her consort, of 20 guns, escaped but was soon overtaken and left in company with the *Alliance*.[473]

Captain Niel's Whig privateer *Bold Attempt* and Captain Ryan's Dunkirk frigate *La Colombe* arrived at Hellevoetsluis on Thursday, April 26 with the English privateer *Kitty*. This was the 22nd prize taken in a span of five weeks.[474]

La Dame de Granville captured seven or eight prizes valued at about 700,000 livres before April 27.[475]

The HM Armed Ship *Leith*, a Greenlandman, captured the Dunkirk privateer *Necker*, carrying 18 guns and 85 men, and sent her to Lerwick, Shetland, before April 28. The *Necker* first gave chase to the *Leith* which found she could not escape, so she lay to and prepared for battle. The *Necker*, suspecting her to be a frigate, declined an engagement and sheered off. The *Leith*, in turn, gave chase. The *Necker* crowded her sails and sprung her topmast. As the *Leith* approached her quickly, the *Necker* threw her guns overboard to facilitate her escape. When the *Leith* overtook her, the *Necker* had nothing with which to defend herself and fell an easy prey. She had three hostages on board, one of whom was ransomed for £800. Her officers were put aboard the *Leith*, which was returning from convoying ships to Shetland. The crew proceeded to Edinburgh by land.[476]

Two French frigates met a Dutch East Indiaman at sea on Friday, April 27. The Dutch did not know of the declaration of war between Holland and England. The frigates conducted her safely to Cadiz. They went out again on their cruise and fell in with two 20-gun ships a few days later. They were the *Charlotte* from London and the *Phoenix* from Bristol, which they captured and brought to Cadiz.[477]

The 20-gun St.-Malo privateer *de Bourgois* captured six homeward-bound merchantmen off Newport before May 2 1781.[478]

Admiral Rodney captured the brig *Atlantick* at St. Eustatius and sent her to Plymouth, where she arrived on May 13. She sailed in company with 32 merchantmen under the convoy of four men-of-war. They fell in with seven French ships in latitude 49.26 N longitude 8.18 W about 40 leagues from land, on Saturday, May 2. The commodore immediately hoisted the signal to disperse, but the captain of the *Atlantick* said he saw many of the leeward ships captured.[479]

Captain Collins's HMS *Aurora* fell in with *Le Comte de Guichen* in the Celtic Sea on May 3. She was a Morlaix privateer lugger carrying 16 guns, 10 carronades and swivels, and 80 men. She had been previously called the *Black Princess* and was cutter-rigged, first commanded by Luke Ryan then by a Mr. McCarty.[480]

M. la Motte Picquet entered Brest on Tuesday, May 8, with 21 merchant vessels and a privateer, part of the British fleet he captured off the Lizard. They also sank a merchant ship and a privateer. The fleet was bound from St. Eustatius to England under convoy of two ships-of-the-line and two frigates.

Two French privateers later captured six merchant ships. The others escaped with the men-of-war and frigates. The cargoes consisted of 8,485 hogsheads of white sugar, 2,275 hogsheads of tobacco, 1,100 elephant teeth, 9332 tierces of coffee, 1,389 hides, 300 bales of cotton, 293 hogsheads of ginger, and eight tierces of indigo. The ships and their cargoes had an estimated value of 16,456,375 French livres.[481]

The Plymouth privateer *Alexander* recaptured a large ship from St. Eustatius about 30 leagues west of Scilly. The *Alexander* retook her from the French and brought her to Plymouth on Sunday, May 13.[482]

Commander James Wallace's 64-gun HMS *Nonsuch* fell in with a 90-gun French flagship in the Bay of Biscay about mid-May. The two had a very severe engagement during the night in which the *Nonsuch* lost 23 men killed and 47 wounded. The French vessel escaped to a French port.[483]

Rear Admiral Rowley's squadron captured a French brigantine bound from La Rochelle to Cape François before Wednesday, May 16.[484]

A French privateer, of 14 6-pounders, attacked an English brig with a few small guns off Balmbrough Castle (Bamburgh Castle, England) on Thursday morning, May 17. They engaged for about two hours before the brig got off by running to shore under the castle guns, which forced the privateer to sheer off. The privateer sent her boats to cut out the brig but Captain Horsall, commanding part of the Yorkshire militia, beat them off with the assistance of the castle guns. The brig then got to Holy Island harbor.

A little later the same morning, the privateer attacked a brig off Sunderland Point. The brig engaged the privateer heading toward Balmbrough with the privateer chasing her in a running fight. The privateer then broke off the engagement.[485]

The Guernsey privateer *Eagle*, mounting only 12 6-pounders, captured the French privateer *Ajax* in latitude 39.23 on Saturday, May 19. The *Ajax*, from St.-Malo, mounted 24 guns, 9- and 6-pounders. She lost four men killed and seven wounded in the 28-minute action.[486]

The Jersey privateer *Friendship*, mounting 14 6- and 9-pounders, fell in with a French privateer of 18 guns off Scilly on Monday, May 20. The two were engaged for some time but became separated and lost sight of each other with nightfall accompanied by a gale.[487]

The same day, a French privateer cutter appeared off Dunbar at 9 AM, greatly alarming the inhabitants. She was in chase of a smack and the privateer *Thistle*, both belonging to Dunbar. Both vessels anchored close to the harbor for shelter. The French cutter, crowding all the sail possible, bore right in on them.

The local militiamen mustered along the pier and prepared to protect the town and vessels as best they could. The French fired a broadside, which was returned, and the engagement continued for 1½ hours when the French privateer sheered off. A great many cannonballs fell in the streets.[488]

Captain Langmure's *Commerce* fell in with a 22-gun French privateer between Dungarvan and Youghall, Ireland, on Friday night, May 25. They engaged for one hour before the *Commerce* beat off the privateer.[489]

Captain William Pierre Williams, of the HMS *Flora*, in company with Captain Pakenham's HMS *Crescent*, discovered two Dutch frigates near Ceuta, Morocco, about 5 AM on Thursday, May 24. They prepared for action, but an approaching storm obliged them to wait for a more favorable opportunity. The storm abated at 7 PM and the British frigates kept the Dutch frigates in sight throughout the night. They approached the Dutch vessels at daybreak and began the action at close range at 5 AM. The engagement continued for 2¼ hours before the Dutch surrendered. They proved to be Captain Peter Melville's frigate *Castor* from Rotterdam, carrying 26 12-pounders and 10 6-pounders and a crew of 230 men, and the frigate *Brill*, mounting 26 12-pounders, two sixes, and eight 4-pounders. A shot carried away the *Crescent's* main and mizzen masts, forcing her to strike her colors. However, the *Flora* got her head toward the *Crescent* and prevented the Dutch from taking possession of her.

The *Flora* had nine men killed and 32 wounded, 18 mortally. The *Crescent* lost 26 men killed and 67 wounded, two of them mortally. The *Castor* lost 22 men killed and 41 wounded, 11 of them mortally. A French frigate retook the *Castor* about five days later. The British fired 1,200 shots and 5,000 pounds of powder.[490]

Captain Daniel's (or Davis's) ship *William* arrived at Port Royal, Jamaica, from the coast of Africa on Saturday, May 26, with 350 choice slaves on board. During her eight-week passage, she fell in with the privateer *Secour*, which had taken a French packet boat bound from Île-de-France (Réunion and Mauritius) to France. The dispatches were delivered to Captain Daniel, who brought them to Kingston for the inspection of the government. The commander of the *Secour* did not have enough crewmen to guard the prisoners, so he took what he could from the vessel and let her depart.[491]

Lieutenant Douglas's HM Cutter *Resolution* captured Louis le Chevalier's French privateer *Bienvenu*, carrying 10 carriage guns, six swivels, and 41 men, about May 27. She was from Dunkirk and taken to Tinmouth. She was in sight of the privateer *Antigallican* when taken.[492]

The 32-gun French frigate *Josephine* took Captain Brander's *Aurora* eight leagues off the Lizard on Monday, June 4, 1781. She was bound from Lisbon to London with wine and taken to Havre de Grace (Le Havre).[493]

Captain Bligh's HMS *Nemesis* took the Dunkirk privateer cutter *Alliance* or *Black Princess* after a four-hour chase about 6 leagues south of Waterford harbor on Tuesday, June 5. The *Alliance*, commanded by John Lauder, a Whig, carried 16 6-pounders, 20 9-pounders, and 87 men. She was eight days out from Morlaix and had captured nothing.[494]

Captain Molstron's Dunkirk privateer *Vulture*, of 16 6-pounders, 20 9-pounders, and 120 men, took Captain Jenkins's privateer cutter *St. Peter* and brought her to Morlaix on June 6. The same day, Lieutenant George's HM Cutter *Rambler* took the French privateer brig *Union*, of six guns, 11 swivels, and 57 men, after a short action off Shoreham. The prize was from St.-Malo and taken to Spithead on June 9.[495]

Captain Cadogan's HMS *Licorne* took a French Guineaman with a rich cargo of gold dust and ivory which arrived at Port Royal, Jamaica, on June 15.[496]

Captain Evans's HM Frigate *Charlestown* arrived at Halifax on Thursday, June 14, and brought a valuable French prize which he captured off Cape Cod. The prize was bound from France to Boston with gunpowder, small arms, brandy, flour, wine, and many other valuable articles. Several other store ships sailed at the same time, laden with all kinds of military stores for the French army at Rhode Island and clothing for the Continental Army.[497]

A French privateer cutter captured six vessels at the mouth of the River Tees, within sight of Hartlepool, England, on Thursday, June 14. Five of the vessels were ransomed and one carried out to sea.[498]

Lieutenant Berkeley's cutter *Liberty*, in company with the HM Sloop *Alderney* and the Custom House Cutter *Hunter*, captured Captain Fre. Barthelemy Blouin's two-gun, 21-man Dunkirk privateer cutter *La Puce* and the *Ferret*, of 12 carriage and 16 swivel guns, on Tuesday, June 19.[499]

The Crown privateer *Associate* took the 18-gun French privateer *Triton* at the mouth of the Shannon River and brought her to Limerick before June 21.[500]

Two Crown revenue cutters captured a French lugsail privateer and brought her to Aldborough about 7 PM on Thursday, June 21. She was bound from Dunkirk to Holland with some dispatches which were thrown overboard and sunk before she struck. The cutters had six men slightly wounded; the privateer had two men killed and five wounded.[501]

Captain de Latouche's French frigate *Hermione* crowded her sails at dawn on Sunday, June 24, and chased a vessel in a weak northwest wind. The vessel hoisted American colors, fired a gun, and continued the chase. The *Hermione* fired several guns at her to slacken sails at 7 AM. As she was out of range of the cannonballs, she continued to be chased. As the *Hermione* approached her at 9 AM, the vessel turned about and came athwart the *Hermione*. She was a 20-gun privateer from Salem returning from a cruise on the coast of Ireland where she captured seven prizes.[502]

Captain Donaldson's letter of marque *Alexander* engaged a French privateer for an hour before June 26. She might have captured the privateer if a fire had not broken out in the privateer's powder room, which blew her up along with all her crew.[503]

Master Thomas Cockrill's pink *New Recovery* was bound from Newcastle to Redbridge with coals on Thursday, June 28. She fell in with a French privateer cutter of 10 carriage guns, some swivels, and small arms off Ensbury Head. They engaged for 2½ hours before the French privateer was forced to sheer off. The *New Recovery* mounted only three carriage guns and had nine men and boys on board. Her fore-topmast, mizzen topmast, and jib boom were all shot away and her sails and rigging shot to pieces. She received a number of shots in her hull but none of her crew were harmed. When the engagement began, she had a brigantine from Sunderland in company which had 10 portholes and was supposed to mount six or eight guns. When the master of the brigantine saw the pink's fore-topmast gone, he crowded sail and went to Portsmouth, where he arrived on Friday, the 29th.[504]

Captain de la Villeneuve Cillard's 36-gun French frigate *Surveillante* captured a schooner bound from the West Indies to New York and sent her to Newport before June 30. Two days earlier, she fell in with a British 50-gun ship, believed to be the *Isis*, which she engaged for some time. The *Isis* had her foremast shot away in the action. When another vessel, believed to be her consort, came into sight, Captain de la Villeneuve Cillard thought proper to retire.[505]

Before June 30, the Crown privateer *Enterprize* captured the 16-gun *Chevalier Luzerne* bound from Lorient to Philadelphia. Also, Captain Carlyon's *Lively* captured the privateer *Marquis d'Aubiterre*, from Brest, with 12 6-pounders and eight swivels, and retook two brigs that the privateer was convoying into port.[506]

Captain Stephen Decatur, Sr.'s Philadelphia privateer ship *Royal Louis* took the New York sloop *Phoenix* in July 1781. She was previously captured by a French frigate and retaken by the HM Sloop-of-War *Swallow*. An officer was conducting her to New York when Captain Decatur retook her and brought her to Philadelphia.[507]

Dunkirk privateers captured 17 prizes between July 1 and August 1, 1781. Nine of them were retaken and eight were ransomed.[508]

The HM Frigate *Charlestown* captured an 800-ton French ship and brought her to Halifax before July 2. She was a very valuable prize and was one of a fleet of 14 vessels that arrived in Boston. She was blown from her anchors at the lighthouse in a violent wind storm. She was loaded with clothing, provisions, arms, and a great quantity of flour.[509]

The British grand fleet, returning from Gibraltar, captured seven French ships-of-the-line under the command of M. la Mothe Picquet before Tuesday, July 10.[510]

Captain Biggs's HM Frigate *Amphitrite* captured a very large store ship of 700 or 800 tons named the *Stanislaus* before July 14. Her cargo consisted of a large quantity of articles for the French army at Rhode Island, including one 16-inch mortar, the largest ever known in America.[511]

Before July 19, two frigates at Sligo captured a Whig privateer, mounting 22 9-pounders on one deck and several howitzers, and a French privateer, carrying 16 6-pounders and four 3-pounders on her quarter deck. These privateers had taken several vessels on the west coast of Ireland and were in close pursuit of a heavily laden brig in Sligo Bay. Also, the Guernsey privateer *Holdernesse* captured the French ship *St. Beaujolais* and brought her in. She was bound from Martinique to Bordeaux with sugar and cotton valued at £12,000.[512]

Captain Donovan, of the revenue cutter *Waller*, secured the quartermaster of the French privateer ship-of-war *Tartar* and lodged him in the Skibbereen jail on Friday, July 20. He was concealed on board a pilot boat in Baltimore harbor, intending to cut out a Dutch prize anchored in that harbor. The crew of the pilot boat were also secured and the privateer was off the coast.

Four men were put in the Cork County jail on Friday, August 3. One of them was an officer belonging to the *Tartar*. The others were pilots belonging to Crookhaven. They were found reconnoitering the southwest coast of Ireland in order to capture some vessels there. They intended to take a Dutch prize anchored in Baltimore harbor on the night of their capture by Captain Donovan.[513]

Captain Griffiths's New York brig *Defiance* fell in with two privateers from St.-Malo, the 20-gun *Le Frederick* and the 12-gun *Tartar*, off Shellick Rock to the North of Cape Clear on Friday, July 20. They ransomed Captain Griffiths and left him cruising from the Cape to the Misen Head, Ireland, for four days.[514]

The Glasgow privateer *Robust* captured the French privateer *Favourite* and brought her to Penzance before July 22. She was from Havre de Grace, mounted 12 guns, and had a crew of 49 men. She was taken out of the Downs by 18 of her crew who convoyed the other part of the crew. They brought her to Calais, where they sold her for £3,000. A hostage on board was ransomed for £500.[515]

The Limerick privateer *Briton*, carrying 18 6- and 9-pounders, had an engagement with a French privateer which lasted two hours and 20 minutes before July 26. The French had 16 men killed and 12 wounded. The *Briton* had 11 men killed and nine wounded and all her rigging shot away. The French, finding the *Briton* would not strike, took advantage of her condition and sheered off. The *Briton* returned to Limerick on July 26.[516]

The Limerick privateer *Thunder* captured two French privateers and brought them to Limerick on July 26. They were the same vessels that patrolled the Irish coast for more than three months and had nine hostages on board. One of the privateers mounted 10 6-pounders. The other had eight guns, 6- and 9-pounders, and a number of swivels. They sailed from Dunkirk on April 2 with six months' provisions on board and captured 28 vessels during their cruise.[517]

The Liverpool privateer *Harlequin* captured Master John Simmons's French vessel *Ruzi* and sent her to the Cove, Guernsey, where she arrived on July 26. She was returning home to Brest with naval stores from Rhode Island.[518]

Before July 27, the Dunkirk privateer *La Fantaise* captured Captain Wage's *Betsey and Polly*. She was bound from Exon to Liverpool and was ransomed for 120 guineas. Also, Master Patrick Dowlin's 16-gun Dunkirk privateer lugger *Fanny* took Captain Isaac Kelsick's brig *Pallas* about one league from the Saltees. She was bound from Workington to Cork with coals and was ransomed for 500 guineas. Some of the privateer's crew told Captain Kelsick's men that they had 25 hostages on board and that their ransom bills amounted to nearly £40,000.[519]

The English privateer *Live Oak* took the French ship *Theresa* bound from Marseilles to Nantes and brought her to Kinsale before July 29. She sailed on June 8 but met with bad weather, sprung a leak, and returned to port where she was repaired.[520]

Captain Fraga's Liverpool privateer *Harlequin* took a French snow and sent her to Cork before Monday, July 30. She was bound from France to Boston and valued at 500,000 livres.[521]

The crew of a French privateer landed at Beaumaris on Tuesday, July 31, and carried off 30 sheep, some pigs, and poultry. Early the next morning, they attempted to land again, but the militiamen mustered and were determined to oppose them. The French returned to the vessel which fired several guns but did no damage except knocking down an old hovel which served as a shelter for cattle.[522]

Before August 3, 1781, Admiral la Motte Picquet's squadron captured a fleet of 18 British ships bound from Lisbon to Newfoundland. Only their convoy escaped. The same squadron also took almost all of Admiral Rodney's vessels from St. Eustatius. French and Whig privateers captured the *New Adventure* and the *Hope* bound for the West Indies and brought them to France. In addition, the French privateer *Flora* took the Guernsey privateers *Quincey*, of 14 guns, and *Hector* after an engagement of 1½ hours.[523]

The French brig *Lafayette* captured the HM Tender Brig *Kitty* after a short engagement on Friday, August 3. The *Kitty* was in search of the fleet.[524]

Two French privateers cruising on the Irish coast captured more than 20 vessels in 10 days between July 25 and August 4, 1781. Sixteen of these vessels were ransomed.[525]

The 80-gun *St. Esprit*, of Admiral de Grasse's squadron, suffered considerably from the fire of the 74-gun HMS *Russell* in an action with Admiral Hood before August 9. She had 48 men killed and nearly double that number wounded.[526]

The HM Frigate *St. Margaretta* captured *Le Juring* bound from Saint-Domingue to Nantes with sugar and brought her to Cork on August 9.[527]

French and Dutch privateers plundered the inhabitants along the coast of Milford in early August. They took a vessel out of the harbor during the night of Saturday, August 11. Only a man and boy were on board, probably sound asleep from fatigue due to what they had undergone the day before.[528]

A French privateer cutter sank two coasting vessels off Wicklow Head on Sunday, August 12. Captain Cooper, of the HMS *Stag*, sent his second lieutenant, Mr. Lewis Vickers, in the cutter *Hope* to search for the privateer. He fell in with her off Bardsey Island on August 16. She proved to be the *Chardon*, carrying 20 6-pounders and 150 men, commanded by John Kelly, an Irishman. Lieutenant Vickers engaged the *Chardon* for an hour and 10 minutes when he was wounded in the thigh by a musket ball. All the officers of the *Hope* were either killed or wounded, so she was forced to submit. She had only 12 4-pounders and 55 men on board, six of whom were killed and 16 wounded.[529]

That night, the HMS *Solebay* took a French lugger to New York. She was bound from Lorient to Rhode Island with dry goods valued at £15,000.[530]

A French privateer captured a sloop off Hartland the week of August 12. She had been discharging tea at Newton. Within a few days, 11 other vessels were taken at the same place. The captain of one of them, named Tudball, of Minehead, offered to ransom his vessel for £600 but was refused.[531]

Captain Myles Urion's Loyalist privateer whaleboat *Ladies Delight* (or *Lady's Delight*) captured five prizes before August 25. Her crew boarded and took a sloop mounting six 4-pounders on Monday, August 13. She had on board part of the cargo of the *Porpoise* bound from Havana to Philadelphia. The *Porpoise* had been run ashore by some Loyalist cruisers.

The *Ladies Delight* captured a French brigantine bound from Cape François to Boston with sugar and molasses and sent her in the same day. She also captured a sloop bound from St. Thomas to Philadelphia with a cargo of rum and sugar and Captain Charles's sloop *Delight*.[532]

Seven French frigates with 32 transports were about six leagues off Guernsey when a privateer captured two of them and brought them to Guernsey before August 14.

They had the enemy signals on board. It was generally believed that the French were preparing to attack Jersey or Guernsey.[533]

The French frigate *Résolu* captured a large transport ship, a brig laden with stores, and a brig bound from Madeira to Québec with wines which she brought in with her on Saturday, August 18.[534]

Captain Cadogan's HMS *Licorne* and Captain Perkins's tender schooner *Punch* returned to Kingston from cruises on Sunday, August 19. The *Licorne* brought in a French brig, part of the homeward-bound convoy to Saint-Domingue. She was laden with sugar and was taken out of a harbor near Cape François by the *Licorne*'s boats.[535]

The French frigates *Hermione* and *Astrée* captured Captain Cobb's *Lockhart Ross* before August 20. She was bound from Québec to Cork and taken to Boston.[536]

The French privateer *Le Chardon* captured and ransomed the following vessels before August 20, 1781:

- Captain Lipson's *Tryal* for £450;
- Captain Lawrence's *Speedwell*, bound from Workington to Dublin, for 300 guineas;
- Captain Mortimer's *John*, bound from Liverpool to Penzance, for 550 guineas;
- Captain Watson's *John*, bound from Wexford to Whitehaven, for 300 guineas;
- Captain Alexander's *Johnson*, bound from Liverpool to Cork, for £300;
- Captain Hodgson's *Elizabeth*, bound from Neverstone to Newham, for 280 guineas;
- Captain Peters's *Hope*, bound from Cardiff to Dublin, for £100;
- Captain Man's *Jane*, bound from Cork to Liverpool;
- Captain Dawson's *James and Ann*, bound from Wicklow to Bardskay, for 200 guineas;
- Captain Bonow's *Molly*, bound from Alverstone to Cardiff, for 200 guineas;
- Captain Huddeston's *Powel*, bound from Dublin to Whitehaven, for £200;
- Captain Bell's *James and Ann*, from Maryport to Newry, for 100 guineas;
- Captain Richards's *Speedwell*, bound from Guernsey to Crecton, for £500;
- Captain Walters's *George*, from Ulverstone, Tasmania, for 375 guineas;
- Captain Cunningham's *Molly and Betty*, bound from Newbury to Chester, for £130.[537]

The HMS *Solebay* captured Master Jean B. Bublel's lugger the *Aimable Elizabeth*, bound from Lorient to Philadelphia with dry goods and wine, and brought her to New York between August 11 and 22.[538]

The French and Spanish captured about 30 British ships near the English Channel before August 22.[539]

A 40-gun British ship captured the French ship *Marquis de Lafayette* off Cape Clear after an engagement of three hours before August 25 and before two 74-gun ships came up. The French ship was bound from France to America with clothing.[540]

Count de Grasse's fleet of 28 ships-of-the-line captured a packet from Charleston with Lord Rawdon on board before August 26.[541]

The French privateer *Duc de Nivernois*, carrying 16 guns, 9- and 12-pounders, and full of men, was sunk within three leagues of Aberdeen in an engagement with Captain Johnson's privateer *Mansfield* about August 28. All the crew were drowned except for five men who were taken up with great difficulty by a boat from the *Mansfield*.[542]

Captain Buchannan's privateer ship *Goodrich*, belonging to Messrs. Shedden and Goodrich, took the schooner *Industry* bound from North Carolina to Boston in latitude 36.28 on Monday, August 27. A French fleet of 11 vessels chased the *Goodrich* and brought her to. The *Industry* arrived at New York during the week of September 2.[543]

The 32-gun French privateer ship-of-war *Sartine* took 15 prizes in the Irish Channel in the course of three months, June to September 1781. The prizes were ransomed or sent to French ports.[544] The French frigate *Amphitrite* arrived in Brest Road with an eight-gun English privateer in early September.[545]

Two French men-of-war took the HM Frigate *Crescent* and her prize, a Dutch frigate (the *Castor*?), and brought them to Lorient before September 1, 1781.[546]

The HM Frigate *Assurance*, of 44 guns and 10 carronades, from Halifax, and Captain Douglass's 50-gun *Chatham* had a severe engagement with the 32-gun (26 of them 18-pounders) French frigate *Magicienne* at the entrance of Boston harbor on Saturday morning, September 1. The *Magicienne* was arriving from Piscataqua (Portsmouth, New Hampshire), convoying the *Marie-Françoise*. She was obliged to strike her colors after a conflict of nearly 1½ hours at half pistol range. She had 60 men killed and more than 40 wounded. The *Chatham* had two men killed and six wounded. Both ships were badly damaged. The *Marie-Françoise* reached Alderton Point, at Hull, Massachusetts, that evening.[547]

Before September 3, the Jamaica convoy captured the large French ship *Marquis de Lafayette*, armed *en flute* and laden with clothing for the Continental Army. Admiral Darby's fleet took the 18-gun St.-Malo privateer *Le Frederick* and the French brig *Voyageur*, from Bayonne, and sent them to Plymouth.[548]

The HMS *Zebra* fell in with a fleet of French ships-of-the-line and frigates 60 leagues off the Virginia Capes on Monday, September 3.[549]

A small victualing sloop which sailed from Rhode Island with Admiral de Barras's fleet returned to Providence on Wednesday evening, September 12. Her rudder and sails were damaged and she was unable to keep up with the fleet. She lost sight of them in the evening of September 4. They captured two transports bound from Charleston to New York with some soldiers and a number of women and children on board.[550]

Captain Stanhope's HM Frigate *Pegasus* fell in with a French fleet of about 12 ships-of-the-line and several vessels under their convoy heading toward Virginia on Tuesday, September 4. Captain Stanhope, having seven vessels under convoy, made the signal for them to disperse, which they did immediately. Three of the vessels were captured.[551]

Battle of the Chesapeake

While General George Washington was marching south on Thursday, August 30, Admiral François Joseph Paul Comte de Grasse arrived in the Chesapeake Bay with his entire fleet of 24 ships of the line. He debarked 3,000 French troops a few days later to join General Marie-Joseph du Motier, Marquis de Lafayette.

General Charles Cornwallis wrote a coded message to General Henry Clinton on August 31, telling him that he could clearly see the sails of about 40 enemy vessels between Cape Charles and Cape Henry off the Virginia coast, "mostly ships of war and some of them very large." Clinton responded that he would try to help Cornwallis, either by sending reinforcements or by mounting a diversion. Clinton decided he could not send reinforcements until the Royal Navy could transport them or protect them on the long march overland. He decided to mount a diversion instead. He sent Benedict Arnold on a raid on Fort Trumbull in New London and on Fort Griswold in Groton, hoping this would convince General Washington to keep troops in New England rather than move them south.

Admiral Thomas Graves, the British naval commander in New York, meanwhile had put out to sea in late August with 19 ships-of-the-line, hoping either to intercept Admiral Louis, Comte de Barras's squadron or to block de Grasse's entry into the Chesapeake. He failed to find de Barras, and, when he arrived off Hampton Roads on September 5, he found de Grasse already in the bay.

When Graves saw the French ships coming out past Cape Henry, he ordered his fleet to reverse their order in the battle line. Admiral Samuel 1st Viscount Hood, who preceded the fleet, now occupied the rear. He assumed that Graves would attack the French, who had not yet formed for battle. Graves delayed for an hour, giving de Grasse time to finish drawing up his battle line. Around mid-afternoon, Graves ordered the attack.

De Grasse knew that Admiral de Barras was on his way from Newport to the Chesapeake with General Jean Baptiste Donatien de Vimeur Comte de Rochambeau's siege artillery. He could not let the British fleet intercept him, but he had to wait for the tide to turn. When the tide turned, around noon, de Grasse ordered his ships to prepare for battle.

The French, who had more ships and greater firepower, sallied forth to meet Graves. The action commenced at 4:15 PM and continued for two hours. Both fleets had almost ceased firing, except for some ships to the leeward, about 6:30 PM, and they were edging southward. The firing ceased on both sides at 7 PM. Both fleets were badly damaged in the inconclusive engagement. The British suffered more damage because the French had greater firepower. The British lost the only vessel sunk in the battle—the 74-gun *Thunderer*, which sank two days later.

The action had not resumed by 6 AM the following morning and a British frigate chased the privateer ship *Marquis de Lafayette* which soon lost sight of the fleets. The *Marquis de Lafayette* returned to Newport on Tuesday, September 11. For all practical purposes, the victory lay with the French. While the fleets maneuvered at sea for five days following the battle, de Barras's squadron slipped into the Chesapeake, and the French and Continental troops got past the British fleet into the James River. Then, de Grasse returned to the Chesapeake on Monday, September 10, where he joined de Barras's squadron with several heavy cannon and tons of salt beef aboard his ships. The combined French fleet now numbered 35 ships-of-the-line.

Graves thought the enemy now had "so great a naval force in the Chesapeake that they [were] absolute masters of its navigation." He turned to Admiral Hood, his second-in-command, for advice. Hood replied, "Sir Samuel would be very glad to send an opinion, but he really knows not what to say in the truly lamentable state we have brought ourselves." Graves decided his only alternative was to bring his "shattered fleet" to New York to refit. The Battle of the Chesapeake confirmed French command of the Chesapeake and sealed the fate of Cornwallis's army.[552]

The South Carolina frigate *South Carolina* took the privateer *Alexander* off Dogger Bank on Thursday, September 6. The *South Carolina* carried 40 guns, 20 of which were French 36-pounders, equal to English 42-pounders. Her quarter guns were French 12-pounders. She had a crew of 556 men and was laden with a large quantity of plate, clothing, arms, and military accoutrements for 30,000 land troops. She also had 26 passengers, including some members of Congress. She sailed from the Texel on August 13 and captured and burned a cutter from Berwick a few days before she took the *Alexander* (c. September 2, 1781). She took eight of the *Alexander*'s crew on board and put 26 French soldiers with an officer, a Whig prize master and mate on board.[553]

Captain Stanhope's HM Frigate *Pegasus* fell in with several French men-of-war less than 60 leagues from the Chesapeake Bay on September 6 and 7.[554]

A British man-of-war captured a 44-gun French ship bound from Martinique to Nantes and sent her to Lisbon before September 8. Upon request from the French ministry, the Portuguese laid an embargo on the French ship.[555]

Captain Biggs's HMS *Amphitrite* and Captain Rogers's *General Monk* captured an American prize on Saturday, September 8. Captain de la Peyrouse's *Astrée* chased them the following day and recaptured the prize.[556]

The Spanish made several unsuccessful sallies on the island of Minorca before the Duc de Crillon, a French general in the Spanish service, landed on the island with 8,000 Spanish troops. They took possession of it except for the Citadel (St. Phillips), to which the enemy withdrew, on Thursday, September 11. They captured three British frigates and more than 100 merchantmen and privateers along with all sorts of provisions and merchandise.[557]

A fleet of about 90 French merchant vessels arrived at Martinique under convoy of two frigates on Monday, September 17. On their 18-day passage, they captured a 44-gun British man-of-war and two sloops and brought them to Martinique.[558]

Two English custom house cutters took Robert Burnet's Dunkirk cutter mounting 18 9-pounders and brought her to Poole during the week of September 23. As the Dunkirk cutter was too fast and of superior strength to either of the British cutters, the British formulated the following stratagem: the smaller revenue cutter would head toward the Frenchman and the other would give chase, firing her bow chases, at intervals, loaded only with powder. When Captain Burnet noticed the largest cutter had a union flag flying, he headed to give protection to the one she chased. He was astonished to find one cutter firing a broadside on his bow and the other on his quarter. Finding all resistance ineffectual, he ordered his colors to be struck.[559]

Captain Luke Ryan's privateer *Tartar* took a large French merchant ship and brought her to Beaumaris before September 27. She was bound from France to the West Indies.[560]

Captain Falkner's privateer *Seven Sisters* arrived at St. Mary's, Scilly with the French ship *Aimable Marie* on Thursday, September 27. She was bound from La Rochelle to the West Indies with bale goods. She separated from the convoy in a storm on September 23 and had to throw part of her cargo overboard to keep from sinking.[561]

The St.-Malo frigate *Aigle* took three British ships belonging to the Québec fleet before September 29. One was the *Admiral Rodney*, another the *General Vaughan*.[562]

Captain Man's HMS *Cerberus* captured the French privateer *Duc de Rettisac*, of 26 6-pounders and 116 men, and sent her to Plymouth before September 29.[563]

Before October 2, 1781, a British frigate captured a French privateer of 24 guns and 150 men after a smart engagement. The Jersey privateers *Fox* and *Tartar* also captured two large French merchant ships. They were bound from La Rochelle to Saint-Domingue with bale goods and were part of a fleet of 20 vessels which sailed under convoy of four ships-of-the-line but became separated.[564]

Captain Waters's Crown privateer *Nancy* captured the French privateer *Dalon* and brought her to Waterford by October 6. The *Dalon* carried 14 guns, 6- and 9-pounders, 90 men, and seven hostages.[565]

Captain Duncan's HMS *Medea*, returning to England from New York, fell in with commander Edward M'Carty's privateer brig *Black Princess* in latitude 50.26 N longitude 11 W on October 9. After a five-hour chase and firing several shots which carried away her main topmast, the *Black Princess* struck. She carried 26 guns, 24 of which were 9-pounders, the other two 12-pounders, and a crew of 179 men. She threw 22 of her guns overboard in an attempt to escape. Her crew was committed to prison in England. The *Black Princess* is referred to as a French privateer, but she was one of Benjamin Franklin's privateers.[566]

Before October 13, two Jersey privateers took a large French ship bound from Nantes to the West Indies with bale goods. The HM Frigate *Carysfort* took a large ship and brought her to Sandy Hook. She was bound from Boston to Martinique with masts, some of them large enough for 74-gun ships. She also took a ship bound from Cadiz to Boston. The privateer *Sea Dragon*, belonging to Seaford, captured a French lugsail privateer. She had just taken a corn vessel bound to London and ransomed her for 1,000 guineas.[567]

Commodore Johnstone's British fleet fell in with six Dutch East India ships off the Cape of Good Hope on the way to St. Helena on Sunday, October 14. The fleet captured five of the homeward-bound Dutch ships and the French frigate *Monsieur*, which convoyed them along with a 64-gun ship. They burned one of the vessels. The ships had an estimated value of £100,000 each.[568]

Captain Folger's schooner *Antelope* arrived at Baltimore on October 15 and reported that the French and Spanish fleets commanded by the Comte de Guichen and Don Luis de Cordova were cruising between Ushant and Cape Clear. The fleet of 48 ships-of-the-line had taken a number of rich British merchantmen from the West Indies.[569]

The 18-gun privateer *Squirrel* captured a small French privateer lugger, mounting eight 6-pounders and six swivels, off Scilly before October 16. The privateer had just taken a coasting vessel and ransomed her for 60 guineas.[570]

Before October 18, two English cruisers captured two French vessels of 500 tons each laden with clothing for the French troops in the West Indies. They sailed under a convoy of a 40-gun frigate and were taken the day after they sailed from France. The frigate returned to La Coruña in a shattered condition after engaging one of the British cruisers·

The 18-gun English privateer *Amazon* and the 12-gun privateer *Jason* captured the 40-gun French frigate *La Bellipotent* after an engagement of 1½ hours and brought her to Madeira in such a shattered condition that she could barely stay afloat.[571]

The South Carolina navy frigate *South Carolina* had several problems with her crew after she sailed to La Coruña. There were a series of desertions, including one that involved the French sailors stealing a jolly boat and rowing to shore under a hail of musket fire. Commodore Alexander Gillon had to quell a mutiny of his French sailors and Luxembourg marines at La Coruña and some of his men were seriously wounded. He rebuilt his crew with Irish deserters from the Spanish Army and sailed from Spain on October 17. He captured the *Venus* near the Madeira Islands on Saturday, October 21. The *Venus* was bound from Newfoundland to Lisbon with 1,600 quintals of saltfish. She was slower than the *South Carolina*, so Commodore

Gillon ordered her towed behind the frigate. He also placed the French crew that had mutinied in La Coruña on board the *Venus*.

The *South Carolina* then sailed to St. Croix and toward Charleston in December. Commodore Gillon did not know whether the city was still in British hands or not and decided to risk taking a look. The *South Carolina* sailed past Sullivan's Island and entered the harbor on December 31. When she saw three British men-of-war approaching, she left by way of the south channel and headed south toward a Spanish port.[572]

The Comte de Grasse's squadron, in the Chesapeake Bay for the siege of Yorktown, captured the following prizes:

• the *Cormorant*, of 13 guns and 130 men;
• the *Queen Charlotte*, of 13 guns and 50 men;
• the *Sandwich*, of 12 guns and 119 men;
• the *Good Intent*, of 10 men;
• the *Worthy*, a pretended flag with six men on board;
• the *Loyalist*, of 24 guns;
• the HM Frigate *Iris*, of 32 guns;
• the HM Frigate *Richmond*, of 32 guns;
• a sloop, of 100 men;
• two transports with provisions and stores.[573]

Admiral de Grasse's fleet captured Admiral Rodney's HMS *Sandwich* and two 74-gun ships with a convoy of 35 vessels bound from the West Indies to Europe. They were taken to Brest.[574]

The French frigates *Hermione*, *Surveillante*, and another vessel captured the *Phillip* bound from Porto to New York with a cargo of wine, oranges, and lemons and a large quantity of delicacies and dried preserves. Captain de Latouche gave his officers a large portion of the boxes and kept most of them in reserve as gifts for captains of the fleet and his lady friends.[575]

The French fleet captured a vessel bound from Bristol to Cork on Saturday, November 3, 1781 and sent her to France.[576]

The French captured the HMS *Iris*, in company with the *Richmond* and the *Guadeloupe*, on November 10. The *Iris* was an American-built vessel, called the *Hancock*, and taken by the 44-gun HMS *Rainbow* July 7–8, 1777. She was a fast sailer and had taken so many prizes in America that the officers all made fortunes.[577]

Captain John Bazeley's HMS *Amphion* captured a French brig with clothing for the Continental Army and sent her to Sandy Hook, where she arrived on Wednesday, November 28. The HMS *Centurion* captured a small French brig bound from New London to Philadelphia with provisions before November 29.[578]

Captain Lutwidge's HMS *Perseverance* captured M. de Chabond's French cutter *Alart*, carrying 18 guns (12 18-pounders, two 9-pounders, and four 6-pounders) and 124 men, after an 18-hour chase and sent her to New York on Wednesday, December 12, 1781. She formerly belonged to Liverpool and was bound from Rhode Island to Martinique.[579]

France decided, in the summer of 1781, to send reinforcements of ships and supplies to Admiral François de Grasse who was then in the West Indies. However, the supplies and transports could not be gathered until the end of the year. Rear Admiral Luc Urbain de Bouexic, the Comte de Guichen, and his fleet of 12 ships-of-the-line would accompany this convoy until it was past the Bay of Biscay and would then proceed to Cadiz. The squadron had increased by five ships destined for de Grasse and another two bound for the East Indies by the time of departure on December 10.

The Comte de Guichen sailed from Brest with 1,062 soldiers and 548 sailors. They had spent several days in heavy squalls and some of the vessels lagged behind the rest of the fleet. The weather was improving rapidly as he sailed with a southeast wind. As the weather cleared, the French could see a fleet of 12 ships-of-the-line, one ship of 50 guns, four frigates, and a cutter to the windward. This was Rear Admiral Richard Kempenfelt's fleet, which had left England on December 2 in search of Guichen and his convoy.

The HMS *Victory* sighted a frigate 159 miles west of Ushant soon after daylight on Wednesday, December 12, and observed several ships-of-the-line a considerable way ahead of her at 10:30 AM. The *Victory* tried to cut them off and succeeded in part.

Guichen deployed his ships ahead and leeward of the convoy. As Kempenfelt's fleet attacked, the vessels of the convoy dispersed in all directions. When the *Victory* got among the convoy, the 84-gun French ship *Triomphant*, which had kept up with them, bore down to join their squadron. She passed close to the *Edgar*, the leading British ship, and gave her a smart raking fire which had little effect. The *Edgar* responded with a broadside to the enemy's stern.

The 74-gun *Active* defended the lagging vessels and fought the British for 1½ hours before they captured 14 French vessels, mostly supply ships. They could not take possession of all of them as evening and stormy weather were approaching. They captured 15 prizes that had a considerable value in financial terms but were even more important in naval and military terms. The captured ships were chiefly laden with artillery and ordnance and had more than 900 troops on board. They included:

- Lieutenant Pierre Scolan's 350-ton frigate *Emilie*, carrying 31 sailors, 149 soldiers, including a colonel and a lieutenant of infantry, and a cargo of 10,000 bullets, bar iron and brass, sailcloth, threads, and 16 pieces of cannon. She was taken to Portsmouth.

- Sieur le Coudrais's 390-ton *Guillaume Tell*, carrying 33 seamen and a cargo of bullets, soldiers' uniforms, accoutrements, flints, grenades, bombs, 535 barrels of powder, each weighing 200 pounds, bar iron, rum, and provisions.
- Jacques François Brisson's 160-ton *Sophia*, carrying 22 seamen and loaded with biscuits, 8-inch bombs, grenades, 29 chests of arms, provisions, cordage, and sailcloth. These ships were from Brest and taken to Portsmouth.
- Lieutenant Sieur Videaux's 300-ton *London*, carrying 48 seamen and 201 soldiers and a cargo of sheet lead, several chests of small arms, ammunition for the artillery, soldiers' uniforms, bales of cloth, four months of provisions for the soldiers and six for the seamen, and some merchandise for a private account.
- Lieutenant Sieur Pomelle's 300-ton *Minerve*, carrying 38 seamen and a cargo of bombs, bullets, 55 chests of small arms, 10 cases of ammunition for the artillery, and a quantity of biscuits and merchandise for a private account. The *London* and *Minerve* were both from Brest and taken to Milford.
- The *Amitié Royal*, carrying 60 seamen and 111 soldiers, with a cargo of 230 barrels of wine, 100 barrels of beef and pork, and a great quantity of other provisions, 20 tons of ball, 150 muskets, 20 tons of musket cartridges, tents, and other military supplies. She was from Brest and taken to Tenby.
- Sieur Dupois's 600-ton *Abondance*, carrying 90 seamen and 248 soldiers and a cargo of artillery, ammunition, and provisions. She was from Brest and taken to Plymouth.
- Sieur de Sourde's 190-ton *Héros*, carrying 30 seamen and an unknown cargo. She was from Brest and taken to Plymouth.
- Sieur Jean Baptiste Tierenier 240-ton *Victoire*, carrying 21 seamen and a cargo of 350 barrels of wine, 250 half barrels of pork, and 32 pipes of brandy. She was from Brest and taken to Plymouth.
- Sieur Jacques Boutel's 500-ton *Mercure*, carrying 45 seamen, some officers, 10 valets, and a cargo of 100 bales of cloth, 150 jars of oil, 80,000 bricks, 3,500 barrels of flour, 60 barrels of wine, various merchandise, and four carronades.
- Jean Baptiste Harinondes's 400-ton *Généreux*, carrying 40 seamen, 193 soldiers, and a cargo of 100 barrels of wine, 60 barrels of flour, 30,000 bricks, wine, brandy, beef, pork, biscuit, and various other articles. She was from Brest and taken to Plymouth.
- Sieur François Carousin's 160-ton *Marguerite*, carrying 20 seamen, one officer, and a great quantity of soldiers' uniforms, wine, brandy, wet and dry provisions. She was from Brest and taken to Plymouth.
- Sieur Pierre le Vigot's 250-ton *Sophia*, with 30 seamen and a cargo of bronze cannons, bullets, cartouches, field magazines, trunks, muskets, and provisions. She was from St.-Malo and taken to Plymouth.

- The 350-ton *Africain*, carrying 40 seamen, 160 soldiers, and a cargo of 100 barrels of red wine, 12 barrels of brandy, 30 chests of firearms, and a great quantity of other provisions. She was from Brest and taken to Plymouth.

The British fleet formed a line of battle at daylight the next day, but, as the enemy force was so much superior, the British declined to engage. The *Triomphant* was seen in the French line, missing her main topmast. Captain Sir Richard Pearson's HMS *Arethusa* arrived at Spithead on Monday afternoon, December 17.

The British captured another vessel, which was sent to Falmouth. They also sank two or three French transports. They captured a total of 1,062 soldiers and 548 sailors. The remaining convoy ships were either lost or dispersed by a severe storm a few days later. Only two ships-of-the-line, the 84-gun *Triomphant* and the 74-gun *Brave*, and five transports continued the voyage to the West Indies. The others returned to Brest.[580]

A British frigate captured a brig bound from Lorient to Philadelphia with silks and other valuable dry goods and sent her to Philadelphia, where she arrived on Wednesday, December 19. The frigate parted company with a French brig laden with naval stores two days earlier. The French brig was bound from the West Indies when she was captured by Captain Ross's privateer brig *Perseverance*.[581]

The Crown privateer *Fox* took the French prize *La Marie* and brought her to Clyde before December 25. She was bound from Nantes to Saint-Domingue.[582]

1782

General Cornwallis's surrender at Yorktown did not end the war. It dragged on for another year and a half before the peace treaty was signed. John Bazeley's HMS *Amphion* captured M. de Barras's (nephew to Admiral Comte de Barras) copper-bottomed sloop-of-war *Bonetta* and sent her to New York, where she arrived on Thursday, January 10, 1782. She was captured by the French fleet in October 1781 at the surrender of Yorktown. She sailed from the Virginia Capes on January 1, 1782 with 110 French soldiers and sailors on board besides her crew. The French troops on board had been left in the hospitals at Yorktown when the Comte de Grasse's fleet sailed for the West Indies. The *Bonetta* was bound from Martinique to deliver those troops and was taken off Cape Hatteras on January 3.[583]

A 50-gun French frigate was chasing a British ship off the back part of Guernsey and captured her before January 7. The frigate was bringing her prize to Betancos (Betanzos, Spain). In the strong wind, she ran on a rock with such force that she broke apart in half an hour in sight of the people on shore. The prize was taken into the harbor. Another French ship, which was in company, took up part of the crew; the rest drowned.[584]

The Crown frigate *Stag* took the very successful French privateer *Terror of England* before January 8.[585]

A French fleet of 10 ships-of-the-line captured Captain Christie's 50-gun HMS *Hannibal* off the north end of Sumatra on January 17 or 18. The British fleet only numbered eight ships-of-the-line.[586]

Crown forces captured four large French merchantmen bound from Saint-Domingue to Nantes and brought them to Newfoundland before January 23.[587]

A French brig captured the HMS *Greyhound*, with Lord Charles Cornwallis on board, off the coast of Scilly before January 24. The captain of the brig took out several English sailors into his own vessel and put eight Frenchmen and a prize master into the *Greyhound*, with directions to head to the first French port. Before they came near the French coast, a violent storm arose and the vessel was in danger of being lost. Lord Cornwallis proposed to the master to restore the ship to the command of the Englishman, pledging his honor that it would be returned. The Frenchmen complied and the vessel was brought to Torbay where Captain McBride received Lord Cornwallis. The *Greyhound* was returned to the Frenchmen.[588]

The Boston privateer *Renown*, carrying 14 9-pounders and 65 men, captured Captain McEvers's ship *Venus*, bound from New York to Lisbon, and sent her to Martinique before January 26.[589]

A French privateer entered the port of Luanco with a captured British frigate on Sunday, February 17, 1781. The prize, which formerly belonged to the Dutch, was headed to Gibraltar with provisions.[590]

John Gerardeau, a French gentleman from the east end of Long Island, sailed from Baltimore on Monday, February 18, in a small schooner called the *Sally*. She was loaded with 80 barrels of flour for Yorktown. The next day, the New York vessels *Jack-o'-Lanthorn*, carrying 20 men and three guns, and the *Sukey*, carrying 30 men and four guns, took her off the horse shoe near Yorktown. Mr. Gerardeau had only two men besides himself in his schooner. They were taken on board the privateers and replaced by two crewmen from the privateers with orders to proceed to New York.

En route, one of the privateer's crewmen ordered the Frenchman to do some business aloft, but he did not understand him; neither did he understand the duty of a seaman. The privateer's man began to beat him with a rope's end for disobedience. The Frenchman picked up a club and knocked the man over. The helmsman ran toward him with the tiller, but the Frenchman evaded him by dodging around the mast, gave him the first blow, and threw him overboard. He regained control of the vessel. Being ignorant of navigation, he headed before the wind and ran on a shoal on the back of Long Island at night. He made a fire as a signal and was taken off by a whaleboat in the morning. His vessel was beaten to pieces by the sea.[591]

Captain Chenard's St.-Malo privateer *Duc de Chartres* took the *Pallas*, of about 350 tons, from New York on Wednesday, February 20, and brought her to Brest.[592]

The HMS *Garland*, *Amphion*, and *Centurion* captured the French armed ship *Persévérance* and sent her to New York where she arrived on February 22. She was bound from Cape François to France with 200 hogsheads of sugar, 200,000 pounds of coffee, and cotton. She was one of 150 vessels which sailed from Cape François on January 13 under convoy of six ships-of-the-line.[593]

A Dunkirk privateer captured the *Nelly*, from Tortola and Cork. She was ransomed for 5,000 guineas and arrived at Milford before February 26.[594]

The Jersey privateer *Sprightly* took the French ship *Elizabeth* and brought her to port on March 1, 1782. She was bound from Nantes to Saint-Domingue with 4,000 muskets, 16 barrels of gunpowder, and other stores. She was one of the convoy that sailed from Nantes on February 28.[595]

The French frigate *Eméraude* arrived at Newport on Tuesday, March 26, after a 42-day passage from France. She sailed in company with a fleet of 150 vessels bound to the West Indies. Seven of them were ships-of-the-line. The *Eméraude* brought about £80,000 in specie to pay the French troops. She retook three prizes and attempted to get into the Chesapeake Bay with them, but she was chased by a British 64-gun ship which was up the bay under French colors. She sank her prizes after taking out some of the most valuable articles. One of the prizes was said to be worth £10,000. She then attempted to get into the Delaware Bay but was prevented by a British 54-gun ship and some frigates in the river. She then headed to Rhode Island.[596]

The 50-gun *Jupiter* and the 32-gun *Mercury*, part of Commodore Johnstone's British squadron, took a 13-gun French privateer off Beachy Head and sent her to Gosport before March 11.[597]

The French privateer *Madame* captured Captain Gibbons's *Sandy Point* before March 15. She was one of the last outward-bound vessels of the West India fleet. *La Madame* also took three other vessels belonging to the same fleet.[598]

Commander Kergorica de Emmaria's French frigate *Sybil* took the New York privateer brig *Delight* in the Chesapeake Bay on Friday, March 22. She arrived at New York the week of April 1, 1782.[599]

A French frigate carried the privateer *Swiftsure* to Toulon before March 28. She was wholly manned by Irish and had five men killed and 15 wounded.[600]

A French frigate captured a Crown privateer in the Chesapeake Bay before April 6, 1782. The French frigate had her guns housed and was mistaken for a merchantman. The privateer did not realize her mistake until it was too late. After exchanging the privateer's crew, the French sent her off on another cruise.[601]

Before April 8, the French frigate *Sybil* took the New York privateer brig *Lark* in the Chesapeake Bay. The *Lark* carried eight 6-pounders and 24 men, and was brought to Yorktown.[602] Several French and Dutch vessels were captured near Jersey and sent to different ports. Two French lugsail privateers took three vessels bound from Dublin to Bristol and Liverpool. One was taken to Havre de Grace (Le Havre) and the other to Dunkirk. The privateer *General Conway* captured a large Dutch ship off Jersey. She was bound from St.-Malo to Amsterdam with bales of silk and other goods and two French families and their effects. She was taken to Jersey along with a small French sloop which was in company.[603]

Captain Moore's Dublin privateer *Fame* captured two French vessels bound from Marseilles to Saint-Domingue on the Forehand, on the Barbary coast, before April 8. They were Captain Fougne's *Marianna Wype* and Captain Bernard's *Activité*. Their cargoes were valued at 8,000 livres each. The *Fame* captured two more of the five vessels which sailed from Marseilles together.[604]

A 36-gun French frigate sailed from Brest in company with about 40 transports and some men-of-war. She retook three brigs on the New York coast that had been captured by Loyalist men-of-war and privateers. As they were of little value, the crews were taken out of the vessels which were scuttled and sunk before April 16.[605]

Before April 16, the French frigate *Sybil* took Captain Jesse Turner's New York privateer *Trimmer*, of eight 6-pounders and 24 men, and brought her into the York River.[606] The British man-of-war *Agamemnon* captured some French transports with cables and cordage sufficient to completely equip six ships-of-the-line. They also captured 4,000 complete soldiers' uniforms, some wine and flour.[607]

Captain Maitland's 90-gun *Queen* came up with and captured the 64-gun *Actionnaire*, armed *en flute*, on Tuesday night, April 16. She was bound for the East Indies with 11 chests of Dutch money and masts for three 74-gun ships.[608]

Captain Collins's *Aeolus* took Sieur Dugue de Laurest's French privateer ship *Aglae*, from St.-Malo, off Cape Cornwall on Thursday, April 18 after a chase of eight hours. She carried 20 guns, 6- and 9-pounders, and 121 men. She had been out six days and had not taken anything.[609]

Mona Passage

Admiral Sir Samuel Hood separated from the fleet with 10 ships-of-the-line, a frigate, and a fireship at 2 PM on Thursday, April 18. A lookout sighted five ships in the Mona Passage (between the Dominican Republic and Puerto Rico) at 6 AM the following morning, and Admiral Hood gave the signal for a chase at 6:30. The 74-gun *Valiant* and the 64-gun *Belliqueux* caught up with the French ships at 2 PM and, after a short engagement, captured the 64-gun ships *Caton* and *Jason*, the 32-gun frigate *Aimable*, and the 18-gun sloop *Cérès* on Friday, April 19. These ships had escaped through the Mona Passage only the day before. Sir James Wallace's *Warrior* was left within gunshot of the *Astrea*, which mounted 44 18-pounders on one deck. They continued to chase after another frigate, which escaped in the night.[610]

Vice Admiral Barrington's HMS *Britannia* and his British fleet chased a French fleet at 3 PM on Saturday, April 20, about 23 leagues off Ushant. At 12:45 AM, Captain Jarvis's 80-gun HMS *Foudroyant* engaged the French commodore's 74-gun and 700-man ship *Pégase* for between three-quarters of an hour to an hour and a half. When Captain Jarvis's *Foudroyant* came alongside her, the *Pégase* surrendered.

Captain Jarvis was slightly wounded in the hand in the close engagement. The *Pégase* was convoying a fleet of 18 vessels laden with stores, provisions, and ammunition, in company with the 74-gun *Protecteur*, the 32-gun *Andromache* and the two-decker *Auctionnaire*, armed *en flute*. They left Brest on April 19 and were bound to Isle de France.

The *Pégase* arrived at Spithead and the following prize vessels arrived at Plymouth:

- *La Fidélité* with 187 troops and stores;
- *La Bellone* with 147 troops and stores;
- *La Lionne* with 180 troops and stores;
- *Le Duc de Chartres* with stores and arms.[611]

Captain Conway fell in with the 14-gun French lugger *Le Barnadine* about 10 leagues south of Scilly on Tuesday, April 23. He took her and retook a 10-ton Scottish lugger which she had captured.[612]

Admiral Barrington fell in with another outward-bound French fleet of men-of-war and transports on Thursday, April 25. He took four ships-of-the-line, three frigates, and 17 other vessels with stores and troops.[613]

The Weymouth privateer *Surprize* took the 200-ton French transport *Henry* before May 15, 1782. She was bound from Brest to the Isle of Rhee with cannons, 200 tons of gunpowder, and ammunition. She was intended to go under convoy with 34 other vessels bound to the East Indies. She had on board 100 officers and soldiers or sailors who were taken to Weymouth.[614]

Captain Newel's HMS *Princess Caroline* and the HMS *Zebra* fell in with and took the large French privateer *Tartar* from Port-au-Prince about May 25. She was quite new, mounted 24 guns, and had a crew of 200 men when she sailed. But, having manned three small prizes taken in her six-week cruise, her crew consisted of 180 men when she was taken. All but three or four were put aboard the British ships, and between 60 and 70 British sailors were put on board the *Tartar*. The following day, a violent gust of wind overset her and she sank off Tybee in seven fathoms of water. Most of the crew were below and were immediately drowned. Others saved their lives by clinging to the upper parts of the masts and rigging. Of these, 14 made a sort of raft and pushed off from the wreck and probably landed somewhere near Beaufort, South Carolina.[615]

The French frigate *Hermione* sailed from Newport on June 16 to convoy, from Dartmouth, a prize Irish brig which she had taken on her cruise prior to her engagement with the HMS *Iris*. The prize arrived at Newport on Friday, June 23.[616]

Captain Ingersoll, on his outward-bound journey from Salem, Massachusetts, in a four-gun letter of marque brig, took a sloop laden with naval stores and brought her to Cape François where she was sold.

On his homeward-bound journey, Captain Ingersoll took two vessels before June 20. One was bound to Long Island with lumber; the other was a small sloop loaded with rum and sugar. She was retaken in sight of a New York privateer, carrying eight carriage guns and a crew of 20, which had taken her earlier. After manning these two prizes, Captain Ingersoll had only four crewmen left. He gave chase to the privateer in order to deceive her regarding the weak state of his vessel. His ruse succeeded and the privateer sailed away, leaving Captain Ingersoll to proceed to port with his prizes.[617]

The combined French fleet met a British fleet of 18 vessels in latitude 47.36 N and 15.20 W on Tuesday, June 25. The fleet was escorted by the 50-gun HMS *Portland*, the 32-gun *Oiseau*, the 24-gun *Danae*, and the sloop *Merlin*. It was destined for Québec and Newfoundland. The French ships took the 18 vessels but could not come up with the ships that convoyed them.[618]

Captain Edward Pellew's HMS *Artois* was sailing down the coast of Ireland, headed to Dublin, on Sunday, June 30. She sighted a cruiser in the southeast quarter about 14 leagues south by west of Dublin at noon and immediately gave chase. The cruiser hoisted French colors at 5 PM and fired a few stern chases. Finding the *Artois* was almost alongside her, she struck her colors. She proved to be the *Prince de Robecq*, carrying 22 12- and 9-pounders and 173 men under Lieutenant de Frégate M. Pierre Vanstable. She was almost new and had been 12 days out of Dunkirk but had taken nothing.[619]

The French, Spanish, and Dutch fleets totaling 46 ships-of-the-line joined forces and were cruising in the English Channel where they fell in with and captured 22 out of a fleet of 26 vessels bound to Québec at the beginning of July 1782. Only four vessels escaped.[620]

The English privateer *Liverpool* took a French East Indiaman valued at £40,000 and took her to Ireland before July 3.[621] British cruisers captured two large French ships laden with tobacco and sent them to London before July 6.[622]

Captain Hall's New York privateer schooner *Surprize* took Captain Baker's Whig schooner *Luck* in latitude 36 N, longitude 60 W on Monday, July 8, and sent her to New York on Saturday, July 13. She carried four guns and 12 men and sailed from the Chesapeake Bay to Cape François in company with 16 merchantmen under convoy of the French frigate *Sybil*. She left the fleet two days after their departure.[623]

Captain McBride's *Artois* arrived at Plymouth with four prizes before Tuesday, July 16. They were part of a convoy of 23 vessels, consisting of transports full of troops, several store ships, and victuallers under the protection of the 74-gun ship *Pégase* and the 60-gun ship *Protecteur*. They were bound from Brest to the East Indies. After the vessel struck to the *Artois*, Vice Admiral Barrington chased the rest of the fleet and captured 13 of them.[624]

Captain de Montperoux's French ship *Le Dauphin Royal*, M. de Bordeleau's 50-gun *Le Sagittaire*, and M. Angle's 50-gun *Expériment* sailed from Cape François on Tuesday, July 9, and arrived at Fort Royal Bay on Sunday night, July 21. En route they captured the 20-gun Liverpool ship *Pitt* and brought her with them.[625]

A French fleet of 13 ships-of-the-line, three frigates, and a cutter sailed off Cape Henry on Sunday, July 28. Commander Elliott Salter's 36-gun HMS *Santa Margaretta* chased Vicomte Montgulote's 30-gun (12- and 6-pounders), 44-man French frigate *Amazone* at daybreak on Monday, July 29. The *Amazone* was accompanied by six large ships which veered and chased the *Santa Margaretta* until 3 PM when they tacked and headed west. Captain Salter lost sight of the large ships and pursued the *Amazone*, hoping to bring her to action. The *Amazone* also tacked to meet the *Santa Margaretta*.

The action began at 5 PM. When they came within a cable's length of each other, the *Amazone* opened fire from her starboard guns. The *Santa Margaretta* held her fire until she could rake her at the moment of veering. When the opportunity presented itself, the *Santa Margaretta* fired her starboard guns and closed to within pistol range. The action continued for 1¼ hours before the *Amazone* struck her colors. Vicomte Montgulote was killed at the beginning of the action, and the *Amazone* lost her main and mizzenmasts and had 4 feet of water in the hold.

When the British took possession of the *Amazone*, they transferred the prisoners to the *Santa Margaretta* and repaired her damage so they could get out of range of the great ships. The *Santa Margaretta* towed the *Amazone* all night. Early the following day, she saw 13 French ships-of-the-line bearing down upon her. Captain Salter transferred all his men and officers from on board the prize and would have sunk the *Amazone* if he could have removed all the prisoners. They numbered a great many, 50 of whom were badly wounded. The *Santa Margaretta*'s mast was shot through several places; the foremast and fore, main and mizzen topmasts and several of the yards were damaged, and she was hulled in several places. Every sail was unfit for service, shot full of holes, and torn in tatters. The first broadside killed midshipman Dalrymple, son of Sir John Dalrymple. The *Santa Margaretta* lost five men killed and 17 wounded. The *Amazone* lost 70 killed and more than 70 wounded. Every officer was either killed or wounded before she struck. A small breeze sprung up, preventing the British from taking possession and she escaped with much difficulty.

The British also captured:

- *Lion* of 500 tons, 10 guns, and 260 men;
- *Grand Sarpedon* of 600 tons, 10 guns, and 50 men;
- *Bellona* of 500 tons, 10 guns, and 250 men;
- *Fidélité* of 500 tons, 8 guns, and 234 men;

- *Duc de Chartres* of 350 tons, 10 guns, and 30 men;
- *Superbe* of 600 tons, 16 guns, and 60 men;
- *Honore* of 400 tons, 10 guns, and 30 men;
- *Villa Nova* of 900 tons, 20 guns, and 44 men;
- *Amphion* of 900 tons 30 guns, and 44 men;
- *Marquis de Castries* of 600 tons, 16 guns, and 30 men;
- six other vessels.

The captured soldiers belonged mostly to the Regiment de Suisse. The vessels were laden with all kinds of provisions and naval and military stores destined for Mauritius.[626]

Captain McKown's 12-gun ship *Molly* took two prizes on her passage from Liverpool to Jamaica. One was a Spanish schooner with wines, the other a brig from Bordeaux. The *Molly* ran aground on the Diamond, coming into the road to St. John's, Antigua, on Thursday afternoon, August 8, 1782. She was lost but most of her cargo was saved and her prizes got into port safely.[627]

The Comte de Vaudreuil's fleet of 13 French ships-of-the-line and four frigates from the West Indies arrived at Boston on Friday and Saturday, August 9 and 10. They brought in a retaken French frigate of 36 guns which had struck to a British 44-gun ship after a severe conflict. The British were going to burn her but were prevented from doing so by a couple of Whig frigates which came up in time. They also brought in Captain Phipps's 12-gun ship *Allegiance* bound from the Penobscot to the West Indies, the *General Greene* from New York, and three or four other vessels.[628]

The HM Frigate *Foudroyant* captured the 74-gun *Le Pégase* before August 9. She was put into commission in the British Navy at Portsmouth and the command given to Captain George Berkeley.[629]

The French frigate *Emeraude* arrived in the Chesapeake Bay from Boston about mid-August. On her passage, she took the 16-gun British sloop-of-war *Polecat*, formerly the *Navarre* of Philadelphia.[630]

The Glasgow privateer *Favourite* took a French merchant ship bound from Bordeaux to Martinique. The captain destroyed the dispatches and all his papers before he was taken and carried into the Clyde before August 19.[631]

Two French frigates captured the 50-gun *Experiment* and brought her into the Chesapeake Bay before August 29. She was a new ship.[632]

Captain Boyd's *Québec*, bound from Québec to London, took a French privateer of 13 guns and carried her to Peterhead before August 30. Also, the Liverpool privateer *Raven* took the French privateer *Mollineux*, carrying 18 9-pounders and 94 men, and took her to Scilly.[633]

The French captured three 74-gun British men-of-war and all the English companies' ships about early September 1782.[634]

A French privateer, commanded by a man known as Laughing Dick, of Essex, and his crew of 16 men, mostly English, captured a sloop off Margate at 7 AM on Monday, September 2. They brought her a few miles out to sea, put a few men on board, and sailed in search of more prizes. When she got as far as the Reculvers, a gun was fired from the fort and three armed boats, with only two rounds of ammunition, went off in an attempt to retake the sloop. The privateer, upon seeing this, hoisted all her sails and returned to take care of her prize. The boats and the privateer came up with the sloop at about the same time. A few guns were fired and the privateer, after sailing round and round her for some time, took her men out in a boat belonging to the sloop and then left. The boats immediately took possession of the sloop and brought her safely into the harbor.

The privateer came in sight again soon afterward, apparently intending to capture a vessel laden with ordnance stores a short distance from her. Three boats, well-manned and armed, went off to engage the privateer about 2 PM. They came up with her in the Queen's Channel. One of the boats exchanged a few shots with her. A British cutter appeared at 4 PM. The privateer sailed away and the boats returned safely into port.[635]

Captain Stout's Crown letter of marque *Triumph* arrived at Montego Bay on Tuesday, September 3. On his passage, Captain Stout fell in with a French brig mounting 18 guns and full of men which he engaged for three-quarters of an hour before she sheered off. The *Triumph* received little or no damage, except in her sails and rigging. The brig probably had a number of killed and wounded as her crew attempted to board the *Triumph* twice and were much exposed to the *Triumph*'s fire.[636]

Captain de Latouche Tréville's return to America

The two French frigates *Aigle* and *Gloire* were not more than about 200 leagues from the shores of North America, at 39° 10' latitude and 67° 53' longitude, the night of September 4. The lookout announced, about midnight, that he discovered a large ship which turned out to be the *Hector*, a 74-gun vessel commanded by Captain John Bourchier. The French had lost her in the battle of April 12, 1782, which is now known as the Battle of the Saints. She was the lead ship of a fleet returning to England from the West Indies. The *Gloire* fired the first shots and Captain de Latouche hurried to her assistance, but it took him more than three-quarters of an hour to get into position. Meanwhile, the *Gloire* fought the *Hector* alone.

The *Gloire* continued to maneuver to find the best position before firing her broadsides. Captain de Latouche placed himself between the two vessels about 4:15 AM and joined the fight. He thought the *Hector*'s crew was ready to board the *Aigle* so he let them because he had 500 fighting men aboard with several army officers eager for a fight. As one of the *Hector*'s yards got caught in the *Aigle*'s mizzen shrouds, Captain de Latouche fired a broadside and ordered his men to board the

Hector, which attempted to escape without firing a single shot. The vessels were so close together that the artillerists fought each other with their rammers. As the two ships separated, they renewed the combat at musket range. The *Hector's* rigging was so badly damaged that she could maneuver only with great difficulty, permitting the *Gloire* to continue fighting for almost three-quarters of an hour without receiving any return fire.

The French would have retaken the *Hector* but the lookouts discovered a number of vessels to the windward. It was the rest of the British fleet coming to the *Hector's* assistance under full sail. Captain de Latouche, according to his orders not to chase any ships and to avoid any action that would deter him from his mission, gave the signal to regroup. However, the *Gloire* was at half musket range from the *Hector*, and Captain de Vallongue considered it too dangerous to execute the maneuver which would force him to expose his stern to the large enemy vessel. He preferred to engage in combat. The *Hector* fired a volley, which the *Gloire* returned into the *Hector's* stern.

The *Aigle* lost four men killed and 13 wounded, four mortally, in the two-hour and 50-minute engagement. The *Gloire* had only two killed and two wounded. The *Aigle* received five cannonballs in her masts and 70 in her sails. The *Gloire* was hulled a few times. The sails and rigging of both frigates were damaged but not seriously enough to affect their sailing.

The *Hector* had nine men killed and 33 wounded, many of whom would die in subsequent days. She had received 85 shots in her sides in the harbor at Port Royal, Jamaica, on April 12 which were plugged up, and a number of shots in her hull in this three-hour action. Her masts were tottering, her sails were torn to shreds, and she had been hulled several times. Captain Bourchier was severely wounded in the arm and back. He attempted to sail to Halifax but the winds toppled his masts on September 17 and he lost his rudder. The officers kept the desperate crew at the pumps by force of arms for 14 days when she fell in with a privateer snow belonging to Tortola. The *Hector* foundered about 300 leagues from the shore and almost all on board perished. The surviving officers and men were forced to abandon her and seek safety. Captain McLean's HMS *Lord Hood* discovered some survivors near the Grand Bank of Newfoundland on October 3 and managed to save them at great risk. He entered the harbor of St. John's, Antigua, 10 days later and landed the *Hector's* remaining 250 crewmen who had been without water or provisions for several days.

Meanwhile, eight British ships-of-war, under Admiral Pigot, chased the *Aigle* and *Gloire* to the Delaware Capes on Thursday, September 5. They were bound from France to Philadelphia with £90,000 in cash for the French army. the British might have captured the two French frigates had it not been for the treachery of a pilot who was taken by Captain de Latouche in the *Raccoon*, a small English sloop-of-war. The *Gloire* touched ground at the Shears, but got over after receiving some damage and reached Philadelphia. The *Aigle* ran aground near the upper part of the Shears.

The passengers got on shore safely with most of the cash. Captain de Latouche, who commanded the *Aigle*, finding he could not save his ship, cut away her masts and scuttled her. But some of the British frigates raked the *Aigle* before Captain de Latouche could land his crew. The *Aigle* also had on board the crew of a New York privateer, formerly the *Charming Sally*, which she had taken in sight of the British fleet. Some of the prisoners concealed in the hold plugged the holes and prevented the vessel from sinking. She was taken to Sandy Hook where she arrived on September 24.[637]

The French frigate *Aigle* sighted land, a brig, and three ships of two and three masts Thursday morning, September 12. The *Aigle*, in company with the *Gloire*, captured the British brig of war *Raccoon*, carrying 14 guns and 72 men, near Cape James at the southern entrance to the Delaware Bay. The northwest wind forced them to tack to enter the bay. Captain de Latouche hoisted signals which he agreed upon with the coastal pilots the previous year. The entrance to the bay was filled with sandbars that marked channels of different depths. It was very risky to attempt to enter without a pilot. As night fell, about 9 PM, Captain de Latouche decided to anchor, three leagues east of Cape James. He sent his boat ashore to search for a pilot at Lewistown (Lewes, Delaware), but the wind dashed the boat against the bluff. Most of the sailors were drowned and the officer escaped with great difficulty.

Five vessels appeared to the southeast at dawn on the 13th. The wind was from the northeast. Captain de Latouche immediately set sail and rapidly approached the entrance to the bay. A British frigate and two other vessels chased the French. The *Aigle*, *Gloire*, and *Raccoon* entered under small sails and with probe in hand. Captain de Latouche soon learned that there was an excellent river pilot on board the *Raccoon*. He immediately offered the pilot 500 Louis d'or if he would take charge of the frigates and bring them to safety. He threatened to hang the pilot if they went aground.

Under instructions from the pilot, the two frigates turned around to gain entry to the correct channel but found it blocked by the British. Captain de Latouche decided to go up a channel which proved to be a dead end. The British hesitated to engage in this dangerous channel and dropped anchor to await the high tide. The *Gloire*'s boat went ashore that morning and returned with some pilots who considered the situation hopeless.

Captain de Latouche decided to put ashore the dispatches from the court, the money, and the passengers he had aboard. The *Aigle* ran aground and the outgoing tide lay her on her side, rendering her artillery useless. The frigate had to be scuttled to avoid falling into enemy hands. Captain de Latouche had the masts cut and ordered the master carpenter and master caulker to make three large holes in the hold wide enough to render the ship inoperable. An enemy frigate approached athwart the *Aigle* to cannonade her. She opened fire at 8:30 PM, killing three men and wounding five. Captain de Latouche attempted in vain to return fire with his stern chases, which fired three shots to no avail. For the safety of his crew, he ordered them to lie prone on deck and had all of the sick and wounded brought up. He thought of blowing up the *Aigle* by setting fire to the powder magazine but he decided not to do so. His boats escaped with about 40 men. Latouche and his officers were taken aboard the HMS *Vestal* and then aboard the 64-gun HMS *Lion* in the middle of the night.[638]

The officers and passengers of the two French frigates *Aigle* and *Gloire* were landed on the starboard shore of the Delaware River on Tuesday, September 17. The Baron de Vioménil sent his boats back to the frigates, about 3 leagues away, with a request to send the treasure contained in the two frigates to him. Even though they were in greater danger than before, they carried out their business with great difficulty. Two boats, containing about 100 armed Loyalists each, attempted to take those in charge of the money. They had almost taken it when the boats of the *Aigle* came up and prevented them from doing so. The Loyalists sheered off in a hurry. The money was sent to Philadelphia under the care of the aide-de-camp and six officers of the Royal Regiment of Artillery and Lauzun's Legion.[639]

The crew of a French privateer tried to get near shore within 2 miles of Galloway to seize some live cattle before September 9. They ran aground and were stuck until the privateer *Duke of Portland* and a sloop took possession of the privateer. By this time, the crew had left her. The privateer was a new vessel and carried 16 guns, 9- and 12-pounders, and was brought to Galloway.[640]

The Jersey privateers *Recovery* and *Friendly* returned to port with two prizes on September 9. One was a French ship bound from Rochelle to Amsterdam with woolen cloth and silks; the other was the *St. Adonus de Didymus*, a Spanish ship from Cadiz, with a cargo of wool and cochineal. The two prizes were worth at least £40,000.[641]

The British captured the 1,064-ton French frigate *Hébé* and brought her to Plymouth on Tuesday, September 17. She mounted 38 guns but was fit to carry 46.[642]

M. de Vaudreuil took Captain Casey's ship *Thomas* bound from the Penobscot River to Jamaica. She had a cargo of lumber and was later retaken by commander McNamara Russel's HMS *Hussar*. She was ordered to New York but was unfortunately wrecked off Cape Sable before September 19. The crew was saved but the vessel was totally lost.[643]

A privateer brig, under French colors, chased Captain Carr's *Parnassus* and captured her after a short engagement on Tuesday, September 24.[644]

British cruisers took the large French ship *Sophie*, of 24 guns and 140 men, and sent her to New York on Thursday, September 26. She was bound from France to Philadelphia with clothing for the French troops.[645]

The privateer *Comte de Vaudreuil*, from Bordeaux, took a ship bound to New York with provisions and sent her to Boston about November 1, 1782. She captured 12 other prizes during the month of October and sent them all to Boston.[646]

The HMS *Jason* took the 22-gun Whig ship *Jolly Tar* and sent her to New York on Thursday, October 3, 1782. She was bound from Baltimore to Havana with flour and tobacco under convoy of the French frigate *Emeraude*. The *Jason* also took a brig belonging to the same convoy with a similar cargo which arrived at New York on the evening of October 3.[647]

Captain de Latouche's French frigate *Hermione* captured the 11-man brig *Anna* off Ushant on Saturday, October 9. She had a cargo of sugar, rum, and Campeche wood from Jamaica. Two days later, the *Hermione* captured the four-man sloop *Marie*. She was bound to Lisbon with a cargo of dried fruit and wine from Malaga. The *Hermione* also captured the six-man brig *Pelican* on Monday, October 12. She was bound from Portugal to Newfoundland with salt.[648]

British cruisers captured two large French privateers, which had been cruising on the coast of Ireland for some time, and sent them to Waterford before October 10.[649]

Robert Steriker's Dover letter of marque *Martha* took Captain Guillaume Ripner's Dunkirk privateer *Adventurer* and brought her to Dover harbor the week of October 13. The *Adventurer* carried 10 3-pounders and 40 men. Her captain had been captured eight times during the war.[650]

Captain John Butchart's HMS *Argo* captured the French *Dauphin*, *en flute*, bound from Rochefort to Martinique on Wednesday, October 23. She mounted 32 9-pounders and had a crew of 348 men. Her cargo consisted mostly of provisions and artillery for the French islands. She also had linens and India goods on board. She was brought to Carenage, Saint-Domingue, on October 24.[651]

Before October 28, a squadron under the command of M. Suffren took Captain Cox's HM Sloop-of-War *Chacer* in the East Indies. She was believed to be bound from Bengal to Madras with money on board. Also, the East Indiaman *Chapman* captured the French transport *Oreston* in the road of Negapatam (Nagapattinam). The *Oreston* mistook it for a friendly port. She had on board the surgeon of the 50-gun *Hannibal* captured by de Suffren as well as the French Surgeon General and 14 assistants.[652]

A French privateer took Captain Season's *Dispatch* bound from London to Fowey and another ship bound from Ipswich, Massachusetts, to Plymouth, England, between Start Point and the Brawle on Sunday, November 10, 1782.[653]

The Guernsey privateer *Hannibal* captured a French packet boat before November 14. She was bound from Boston to Brest with dispatches which were thrown overboard before she struck. She was brought to Lisbon where she sank soon afterward. The crew were taken out a few minutes before she sank.[654]

The Jersey privateer *Discovery* took a large Whig prize bound from Philadelphia to Amsterdam with 540 hogsheads of tobacco, 60 barrels of rice, 30 casks of indigo, and a quantity of furs. The *Discovery* brought her to Jersey before November 16. Her captain and nine crewmen were French; the rest of the crew were from Boston.[655]

The Crown privateer *Hibernia* captured the 10-gun French privateer *Duc de Valois* with a vessel from Elsineur, Denmark, under convoy. She brought them to Sligo before November 20.[656]

Before November 22, the English *Marquis of Rockingham* and the privateer *Fly* captured the 20-gun French privateer *Marquis de Tallad* and brought her to Kinsale. Captain Zwartje's *Vreyheyd* was taken and brought to Guernsey. She was bound from St.-Malo to a Dutch port with bale goods, silks, and other valuable goods. A French ship, which sailed in company, left her as soon as she perceived the *Vreyheyd* in danger. Captain Williams's English privateer *Mercury* captured the eight-gun Dunkirk privateer *Fort Louis*. The *Fort Louis* had just taken a ship which she sent to France so Captain Williams immediately set out to search for her.[657]

In December 1782, The English privateer *Carlisle* captured the French privateer *Le Dauphin* after a smart engagement and brought her to Galway. She was a new vessel on her first cruise. She mounted 18 guns and some swivels. Also, the English privateer *Adventure* captured the French 16-gun privateer *St. Brieux* on the coast of Portugal after an engagement of one hour and brought her to St. Ubes. She was sold to an English captain who lost his ship in a recent storm. The Irish privateer *St. Patrick* picked up a large French ship at sea and brought her to Londonderry. She had 7 feet of water in her hold and jury masts. Her crew had deserted her. She had a few bags of cotton, wool, and a small quantity of indigo on board. The rest of her cargo had probably been thrown overboard.[658]

The Crown privateer *Hercules* captured the French privateer *M. de la Constantia*, of 12 guns (12- and 9-pounders), on the coast of Ireland after a smart engagement and took her to Sligo before December 3. She had on board a hostage from a vessel belonging to Limerick which she had taken the day before.[659]

The Crown privateer *Jupiter* captured a French ship from Guadeloupe with about half her lading of sugars, coffee, and indigo and brought her to Guernsey before December 7.[660]

Captain Casey's New York privateer ship *Juno* captured a brig loaded with West India produce and a French polacre from Marseilles with a cargo worth £15,000 and a number of other articles of undetermined value before December 11.[661]

Captain James Lutterell's HMS *Mediator* sighted five vessels at 7 AM on Thursday, December 12 and chased them. They formed a line of battle at 8 AM and waited for the British. Captain Baudin's 36-gun, 130-man frigate *Eugène* was the lead ship. She was bound to Port-au-Prince flying a French pendant and ensign. Next to her was a Whig brig of 14 guns and 70 men. She was flying Congressional colors. Next to her came Captain de Folligne's *Menagère*. She was a two-deck ship the length of a 64-gun ship, armed *en flute*, and flying a French pendant and ensign. She mounted 26 long 12-pounders on her main deck and four 6-pounders on her quarter deck and forecastle. She had a crew of 112 men and was laden with gunpowder, naval supplies, and bale goods for the French at Port-au-Prince. Then came Captain

Stephen Gregory's *Alexander*, carrying 24 9-pounders and 102 men, and flying a French pendant and a Congressional ensign. Captain Gregory appeared to be an Irishman, but he had a commission from Congress. Then came the *Dauphin Royal*, of 48 guns and 120 men, bound to the East Indies flying a French pendant and ensign.

The *Mediator* bore down on the French with all sails set. She received a few shots from the *Menagère's* upper deck at 10 AM and then from the rest of the line as she continued to approach. When she approached the rear of the French line, it broke. The brig and the *Dauphin Royal* sailed away from the rest. The *Mediator* bore down at 11 and cut off the *Alexander* from her consorts. The first broadside made her strike her Congressional colors. The *Menagère* and *Eugène* continued firing at the *Mediator* for some time before they sailed away. The crew of the *Mediator* boarded their prize and took out 100 prisoners.

They then chased the *Menagère* at 12:30 PM and began firing at her at 5 PM. They covered themselves with smoke to prevent the *Menagère* from aiming at their masts. They fired a few broadsides at each other at 5:30 but a sudden squall came up at 6, obliging the *Mediator* to break off the engagement to deal with the knee-deep water on deck. They began firing at each other again at 7 and continued until 9 PM when the *Menagère* yielded. The *Mediator* lost her main topgallant mast and fore-topgallant yard. The *Alexander* joined the *Mediator* at 11 PM.

At daybreak, they could see that the *Dauphin Royal* had lost her main topmast and was disabled. The brig lost all her masts except part of her lower masts. Captain Lutterell declined to pursue them because he had put 50 men on board the large ship and 20 on board the *Alexander* and had manned the Spanish prize, leaving him with only 190 men to work his ship and guard 340 prisoners.

Captain Stephen Gregory, of the *Alexander*, plotted with the prisoners to rise and take the *Mediator* at 10 PM on Saturday, December 14. However, Lieutenant Rankin, of the marines, had taken the precaution of ordering all the gratings of the hatches in the lower gun deck to be locked-down with capstan bars, leaving only enough room for one man to come up on deck at a time. The mutiny was prevented without bloodshed, as the prisoners found no passage where they could come up on deck. The *Menagère* had four men killed and seven or eight wounded. The *Alexander* had six men killed and eight or nine wounded.[662]

The privateer *Restoration* arrived at Liverpool before December 28 with a French prize bound from Cherbourg to Saint-Domingue with bale goods. She was a new vessel and carried 12 9-pounders and 40 men, two of whom were English and two Irish.[663]

The HMS *Lion*, in company with Sir Jacob Wheat's HMS *Cerberus*, captured a French brig off the Virginia Capes on Monday, December 30. She was from Martinique, loaded with West India produce. The *Lion* arrived at New York on Saturday, January 4, 1783.[664]

1783

Captain Bazely's 32-gun HMS *Amphion* and Captain Christian's 28-gun HMS *Cyclops* fell in with a fleet of French and Whig ships and other vessels on Tuesday, January 7, 1783. They took five vessels and a French corvette or sloop-of-war.[665]

The East Indiaman *Mars*, which had been equipped for war at Malaga, and the French privateer *St. Thérèse* captured the English ship *Betsey* before January 9. She mounted 24 6-pounders and was anchored under the fort of Rioush.[666]

The HMS *Amphion*, HMS *Cyclops*, and HMS *Diomede* captured Master Martinong's ship *Le Frier*, a French sloop-of-war, a Portuguese ship, and a Philadelphia-built ship on Saturday, January 11. They sailed from Cape François on December 27, 1782 in company with 20 other vessels under convoy of Captain Le Comte de Keragou de Leomaria's 36-gun French frigate *Sybil*. They separated from the *Sybil*, which was engaged with a British frigate in latitude 27 on January 2.[667] The *Amphion*, *Cyclops*, and *Diomede*, along with the *Bonetta*, captured Captain Allorme's 16-gun ship *New Polly* and the polacre *Two Brothers* bound from Cape François to the Chesapeake with cordage, rum, wine, and salt on the same day. The British frigates took the *Montague* and two other vessels from the French fleet. One of the vessels was thought to be a Whig sloop-of-war under French colors. The prizes were taken to White Stone.[667]

Captain Oliver Reed's privateer schooner *Rochambeau* retook a brig bound from Cape François to Providence and sent her to Newport on January 22. He also took another vessel bound from Antigua to Penobscot, Maine.[668]

Commander Thomas Macnamara Russell's 20-gun, 160-man HMS *Hussar* fell in with M. Le Comte de Keragou de Leomaria's French frigate *Sibyl*, carrying 350 men and 42 guns (28 12-pounders on the lower deck, eight sixes on the quarterdeck, and six sixes in the forecastle) in the Soundings at latitude 36.20 on January 22. The *Hussar* disabled the *Sybil* by carrying away her masts and bowsprit in a one-hour engagement. Captain Cotes's 50-gun HMS *Centurion* soon appeared to the windward and the HM Sloop *Tarrier* about 5 miles to the leeward. The *Hussar* came up again and renewed the action. After the third broadside from the *Hussar*, the *Sybil* was sinking. Her powder was drowned and she attempted to flee. The *Sybil* had a very large sum of money on board to pay the expenses of refitting the Comte de Vaudreuil's fleet which sailed from Boston to the West Indies. The British frigates captured between 250 and 270 French sailors.[669]

Captain Stephen Patie's *Aimable Catichette*, prize to the HMS *Amphion* and the HMS *Cyclops*, ran on shore on the back of Staten Island on Monday night, February 10. She was bound from Guadeloupe to Virginia. The captain of the *Amphion* ordered two officers and 12 men to take his prize to New York. They left three Frenchmen and the cabin boy on board.

When Captain John Storer was informed that some small craft from New York were unlading *Aimable Catichette* on Sunday, he pushed out about 8 PM with five other gunboats to try to take some of them. A gunboat with a lieutenant of the armed brig *Keppel* and 27 men was sent down from New York city to protect the vessel. The crew was overpowered and compelled to surrender after a long conflict. Captain Storer's men also took two pettiaugers loaded with West India produce at the same time. The prizes and prisoners were all taken to Brunswick before March 1.

The *Aimable Catichette* was within sight of the lighthouse at Sandy Hook at 6 PM on Saturday, February 22. The three Frenchmen, realizing they were going to be put aboard a prison ship, forced the cabin, got hold of the two officers' cutlasses and pistols, and armed themselves with a pistol in one hand and a cutlass in the other. They went up on deck where they found the lieutenant and a midshipman. Seeing the prisoners armed and threatening them with instant death, they cried quarter and were taken into the hold. Soon afterward, the Frenchmen perceived that their prisoners were working to get out of the hold. They were breaking a hole to get into the powder room in order to come out by the scuttle of that room. The French prevented this by repeated blows of the cutlasses upon the scuttle and the use of trunks put on its lid. The French took a chest of arms out of the powder room and heaved it overboard.

The captain found the currents too strong, so he ran the brig ashore at 3 AM on the 23rd. Once ashore, he hoisted the French colors and fired several shots as a sign of distress. As the hold was filling with water, the Frenchmen allowed their prisoners to come on deck but ordered them to cut down the mainmast. As they were doing so, a boat rowed toward the vessel with three Whigs aboard. One of them came on board and the other two went ashore, saying they were going to get more help to dislodge the ship and secure the British.

The same boat returned at noon with six men armed with cutlasses and guns. They joined the 14 British and attacked the three Frenchmen and took their arms from them. They then plundered and stripped them, sent them ashore, and delivered them to a British major on Staten Island who put them in a wagon, escorted by three men, to conduct them to the place of embarkation for New York where they were going to be put on a prison ship. They somehow escaped and made their way to Philadelphia before March 15.[670]

The HMS *Amphion* and the HMS *Cyclops* captured the large 16-gun French ship *Lamlaset* and the brig *Charming Betsey* bound from Guadeloupe to Virginia with rum, sugar, and coffee and sent them to New York where they arrived on Saturday, February 22.[671]

The HMS *Diomede*, HMS *Québec*, and HMS *Atalanta* captured a ship from Nantes, mounting 22 9-pounders, a ship from Bordeaux with 16 6-pounders, another ship and a brig from Bordeaux, and brought them to New York on Thursday, February 27.[672]

In early March 1783, a British cruiser captured a brig from France bound for an eastern port with a cargo of dry goods and ordered her to New York. She was retaken by some Whig prisoners on board who were joined by some of the British. They ran her ashore near Guilford, Connecticut, where her cargo was removed. The British also captured a large French ship which was retaken at Gardiner's Bay, on the east end of Long Island, and brought to New London. She was worth £80,000.[673]

Captain Leslie's 28-gun HM Frigate *Enterprize* captured the homeward-bound French East Indiaman *d'Estaing* and was towing her toward Portsmouth before March 5.[674]

The HM Frigates *Amphion* and *Cyclops* captured the 16-gun, 300-ton French ship *La Favorite* and sent her to New York on Saturday, March 22. She sailed from Bayonne, France, bound to Philadelphia with brandy, dry goods, and cordage on January 1.[675]

The HMS *Ceres* captured a sloop from Rhode Island bound to Cape François with onions and oil and brought her to St. Kitts on Thursday, March 27.[676]

The French 64-gun ship *Solitaire* fell in with Captain Collins's 64-gun HMS *Ruby* before Wednesday, April 2. They fought for 40 minutes before the *Solitaire* struck her colors. She lost a great number of men; the *Ruby* had no losses.[677]

This action marked the last of the naval engagements of the Revolutionary War, though the French would continue to fight in India until June 1783.

Though many of the skirmishes outlined above did not, in themselves, significantly alter the course of the war, the near constant activity undoubtedly kept the respective warring countries on the alert, reminding them not to be lulled into a false sense of security and requiring both the British and the French to keep their armies and navies on alert throughout the conflict—at very great expense.

CHAPTER 5

Military Aid

Tensions between Versailles and London had reached a climactic point by the summer of 1777 because the French allowed American privateers to use their ports. French military preparations were nearing completion and King Louis XVI was ready to agree to a proposal of war. However, when Vergennes approached the Spanish, he found they were less receptive to war than they were a year earlier. Spain proposed that she and France mediate the conflict between Britain and America. France, feeling abandoned by Spain and exposed to potential British retribution, banned American privateers from her ports.

News of the American victory at Saratoga in October 1777, a victory in which arms supplied by France played an important role, reached Versailles on December 3, 1777 and convinced King Louis to recognize the United States and to sign treaties with the American delegation in Paris. The Treaty of Amity and Commerce, signed on January 7, 1778, opened French ports in the Caribbean to American commerce and the French pledged to protect American commercial shipping.

The formal Treaty of Alliance, signed on February 6, 1778, pledged France's military support to the United States should hostilities commence between France and Great Britain. It also gave the French the right to conquer territory in the Caribbean. France officially recognized the United States as a sovereign nation on March 20, 1778, and a plenipotentiary was dispatched to represent France in America.

Although war between France and Great Britain formally began on July 10, 1778, following a naval skirmish between the two countries off the coast of France on June 17, many French officers had started to travel to America in 1777 with the tacit approval of King Louis and at their own expense.

Marie-Joseph Paul Yves Roch Gilbert du Motier, Marquis de Lafayette, was the most famous of these officers but he was not the first or the only one to arrive. Others who came to America in 1777 include Charles-François Sevelinges Marquis de Brétigny, Pierre Colomb, Charles-François Vicomte Dubuysson des Hays, Matthias Alexis de Roche Fermoy, René Etienne-Henri de Vic, Gayauld de Boisbertrand, Jean-Joseph Gimat de Soubadère, Jean Baptiste Gouvion, Michel-Gabriel Houdin de Saint-Michel, Jean-Baptiste-Joseph Chevalier de Laumoy, Augustin Mottin de la Balme, Luc de La Corne, Louis le Bègue de Presle Duportaïl, Louis-Pierre Penot Lombart, René Hippolyte Penot Lombart de Noirmont, Philippe François Rastel Sieur de Rocheblave, Ann-Louis Toussard, Philippe Charles Jean Baptiste Tronson du Coudray, Armand Charles Tuffin, Marquis de la Rouërie, François-Louis Teissèdre de Fleury, Pierre-Jean-François Vernier. There were many more men and officers who came in the period 1778–81. Admiral d'Estaing came with a fleet and some soldiers in 1778. Count de Rochambeau arrived with an army of about 7,000 men and navy of 5,000 men under Admiral de Ternay in 1780. More soldiers and sailors came with Admiral de Barras in 1781, as did a few regiments from the West Indies.

Brandywine

Probably the first action of the Revolutionary War that included a Frenchman occurred on July 15, 1777, when François-Louis Teissèdre de Fleury of Anthony Wayne's regiment captured the British flag at Stony Point, New York.

General William Howe left New York on Wednesday, July 23, 1777, with an army of 13,000 men on about 260 ships. After maneuvering in New Jersey, he sailed down the coast and up the Chesapeake Bay to Head of Elk (now Elkton, Maryland, a small town at the head of the Elk River), arriving on Monday, August 25.

General George Washington planned a general engagement to defend the city of Philadelphia in 1777. He placed his army at Chadd's Ford on Brandywine Creek on Tuesday, September 9, in an attempt to block General Howe's probable route from the Chesapeake Bay to Philadelphia. Because he did not have an accurate map of the area, he relied on erroneous information that there was no ford across the creek immediately to the north of his position.

Lieutenant General Wilhelm von Knyphausen marched the left of the Crown army to New Garden and Kennett Square on the afternoon of September 9, while General Charles Cornwallis moved to Hokessen's Meeting House with the right. Both joined the next morning at Kennett Square. They were within 3 miles of the Continental advance parties.

The entire Crown army advanced in two columns at daybreak on Thursday, the 11th. General Knyphausen now commanded the right, which consisted of four Hessian battalions under Major General Sterne, the first and second brigades of British, three battalions of the 71st Regiment, the Queen's American Rangers commanded by Captain James Wemys of the 40th Regiment, and one squadron of the 16th Dragoons under Major General Grant. They had six medium 12-pounders, four howitzers, and the light artillery belonging to the brigades. This column took the direct road to Chadds Ford, which is 7 miles from Kennett Square. Brigadier General William Maxwell's advance light corps engaged them on the other side of the creek and repulsed them twice and dispersed a body of 300 Hessians. These light troops were engaged with the Hessian advance parties most of the day. Nevertheless, General Knyphausen's column arrived in front of the enemy at 10 AM.

The other column, the main force of 12,500 men, under the command of Lord Cornwallis, Major General Charles Grey, Brigadier Generals Edward Mathew (often misspelled Matthews) and James Agnew, consisted of the mounted and dismounted chasseurs, two squadrons of the 16th Dragoons, two battalions of light infantry, two battalions of British and three of Hessian grenadiers, two battalions of guards, the 3rd and 4th Brigades with four light 12-pounders and the artillery of the brigades. They marched about 12 miles to the banks of the Brandywine, crossed at the first breach at Trimble's Ford and the second at Jeffrey's Ford about 2 PM, and proceeded 3 miles east, following Great Valley Road (no longer in existence). They then took the road to Dilworth to circle around the Continental right flank at Chadd's Ford in a maneuver similar to the one General Howe used on Long Island to attack Major General John Sullivan from the rear.[1]

General Washington ordered General Sullivan's, Brigadier General William Alexander's (Earl of Stirling), and Brigadier General Adam Stevens's divisions to advance and attack them about 3 PM. These divisions advanced about 3 miles and fell in with the advancing Crown forces. They engaged in a heated contest that lasted about an hour and a half without intermission, when the Continentals began to give way because many of them had expended their ammunition.

Lieutenant General Knyphausen led 5,000 men to attack the center of the Continental line. His Hessian troops met constant fire from General Washington's sharpshooters opposite the ford. British cannons opened fire at 4 PM. General Cornwallis drove the Continentals back to Dilworth, where General Sullivan regrouped his men. General Cornwallis also regrouped his men to keep up his attack, even though four of his battalions had lost their way in the thick woods between Birmingham Meeting House and Dilworth. He forced General Sullivan out of Dilworth, but General Washington brought his reserve under Major General Nathanael Greene to cover Sullivan's retreat to Chester. Fighting continued until dark.

While this action occurred on the right, the British opened a seven-gun battery on the left, opposite one of an equal number. Brigadier General "Mad Anthony" Wayne and a division of Pennsylvania troops with Brigadier General William Maxwell's light corps on the left and Brigadier General Francis Nash's brigade on the right formed the left wing. The batteries on both sides kept up an incessant cannonade that created so much smoke that the British infantry managed to cross the creek unseen and took possession of a hill opposite General Wayne. A very severe action began between the two sides. The British made several attempts to cross the low ground between them and were repulsed each time.

Toward nightfall, General Washington ordered a retreat and retired to Chester for the night. General Knyphausen took advantage of the withdrawal of the Continental troops to cross Chadd's Ford and come to General Cornwallis's assistance. After crossing the ford, Knyphausen's men encountered Cornwallis's four battalions and took them along. The two British columns met after nightfall but were too exhausted to pursue the Continentals any further. They had lost 577 killed and wounded and six missing. Hessian casualties accounted for only 40 of the total.

General Washington suffered a serious defeat but not as bad as at New York where he nearly lost his army on August 26, 1776. He had lost 11 guns, and between 1,200 and 1,300 casualties: 400 as prisoners, 300 dead, and about twice as many injured, including General Marie-Joseph du Motier, Marquis de Lafayette, who was wounded in the left thigh and needed two months to recuperate. It could have been worse. The casualties could have included General Washington, as the account below illustrates.

Major Patrick Ferguson, of the Royal Welch Fusiliers, scouting ahead of his men, heard the sound of horses' hooves and took cover, unaware at the time of the presence of Washington and Lafayette. He records:

> We had not lain long… when a rebel officer, remarkable by a hussar dress, passed towards our army within a hundred yards of my right flank, not perceiving us. He was followed by another dressed in dark green or blue, mounted on a bay horse, with a remarkably large cocked hat.
>
> I ordered three good shots to steal near… and fire at them, but the idea disgusted me. I recalled the order. The hussar in returning made a circuit, but the other passed again within a hundred yards of us, upon which I advanced from the woods towards him.
>
> On my calling, he stopped, but after looking at me, proceeded. I again drew his attention and made signs to stop but he slowly continued his way. As I was within that distance at which in the quickest firing I could have lodged half-a-dozen of balls in or about him before he was out of my reach, I had only to determine. But it was not pleasant to fire at the back of an unoffending individual, who was acquitting himself very coolly of his duty, so I let him alone.
>
> The day after, I had been telling this story to some wounded officers who lay in the same room with me, when one of our surgeons, who had been dressing the wounded rebel officers, came in and told us they had been informing him that General Washington was all the morning with the light troops and only attended by a French Officer in a hussar dress, he himself dressed and mounted in every point as above described. I am not sorry that I did not know at the time who it was.

Major Ferguson might have shot Washington and perhaps ended the war at Brandywine. Major Ferguson himself had his right elbow shattered in the battle. Ferguson modified and improved the design of a breech-loading rifle that his company of Royal Welch Fusiliers used in this battle. General Howe went on to occupy Philadelphia on September 26.[2]

A party of British light horsemen attacked two squadrons of Continental light horsemen near Philadelphia on Saturday, November 8, 1777. The British drove them, capturing a major, a French officer and some horses, and a dragoon.[3] Discounting the French Canadians involved in the siege of Québec, these were the first French to be taken prisoner. Captured officers were generally treated better than enlisted men and often paroled (given a conditional release after promising not to bear arms).

Swedesboro

In the spring of 1778, General William Howe's army needed to forage for food and supplies, which became increasingly scarce as General George Washington's army also foraged in the same areas. The fertile fields in southern New Jersey provided excellent opportunities. Lieutenant Colonel Charles Mawhood commanded one of these foraging parties comprising the 17th, 27th, and 46th British Regiments, Lieutenant Colonel John Graves Simcoe's Queen's Rangers (a mixed force of 270 Loyalist infantrymen and 30 dragoons), and the Loyalist New Jersey Volunteers.

The detachment of 1,200 to 1,300 men set out from Philadelphia and crossed the Delaware River to Salem on Thursday, March 12, to collect forage and cattle and to destroy salt works. They brought with them four cannon, two howitzers, and provisions for two weeks. Captain Charles Phipps's frigate *Camilla* provided security for six transports anchored in the Delaware River close to Salem, which Lieutenant Colonel Mawhood expected to fill with cattle, horses, and forage.

Mawhood's party landed about 6 miles from Salem at 3 AM on Tuesday, March 17, and destroyed James Smith's house at Alloway's Bridge. James Smith (son of Claudius Smith, "a notorious offender") and one Benson of Long Island had all committed many daring robberies. They were captured at the house of Nathan Miller in Smith's Clove (now Monroe, New York) on Saturday night, February 6, 1779, and jailed.

Colonel Elijah Hand hastily assembled local New Jersey militia units to oppose the raiders. One group of 300 militiamen under Colonel Asher Holmes guarded Quinton's Bridge 3 miles southeast of Salem. This was the middle of three bridges in Salem County that crossed Alloways (Alewas, Aloes) Creek, on the road that ran from Salem to the Maurice River and Millville in 1778. The bridge, which was a wooden drawbridge made of rough-hewn planks, was named after Tobias Quinton (Quintin, Quintan), the first English settler along Alloways Creek.[4]

The militiamen were positioned on the eastern side of the creek in some slight earthworks. They had taken up the planks of the bridge for further security. Mawhood sent a detachment of 70 men from the 17th Regiment to the two-storied Wetherby's Tavern on the west bank of Alloways Creek on March 18 to screen the bridge and allow the foraging party to proceed unmolested. He also concealed the Queen's Rangers to strengthen this party. He placed part of the Rangers under Captain Charles Stephenson in the tavern. Captain John Saunders commanded another group behind a fence in back of the tavern, while Lieutenant Colonel Simcoe commanded the rest in the woods farther back.

Mawhood and Simcoe stationed the troops of the 17th Regiment in the open, while the other units secretly took their positions to create a trap. Mawhood then ordered the 17th to retreat from their exposed location. The militiamen fired their muskets at the departing Crown forces, re-laid the bridge planks, and crossed the creek in pursuit. About 100 militiamen occupied the high ground near the bridge, while Captain William Smith led the other 200 in pursuit, unaware that the Rangers lay in wait. The militiamen passed Wetherby's Tavern and proceeded up the road from the bridge when a French officer heard someone stifle a laugh behind the fence. He looked down, saw the Rangers, and galloped off. He was fired at, wounded, and captured.

Captain Smith ordered a retreat. The militiamen began running back up the road toward the creek when Captain Stephenson's company came out of the tavern to block their escape. The militiamen were caught between two fires and panicked. They fled south, off the road, and across the fields to cross the stream above the bridge. Captain Stephenson drove them across the fields. Captain Saunders pursued them. The hussars were let loose upon them, followed by Colonel Mawhood's battalion.

Colonel Simcoe sent the 30 mounted hussars of the Rangers to harass the retreating militiamen. Several were taken prisoners. Mawhood and the 17th Regiment joined the rout, accompanied by Simcoe's Rangers from the woods. The hussars of the Rangers cut down many of the militiamen and shot or drove more into the creek, where they drowned. Captain Smith was wounded twice, had his horse shot from under him, and was captured. The Rangers had one hussar mortally wounded by a man whom he had passed and not disarmed in his eagerness to pursue. The man was killed by another hussar.

The 100 militiamen who had remained near the bridge managed to recross before Mawhood sprung his trap. Andrew Bacon grabbed an axe and cut away the drawbridge section of the bridge to keep the Redcoats from crossing. He was severely wounded and crippled for life. Colonel Elijah Hand and a company of Cumberland County militiamen arrived at the eastern bank of the creek with two cannon at this time. They stopped the British advance and provided cover for the survivors.

There is no official count of casualties incurred by Congressional troops, but the death toll was heavy—30 to 40 killed and an unknown number of drowned. The Crown forces lost one hussar, mortally wounded. The affair was called a massacre in New Jersey, but it was a well-planned and well-executed trap sprung on unsuspecting and militarily naive militiamen. The engagement aroused strong feelings against the New Jersey Loyalists for their participation in the ruthless pursuit and slaughter of their countrymen.

Barren Hill

General Henry Clinton had been appointed to replace General William Howe, who had resigned his command of the Crown forces in North America. News that the French would support the Congressional cause persuaded Clinton to consider moving his troops to New York City. He feared the French navy would block the mouth of the Delaware River and trap him in Philadelphia.

General George Washington's army was camped at Valley Forge, about 20 miles northwest of Philadelphia. His spies told Washington that the British planned to evacuate Philadelphia, but Washington did not know when they would leave or whether they would travel by land or by sea. He also wondered if the Redcoats would attack Valley Forge before leaving. He needed more intelligence, so he selected 20-year-old Major General Marie-Joseph Paul Yves Roch Gilbert du Motier, Marquis de Lafayette, for this mission.

Lafayette was one of the few senior major generals in camp and the most prominent of all Frenchmen serving with the Continental Army at that point. Washington regarded him as a son and selecting him would honor the new French alliance. Washington entrusted him with about 2,200 Continentals, militiamen, and Native Americans—approximately one-third of the strength of his army—and sent them with some horses and five cannons to obtain the needed intelligence.

He instructed Lafayette "to be a security to this camp and a cover to the country between the Delaware and the Schuylkill, to interrupt communications with Philadelphia, to obstruct the incursions of the enemy's parties, and to obtain intelligence of their motions and designs." He also reminded Lafayette: "You will remember, that your detachment is a very valuable one, and that any accident happening to it would be a very severe blow to this army."[5]

Lafayette led his troops out of Valley Forge at 10 AM on Monday, May 18, 1778 under overcast but clearing skies. They crossed the Schuylkill River at Swede's Ford, near present-day Norristown, then followed the Ridge Road until they got to Barren Hill, about halfway between Valley Forge and Philadelphia. They made camp on top of Barren Hill, just south of Matson's Ford, where they stayed for two nights. (The site, now called Lafayette Hill, is occupied by the Masonic Lodge on Ridge Pike where a stone commemorates Lafayette's encampment.)

A network of roads from every direction converged here. The Manatawny or Ridge Road from Philadelphia, via Germantown, passed through Barren Hill on its way north to Swede's Ford. A road from Whitemarsh and Chestnut Hill in the east crossed Ridge Road in the village; and another road from Germantown crossed Ridge Road about a mile north of Barren Hill near Matson's Ford.

The ridge and the river on his right flank gave Lafayette a sense of security. He placed Brigadier General Enoch Poor's brigade of New York and New Hampshire Continentals in the center on top of the hill on a small elevation south of the church facing south. He placed his five fieldpieces in front of this line. He positioned the Connecticut Continentals and Brigadier General James Mitchell Varnum's brigade of Rhode Islanders at St. Peter's Lutheran Church and its burial ground on the left as well as at several stone houses that could be turned easily into miniature fortresses.

The road they followed from Valley Forge, in their rear, could also serve for retreat if necessary. Captain Allen McLane's dragoons and about 50 Oneida warriors patrolled the Ridge Road about a mile south of the camp as pickets in front of the detachment. Brigadier General James Potter's 600 Pennsylvania militiamen guarded the road network on the far left, at Whitemarsh, that led to Lafayette's rear. Lafayette himself was in the center of camp, aided and protected by two companies of Washington's personal lifeguard.

Lafayette had all the roads covered as well as the three fords across the Schuylkill in the event of a retreat. He then had McLane send spies into the city to gather intelligence about troop movements in Philadelphia.

The British were celebrating a spectacular event known as the Mischianza to honor their commander, General Howe, prior to his departure. The wild party began on Monday, May 18, and lasted into the early morning of the 19th. Loyalist informers and scouts informed the general at the party that Lafayette and a force of Continentals had occupied Barren Hill. Howe decided to lead an expedition personally to trap "The Boy" after everyone had recovered from the party.

Even though General Henry Clinton was technically in command from May 11 on, General Howe retained his leadership role until he departed on May 24. The capture of Lafayette would be a fitting end to his service in North America. He took most of his army out of Philadelphia, leaving General Alexander Leslie to guard the city with 2,300 men. He divided his troops into four parts. Howe personally led the main body, about 6,000 men, accompanied by Clinton and Admiral Richard Howe. They marched out of Philadelphia at 5:30 AM on Wednesday, May 20, 1778. They proceeded up the Limekiln and Old York roads to Germantown, where they took the Ridge Road directly toward the center of Lafayette's camp at Barren Hill.

When the dragoons at the head of the column suddenly came upon the Oneidas on picket duty on the Ridge Road, the terrified Oneidas, unaccustomed to mounted troops, sprang up with terrifying whoops and yells that frightened both the horses and the dragoons. The dragoons and the Oneidas fled in opposite directions.

Major General Charles Grey took a few dragoons and 2,000 grenadiers up past Chestnut Hill to strike Lafayette's left flank. Captain Johann von Ewald guarded the ford at Levering's Mill near the falls of the Schuylkill with some jaegers and horses. Howe used a maneuver similar to the one he used successfully at Long Island and Brandywine. He sent the main columns in a frontal attack and a flanking column to the rear, trapping the Continentals between the two columns with no escape, to the front or rear.

The flanking column of 5,000 men and 15 guns under Brigadier General James Grant left first at 10:30 PM on May 19. They took the road for Frankford and New York to deceive enemy spies. These troops comprised the best of the army. The dragoons led the column, followed by the Queen's Rangers, both light infantry battalions, the guards, three line regiments, and 15 cannon. They marched north and circled west along the Old York Road to Church Road. They then took the Skippack Pike to the Broad Axe Inn, where they turned left on today's Butler Pike. They marched past the Plymouth Meeting to the junction of the Ridge Road near today's Conshohocken, about 1½ miles north of Barren Hill. They planned to box in the Continentals on three sides with the river on the fourth, forcing them to surrender in the face of such overwhelming numbers. They would spring the trap the next morning.

Lieutenant Colonel Simcoe's Queen's Rangers successfully got behind Lafayette without his knowledge, arriving at their position about daybreak. A Captain Story, of the Pennsylvania militia, who lived along the Wissahickon Creek at Farmar's Mill, north of the junction of the Bethlehem and Skippack roads, heard the troops on the road. He saw the red coats and jumped out his window in his nightclothes and raced to warn Lafayette of the danger. When he reached the camp, Story found the troops asleep. He met Lafayette's surgeon and informed him of the British march. When the surgeon went to Lafayette's tent, the general was interviewing a young lady spy who was going into Philadelphia that day to observe the British. The news did not disturb Lafayette as he had sent some dragoons in red coats to General Potter and his militia. Maybe Story had seen them.

General Grant had already seized the crossroads behind General Lafayette's camp. Lafayette sent couriers to Valley Forge, 11 miles away, requesting Washington for help. They returned with reports that the British had cut off all roads to the rear. Captain McLane and his dragoons, in front of the camp, had also run into the troops coming from Germantown. They captured two grenadiers at Three Mile Run who gave McLane the whole story. McLane immediately sent word to Lafayette who now realized he was caught between two enemy forces who held the roads to the nearest fords—Swede's, Bevin's, and Matson's.

Panic began to spread in the Continental camp as the men thought they were surrounded. Lafayette remained calm in the confusion. His surgeon had returned with information about a secret and hidden path that ran from Barren Hill down to the river and then along it to Matson's Ford 3 miles away. The drop was so sudden, so concealed by the height above, that Lafayette could march his army immediately out of both Grant's and Grey's sight.

If the Continentals could delay General Grant, the rest of the army might be able to retreat. Lafayette sent more men to St. Peter's Church and the burial grounds in an attempt to block the British advance. He also formed columns to march toward the British as if they were going to attack. This action confused Grant, who could not decide what to do. He pulled in his pickets, leaving the bluff overlooking Lafayette's escape route totally uncovered. Although Grant's force was closer to Matson's Ford than to Lafayette's position, Grant wondered what the attack meant, giving Lafayette an opportunity to evacuate his troops who marched in platoons taking the hidden road to the ford with Poor's division in the lead.

At Matson's Ford, the Schuylkill River ran about 3–4 feet high with a rapid current. The Continentals linked arms to cross without losing anybody. As the last troops crossed, a brisk skirmish ensued over the two guns, which were the last to cross. The retreat was successful and the guns were saved. The Continentals quickly set up defenses on the heights of the west bank to defend against a British attack which did not come.

The Redcoats on top of the bluff saw the Continentals escaping and begged General Grant for permission to attack. He refused, believing it was a trick to draw him away from the main attack at the church because he saw the enemy columns coming right at him through the woods in front of him.

Realizing that something was wrong, General Washington, in Valley Forge, had three cannons fired as an alarm to alert the entire army to assist Lafayette. Even though some troops got across Sullivan's Bridge, they were not needed. Grant's column alone outnumbered the Continentals two to one; but the Continentals were moving to his rear and preparing to strike him in the front. He now found himself trapped between two Congressional forces and about to be captured rather than being the captor. He decided to strike out at the attackers to his front.

After most of his troops were safely on their way, Lafayette withdrew his men from the churchyard area. As the rear guard proceeded down the river path with two additional cannons, General Grant mistook them for the van and ordered an immediate advance on St. Peter's and Barren Hill. Grey's troops met Grant's at Barren Hill which was now empty.

General Grant sent Brigadier General William Erskine down the Ridge Road to meet General Howe, who was leading his column toward Barren Hill. When he received Erskine's news of Lafayette's escape, Howe turned his men about and marched back to Philadelphia, where they arrived about 2 PM.

General Grant sent his cavalry in pursuit, but they took the Spring Mill Road instead of the more direct route and failed to get to the riverbank in time. When they arrived, they clashed with the Continental rear guard. Both sides suffered casualties, with the Continentals losing between nine and 40 men killed, wounded, or missing and the Crown forces losing an undetermined number, including seven dragoons killed at Matson's Ford. Grant and his column arrived in Philadelphia in the evening. Some of his officers were so angry with him, they would not speak to him.

Lafayette and his troops proceeded to Gulph Mills and then to Swede's Ford again. The following day, May 21, they crossed the Schuylkill again and returned to their former campground on Barren Hill where they stayed for another three days before rejoining Washington at Valley Forge.[6]

Monmouth

As General Henry Clinton prepared to depart Philadelphia in 1778, General George Washington had high hopes of winning the war by a cooperative effort between his army and the French fleet. Admiral Jean Baptiste Charles Henri Hector, Comte d'Estaing—with a French naval squadron of 25 warships, including

11 ships-of-the-line and transports carrying 12,638 men—left France in May to sail for the American coast. D'Estaing's fleet was considerably more powerful than any Admiral Richard Howe could immediately concentrate in American waters. The strategic initiative passed from British hands for a brief period in 1778 and General Washington hoped to make full use of it.

Sir Henry Clinton had already decided, before he learned of the threat from d'Estaing, to move his army overland to New York, largely because he could find no place for 3,000 horses on the transports along with his men and stores and the hundreds of Loyalists who claimed British protection. He began evacuating Philadelphia on Thursday, June 18, 1778. At the same time, he sent 5,000 men to attack St. Lucia, an important French harbor in the West Indies. He also sent 3,000 men to Florida and smaller detachments to Bermuda and the Bahamas.

Clinton headed toward New York with 10,000–17,000 men in very hot and humid weather with frequent downpours. His men carried 80-pound packs, and their heavy woolen uniforms were soggy and painful to wear. He also had an immense baggage train of 1,500 wagons and 5,000 horses. The wagon train stretched 12 miles along the road. Lieutenant General Wilhelm von Knyphausen commanded the guard, which required almost half the army.

General Washington had gathered about 12,000 men by the time Clinton left Philadelphia. He immediately occupied the city and began to pursue Clinton, undecided as to whether he should risk an attack on the British column while it was on the march. His Council of War was divided, though none of his generals advised a "general action." The boldest, Brigadier General "Mad Anthony" Wayne, and the young Major General Lafayette, urged a "partial attack" to strike at a portion of the Crown forces while they were strung out on the road. The most cautious, Major General Charles Lee, who had been exchanged and had rejoined the army at Valley Forge, advised only guerilla action to harass the enemy columns.

At the same time, Major General Horatio Gates advanced from the north to prevent Clinton from crossing the Raritan River to Amboy. Clinton, taking personal command of the rearguard, turned right and headed toward Sandy Hook at the mouth of the Hudson River, where ships were waiting to carry them to New York.

On June 23, Washington sent an additional 1,500 men to help the New Jersey militia harass the Crown troops. Later in the day, he sent another 1,400 men and Colonel Daniel Morgan's 600 riflemen, bringing the number of men pursuing Clinton to over 5,000.

Washington's much less heavily encumbered army moved faster, closing in on Clinton's left flank and harassing him, threatening to overtake him. Patrols demolished bridges ahead of him. The Continentals were close to trapping Clinton, who covered less than 30 miles in five days, when he turned northeast toward Monmouth Courthouse on Thursday, June 25. The midday heat grew more intense. The soldiers became more exhausted and ill tempered.

On June 26, Washington decided to take a bold approach, though he issued no orders indicating an intention to bring on a "general action." He sent forward an advance guard, composed of almost half his army, to strike at the rear of the Crown forces, when Clinton moved out of Monmouth Courthouse on Saturday morning, June 27. Washington met with Lee, Lafayette, Wayne, and others that afternoon. They decided to move against the enemy. Lee claimed the command from Lafayette when he learned the detachment would be so large. He was to attack east of the town, while Washington supported him with the main body of the army.

At 4 AM on June 28, Clinton sent Von Knyphausen's division ahead with the baggage train. Cornwallis would follow with a larger force of three brigades: the Guards, two battalions of British grenadiers and the Hessian grenadiers, two battalions of British light infantry, the 16th Dragoons, and Colonel John Graves Simcoe's Queen's Rangers, a Loyalist unit.

Washington received a report of enemy movements by 5 AM, but Lee wasn't ready to move until 7 AM. As the Crown forces passed Monmouth County Courthouse on that hot Sunday, General Charles Lee's 5,000 men advanced over rough ground that had not been reconnoitered and made contact with Clinton's rearguard. Clinton outnumbered Lee by about three to two. He sent an urgent message to Knyphausen for reinforcements and ordered an attack, hoping to gain the advantage before Washington arrived. Lee's 12 guns opened fire. Clinton reacted quickly and maneuvered to envelop the Continental right flank. Lee, feeling that his force was in an untenable position, began a retreat that became quite confused in the appalling heat. The British grenadiers pressed hard against the Continental front, while the light infantry and 16th Light Dragoons raced round their left flank.

There was much confusion among Lee's commanders and aides. Lafayette withdrew from one position to take another. The other commanders, uninformed of the order, interpreted this action as a retreat and ordered their units back as well. This caused a general withdrawal which Lee could not stop. Washington rode up amidst the confusion and, exceedingly irate to find the advance guard in retreat, exchanged harsh words with Lee. Washington then assumed direction of what had to be a defense against a counterattack. He rallied the disorganized troops and formed a new line (along the road that now borders the cemetery (just past the intersection of County Road 522 and U.S. 9). He held his position until the main body arrived to take up positions a half mile to the west. The Continentals met the attacking Crown forces with volleys of musketry and artillery. The battle that followed in the afternoon heat involved the bulk of both armies and lasted until nightfall, with both sides holding their own in one of the longest battles of the American War for Independence.

When Lee ordered a retreat, Mary Ludwig Hays's husband John served on the gun crew. The temperature was around 100 degrees. Molly brought pitcher after pitcher of cool water from a spring to the troops, earning her the nickname of Molly Pitcher. She also tended the wounded and once hoisted a disabled soldier onto her shoulders and carried him to safety. On one of her water trips, Molly found her husband with the artillery, replacing a casualty. John fell wounded, leaving the gun crew with too few men to serve it. They were about to drag it to the rear when Molly took the rammer staff from her husband's hands and joined the crew, swabbing the barrel under heavy fire.

Joseph Plumb Martin recorded the event:

> While in the act of reaching for a cartridge and having [one foot] as far from the other as she could step, a cannon shot from the enemy passed directly between her legs without doing any damage than carrying away all the lower part of her petticoat. Looking at it with apparent unconcern, she observed that it was lucky that it did not pass higher, for in that case it might have carried away something else, and then she continued upon her occupation.[7]

Clinton sent strong forces to attack both of Washington's flanks. One column marched up Wemrock Road to attack Greene, who turned his artillery on Comb's Hill against them. The troops that attacked the left flank were beaten back by a wild bayonet charge that some historians believe was the turning point of the battle.

Meanwhile, the British grenadiers tried to break the center of the line with repeated assaults. Eyewitnesses reported an entire line of grenadiers collapsed from exhaustion in the intense heat as they charged up the slope. The Continentals pushed the Crown forces back and pursued them. Washington urged them on, riding up and down encouraging his men, seemingly unconcerned for his safety. He was only 30 or 40 feet from the enemy at times.

For the first time, the Continental troops, trained by Major General Friedrich Wilhelm von Steuben, fought well with the bayonet as well as with the musket and rifle. Their battlefield behavior generally reflected their Valley Forge training. Nevertheless, Washington failed to strike a telling blow at the Crown forces for Clinton slipped away in the night and, in a few days, completed the retreat to New York. General Charles Lee demanded and got a court-martial at which he was judged guilty of disobedience of orders, poor conduct of the retreat, and disrespect for the Commander in Chief. He was suspended from command for 12 months. Congress later approved the sentence, which prompted Lee to write an insulting letter to the Congress, which expelled him from the army and ended his career.

The Continentals lost about 369 men (76 killed, 161 wounded, and 132 missing). The Crown forces lost about 358 killed and wounded. Many of the missing dropped because of heat exhaustion and later rejoined their units. About 37 Continentals and 60 Crown troops died of sunstroke (or heat exhaustion). Washington recorded that his men buried more than 249 enemy dead. Some historians believe the Crown forces lost more than 1,200 men in this one battle—about one-quarter of the troops involved in the battle if half of Clinton's army of 10,000 was occupied protecting the wagon train. The Continentals almost lost some people who would become notable. Alexander Hamilton almost got killed when his horse got shot out from under him. Lieutenant Colonel Aaron Burr recklessly pursued the enemy until their guns began killing the men around him.[8]

Fort Massac

France transferred its colony of Louisiana to Spain in 1762, in the secret Treaty of Fontainebleau, to induce Spain to enter the Seven Years War (French and Indian War, 1756–63), as a French ally. When Great Britain won the war in 1763, she acquired nearly all of Louisiana east of the Mississippi River. Spain kept the larger western part which lay across the Mississippi from West Florida and retained the name Louisiana.

The predominantly French people were surprised and angry to now have a Spanish government. As Spain considered Great Britain her main rival in colonial North America, the Spanish, mostly in New Orleans, supplied the revolting colonies with arms, ammunition, and provisions during the American War of Independence, as early as September 1776, hoping to eliminate the British presence. When Bernardo de Gálvez was appointed governor-general of Louisiana in 1777, he accelerated the flow of supplies up the Mississippi and strengthened the defenses of his province. Meanwhile, the Crown forces reinforced their posts in West Florida and were prepared and waiting when Captain James Willing resumed his raids.

Illinois became part of the French colony of Louisiana in 1717. With the defeat of the French in the Seven Years War, the French ceded the Illinois region to Great Britain. The British failed to make friends with the French settlers, many of whom moved west across the Mississippi River.

The French built Fort Massac in 1757 but abandoned it long before George Rogers Clark arrived in the summer of 1778. Clark and his Kentucky Long Knives rested at the site before their arduous overland march to capture Fort Kaskaskia, built by the French along the Kaskaskia River in 1736. The settlement of 80 stone houses became the largest French colonial settlement in the Illinois region. The townspeople partially destroyed the fort to keep it out of British hands. The British took it over in 1763 and fortified a Jesuit mission in the village, which they called Fort Gage.

The British left many of the former French outposts lightly defended during the American War of Independence, for they had gathered their western forces in Detroit. Twenty-three-year-old George Rogers Clark, of Virginia, an explorer of the Ohio Valley, had secret orders from Patrick Henry, governor of Virginia, to capture the town of Kaskaskia and nearby Fort Gage. They expected that this might lead to the capture of the entire Northwest and open the Mississippi and Ohio rivers to Spanish supplies from New Orleans. Spain was an American ally at the time.

George Rogers Clark planned to establish several settlements in the area north of the Ohio River during the American War of Independence. He and a small band of fewer than 200 men, called the Kentucky Long Knives, sailed down the Ohio River in the summer of 1778. They covered 120 miles in five days, landing at the site of where they planned a surprise overland attack on Kaskaskia. After a night crossing of the Kaskaskia River, Clark surrounded the town. When the French commander learned of Clark's approach, he mustered the militia, but he surrendered on Saturday, July 4, 1778 without firing a single shot.

Although the British were fairly tolerant of the inhabitants and their cultural and religious beliefs, the former French citizens disliked living under British rule. They much preferred Clark's benevolent leadership, which won their allegiance to the state of Virginia. These new allies would become valuable in Clark's conquest of the region.[9]

Clark and his men then proceeded to capture Cahokia and other British forts, which allowed Virginia to claim jurisdiction over the Illinois territory north of the Ohio River.

Newport

Admiral d'Estaing sailed to the Virginia coast and then moved northward. He arrived off the coast of Delaware with 12 ships-of-the-line, three frigates, and some 4,000 French soldiers in late June 1778. He proceeded to New York to try to capture Sir Richard Howe's fleet of nine ships in New York harbor. However, when he arrived off Sandy Hook, New Jersey, on July 9, he discovered that the water was too shallow for his ships to get at the British fleet. General Washington and d'Estaing decided instead to attack the British at Newport, Rhode Island, the second largest British seaport at the time.

The British had held Newport since December 1776. General Sir Robert Pigot now defended it with only 3,000 men. Major General John Sullivan commanded about 1,000 Continental soldiers. He called out about 6,000 militiamen. General Washington sent him 3,000 more Continentals under Lafayette, bringing the total Congressional force in Rhode Island to 10,000 troops in July 1778.

D'Estaing sent two men-of-war up the Narragansett Passage (Middle Passage) and two frigates up the Seaconnet (Sakonnet) Passage on Wednesday, August 5, 1778. French Admiral Pierre André de Suffren de Saint Tropez led the two frigates into the Sakonnet, causing panic in the British fleet. Fearing the loss of their ships to the French fleet waiting outside Narragansett Bay, six British ships ran aground trying to escape. The 32-gun frigate *Cerberus* ran aground trying to get down into Newport harbor. Her captain set her afire and she blew up.

The 32-gun frigates *Juno*, *Orpheus*, and *Lark* met a similar fate as did the 16-gun *Kingfisher* and the troop transport *Pigot Galley*. The *Orpheus* was run on shore at Almy's Point and the *Lark* and *Pigot* at Freeborn's Creek. After the crews had landed, they were set on fire. The *Orpheus* blew up about 7 o'clock; the others not until close to 12. The *Kingfisher* drifted to High Hill in Tiverton, where she was blown up by British explosives. The 32-gun *Flora*, the 18-gun *Falcon*, and several transports were scuttled to block the entrance to Newport harbor. Three other ships were set afire and drifted across the Sakonnet where they ran aground. The crew of one of the ships abandoned her with loaded guns. When the fire reached the touchholes, it ignited the charges, firing the shot uncomfortably close to the barracks on Sandy Point. The French ships approached this point but remained at a safe distance when they saw the enemy ships in flames. With most of the British vessels in the area scuttled, the French commanded the sea. On August 8, as planned, the French then sailed the rest of the fleet to prepare for the Battle of Rhode Island.[10]

In the first week of August, Sullivan's army was camped at Tiverton, Rhode Island. The French landed on Conanicut Island (Jamestown Island) in Narragansett Bay. The Congressional forces planned to cross at Tiverton and move down the east side of Rhode Island (now called Aquidneck Island), while the French would land on the western side, hoping to trap General Sir Robert Pigot on the island.

Despite being known as a naval battle, neither side in the naval battle of Rhode Island, as overviewed below, actively engaged the other. Admiral Richard Howe had received a squadron of 13 vessels from England, bringing his fleet to 36 warships. He came north to challenge Admiral d'Estaing, who sailed out to meet him with his 12 ships which were larger and had more firing power than Howe's. Howe's fleet carried 1,064 guns compared with d'Estaing's 834 guns, but the French guns were of higher caliber.

The two fleets dogged each other for two days when, on the night of Tuesday, August 11, a hurricane scattered both fleets and forced the ships to engage in combat individually. D'Estaing's flagship, the 84-gun *Languedoc*, engaged the 50-gun *Renown* in a brief but indecisive action on the 13th. The 80-gun *Marseillais* fought the 50-gun *Preston* until darkness forced an inconclusive end to the engagement. The 74-gun *César* was defeated by the 50-gun *Isis* but remained in action on the 16th. The storm badly damaged many of the ships, rendering them unseaworthy. The HM Frigate *Apollo* lost her mast as did the 80-gun *Tonant*.

Howe's fleet returned to New York to refit. The French returned to Rhode Island on the 20th but d'Estaing refused to cooperate with Sullivan, whom he disliked. He sent an officer to inform Sullivan that he had returned as promised but could not remain to assist him. He sailed to Boston around midnight on August 21 to refit his ships, after which he sailed away to Martinique.[11]

When General Sullivan learned that d'Estaing had withdrawn, he was forced to retreat and roundly chastised the French. His comments almost led to a duel with Lafayette and sparked anti-French rioting in Boston and Charleston.

Vincennes

Indiana was part of the colony of Virginia during the American War of Independence. The fur trade was the main source of the economy. The Native Americans favored the French who treated them as equals, but the British slowly won them over because they paid higher prices for the furs and traded firearms. The French and the British fought over the fur trade for many years. With the defeat of the French in the Seven Years War, the British claimed Indiana and other regions. They began to occupy the Indiana region in 1777.

Lieutenant Colonel George Rogers Clark planned to take control of the Ohio Valley away from the British in 1777. He captured Fort Kaskaskia in Illinois on Saturday, July 4, 1778, followed shortly afterward by Fort Massac. He then turned his attention to Vincennes, Indiana, which he captured that same summer, but he had to surrender it back to the Crown forces in December. Because of the importance of this post, Clark set out from Kaskaskia with about 130 American and French soldiers to recapture it, which he did on Thursday, February 25, 1779, after an arduous trek.

The French built a series of military posts between the Great Lakes and the Louisiana territory. The one built in Vincennes was constructed in 1731 and named for the builder and first commander, François Marie Bissot, Sieur de Vincennes. A permanent settlement grew up around the post in the next few years. The British acquired the post from France after the Seven Years War and renamed it Fort Sackville for a British government official.

The British dominated a large portion of the Trans-Appalachian frontier. The Proclamation of 1763 which officially ended the Seven Years War forbade the settlement of lands west of the Appalachian Mountains. There were many Native American tribes located between the Appalachian Mountains and the Mississippi River. Although never unified, the warriors from these tribes greatly outnumbered both the British and the Americans and constituted a strong military force on the western frontier. American settlement west of the Appalachian Mountains posed a threat to Native American tribes' way of life and caused most of them to favor the British.

British officials actively encouraged the Native Americans to attack the frontiersmen beginning in 1777. The British supplied the warriors with weapons and ammunition and rewarded them with gifts when successful war parties returned with scalps and prisoners. From their posts north of the Ohio River, the British sent Native American war parties against those settlers who ignored the proclamation line, including those in Kentucky (also a part of Virginia at that time).

Colonel George Rogers Clark organized the Kentucky militia to defend against these raids. Not content to wait for the attacks, he took his plan to Patrick Henry, governor of Virginia, and gained approval for a major offensive campaign. He planned to lead a force of frontiersmen into the Illinois country and strike at the source of Native American raids.

Clark captured the British posts at Kaskaskia and Cahokia along the Mississippi River, near St. Louis, in the summer of 1778. French settlers occupied these posts after the Seven Years War. They disliked living under British rule, so Clark quickly gained their support. Father Pierre Gibault and Dr. Jean Laffont volunteered to travel to Vincennes on Clark's behalf. That settlement also gave its support to Clark, but the French at Detroit, Michigan, and other northern posts continued to support the British.

British Lieutenant Governor Henry Hamilton (The "Hair Buyer") received news about the fall of the three outposts by August 6. He left Detroit in early October 1778, with a mixed force of English soldiers, French volunteers and militiamen, and Native American warriors, intending to retake Fort Sackville in Vincennes. Picking up Native American allies along the way, his force numbered about 500 when he arrived at Vincennes 71 days later (Thursday, December 17, 1778).

Clark left Captain Leonard Helm in charge at Vincennes. With only a few men on whom he could depend, Helm had no hopes of defending the fort against Hamilton's force. Hamilton recaptured the fort on Thursday, December 17, and the French settlers, faced with overwhelming force, returned to British allegiance.

Hamilton allowed most of his force to return home for the winter, as was customary in 18th-century warfare, postponing his intended invasion of the Illinois country. He planned to muster his forces in the spring for an attack on Clark's posts on the Mississippi River. Victories there would pave the way for a joint effort with tribes from south of the Ohio River to drive all American settlers from the Trans-Appalachian frontier.

Francis Vigo (Joseph Maria Francesco Vigo), a merchant and supporter of the Whig cause, left his home in St. Louis and headed for Vincennes, unaware that the fort was in British hands. He was taken prisoner near the settlement, held for several days and released, his captors not realizing Vigo's involvement with the Congressional forces. Vigo returned to St. Louis and then went to Kaskaskia, 50 miles south, where he provided Clark with valuable information concerning the military situation in Vincennes and Hamilton's intent to attack in the spring.

Clark, determined to capture Hamilton, set out from Kaskaskia on February 6, 1779, with his force of approximately 170 Whigs and Frenchmen. They covered the distance in 18 days. About 10 miles from Vincennes, they found themselves in country flooded with icy water which they had to wade through—sometimes shoulder-deep. They arrived in Vincennes after nightfall on Tuesday, February 23.

The French citizens greeted Clark's men warmly and provided them food and dry gunpowder. Clark's men surrounded the fort, which was now defended by approximately 40 British soldiers and a similar number of French volunteers and militiamen from Detroit and Vincennes. The French troops were not inclined to fire on the enemy when they realized that the French inhabitants of the town again sided with the Whigs.

Clark brought, from Kaskaskia, flags sufficient for an army of 500. He had them unfurled and carried within view of the fort, giving the impression he had a much larger army. His soldiers, experienced woodsmen, armed with the famed long rifle which was accurate at longer ranges than the defenders' muskets, could maintain a rate of fire that convinced the British that they indeed faced a large army.

Clark ordered the construction of tunnels, from behind the riverbank a short distance from the fort, to plant explosive charges under the fort walls or beneath the powder magazines. His men also built barricades and entrenchments to provide additional cover.

Hamilton considered surrendering and requested that Clark meet with him at the nearby church, St. Francis Xavier Catholic Church. He tried to get liberal conditions, but Clark insisted on unconditional surrender. After a long and heated discussion, they failed to agree upon acceptable terms and each commander returned to his respective post.

A Native American raiding party which Hamilton sent out to attack the settlers along the Ohio River returned to Vincennes at this time, during a lull in the battle. They saw the British flag flying as usual from the fort and began yelling and firing their weapons in the air. They realized their mistake too late, when the frontiersmen killed or wounded several of them and captured others.

Clark ordered five of the captured warriors to be tomahawked in full view of the fort in retaliation for the raids in which numerous men, women, and children had been slaughtered. The executions were intended to demonstrate to Native American observers that the redcoats could no longer protect those tribes who made war on the settlers and to put pressure on the British who sensed they could suffer the same fate.

Hamilton reluctantly agreed to Clark's final terms, which were just short of unconditional surrender. He described his thoughts at having to surrender: "The mortification, disappointment and indignation I felt, may possibly be conceived..." The defeated British Army marched out of Fort Sackville and laid down their arms at 10 AM on Thursday, February 25, 1779. Clark had the American flag raised above the fort and 13 cannon shots fired in celebration. An accident during the firings severely burned several men, including Captain Joseph Bowman, who died six months later and was buried in the church cemetery adjacent to the fort. The surrender of Fort Sackville marked the beginning of the end of British occupation and control of the western frontier of America.

Even though he was unable to achieve his ultimate objective of capturing Detroit, Clark successfully prevented the British from achieving their goal of driving the Whigs from the Trans-Appalachian frontier. His brilliant military activities caused the British to cede to the United States a vast area of land west of the Appalachian Mountains. That territory now includes the states of Ohio, Indiana, Illinois, Michigan, Wisconsin, and the eastern portion of Minnesota.[12]

Ouiatenon

After Colonel Clark recaptured Vincennes, he learned that the British were sending supplies from Detroit to Vincennes. He sent Captain Leonard Helm and 50 men up the Wabash River to intercept the convoy, which they did on Friday, February 26, 1779. Helm returned on March 5 with the provisions and 40 British and French prisoners.[13]

Stanyarne's and Eveleigh's plantation

Brigadier General William Moultrie ordered Captain James Pyne (or Payne) to "proceed… to Stono-ferry, there you are to endeavor to destroy a bridge of boats the enemy have thrown over the river. In your passage up, and on your return, you are to sink, burn, and destroy any of the enemy's boats or vessels that you may meet with." He took three galleys up the Stono River to harass the British on Tuesday, June 22, 1779. The captains of the other galleys were Paul Frisbie and Boutard.

Brigadier General Casimir Pulaski and his Legion were ready to support the landing of Colonel Marquis de Brétigny and his Corps of Frenchmen, who were with the galleys and were to try to make a landing, if possible. The galleys sailed through the Wappoo Cut during that night but did not find any bridge of boats. The British were unable to get enough boats to build the proposed bridge, so the galleys passed by Gibbes's plantation undetected. However, they were fired upon "with field-pieces and small arms" for 45 minutes when they passed Stanyarne's plantation.

Captain Pyne captured a British schooner during the fight and silenced the batteries at the plantation. He then continued up the river to the next bluff, where "a battery consisting of 3 field-pieces and a great deal of musketry" fired upon him again. The galleys managed to silence that battery also. The vessels then anchored at Eveleigh's plantation as the sun was rising and the tide was going out.

When the sun came up, the sailors realized that there were 1,200 Crown troops at Eveleigh's plantation and cannons were entrenched on the causeway leading to it. Although the galleys were safe where they were, moving in any direction would place them "within pistol shot of their intrenchment" so Captain Pyne decided to wait until dark.

Aware that the galleys were nearby, the Crown forces sank a schooner in the river to block the enemy's escape. The Carolina gunners fired cannonballs into the Crown camp throughout the day. The vessels rushed down the river after nightfall, running the gauntlet of men and cannons (the largest were 9-pounders) firing along the riverbank. The galleys returned fire only when necessary as they were low on ammunition. Captain Boutard's galley, in the rear, received the heaviest fire, which killed six men and wounded several others. All three galleys returned with the British schooner as their prize.[14]

Stony Point and Verplanck's Point

General Henry Clinton tried to draw General George Washington into a general engagement in the summer of 1779. He occupied Stony Point on the west side of the Hudson in May and Verplanck's Point on the opposite shore on June 1. This was an important link between the Continental forces in New York and New England. Clinton then began to enlarge the earthen forts at these points by cutting down trees and protecting them with an abatis. He left 625 officers and men under Lieutenant Colonel Henry Johnson to defend them.

Washington sent Brigadier General "Mad Anthony" Wayne's brigade of about 1,360 light infantrymen selected from every regiment for their agility, alertness, and daring to retake Stony Point 150 feet above the Hudson River. At first, Wayne was somewhat dismayed by his observations of the position, which was practically immune to attack except by a surprise assault. He decided to target specific objectives rather than mount an all-out assault. His men would advance during the night with unloaded muskets to maintain silence. Any man who fired his musket or panicked in the advance would be punished by death.

Major John Stewart would lead one column of 300 men, advancing on Stony Point from the north through the marshes of the Hudson River. Wayne would lead the second column through the waters of Haverstraw Bay on the south. Each column would be preceded by a "forlorn hope" of 20 men to guide the way for the second group of 150 men who would enter enemy lines first, overcome sentries, and sever the abatis.

Meanwhile, Lieutenant Colonel Hardy Murfree would lead two companies in a diversionary attack on the fort's front in the center. They were the only troops allowed to load their muskets to draw the Crown forces from their posts with musket fire. The others would rely only on the bayonet. Wayne's brigade began to advance around midnight on Thursday, July 15, 1779. They only had to travel about a mile and a half to their objective. They traveled along Frank Road which becomes Crickettown Road. Stewart's column followed what is now Wayne Avenue toward the river.

The sound of hundreds of men moving waist-deep in the water alerted a British sentry who sounded the alarm. The Continentals, unable to return fire, hurried to dry ground where they climbed the rocky slope and entered the British earthworks. Colonel Henry Johnson charged down the hill with six companies to counter what he thought was the main attack. Wayne's column arrived from the south and cut him off from the central redoubt at the top of a huge outcropping of rocks.

Colonel Johnson was caught between Wayne's men and Murfree's column, unable to get back. The Continentals were now in the main redoubt, and he was forced to surrender. The Continentals captured the fort at Stony Point in about half an hour with only 15 lives lost, mostly from volunteers in the forlorn hope (essentially a suicide squad not expected to survive), and 83 wounded. Casualties might have been higher had the defenders not had to fire downhill in the dark. The British lost 63 killed, 74 wounded, 58 missing, and 472 prisoners, including the wounded. One officer escaped by jumping into the river and swimming out to the HMS

Vulture, the same ship that would carry Major John André to his rendezvous with Major General Benedict Arnold 14 months later and take Arnold to safety after his treason. The British occupying Fort Lafayette on Verplanck's Point probably heard the fighting at Stony Point and wondered who won. When the victors fired their guns at the *Vulture*, they knew.

Wayne offered a $500 prize for the first man into the fort, which went to Lieutenant Colonel François Louis Teissedre de Fleury, a French engineer. Fleury was also awarded a silver medal which became a gold one when finally awarded in 1783—the only medal awarded to a European volunteer during the war. Wayne also received a gold medal. He continued to lead the charge despite suffering a head wound from grapeshot. He thought he was seriously wounded and asked his men to carry him to the top of the hill so he could die in the redoubt. Major John Stewart, the leader of the second column, was awarded a silver medal. The action at Stony Point accounted for three of the 11 medals Congress awarded during the war.

General Washington also planned to take Fort Lafayette at Verplanck's Point after receiving word of Wayne's victory at Stony Point. Wayne wrote to him at 2 AM on Friday morning, July 16: "The fort and garrison with Colonel Johnson are ours. Our officers and men behaved like men who are determined to be free." He dispatched the message immediately, but it went astray. By the time the attack force was in position around Fort Lafayette, General Clinton learned of the defeat at Stony Point and sent reinforcements. The Continentals abandoned their plans to take Fort Lafayette.

Washington could not spare enough men to defend the fort. He destroyed and abandoned it two days later. Clinton reoccupied it the following day, July 19, but withdrew in October. The battle at Stony Point had little tactical importance, but it boosted morale.[15]

Savannah

As a result of the anti-French sentiment after the events in Rhode Island and in line with his government's instructions to regain territory for France, Admiral d'Estaing took his fleet south to attack British colonies in the Caribbean. He was able to capture Grenada but was recalled to aid in the siege of Savannah.

Admiral d'Estaing's fleet of 33 warships (totaling more than 2,000 guns) and army of 4,450 arrived off Savannah on Wednesday, September 1, 1779. Major General Benjamin Lincoln and Brigadier General Casimir Pulaski joined them with over 2,100 men. The three divisions (d'Estaing's; General Arthur, Count de Dillon's; and Colonel Louis Marc Antoine Vicomte de Noailles's) of the French army encamped east of the Ogeechee Road and the Continental troops camped to the left of the French all the way to McGillivray's plantation on the Savannah River.

The British sent out patrols to determine the location of Admiral d'Estaing's fleet as it approached Georgia. The HMS *Rose* went out of Savannah on Friday, September 3, 1779 to investigate a report of several large ships. She returned with news that the French ships were near the coast.

The 74-gun ship-of-the-line *Magnifique* captured the sloop *Polly* and her crew on Monday, September 6. Five French sailors boarded the *Polly*, but that night a gale blew her away from the French fleet toward Tybee. The French sailors, unaware of their location, sailed the *Polly* up the Georgia coast. The English prisoners on board added to the confusion by telling their captors that the Savannah River was the entrance to Charleston, South Carolina.

The crew sailed the *Polly* in the mouth of the river and anchored, whereupon she was captured. The sailors informed their captors that the French fleet consisted of the 74-gun *Magnifique*, the 64-gun *Sphinx*, two frigates, a schooner, and a cutter, all bound to Boston for masts and spars.[16]

The French fleet sailed into Charleston harbor on Friday, September 3, 1779 and arrived off the coast of Georgia the following day when a British lookout sighted five French men-of-war and several sloops and schooners approaching Tybee Island.

The *Paris Gazette* reported that the troops landed there consisted of 2,979 "Europeans" and 545 "Colored: Volunteer Chasseurs, Mulattoes, and Negroes, newly raised at St. Domingo." The Volunteer Chasseurs, called the Fontanges Legion after its French commander (Major General Vicomte François de Fontanges), included young men who would become famous in the Haitian revolution, such as Pierre Astrel, Pierre Auba, Louis Jacques Beauvais, Jean-Baptiste Mars Belley, Martial Besse, Guillaume Bleck, Pierre Cangé, Jean-Baptiste Chavannes, Pierre Faubert, Laurent Férou, Jean-Louis Froumentaine, Barthélemy-Médor Icard, Gédéon Jourdan, Jean-Pierre Lambert, Jean-Baptiste Léveillé, Christophe Mornet, Pierre Obas, Luc-Vincent Olivier, Pierre Pinchinat, Jean Piverger, André Rigaud, Césaire Savary, Pierre Tessier, Jérome Thoby, Jean-Louis Villate, and Henri Christophe, future King of Haiti. Christophe was 12 years old at Savannah. He volunteered as a freeborn infantryman and served as orderly to a French naval officer.

Upon learning about the arrival of the French fleet, Major General Augustine Prevost ordered all his troops posted outside Savannah to prepare to come join him in Savannah. Captain James Moncrieff, of the British engineers, sailed down the river on Wednesday, September 8, with 100 men and a howitzer to strengthen the outposts and batteries at Tybee. The schooner *Rattlesnake* followed them with three officers and 50 men. Captain Moncrieff burned the fort on the 10th and returned to Savannah with the garrison.[17]

D'Estaing's fleet captured the 50-gun *Experiment*, the frigate *Ariel*, and two store ships carrying the £30,000 payroll for the Savannah garrison, along with Brigadier General George Garth who was on his way to take command of the British forces in Georgia. The French off-loaded their heavy cannons and mortars at Thunderbolt and Causton's Bluff on Saturday, September 11. The heavy rains slowed their progress, as they had to haul the heavy guns about 5 miles from the landing sites. The French troops began landing at Beaulieu, on the Vernon River, that night. They unloaded more artillery that had to be dragged about 15 miles to their emplacements. Meanwhile, the British in Savannah continued to build fascines for their defenses. They sank six British ships in the river to block the French.

Major General Benjamin Lincoln hurried south with 600 Continentals, Count Casimir Pulaski's 200 legionnaires, and 750 militiamen to join d'Estaing. He reached Cherokee Hill, just west of Savannah, on September 15. The following day, d'Estaing demanded that General Prevost surrender the city, but he gave Prevost 24 hours to consider the terms. This gave Prevost enough time to strengthen his defenses and receive reinforcements of Colonel John Maitland and 800 Regulars from the garrison at Beaufort, South Carolina, after a remarkable forced march through swamps, marshes, and streams. Colonel John Harris Cruger was on his way from Sunbury with the 1st Battalion of de Lancey's brigade.

D'Estaing got upset as the Redcoats dug their trenches. He sent Prevost a letter saying, "I am informed that you continue intrenching yourself. It is a Matter of very little Importance to me, however for Form's sake, I must desire that you will desist." With his total manpower raised to 3,250 plus a considerable number of militiamen and armed slaves, Prevost declined to surrender. Unfortunately, the Franco-American force had to hurry its attack because d'Estaing was unwilling to risk his fleet in a position dangerously exposed to hurricanes, remembering his experience at Rhode Island where he was caught in one. Moreover, his sailors were dying of scurvy at the rate of 35 a day.

Captain William Campbell and 200 British light infantrymen made a sortie on Friday morning, September 17, to attack a covering party of about 200 French at a battery near the barracks. They were repulsed and pursued into their redoubts with the loss of 53 men killed, including Captain Campbell and two other officers, and nearly 100 wounded. The French lost about 26 men killed and 84 wounded, including 10 officers. The French were so eager and impetuous that, instead of waiting for the enemy, they leapt out of their trench, attacked, and pursued them with the bayonet until the cannon from the British redoubts galled them and inflicted their greatest loss.[18]

That evening, "the guns for the retreat were fired an hour earlier than usual as a signal that hostilities were resumed."[19]

Brigadier General Pulaski and his legion, along with Colonel Peter Horry and some of the 1st Regiment Continental Light Dragoons, went in pursuit of Colonel Daniel McGirth on Saturday, September 18. The Continentals trailed McGirth's Loyalists as they drove a large number of "horses, cattle and Negroes to St. Augustine." Pulaski ordered his dragoons to remain near the Ogeechee Ferry, about 15 miles south of Savannah, to intercept any provisions. Meanwhile, he overtook McGirth's party near the Ogeechee Ferry and captured 50 men along with some livestock and slaves. Pulaski returned to the ferry the next day, gathered his dragoons, and returned to camp.[20]

Major General Prevost chose the Spring Hill Redoubt, off the town's southwest corner, as the strongest point of his defense. At 9 PM Wednesday evening, September 22, M. de Guillaume, lieutenant of grenadiers in the regiment of Guadeloupe, of the Viscount de Noailles's division, attempted to capture an advance enemy post at Thunderbolt Bluff on St. Augustine Creek, 5 miles southeast of the city, with 50 picked men. Disregarding the Viscount de Noailles's instructions, they rushed head-on, attacking, with full force, a post which should have been captured by surprise. The Viscount de Noailles, following closely to support him, saw that success was impossible and ordered a retreat. The Crown forces repulsed the French with a lively fire of artillery and musketry that killed six men and wounded several others.

The following day, the Allied armies completely invested Savannah. The siege of the 2,500 British Regulars and Loyalists under Major General Prevost lasted until Monday, October 18. The allied forces began digging siege trenches on September 23 and installed cannons by October 3.

General Prevost had the barracks in the center of his lines pulled down on Monday, September 27, to erect a great battery. A British sortie against the French trenches on Friday, September 24, cost the attackers four killed and 15 wounded, but they killed and wounded 70 Frenchmen. French artillery in siege lines began to bombard the town on Monday, October 4.[21]

A force of Georgia Continentals prevented Lieutenant James French and a detachment of 111 Crown troops from reaching Savannah on Friday night, October 1. The Crown troops, including a detachment of sick and wounded of de Lancey's brigade from the Sunbury garrison, had sailed into the Ogeechee River to escape the French fleet and camped on Savage Point, about 15–20 miles south of Savannah. In addition to de Lancey's invalids, Lieutenant French had command of five vessels—four of them fully armed. The largest mounted 14 guns and was manned by 40 seamen.

Colonel John White, his servant, Captain Augustus Christian Georg Elholm, a sergeant, and three privates were on patrol. They lit fires in the woods around Lieutenant French's camp to make it appear that a whole army was bivouacked there. They then rode around the camp shouting out orders to fictitious units, deceiving the Loyalists into thinking they were surrounded by a larger force. Colonel White demanded the Loyalists surrender and told Lieutenant French that his army so hated the Loyalists that they would slaughter the prisoners if they saw them. Colonel White told Lieutenant French that he would protect his prisoners from the concealed Continental Army and order three guides—half of White's force—to escort the 150 prisoners. Lieutenant French quickly surrendered along with the privateer sloops and a schooner carrying a shipment of salt. Colonel White took them prisoner, along with Colonel Moses Kirkland, of the South Carolina Loyalist Militia, and 130 stands of arms. He then mustered local militiamen who took charge of the prisoners and escorted them to Savannah. The men also burned the five British vessels.

Colonel Kirkland was much despised by the Whigs and had been General Henry Clinton's advisor during the planning of the Southern Campaign that resulted in the capture of Savannah. The Whigs bound him and his son in irons and placed them on board a galley which the British later captured. Kirkland rejoined the Crown forces in Savannah.[22]

Early Monday morning, October 4, allied gunners fired the first shots of a bombardment, hoping to weaken enemy resistance. A furious bombardment by land and sea from 10 mortars and 54 pieces of heavy artillery continued for seven days but killed only a few men. Some drunken French gunners hit their own lines. After being reprimanded, they resumed firing "with more vivacity than precision." The cannonade failed to produce the desired result.

When d'Estaing learned, on October 8, that bad weather was approaching and the assault trenches would not be completed until 10 days later, he abandoned plans to make a systematic approach by regular parallels and prepared for an immediate attack. Major General Benjamin Lincoln, in charge of some 5,000 troops, agreed somewhat grudgingly.

The Allies planned to make a coordinated attack against the Spring Hill Redoubt at 4 AM on Saturday, October 9. Brigadier General Isaac Huger would lead 500 South Carolina and Georgia militiamen in a diversionary attack against Cruger's Redoubt on the White Bluff Road and break through their defenses if possible.

The Crown defenses included the armed brig *Germain* in the Savannah River (near the foot of West Broad Street), which could deliver enfilade fire along the allies' northwest flank. This ship covered the Sailors' Battery (roughly at the present intersection of West Oglethorpe Avenue and Martin Luther King Jr. Boulevard, formerly West Broad Street), so named because it was armed by sailors manning a 9-pounder. The Sailors' Battery covered the Spring Hill Redoubt (now the intersection of Louisville Road and West Broad Street), where Prevost expected the main assault. A line of earthworks and smaller redoubts connected these main posts and a thick swamp protected the western front. A fourth redoubt was located where the brick Continental barracks had been demolished overnight to erect the battery that covered White Bluff Road leading from Savannah to the south. A fifth redoubt was at Trustees' Garden at the northeast corner of the British line.

The French under General Arthur Count de Dillon would emerge from a swamp in a secondary assault against the Sailors' Battery on the British right flank. However, Dillon's men got lost and the Crown forces, in strongly entrenched positions, repelled the attack in what was essentially a Bunker Hill in reverse. The allies suffered staggering losses. British grenadiers of the 60th Regiment and marines charged. Fierce hand-to-hand fighting threw the allies into confusion and finally into flight. After the repulsion of other thrusts, Lincoln gave up. The Fontanges Legion, stationed as a reserve in the rear guard, prevented the annihilation of the allied force. Brigadier General Pulaski led his 200 legionnaires in a cavalry assault that resulted in his death. Martial Besse and Henri Christophe were slightly wounded and returned to Saint Domingue (now Haiti).

Eighteen years later, General Besse visited the United States on official business. He disembarked at Charleston "dressed in the uniform of his grade." Authorities forced him to post a bond as required by South Carolina law for all incoming blacks. When the French consul in Charleston protested that General Besse was a representative of his government and that he was wounded at the siege of Savannah, the bond was remitted.

The French and American allies mounted a direct assault on the Crown forces, who were aided by hundreds of "armed blacks" gathered from the countryside to build redoubts, mount cannon, and serve as guides and spies. Their "incessant and cheerful labours, in rearing those numerous defenses which were completed with so much expedition as to astonish the besiegers, ought not to be forgotten in a history of this memorable siege." They fought a long and bloody battle in the ditch outside the Spring Hill Redoubt, trying to get to the top. The Continentals managed to gain the parapet and planted the South Carolina Crescent and the French colors on it, but they were immediately knocked down. The allies made three attempts to place their colors on the parapet and the Crown forces tore them down each time. Count d'Estaing's standard bearer was shot down and d'Estaing was wounded in the arm trying to reorganize the French forces. When Lieutenant Gray, the Continental standard bearer, was killed, Sergeant William Jasper supported the colors until he was mortally wounded.

None of the French grenadiers managed to get inside the redoubt and many were killed with the bayonet. The Vicomte de Castries reported that the captain of the volunteers from Martinique or Guadeloupe and three-quarters of the company were killed in the trenches and the corps of riflemen was almost completely destroyed. "In less than half an hour more than 2,500 men were killed on the spot." D'Estaing was wounded a second time with a shot through the leg. Colonel Lachlan McIntosh asked him for instructions and was told to circle left so as not to interfere with the French reorganization. This diverted the column into Yamacraw Swamp, where its left flank came under fire from the *Germain* until the end of the battle.

The Congressional forces lost about 444 men, including 80 dead in the ditch and 93 more between it and the abatis. The French sustained approximately 650 officers and men wounded. We don't know the Crown losses, but they range from approximately 55 to 155 men. Most authorities accept the figure of about 40 killed and 63 wounded.

The French army departed the area and boarded their ships on October 20. D'Estaing then sailed away to the West Indies. General Lincoln marched his army back to Charleston, which would fall the next year. The second attempt at

Franco-American cooperation ended in much the same atmosphere of bitterness and disillusion as the first. As in Rhode Island, this affair displayed poor coordination between the Americans and the French. Each allied commander disliked his counterpart and departed Savannah with a mutual distrust. American and French coordination and cooperation would improve at the siege of Yorktown in 1781.

The allied defeat at Savannah confirmed the British as masters of Georgia and paved the way for the offensive that would capture Charleston and most of South Carolina the following year. The British would later evacuate Savannah on July 11, 1782.[23]

Gillivray's plantation

Mr. Gillivray's plantation (on the outskirts of Savannah, Georgia), guarded by "armed negroes"—most likely the Negro Cavalry Company—was the scene of a great deal of skirmishing on Saturday, October 16, 1779. Congressional troops attacked the African American Loyalists but were driven back "from the Buildings on the Plantation into the Woods." The defenders ran out of ammunition and were obliged to retreat. They lost one man killed and three wounded but they captured "two Rebel Dragoons and eight Horses, and killed two Rebels." A British account notes:

> Saturday, the 16th, in the afternoon there was a "great deal of skirmishing on Mr. Gillivray's plantation, betwixt some Negroes and a Party of Rebels and the latter were several Times driven from the Buildings on the Plantation into the Woods. Want of Ammunition, however, obliged the Blacks to retreat in the Evening, with the loss of one killed, and three or four wounded. The Enemy Loss is not known. There was very little firing this Night from the French, who had sent off all their Cannon except two.[24]

The Marquis de Brétigny and eight men in a boat captured a four-gun sloop from New Providence (Nassau, Bahamas) and sent her to Charleston, South Carolina, on Saturday, October 16. The vessel was captured as she came to anchor in the Savannah River.[25]

Cahokia

Spanish Illinois was a buffer between the British in Canada and in the Ohio Valley and the Spanish colony of New Spain. Britain also recognized the importance of Spanish Illinois. General Sir Frederick Haldimand, governor of Canada, authorized Emmanuel Hesse to lead a large force of traders, Loyalists, mercenaries, and several hundred Fox, Sauk, and Winnebago warriors from Detroit to St. Louis. The force left Prairie du Chien on Tuesday, May 2, 1780, under the command of Lieutenant Governor Patrick Sinclair of Fort Michilimackinac. Their objective was to raid the Spanish and French settlement of St. Louis and to capture the outposts beginning with Cahokia. Colonel George Rogers Clark set out on May 13 with a small body of troops. He repulsed the attack on Cahokia on Friday, May 26, with the loss of four killed and five wounded.[26]

On July 11, 1780, French General Jean-Baptiste Vimeur, the Comte de Rochambeau, arrived in Newport with 6,000 troops. This marked the beginning of a new and decisive phase of Franco-American military cooperation. A series of British strategic blunders, the decision of Admiral de Grasse to move his large French fleet north from the West Indies to support the allied armies of Rochambeau and Washington, and the skillful operations of Lafayette in Virginia contributed to the victorious Yorktown campaign and the end of British military power in America.

Although the British had earlier abandoned Newport, Rochambeau's forces were stuck in the port as the result of a British naval blockade. At the beginning of 1781, General Washington wanted to coordinate a Franco-American attack on New York with Rochambeau, but the siege appeared too difficult. In August 1781, Rochambeau helped convince the American leader to move south and strike at the British Army under General Charles Cornwallis in Virginia.

The key to the allied strategy was French Admiral François de Grasse. De Grasse pledged to sail from the West Indies with a fleet of 29 ships and 3,000 troops to support the Franco-American land forces, which marched south to attack Cornwallis at Yorktown. De Grasse was able to defeat a British naval force during the Second Battle of the Chesapeake in September 1781 and prevent reinforcements from reaching Cornwallis.

Miamitown (Fort Wayne)

Colonel Auguste La Mottin de La Balme, a French soldier of fortune, led more than 100 French militiamen toward Detroit to invade Canada in 1780. They traveled across the plains of southern Illinois by horseback and arrived at Vincennes in August. There, La Balme found young Creoles interested in his plan, but when they delayed in forming themselves into a company, La Balme grew impatient and marched north up the Wabash River with his volunteers. They camped at Fort Ouiatenon for about three weeks to drill and await the new company of Creole volunteers from Vincennes. When they still failed to arrive, La Balme and his men resumed their trek up the Wabash. They arrived at Post Miami (now the city of Fort Wayne) where they were not received well by the inhabitants who were loyal to the Crown.

The troops raided the Miami capital of Kekionga (at Fort Wayne) and learned about the Eel River Post, a rich fur trading post near the Miami village of Little Turtle, located about 7 miles southeast of the present community of Columbia City. La Balme left 20 of his troops at Kekionga while he and the rest of his men marched about 18 miles west to the Eel River Post.

A couple of disgruntled French traders who had lost all of their furs in the raid on Kekionga incited the Miami in the neighboring villages and alerted the village of Little Turtle about La Balme's expedition shortly after their departure. The Miami annihilated the troops left at Kekionga and then hurried to Little Turtle to attack the rest of La Balme's force.

Little Turtle (Mishikinakwa) was eager for a fight. He mustered more than 100 warriors even though he had not yet become a chief. Little Turtle and his warriors attacked La Balme's soldiers on Sunday, November 5, killing about 30, including the colonel himself, capturing one, and scattering the rest.[27]

This victory made Little Turtle the principal war chief of the Miamis. When he presented La Balme's scalp, watch, spurs, sword, and official papers to the British commander at Detroit, Little Turtle was rewarded with a gift of military supplies. The Miami tribe, which had been fairly neutral, now sided with the Crown forces. This presented a serious obstacle to Colonel George Rogers Clark's plan to capture Detroit.[28]

Le Petit Fort

Colonel Clark might have been able to capture Detroit with little opposition had he done so in 1779 after his victories at Fort Sackville at Vincennes when Lieutenant Governor Henry Hamilton (The "Hair Buyer") was held prisoner. However, he waited for large reinforcements which never came.

Jean Baptiste Hamelin, a half-breed, led a group of 16 Americans and Creoles from Kaskaskia, Cahokia, and other French settlements to raid Fort St. Joseph, near present-day Niles, Michigan, in December 1780. They chose to attack the British fort on the east bank of the St. Joseph River, less than 10 miles north of the present city of South Bend, Indiana, while the Native American warriors were away hunting for their winter sustenance. The fort did not maintain a regular garrison at that time and was little more than a fur-trading post. The Creoles captured the fort and many bales of valuable furs from the nearby area villages that were stored there.

As the Creoles returned quickly with their captured pelts, a strong force of Potawatomis, probably under Chief Anaquiba (and his son, Topinabee or Topenebee "Quiet Sitting Bear"), who lived just south of the fort, pursued them down Trail Creek in northwestern Indiana. A running fight ensued for several miles along Trail Creek on Tuesday, December 5, according to one account. Major Arent Schuyler De Peyster, British commander at Michilimackinac, Michigan, in his report to Brigadier General Henry Watson Powell on January 8, 1781, presents another account. He says that Lieutenant Dagreaux Du Quindre (or Dagneau De Quindre) and a band of natives and Loyalist traders encountered the Creoles at the Indiana Dunes and recovered all of the furs by defeating Hamelin's forces, killing four, wounding two, and capturing seven near Le Petit Fort which is near Aberconk Village, located inside Indiana Dunes State Park. Le Petit Fort was probably a simple cabin with gardens for growing vegetables surrounded by a palisade. It may have been built by the *coureurs de bois* or illegal traders and most likely served as a warehouse for the furs of traveling merchant-voyageurs and as a trading post. The report read:

> Since the affair at the Miamis something similar happened at St. Joseph's. A Detachment from the Cahokias, consisting of sixteen men only, commanded by a half Indian named Jean Baptiste Hammelain, timed it so as to arrive at St. Joseph's with Pack Horses, when the Indians were out on their first Hunt, an old Chief and his family excepted. They took the Traders Prisoners, and carried off all the goods, consisting of at least Fifty Bales, and took the Route of Chicagou. Lieut. Dagreaux Du Quindre, who I had stationed near St. Josephs, upon being informed of it, immediately assembled the Indians, and pursued them as far as the petite Fort, a days Journey beyond the Riviere Du Chemin where on the 5th December, he summoned them to surrender, on their refusing to do it he ordered the Indians to attack them. Without a loss of a man on his side, killed four, wounded two, and took seven Prisoners, the other Three escaped in the thick Wood. Three of the Prisoners were brought in here amongst whom is Brady a Superintendent of Indian affairs. The rest he suffered the Indians to take to M. Makina. I look upon these Gentry as Robbers and not Prisoners of war, having no commission, that I can learn, other than a verbal order from Mons. Trottier an Inhabitant of the Cahoes...[29]

This small incident increased Native American support for the Crown forces throughout the northern region and created another obstacle to Clark's plans to capture Detroit.

Fort St. Joseph

After the attack on St. Louis, the campaign of 1781 west of the Alleghenies began with a surprise attack on the British Fort St. Joseph. Spain, which had joined the war against the British, sent Captain Don Eugenio Pourré (or Poure) with a force of 65 Spaniards and French militiamen from St. Louis and Cahokia and 60 Potawatomies to capture the British post and its fur traders. Fort Saint Joseph was the closest British post to St. Louis.[30]

Historians give four major reasons for the attack:

1. to establish a Spanish claim east of the Mississippi;
2. to plunder and gain revenge for the British attack on St. Louis;
3. to provide defense against an expected British counterattack on St. Louis the next spring;
4. to assist tribes friendly to Spain to fight the Crown forces.

Most documentary evidence seems to support the last view, especially a letter from Francisco Cruzat, lieutenant governor of Spanish Illinois, that describes an appeal for assistance from two Milwaukee chiefs hostile to the British—El Hetumo and Naquiguen.

The attackers left St. Louis on Tuesday, January 2, 1781 and arrived at Fort Saint Joseph on Monday, February 12. They caught the British unprepared, quickly surrounded the fort, and captured it easily, having struck a deal with a group of 200 nearby Potawatomies to give them half of the goods taken at the fort in exchange for their neutrality.

However, Pourré's force withdrew the following day and returned to St. Louis, staying only long enough to permit Spain to claim, by right of conquest, the valleys of the St. Joseph and Illinois rivers at the end of the war. Some historians say that Spain wanted to lay claim to the region during future peace negotiations. The claim later created problems between Spain and the United States.

George Rogers Clark went to Richmond, Virginia, before the end of 1780 to consult with Governor Thomas Jefferson. They made arrangements for Clark to lead 2,000 men against the British stronghold early in the spring in hopes of adding "an extensive and fertile country" to the "Empire of Liberty." Jefferson made Clark a brigadier general and appointed him to lead the expedition which was to be largely a Virginia affair supported by Congress. Clark encountered many difficulties in obtaining both supplies and men and had to resort to a draft. He mustered 400 men at Pittsburgh and proceeded down the Ohio in August.[31]

Pensacola

When Spain entered the war in 1779, her main area of activity was at sea and along the shores of the Gulf of Mexico. She did not want to appear as supporting the American War of Independence because she saw it as one of ideology and as a threat to her own empire in the New World. When she declared war, it was out of alliance with France, as the kings of the two countries were uncle and nephew. Yet, the forces of Bernardo de Gálvez, the young governor of Louisiana and an experienced soldier, probably helped relieve the pressure on the frontiers of Georgia and South Carolina in 1780 and brought indirect benefits to the Congressional cause in the South. Unlike France, Spain refused to sign a treaty with the United States, but she wanted to recover the possessions which she lost in the Seven Years War.

Bernardo de Gálvez planned to capture Pensacola, Mobile, and other smaller Crown posts on the Gulf coast of West Florida. Brigadier General John Campbell garrisoned the fortified city of Pensacola with 900 worn-out veterans, Irish deserters from the Continental Army, ill-equipped Hessian mercenaries, and untrained Loyalist troops.

The authorities in Havana gave Gálvez considerable opposition as they wanted a primarily naval campaign against Pensacola while Gálvez wanted to take Mobile first to cut Pensacola's supply source and to control the Native Americans in the area. Gálvez also needed more troops, artillery, supplies, and ships which Havana refused to give him. Despite these obstacles, he proceeded with his attack on Mobile.

Gálvez's first fleet sailed from Havana on Monday, October 16, 1780 but was dispersed by a hurricane two days later. Some of the ships sank in the Gulf of Mexico and the rest returned badly damaged. Gálvez put together another expedition of between 8,000 and 10,000 troops with a large train of artillery.

A force of 1,315 men boarded transports and sailed from Havana on Tuesday, February 13, 1781. The convoy of 21 major vessels, including some vessels of war, 35 ships, and several gunboats headed for Pensacola to defend Spanish positions on the mainland. They arrived at Santa Rosa Island, which shielded the Bay of Pensacola, on March 9 and occupied the island. The fleet could not enter Pensacola Bay, however, because of the danger of running aground on the sand bars and because of the British guns. Although Gálvez commanded the expedition, he did not have the authority to countermand an order from the commander of the fleet, Admiral José Calbo de Irazabal.

Gálvez landed on Santa Rosa Island at the mouth of Pensacola harbor at 3 AM on Saturday, March 10. He found the British battery there abandoned. A fort on Barrancas Coloradas (the red cliffs) guarded the harbor opposite Santa Rosa. The fort had 11 guns, including five 32-pounders.

Irazabal almost ran his 74-gun flagship *San Ramón* aground trying to negotiate the tricky bar at the mouth of the harbor. He found it impossible to bring the fleet into the harbor under the fire of Fort Barrancas Coloradas. General Gálvez realized the delay of the squadron and convoy in entering the harbor and feared that a strong wind might force the warships and cargo vessels to set sail to avoid being wrecked upon the shore, thereby abandoning the troops on the island without means of subsistence. He decided to enter the harbor first, convinced that the others would follow him.

The next morning, Gálvez sent Admiral Calbo a 32-pound ball fired by Fort Barrancas Coloradas at his camp on Santa Rosa Island. He also sent a message with the cannonball: "whoever has honor and valour will follow me." The fleet included four ships from Louisiana which Gálvez had the right to command.

At 11 AM on Monday, March 17, Don Juan Riano's sloop *Valenzuela* positioned herself at the entrance of Pensacola harbor, accompanied by the brig *Galveztown* and two small gunboats. Sub-lieutenant D. Miguel Herrera arrived at 4 PM with letters from Colonel José Manuel Ignacio Timoteo de Ezpeleta Galdeano Dicastillo y del Prado, conde de Ezpeleta de Beire to General Gálvez, advising him that he was marching with his troops to join him.

Gálvez embarked in an open boat at 2:30 PM on Sunday, March 18, to go on board the *Galveztown*, formerly William Pickles's *West Florida*, anchored at the mouth of Pensacola harbor. He ordered the captain to hoist the rear admiral's pennant; and the crew fired a salute of 15 guns to further clarify Gálvez's intentions. The

Galveztown then set sail followed by two armed launches and the sloop *Valenzuela*, commanded by Don Juan Riano—Louisiana's entire navy—into Pensacola's harbor.

Fort Barrancas Coloradas had 11 guns and was garrisoned by approximately 140 officers and men. It fired its five 32-pounders on the fleet. Any round shot could have sunk the *Gálveztown*; but Gálvez and his staff stood on the quarterdeck as the shots whizzed above and around the ship. Although the British fired 140 cannon shots, they inflicted no casualties and only minor damage to the ships, piercing the Gálveztown's sails and shrouds. The next day, Calbo, shamed by Gálvez's success, led the rest of the fleet into the harbor.[32]

The Spaniards began landing 15,000 troops on Rose Island (Santa Rosa Island). They then advanced within a mile of Fort George, where they began a subterranean work while their batteries fired incessantly on the fort. The British garrison refused to surrender until a man deserted and instructed the Spaniards to shell the magazine. One shell blew it up, killing about 100 men.

A small British naval squadron arrived from Jamaica, British West Indies, but did not dare to challenge the large fleet. Spanish infantry captured nine British seamen despite firing from the 18-gun HM Sloop-of-War *Port Royal* and the privateer *Mentor*. The Spanish captured the *Port Royal* and destroyed the *Mentor* in the harbor.[33]

Other troops came overland from Mobile, Alabama, and New Orleans, Louisiana, arriving a week later with 2,300 men to help in the siege of Pensacola, the last major British post in the area in early 1781. The French provided an additional 725 soldiers. The Chickasaws and Loyalists sniped at the Spanish camp from cover. They ambushed any soldier foolish enough to wander into the woods alone. The Spanish casualties at this time were caused by the Choctaws, Creeks, Seminoles, and Chickasaws, allied with the British who raided Spanish outposts and attacked stragglers day and night.[34]

The convoy set sail at 2 PM on Monday, March 19, 1781, preceded by the King's frigates. General Gálvez decided to go to the Perdido River in a boat to instruct Colonel Ezpeleta personally about his plans at 5 PM. However, the winds and currents both forced him to return to the camp at 11 PM.[35]

Lieutenant George Pinhorn led a sortie against the Spanish lines on Tuesday, April 12. His men killed one and wounded nine, but Pinhorn was killed in the action. Don Josef Solano's fleet of 20 ships arrived from Havana with 1,600 Spanish and four French frigates carrying 725 French soldiers on Friday, April 19. The Spanish forces included a regiment of the famed Irish Brigade under the command of Lieutenant Colonel Arturo O'Neil. These reinforcements brought Gálvez's army to more than 7,000 men. He was now ready to begin the final phase of the operation.

The Crown forces, which included two battalions of Pennsylvania and Maryland Loyalists, bloodied the Irish Regiment in one sortie, and their 149 cannon and howitzers fought deadly duels with Gálvez's batteries.

Field Marshal Don Juan Manuel Cagigal, the commandant of artillery, the quartermaster general, the major general of the army, and his aides-de-camp went on horseback accompanied by a party of light infantrymen, to reconnoiter the terrain and the distance for opening the trench and to establish the first one at 9:30 AM on Sunday, April 22. The Crown forces discovered them and fired cannon at them, forcing them to retire with one man wounded.

Two companies of French light infantry and the artillery companies arrived in camp that same morning and were assigned a camping place. The troops began disembarking; and, although they came under enemy fire passing before Barrancas Coloradas, they suffered no harm. The troops finished disembarking the next day.[36]

The encampment for the recently arrived troops had also been laid out, with the order that it should be immediately protected by bulwarks because it was in the midst of woods and surrounded by Native Americans who hid in the forest and harassed the troops at all hours.

The Crown forces resumed intermittent fire from cannons, howitzers, and mortars at 9 PM. The fire continued until 1 AM on the 30th and resumed with great intensity at daybreak, delaying the work on the trenches considerably. The Spaniards only built a fascine, widened the trench a little through its widest part, and raised half of the parapet of the mortar and cannon battery outlined the previous day. The guards and workers were happily relieved, at 7 PM, by the same number of troops less 200 soldiers.

Some parties of Native Americans came through the nearby woods toward the camp and fired on the advanced positions, which responded immediately with field pieces and rifles. After mortally wounding a soldier who was resting in his tent, and seriously wounding one officer and one soldier, the braves retreated, under cover of the woods, to the shores of the bay where the Spanish launches came through to unload their cargo. The warriors surprised six sailors who were fishing on the opposite side of the swamp and either killed them or carried them away as prisoners.

The French frigate *Andromanche* entered the port of Pensacola at noon on April 30 to fire on the enemy fortifications from the sea at the same time as the Spanish trench batteries. The French and Crown forces fired on one another as the *Andromanche* passed before Barrancas Coloradas. She received only two or three hits which did not cause much damage.

A deserter arrived at 7 AM and reported that the Crown forces began constructing a battery of small calibre cannons in the glacis of Fort George. The Spaniards spent the entire day widening the trench, perfecting the batteries of cannons and mortars and in finishing the two redoubts without the enemy firing any more. The soldiers and laborers were relieved at 8 PM, and the four mortars were brought to the battery.

The siege involved 23,200 Spanish troops, including seamen; 50 pieces of brass cannon; six 13- and six 9½-inch mortars; an immense field train; and a naval force of 11 Spanish and four French ships-of-the-line, four Spanish and four French frigates, transports, victuallers, and row galleys.[37]

Spencer's Ordinary (Tavern)

The engagement at Spencer's Ordinary is the first encounter of Major General Marie-Joseph Paul du Motier, Marquis de Lafayette's army with General Charles Cornwallis's army in the Virginia campaign of 1781. Cornwallis, now in command in the south, had ended his raids by the middle of June and marched east through Richmond and toward the former capital at Williamsburg. Here, he hoped to receive additional instructions from General Henry Clinton, commander of the Crown forces in North America. Clinton and Cornwallis didn't get along. Clinton's communications to Cornwallis were often confusing and contradictory; but Cornwallis hoped the new orders would be clearer.

Lafayette and his force of about 4,500 men followed Cornwallis, keeping about 20 miles behind. He did his best to give the impression that his force was larger and more powerful than it was, hoping to lure Cornwallis into battle on favorable terms; but Cornwallis ignored him. Lieutenant Colonel Banastre Tarleton and his legionnaires guarded Cornwallis's rear.

Cornwallis had sent Lieutenant Colonel John Graves Simcoe and a large detachment on a foraging mission to the Chickahominy River area on Saturday, June 23. They had gathered a large number of cattle that they were driving to Williamsburg, burning tobacco and other crops along the way. Simcoe's force arrived at Spencer's Ordinary (tavern), about 6 miles from Williamsburg, in the early morning of June 26, a peaceful but hot summer morning.

Captain Johann von Ewald ordered his jaegers to stop and rest their horses and to eat breakfast along the road in front of Spencer's while Simcoe guarded the rear and eventually joined Ewald's men at Spencer's.

Meanwhile, Lafayette's army moved to Bird's Tavern, 10 miles from Williamsburg. Lafayette made his headquarters at Tyre's plantation, halfway between Spencer's Ordinary and Bird's Tavern. When his scouts alerted him to Simcoe's movements, Lafayette sent a large force to trap Simcoe and destroy him. Tarleton's troops, north of Simcoe's men, guarding the rear, never detected Colonel Richard Butler's detachment that caught the Crown forces by surprise while Ewald was asleep. They had marched all night, arriving about an hour away from the Crown forces about dawn. When the Crown forces stopped for breakfast, Butler's men caught up.

While Lafayette's original plan was to cut the road between Cornwallis and Simcoe and attack Simcoe's flank and rear, Butler saw an advantage in surprise and took it without waiting for Brigadier General "Mad Anthony" Wayne's reinforcements. He attacked too hastily. Major William McPherson, with 50 dragoons and 50 mounted light infantrymen, had ridden hard and charged Simcoe's outposts suddenly without waiting for Colonel Butler to get his troops into position. The outposts rode into camp and gave the alarm. When Butler's force charged down the Jamestown Road, they failed to notice the unmounted British dragoons resting in a field to the right of the road.

When the dragoons saw the pickets retreating and spreading the alarm, they saddled up and charged Butler's men unexpectedly and with such force that Major McPherson was knocked from his horse. Vicious saber-to-saber fighting ensued and McPherson managed to escape unharmed.

Simcoe rallied his men and forced the Congressional horsemen to retreat. He also sent a rider to Cornwallis in Williamsburg for assistance. Ewald, awakened by the gunfire and shouting, formed the rangers, the light infantry, the grenadiers, and his jaegers in line in the fields along the road. They moved north toward the ordinary's orchard where they ran into Majors William Call and William Willis approaching quickly with the Virginia riflemen and 150 mounted troopers under Major William McPherson.

Ewald noticed that his line overlapped the enemy's left. He ordered the jaegers to flank the Continentals and strike their rear. He then ordered the British light infantry and grenadiers to execute a bayonet charge. Despite being flanked on the left and attacked in the front with the bayonet, the riflemen waited until the Crown forces were about 40 yards away when they fired a volley into their line, bringing down about half the grenadiers. The Crown troops kept advancing, forcing the riflemen, without bayonets, to retreat to the woods, closely pursued by Ewald's force.

Ewald attacked before the riflemen could rally, throwing them into confusion. However, in the limited visibility caused by the smoke of the musketry hanging low in the woods, the flanking force of jaegers became dispersed in the woods and lost their cohesion and firepower. The hot fight drove the riflemen and cavalry back in hand-to-hand combat. They soon encountered Colonel Butler's Continental light infantry line advancing to support them.

Ewald, realizing that he was now outnumbered by fresh troops, recalled his men and requested Simcoe to order a retreat. The Crown forces withdrew 2 miles along the Williamsburg Road, when they met Cornwallis coming from Williamsburg to support them. Without reliable intelligence on the enemy's location, Cornwallis could not afford to lose men when Clinton was expecting them in New York.

Butler did not pursue the retreating Crown forces because Cornwallis outnumbered him. Nor did Butler want to bring on a general engagement at this point. The Congressional forces claimed a victory and returned to Tyre's plantation and Bird's Tavern. The Crown forces also claimed winning a sizable victory, despite retreating and leaving dead and wounded behind. They later removed the dead and wounded while Cornwallis shielded the area. Real casualty figures are difficult to determine. Simcoe reported 10 killed and 23 wounded. However, Lafayette claimed he inflicted 60 killed and over 100 wounded. The Congressional forces reported nine killed,

14 wounded, and 14 missing; but the British claimed they captured three officers and 28 privates.

Cornwallis returned to Williamsburg where he received orders to send some of his best troops to New York City to reinforce Clinton, who felt himself surrounded by the French and American armies and the French fleet. Lafayette moved his camp almost daily to avoid being caught by surprise.[38]

The British landed at Portsmouth, Virginia, five days later, on May 10, and occupied the town without opposition. General Mathew sent detachments to capture Suffolk, Gosport, and other small towns. The detachments encountered no opposition except in Gosport, where the 100-man garrison of Fort Nelson resisted for a short while before abandoning the redoubt. The defenders burned a nearly completed war vessel and two French ships loaded with tobacco and other merchandise to prevent their capture. The Crown forces sacked the shipyard, ropewalks, and a very considerable store of ship timbers and naval stores at Gosport and burned the town. They also looted the neighboring plantations, destroyed or carried off 130 vessels and 3,000 hogsheads of tobacco. They damaged an estimated £2,000,000 of property before sailing away with all sorts of plunder, without losing a single man.[39]

North Castle and Kingsbridge or King's Bridge

As General Rochambeau's army marched south to join Lafayette, French grenadiers and chasseurs camped on a height to the left of the New York road in front of a pond adjoining the North Castle Meeting House in early July 1781. The rest of the army camped on high ground in back of the pond and the little North Castle River (Kisco River). Their left flank was at the meeting house and their right near a wood. They held an excellent position protected by marshes on the left and nearby mountains and woodland. They could advance toward the enemy in three columns or retire in two: one by way of Pines Bridge, which crossed the Croton River 4 miles to the north of the camp, and the other by way of Ridgebury and Bedford, 22 and 5 miles away respectively. Troops advancing to attack them, especially if numerous, would have to march on the roads, unable to make detours without coming up against woods, mountains, and many insurmountable obstacles. These natural obstacles made the position easy to defend.

Meanwhile, Major General Benjamin Lincoln led the vanguard of the Continental Army (two regiments of light infantry and a detachment of artillery) in an attempt to retake the north end of Manhattan Island. A force of 800 came down from Peekskill in boats during the night of Sunday, July 1. They landed secretly on the New York shore below Fort Knyphausen, formerly Fort Washington. They were to reconnoiter the enemy posts on the northern end of the island and to capture by surprise not only Fort Knyphausen but also Fort Tryon, Fort George on Laurel Hill, the works on Cox Hill at the mouth of Spuyten Duyvil, and those at Kingsbridge.

General George Washington was scheduled to arrive at Valentine's Hill, 4 miles above Kingsbridge, early the next day with the main army.

However, if he deemed it inadvisable to attack them, Lincoln would remain on the mainland above Spuyten Duyvil Creek and cooperate with Armand Louis de Gontaut-Biron, Duc de Lauzun's operation. Lauzun would advance to Morrisania (on the east bank of the Harlem River) to capture, or at least defeat, De Lancey's corps of Loyalists believed to be quartered in that vicinity. In this event, Lincoln would land above Spuyten Duyvil and march to the high ground in front of Kingsbridge. There, he would remain concealed until the beginning of Lauzun's attack to prevent De Lancey from turning Lauzun's right as he cut off the Loyalists' escape over the bridge. Both of these movements depended on surprise to be successful.[40]

General Lincoln decided not to attack the Manhattan Island forts, as the enemy became aware of his movements and he could not surprise them. Colonel James De Lancey's corps had moved farther inland from Morrisania toward Williams's bridge on the Bronx River.

Examining the ground from Fort Lee on the New Jersey shore, Lincoln saw it was occupied by a large force that had just returned from foraging in New Jersey and a man-of-war was anchored in the river between. He abandoned the main plan and went for the second, which failed. He landed his troops above Spuyten Duyvil but another foraging party stronger than his own discovered him and attacked.

Lauzun's Legion, Colonel Elisha Sheldon's dragoons, and a detachment of Connecticut state troops under General David Waterbury arrived, after a hot and tiring forced march, only to find the intended surprise of De Lancey impossible. Lauzun gave his support to General Lincoln and General Washington hurried down from Valentine's Hill.

The Crown forces escaped by boat; and Washington spent the rest of the day in reconnoitering the ground about Kingsbridge, in the event of a future operation. The next day, he withdrew his army to Dobbs Ferry, where the French army joined it on July 6.[41]

Meanwhile, Hessian Lieutenant Colonel Andreas Emmerich and 100 men marched to Phillips's house (Yonkers) in the evening of Monday, July 2. The next morning, a number of wagons, under an escort of 200 foot and 30 mounted jaegers, were to be sent there for some hay. The Crown forces learned, about 10 PM, that General Washington had been at Singsing that afternoon. They decided to leave the wagons within the lines and send a detachment to recall Colonel Emmerich. The detachment left the camp at Kingsbridge at daybreak. An advance guard of a sergeant and 10 men reconnoitered Fort Independence and its environs.

Meanwhile, General Washington planned an expedition to cut off Colonel James De Lancey in the vale and Major Pruschenk, commanding the jaeger horse on Cortlandt ridge. The Duc de Lauzun would march to Williams's bridge at daybreak the following morning. Major General Benjamin Lincoln would go from Tappan and land below Yonkers and General Washington would occupy Valentine's Hill.

As it was not quite day yet, the Crown scouting parties did not perceive the enemy drawn up in line of battle until they were within 10 yards of them. The Continentals fired at them; they returned fire and fell back to a proper distance. The scouts, under fire, tried to gain the height behind the fort. They succeeded in taking possession of the ruins of a house formerly fortified by Colonel Emmerich. From this location, they tried to attack the Continentals to dislodge them from their advantageous position.

The scouts noticed a battalion with flying colors in the fort. That battalion outnumbered them and attacked furiously with the bayonet. Unable to gain any ground, the scouts fell back, under cannon fire, to Charles's redoubt. The Continentals pressed them so hard that they began to lose ground because of the narrow defiles. The cavalry charged the advancing Continentals and stopped them. The jaegers re-formed and resumed the attack with redoubled vigor, driving the Continentals from the fort and down from the heights as far as Deveaux's house. The jaegers then took possession of the ground.

Lieutenant Colonel Ludwig Johann Adolph von Wurmb arrived from Kingsbridge with the rest of the jaeger corps and took possession of the rising ground between the bridge and Fort Independence. He reconnoitered the enemy's new position, extending from Mile Square Road over the heights to Williams's bridge. A thick wood in the rear of the Continentals indicated their intention to conceal their real strength. Repeated intelligence told Colonel von Wurmb that 300 French dragoons covered the enemy's left at Williams's bridge, so he acted carefully, not thinking it advisable to risk another attack.

Lieutenant Colonel Emmerich retreated over Spuyten Duyvil Creek and was cut off by the Continental position. Meanwhile, 200 Regulars had arrived along with Loyalists from Morrisania. It was decided to force the Continentals from their position and to allow Colonel Emmerich an opportunity to advance on Cortlandt's house, still occupied by the Continentals.

The jaegers advanced and took possession of Cortlandt's bridge. The Loyalists and the jaeger advance parties engaged the Continental advance posts and drove them to their main body. The Continentals withdrew to the left and retreated toward Williams's bridge. With the passage now open, Colonel Emmerich was able to leave Spuyten Duyvil. He informed General Friedrich Wilhelm von Lossburg that he drew 200 Whigs into his ambuscade at Phillips's house, killed three, and took nine that the Continentals were moving in two columns toward Cortlandt's bridge. One of the columns had already been seen on Valentine's Hill. The troops were now ordered to fall back to their former position, leaving 100 jaegers at Fort Independence to observe enemy movements. General Washington reconnoitered

Spuyten Duyvil at 3 PM and the troops moved into their lines and to their encampment at 4 PM.

The jaegers lost three men killed; one officer, one sergeant, and 26 men wounded; and five missing. The Continentals suffered considerable losses. Reports said they embarked 101 wounded men at Singsing and sent them up the North River and that a great many died of their wounds before reaching Singsing. They also reported one officer and 17 men who were left dead on the field and 17 stands of arms.[42]

As General Lincoln proceeded along Guard Hill Road with 1,000 men on Tuesday, July 3, he was himself surprised and would have been cut off had the Duc de Lauzun and his hussars not been posted in the rear to protect it. Colonel James De Lancey's dragoons did not dare take on the hussars.

Meanwhile, General Washington took the rest of his army to White Plains and camped at Phillipsburg, sending word to the French army to march as rapidly as possible to North Castle to form a second line in reserve, 20 miles to the rear, in case the Crown forces advanced in considerable force.

When the French appeared to surprise an enemy post at North Castle on Tuesday, July 3, 1781, nearly 3,000 Crown troops marched out in several columns, forcing the French to cross a small stream and form in line of battle behind it. General Lincoln joined up with the French troops but his vanguard fired before they were ordered, alerting the English and enabling them to retire in good order after a brisk fire. General Lincoln had four men killed and 15 wounded; Lauzun's Legion lost none.[43]

Dobbs Ferry

The HM Galley *Dependence* returned to the vicinity of Tarrytown, New York, to annoy the French and Continental troops camped in that area to rest prior to resuming their march to Yorktown in the summer of 1781. The *Dependence* was anchored off Tarrytown together with the frigate *Tartar* and the galley *Crane* on Thursday, July 12. The following morning at 10, the *Dependence* fired eight 24-pound round shots to prevent the Congressional troops from constructing earthworks. The battery cannonaded the ships at 6 PM that evening, forcing them to weigh anchor and row farther up the river. The French, camped along the river 4 miles above Dobbs Ferry, heard the cannonade and mustered, thinking that their camp was under fire. They were later dismissed. The soldiers had barely returned to their tents when they were ordered to send 200 men with six 12-pounders and two howitzers to Tarrytown. The order was countermanded when they were ready to march. Only Major General Robert Howe marched out with a detachment of his own troops.[44]

Continental and French troops exchanged fire with British ships in the Hudson River off Tarrytown on Sunday, July 15. They suffered one killed and one wounded.[45]

Bedford

Eight Westchester Loyalists went out on Tuesday night, July 17, in an attempt to surprise some French officers lodging in a house in front of their camp. On their way, they encountered a patrol of six hussars of the Duc de Lauzun's Legion. An officer and 25 dragoons followed the hussars. The Loyalists hid near the side of the road. The hussars passed without discovering them, but the officer spotted them and was preparing to fire. The Loyalists immediately fired back, shot and killed the officer, rushed out, and fired at the dragoons who rode off as fast as possible.[46]

A party of about 10 of Colonel James De Lancey's Loyalists, under the command of Lieutenant Jeremiah Vincent, proceeded from Morrisania to Samuel Crawford's neighborhood, less than 3 miles from White Plains on Tuesday evening, July 17. There, they fell in with a captain and 30 French hussars who charged the little detachment with their sabers. This forced the Loyalists to leave the road and seek the protection of a fence. Lieutenant Vincent fired and shot the French commander dead. Two of his men also fired and the whole party ran away, leaving their slain captain on the road. A body of French infantrymen immediately advanced briskly. Lieutenant Vincent retreated without any loss.[47]

Oyster Bay

A large body of Continental and French troops was observed in motion in front of Kingsbridge at daybreak on Sunday, July 22. They positioned themselves on the heights from Cortland's house to Williams's bridge and placed strong advanced posts in the old forts: Independence, King's Fort, and others in that line. The Loyalists from Morrisania were forced to retire within British lines but did not have time to bring their stock, which the Continentals seized and drove off.

The Continentals brought two artillery pieces to fire at a scow at Holland's Ferry about 6 AM. The scow was transporting Loyalists from the rear of Redoubt No. 8 on Fordham Heights. The artillery did little damage. General George Washington marched a large column of about 4,000 men, with some cavalry, and a few field pieces and two or three French battalions toward Morrisania Point soon afterward. He came so near the point with some cavalry, that some cannon shots were fired at him, forcing him to withdraw. This column returned in the afternoon and joined the other troops near Fort Independence, where they remained all day without attempting anything further.

The British reinforced Redoubt No. 8 with 20 men and kept the troops stationed near Kingsbridge ready to move if necessary. The French and Continentals killed three or four British and captured eight or 10 on the march. The Continentals lost about two men killed, one wounded, and about five captured.

A Congressional fleet consisting of a large sloop of war, five brigs, and about five whaleboats, all fully loaded with infantry, left Fairfield, Connecticut, and joined a detachment of three French ships from the fleet of Admiral Louis, Comte de Barras, out of Newport. The ships had a battalion of French infantry on board. The Congressional fleet landed their troops on the unguarded beach on the north shore of Lloyd's Neck, Long Island, at 8 AM on July 12. The infantry, with some rangers on the flanks of the column, took a logging road through the woods, guided by Heathcote Muirson, a veteran of many similar raids on Long Island. Muirson had scouted the enemy works a few days earlier and found that the large, well-fortified redoubt mounted only two long 12-pounders which faced out over Oyster Bay. The Loyalist camp extended from the south side of the fort to the causeway connecting the Neck to the mainland. A large parade ground on the land side of the fort extended ½ mile eastward. The fort had an opening with no gate in the southeast corner for wagons to pass through and a picket guard on the eastern end of the Neck overlooking Huntington Bay. However, there were no guards along the intervening shoreline.

The fleet returned into Long Island Sound to watch for enemy shipping. One of the French frigates blockaded Huntington harbor and bombarded the Loyalist fleet in Lloyd harbor, while the large Continental sloop-of-war went to Oyster Bay to blockade that port and to bombard the fort. The infantry followed the logging road for about a mile before turning into the woods for another mile. They planned a "hit and run" assault against the undefended side of the fort and brought no artillery. When they got to the edge of the woods, they displayed into a line formation on the east side of the parade ground.

The Continental sloop-of-war sailed within range of the fort and began to cannonade it at 11 AM. The gunners on the west parapet returned fire and were quickly supported by running fire from Captain Thomas's 10-gun brig *Restoration*, a Loyalist privateer anchored just below the fort. Meanwhile, the French 40-gun frigate in Huntington Bay fired a broadside at the Loyalist vessels in the Lloyd harbor inlet. These included a large, unarmed schooner commanded by Captain Church, the one-swivel gun whaleboats *Henry Clinton* and *Association*, and one or two small coasters which were being loaded with firewood. A shore battery of two long 12-pounder deck guns, which had been landed from a British warship, unexpectedly returned fire from an earthwork dug the day before on the east end of the Neck, overlooking the mouth of Lloyd harbor.

All the Loyalist vessels moved as quickly as they could toward the head of Lloyd harbor to get out of cannon shot. The French ship held her position in Huntington Bay and continued a running fire against the shore battery and the inlet.

About 600–700 Loyalists assembled on the parade ground outside the fort while messengers galloped on horseback to call out all available reinforcements from the nearby towns of Huntington and Oyster Bay. Major Benjamin Tallmadge's allied force of about 450 men marched out onto the parade and halted about 400 yards from the fort, in full view of the Loyalists.

Both sides advanced across the parade ground in a line formation until they came within effective musket range of each other. They then halted, less than 150 yards apart, and began to fire at each other in the hot, midday sun. When it became evident that the smaller attacking force was not going to rout or capture the Loyalist militia, the attackers began to destroy the large number of unprotected huts on the south side of the fort.

While Tallmadge's main force attacked the Loyalist militia to keep them in their position against the outer defenses of the fort, Heathcote Muirson went to the left flank to scout ahead and to guide a French detail to the Loyalist camp. Some of the French troops headed toward the high hill at the south end of the parade with some combustibles. They marched uphill across about 200 yards of open ground covered with tree stumps and low bushes to reach the huts along the main road on the far side of the hill.

The Loyalists perceived this flanking movement by the French as an attempt to place artillery on the hill. This would give them a good field of fire into the fort. The Loyalist gunners hurried to the east parapet of the fort to load and fire the two 12-pounders covering the open ground. A brisk cannonade raked the French position with grapeshot. Heathcote Muirson's arm was severed at the shoulder. The French gathered their casualties and retreated east toward the woods, where they set up a field hospital on the edge of the parade ground.

The Loyalist artillery dashed any hopes of capturing the fort. The French regrouped and joined the main line which retreated slowly and in good order. The Loyalist militia did not pursue the attackers who consisted mostly of regular army troops. The first Loyalist reinforcements of about 50 mounted men from Oyster Bay and Huntington began to arrive and deployed along the West Neck road to protect the southern approach to the fort. A company of 50 Oyster Bay militiamen joined them, but no other attack occurred. Major Tallmadge's troops disappeared into the woods and headed to the beach to re-embark under the protection of a rear guard. They took evasive courses back to the Connecticut shore and the French returned to Newport. The Loyalists patrolled the battlefield and found "a number of surgeon's instruments, a great quantity of lint, bandages, etc., a bayonet, sword, and a very large quantity of port-fire and other materials for burning our houses; also, some few fragments of coats and shirts; and the grass besmeared with blood."[48]

The Loyalists from Lloyd's Neck attacked Middlesex, Connecticut, two weeks later in retaliation for the raid against Fort Franklin. The whaleboat war across Long Island Sound continued for another two years.[49]

Siege of Yorktown

When General Charles Cornwallis set off for Yorktown, he planned to obtain a good seaport and harbor, never thinking that he would have to defend it against a siege from the land. Yorktown had some natural advantages as a naval station. Gloucester lay less than a mile to the north, on the northern bank of the York River opposite Yorktown, and swamps were on the east and west. He intended to fortify Yorktown and Gloucester. Both places were on low ground and would require building exceptionally strong fortifications to make them safe as naval stations. A strong British squadron was expected to sail by October 5, 1781, to take a position between the two towns. A Congressional force coming by sea would have to come from the south.

Cornwallis thought that his men's time and energy could be better employed in other ways. Even using as many African Americans as he could muster, he would have to put the whole army to work either building the fortifications with the few entrenching tools with which his army was supplied or in guarding the working parties. He used the home of Thomas Nelson, Jr., governor of Virginia, as his headquarters during the siege and began constructing an outer line of redoubts and an inner line of earthworks, redoubts, and batteries around the town. Two redoubts, Numbers 9 and 10, strengthened the east end of the line. Two ravines in the rear of the town, Yorktown Creek and Wormley Creek, offered a little protection against an attack. Cornwallis also constructed a series of outworks on both sides of Wormley Creek northwest of Yorktown near the river. This star-shaped redoubt became known as the Fusiliers' Redoubt because some of the Royal Welch Fusiliers manned it.

When General George Washington's army arrived at Yorktown on Wednesday, September 26, 1781, the French fleet was in firm control of the Chesapeake Bay, blocking General Cornwallis's sea route of escape. A decisive concentration had been achieved. Counting 3,000 Virginia militiamen, Washington had a force of about 8,850 Continental and 7,800 French troops—a far greater number than Cornwallis had expected. Cornwallis had an army of only about 7,400 men, including about 2,000 German troops, to defend Yorktown and Gloucester. He concentrated on Yorktown from the beginning.

The Continentals and French prepared for the siege of Yorktown that proceeded in the best military traditions of Sebastien Le Prestre de Vauban under the direction of French engineers. Cornwallis soon realized that he could not hold Yorktown without reinforcements. Even though Clinton promised to send help, Cornwallis knew he could not count on him.

Major Generals Lafayette, Benjamin Lincoln (who had been exchanged after his capture at Charleston, South Carolina), and Friedrich Wilhelm von Steuben each commanded two brigades of Continental troops. General Thomas Nelson, governor of Virginia and a native of Yorktown, commanded the militia. General Jean Baptiste Donatien de Vimeur Comte de Rochambeau commanded the French wing, on the left, which consisted of seven regiments organized into three brigades. Both armies also had their own complements of engineers, cavalry, and artillery. Brigadier General Henry Knox commanded the Continental artillery brigade.

On September 27, Washington ordered his troops to encircle Yorktown within a mile of the British fortifications. The troops encountered no opposition until midday, when they came close to Yorktown where they met a few enemy pickets.

The Crown forces, trapped in Yorktown and under siege by Continental and French forces, lacked forage and slaughtered 600–700 horses. Their carcasses floated down the river almost continually during the siege. When the Crown forces realized that the Congressional troops constructed two redoubts during the night of Saturday, September 29, they began a furious cannonade. The troops continued their work despite heavy cannon and mortar fire. One shot killed three men and mortally wounded another. Rev. Evans, the chaplain, was standing near General Washington when a shot struck the ground nearby, covering his hat with sand. Rev. Evans, much agitated, showed it to the commander-in-chief who replied with his usual composure: "Mr. Evans, you had better carry that home and show it to your wife and children."

The Continental wing on the right, or east side, of the line tightened the circle by moving farther to the right and nearer the enemy. The allied (Continental and French) army established permanent camps that formed a 6-mile-long curve extending from the York River, northwest of the town, around to the south through woods and fields, then east to Wormley Creek. The swamps and marshes of Beaverdam Creek separated the Continental wing on the right and the French wing on the left.

Colonel Alexander Scammel, commanding a regiment of light infantrymen, mistook a few of the enemy's light horsemen for Colonel Stephen Moylan's brigade while reconnoitering some outworks the Crown forces had just evacuated. He thought he knew the officer in the front and was therefore not alarmed. However, two enemy soldiers came up to him on Sunday, September 30. One seized the bridle of Scammel's horse, while the other pointed a pistol at him. As Scammel inquired who they were, a third man rode up and shot him in the back at point-blank range, burning his coat with the powder. At the same time, another soldier thrust his sword at the colonel, who, weakened with his wound, fell to the ground when his horse started at the sound of the pistol firing. The soldiers then plundered the colonel and took him to York as a prisoner. General Washington requested General Cornwallis to allow him to be taken to Williamsburg, where he died of his wounds on Wednesday, October 3.[50]

Cornwallis abandoned his forward position during the night of Sunday, September 30, except for the Fusiliers' Redoubt northwest of Yorktown and Redoubts 9 and 10 close to the river on the east side of the town. The day before, he received information from Clinton that a large fleet and 5,000 men would sail to reinforce him within a few days. He decided that he only needed to hold out for a few days and that he could do so more easily by occupying the inner defense line. As delays inevitably occur in war, Clinton's fleet waited for a favorable wind and tide and actually sailed from New York on the day of Cornwallis's surrender.

The Continentals and French immediately occupied the abandoned fortifications and began additional construction, including a new redoubt. The French advanced against the Fusiliers' Redoubt on the left and drove in the pickets, but the position was too strongly defended. British guns in the main fortifications maintained a heavy and sustained fire on the allies, but they continued to work on new construction, completing it in about four days.

The allies completed preparations for the siege during the first days of October. Advanced detachments, including general officers and engineers, reconnoitered the British lines on Monday and Tuesday, October 1 and 2, and soon determined that they would make the main attack on the left or west. They brought up the heavy guns which had been landed at the James River, 6 miles to the southwest, and fired a few cannon shots from the embrasures overlooking the works the Crown forces were finishing on the gorge.

Gloucester Point

Gloucester was defended by a line of entrenchments across the Point and by about 700 British infantrymen commanded by Lieutenant Colonel Thomas Dundas. Lieutenant Colonel Banastre Tarleton and his cavalry joined him, raising his strength to 1,000. They faced 1,500 Virginia militiamen under Brigadier General George Weedon who were stationed there to check foraging expeditions and to close a possible escape route for the British Army. The Continentals were joined later by 600 French dragoons and 800 French marines.

Another force of Continental and French troops formed an arc across the interior of the point. (A French map of the Yorktown campaign shows the British fort on Gloucester Point as a semicircular structure with its broad, open end on the southeast shore of the point and extending across most of the point. A National Park Service booklet on the siege says the fortifications enclosed the village of Gloucester Point and consisted of a single line of entrenchments with four redoubts and three batteries. Nothing appears to remain of the structures, and route U.S. 17 cuts right through the area it encompassed. Most of the French troops were probably placed east of U.S. 17, extending several miles to the northwest.)

On Tuesday evening, October 2, Lieutenant Colonel Tarleton's Legion of 250 cavalrymen and mounted infantrymen crossed the York River to Gloucester since there was no forage or room for the horses at York and they were useless there.

The following morning, Lieutenant Colonel Dundas, who commanded the post at Gloucester, led detachments from all the corps to forage the country. The wagons and the pack horses were loaded with Indian corn about 3 miles from Gloucester and began to return at 10 AM with the infantry of the covering party. The dragoons in the rear guard formed an ambuscade for some militia horsemen who came by. If the enemy attempted to capture the forage, Colonel Dundas would rush out with the legion and capture them.

The wagons and infantry had nearly reached the York River when the cavalry began to retreat. When they reached the wood in front of Gloucester, Lieutenant Cameron, who had been sent to the rear with a patrol, reported that the enemy were advancing in force. They soon saw a column of dust and then some French hussars. Lieutenant Colonel Tarleton ordered part of the legion, the 17th Regiment, and Simcoe's dragoons to face about in the wood while he and Lieutenant Cameron's party reconnoitered the enemy.

Armand Louis de Gontaut-Biron, Duc de Lauzun's 300 hussars, and Lieutenant Colonel John Francis Mercer's infantrymen attacked Tarleton's Legion while Lieutenant General Claude Gabriel Marquis de Choisy, at the head of a great part of the corps sent to blockade Gloucester, marched down the road with a corps of cavalrymen and infantrymen to support them. The British rear guard was forming at the edge of a wood more than a mile away, in sight of the skirmish, when one of the hussars struck the horse of one of Tarleton's legionnaires. The horse plunged and overthrew Lieutenant Colonel Tarleton and his horse near the French line.

The entire British cavalry, concerned for the safety of their commanding officer, set out at full speed and arrived in such disorder that the charge failed to have any effect on the Duc de Lauzun's hussars who had already formed on the plain. Meanwhile, Tarleton escaped, obtained another horse, and ordered a retreat to reorganize his men.

Tarleton dismounted 40 infantrymen who had just arrived under Captain Champagne. He placed them in a thicket on his right, about 300 yards from the French squadrons. Their fire held off the Duc de Lauzun's hussars; and the Crown forces soon rallied. They immediately prepared to charge the front of the hussars with 150 dragoons while a detachment wheeled upon their flank.

The French hussars retired behind their infantry and a large body of militiamen who had arrived at the edge of the plain. They fired on Tarleton's Legion, who had gathered behind a rail. Tarleton again ordered a retreat and made many unsuccessful attempts to detach the French hussars from their infantry. He reported one officer and 11 men killed and wounded and two officers and 14 French hussars killed and wounded. Captain Johann von Ewald, of the jaegers, reported losing one officer and four men killed and nine men wounded by the lances of the French hussars.

The next day, General de Choisy, reinforced by a detachment of marines, proceeded to cut off all land communications between the country and Gloucester.[51]

Afterward, the allies established their camps closer to the British camp and contained them until the end of the siege. Closing the siege lines around the Gloucester Point fort, the Continentals forced Tarleton to surrender. The Crown forces were paroled in 1782. Tarleton returned to England and never returned to America.

The French made a diversionary attack against the Fusiliers' Redoubt early Saturday evening, October 6, as 4,300 men began digging the first parallel trench between the lines. This trench extended about 2,000 yards and ran approximately parallel to the British inner defense line. The average distance of the line from the British defenses was only 800 yards except opposite Redoubts 9 and 10. The officers put 1,500 men to work digging, while 2,800 men guarded them. By morning, the trenches were deep enough to protect the sappers digging the next day.

The allies placed artillery along the trench and began an immense cannonade on October 9. The French constructed a small defense opposite the Fusiliers' Redoubt from which they could fire their guns against the British ships anchored in the harbor.

All the batteries of the Congressional forces opened fire with a terrible roar early Thursday morning, October 10. General Washington fired the first shot. The batteries fired 60 cannons and mortars until 10 o'clock, silencing the enemy guns. About 3 PM that afternoon, the batteries on both wings opened fire, driving back to Gloucester Point the frigate *Guadeloupe* and the sloop *Formidable*, which covered the advance redoubt from the right on the York River.

Captain Johann von Ewald was seated at table when the first cannon shot was fired. Commissary Perkins was killed at table and Lieutenant Robertson, of the 76th Regiment, lost his left leg. Commissary Perkins's wife was seated between the two men.

The batteries resumed heavy fire at three British ships in the York River in the evening. The French and Continental artillery nearly silenced the British guns. The 40 cannon and 16 mortars fired 3,600 shots on the first day. Red-hot shot from the French battery struck the frigate *Charon*, a 44-gun ship situated to greatly annoy the troops in the battery above the town. The *Charon* caught fire and burned to the water. One transport was also lost. The batteries continued to fire the following day, burning another ship.[52]

Food supplies, even of putrid meat and worm-holed biscuits, were running so low that the British drove African Americans out of the town. The numbers of sick and dead increased daily. A German soldier noted the bodies lying unburied in the town, some of them with "heads, arms and legs shot off."

Stephen Popp in the British lines remembered:

> We could find no refuge in or out of the town. The people fled to the waterside and hid in hastily contrived shelters on the banks, but many of them were killed by bursting bombs. More than eighty were thus lost, besides many wounded, and their houses utterly destroyed. Our ships suffered, too, under the heavy fire, for the enemy fired in one day thirtysix hundred

shot from their heavy guns and batteries. Soldiers and sailors deserted in great numbers. The Hessian Regiment von Bose lost heavily, although it was in our rear in the second line, but in full range of the enemy's fire. Our two regiments lost very heavily too. The Light Infantry posted at an angle had the worst position and the heaviest loss. Sailors and marines all served in defending our lines on shore.[53]

Colonel Philip van Cortlandt, of the 2nd New York Regiment, later recalled:

.. the first gun which was fired I could distinctly hear pass through the town… I could hear the ball strike from house to house, and I was afterwards informed that it went through the one where many of the officers were at dinner, and over the tables, discomposing the dishes, and either killed or wounded the one at the head of the table. And I also heard that the gun was fired by the Commander-in-Chief, who was designedly present in the battery for the express purpose of putting the first match.[54]

General Charles Cornwallis was forced to conclude that "against so powerful an attack, [he could] not hope to make a very long resistance." He had about 3,250 men fit for duty and faced an allied army he estimated at about 16,000 men.

The sappers finished digging a zigzag communication trench 200 yards forward by October 11. About dusk, they began work on a second parallel, completing about 750 yards that night. They continued working for the next three days, but they could not complete the line to the York River on the right because of the two British redoubts, Numbers 9 and 10.

The allies decided to capture the two redoubts on Sunday night, October 14. The French were to attack Redoubt Number 9, the stronger of the two forts, with 120 British and Hessians, and the Continentals would take Redoubt Number 10, defended by 70 men. This would be the last infantry assault of the war. Each force consisted of 400 men. Lieutenant Colonel Guillaume de Deux Ponts, Comte de Forbach, led the French, and Lieutenant Colonel Alexander Hamilton commanded the Continentals.

Both columns began their assault at 8 PM. A "forlorn hope" preceded each column to cut through the abatis. The Continentals advanced with unloaded muskets and fixed bayonets and took Redoubt Number 10 in about 10 minutes. They did not wait for the sappers to chop through the abatis and lost fewer men. The French encountered some difficulties but captured their objective in less than half an hour. Sergeant Joseph Plumb Martin recorded his observations of the assault on Redoubt Number 10:

We arrived at the trenches a little before sunset. I saw several officers fixing bayonets on long staves. I then concluded we were about to make a general assault upon the enemy's works, but before dark I was informed of the whole plan…

The sappers and miners were furnished with axes and were to proceed in front and cut a passage for the troops through the abatis… At dark the detachment… advanced beyond the trenches and lay down on the ground to await the signal for… the attack, which was to be three shells from a certain battery… All the batteries in our line were silent, and we lay anxiously waiting for the signal… Our watchword was, "Rochambeau"… Being pronounced, "Ro-sham-bow," it sounded when pronounced quick like, "Rush on boys."

We had not lain here long before the… signal was given for us and the French… the three shells with their fiery trains mounting the air in quick succession. The word, "up up" was then reiterated through the detachment. We… moved toward the redoubt we were to attack with unloaded muskets.[55]

The French had 15 men killed and 77 wounded taking Redoubt Number 9. The Continentals lost nine killed and 25 wounded. The sappers continued digging the trenches immediately after the capture of the two redoubts, incorporating both into the second parallel by morning.

About 4 AM on Tuesday, October 16, Lieutenant Colonel Robert Abercromby (or Abercrombie) and eight companies of light troops (about 350–400 men) made a sortie near the center of the line against two unfinished redoubts occupied by the French. They spiked seven or eight pieces of cannon and killed 20 French and one Continental before being repulsed with a loss of eight killed and 12 captured. The disabled guns were repaired and soon resumed firing on Yorktown. General Cornwallis was in a hopeless situation. He hoped to get some of his troops across the river, break through the Gloucester lines, and escape to New York. He embarked some of his men in small boats and landed them on the opposite shore before midnight of October 16. A storm scattered the boats and prevented a second trip across.[56]

Surrender

The following day, the defenses of the allied troops were completed. They mounted more than 100 pieces of heavy ordnance that had been in continual operation during the previous 24 hours. The incessant cannonade caused the whole peninsula to tremble and silenced the enemy guns. At 10 AM, on the fourth anniversary of Major General John Burgoyne's surrender at Saratoga, New York and the very day that Admiral Thomas Graves set sail from New York with a reinforced fleet and 7,000 troops for the relief of Yorktown, a drummer began to beat a "parley." The guns ceased fire; a British officer appeared, was blindfolded and taken into the American lines.

General Cornwallis proposed a cessation of arms for 24 hours so commissioners could prepare and adjust the terms of capitulation. General Washington consented to a cessation of hostilities for only two hours. Two or three flags of truce passed in the course of the day. Cornwallis surrendered two days later. Admiral Graves arrived five days too late.

Cornwallis requested that the Loyalist civilians and Continental Army deserters at Yorktown and Gloucester not be punished for supporting the British. He also asked permission for his troops to return to Europe as Major General Horatio Gates had done with General Burgoyne's army at Saratoga. General Washington would not comply with these requests. Because Brigadier General Charles O'Hara did not allow Major General Benjamin Lincoln to march out with drums beating and flags flying at the surrender at Charleston, South Carolina, the British Army would endure the same humiliation at Yorktown.

Cornwallis protested that he was not responsible for O'Hara's harshness at Charleston. One of the Continental negotiators replied, "It is not the individual that is here considered. It is the nation." Washington later agreed to let the British parade to music, provided it was not a parody of any Continental tunes which the British bands enjoyed playing. During the negotiations, soldiers on both sides rested in the sun, and bands entertained each other with music.

The defeated British Army marched out from Yorktown at 2 PM on Friday, October 19, 1781, dressed in new uniforms so they would not have to surrender them to the Continentals. The allies formed two lines, with the French on one side and the Continentals on the other. The French wore white uniforms with black gaiters and their white standards with gold fleurs-de-lis flew above their heads. The Continentals wore darker, drabber clothes; the British turned their gaze away from them. The British Army marched between these two lines to a tune called "When the King Shall Enjoy His Own Again." Someone later switched the name of the piece to "The World Turned Upside Down" to make a political statement.

Cornwallis pleaded illness and did not attend. He sent Brigadier General Charles O'Hara of the British Guards, his second-in-command and the only other general officer on the British side, in his place. General O'Hara tried first to give Cornwallis's sword to General Jean Baptiste Donatien de Vimeur Comte de Rochambeau, acknowledging that the British were surrendering to the French rather than to the Continentals. Rochambeau motioned him toward Washington, who indicated that he should hand the sword to General Lincoln who had surrendered to the British under similar circumstances at Charleston the year before. General Lincoln accepted the sword and then returned it. The troops then marched to the surrender field where they laid down their arms.

Mathieu Dumas, who met the troops and directed them, recalls:

> I placed myself at General O'Hara's left hand… He asked me where General Rochambeau was. "On our left," I said, "at the head of the French line." The English general urged his horse forward to present his sword to the French general. Guessing his intention, I galloped on to place myself between him and M. de Rochambeau, who at that moment made me a sign, pointing to General Washington who was opposite to him.
>
> "You are mistaken," said I to General O'Hara. "The commander-in-chief of our army is on the right." I accompanied him, and the moment that he presented his sword, General Washington, anticipating him said, "Never from such a good hand."

The British soldiers passed between the two lines of allied troops and laid down their arms. Some of them threw their weapons down angrily, as though they wanted to smash them on the ground, until General O'Hara prevented them from doing so. As they marched away, some appeared drunk and many were close to tears, biting their lips or weeping.

Lieutenant Colonel Banastre Tarleton surrendered the troops in the Gloucester lines across the river. Before doing so, he told Lieutenant General Claude Gabriel Marquis de Choisy, the allied commander, that, because of his evil reputation, he feared for his life if left in the hands of the militia. De Choisy excluded some of the militia from the surrender ceremony and everything proceeded smoothly.

The British surrendered 7,247 officers and soldiers and 840 seamen at Yorktown and Gloucester. They also gave up 264 cannon, 6,658 muskets, 457 horses, and over £2,000 (approximately $288,200) in cash. Ironically, there were still 30,000 British and Loyalist troops fit for duty in America. Casualties during the siege were fewer than expected. Total Crown forces casualties were 596 killed and wounded and 8,081 captured. The French suffered 60 killed and 192 wounded during the siege. The Continentals had a total of 24 killed and 65 wounded.[57]

The defeat led to the resignation of Lord North, the end of major British military operations in America, and the beginning of peace negotiations between the Americans and the British.

Under the terms of the Franco-American Alliance, neither ally was supposed to negotiate independently of each other with the British. The American peace commissioners, however, quickly discovered that their goals in ending the war were different from those of the French. Congress had instructed the American delegates to follow the advice of the Comte de Vergennes in their negotiations, and the French minister thought that further war might weaken the British and allow for the conquest of additional colonies in the Caribbean. Vergennes was also worried about the potential power of the United States. The Americans, however, wanted an end to war as quickly as possible, and they were worried about the potential for a French reoccupation of Canada. As a result, the Americans decided to negotiate directly with Britain. Ignoring Vergennes, they were able to gain considerable concessions from the British. Their independent negotiations, however, caused considerable French resentment and laid the foundation for Franco-American tensions during the coming decades.

Despite General Cornwallis's surrender, the Crown forces still held New York City and the main port cities of the South. They continued to raid the lower Chesapeake in 1782 and fighting continued in South Carolina and Georgia and on the Ohio frontier. Both General Nathanael Greene and General Washington maintained their armies in position near New York and Charleston for nearly two more years.

King George III wanted to continue the war, but the British people were overwhelmingly opposed. The ministry fell and a new cabinet that decided the war in America was lost was appointed. General Sir Guy Carleton succeeded General Henry Clinton in the spring of 1782. Shortly after assuming command in New York, he wrote Washington to ask for a cessation of hostilities. With some success, Britain devoted its energies to trying to salvage what it could in the West Indies and in India.

Peace negotiations began in 1781 and dragged on until 1783. The British finally declared an end to hostilities in February 1783. Congress did the same in April. The Peace Treaty of Paris, acknowledging the independence of the United States of America, was formally signed on Wednesday, September 3, 1783 and ratified by Congress in January, 1784. The treaty also defined the boundaries of the new nation, settled fishing rights, and made arrangements for the payment of debts, the treatment of Loyalists, and the evacuation of Crown forces.[58]

Toms River

A major and 13 young British captains rode through the streets of Lancaster, Pennsylvania, up to the Black Bear Inn, shortly before 9 AM on Sunday, May 26, 1782. They entered the tavern and drew lots to settle the reprisal for the hanging of Captain Joshua Huddy. Two drummer boys each carried a hat containing slips of paper. One hat contained 13 names; the other had 12 blanks and a slip marked "Unfortunate." The boys drew 10 blanks before 19-year-old Captain Charles Asgill's name was drawn with the "Unfortunate" slip. Asgill, who was captured at Yorktown, blanched and whispered, "I knew it would be so. I never won so much as a bet of backgammon in my life." The lottery condemned Asgill to death for the murder of a man he had never seen.[59]

General Washington, against capital punishment of an innocent man, found a suitable political solution when Asgill's mother wrote an impassioned plea to the French for his release. The Comte de Vergennes asked King Louis XVI and his queen to write letters requesting Asgill's release to General Washington. Congress voted unanimously, on November 7, that Asgill's life "should be given as a compliment to the King of France." He was set free and sent home. Partisan warfare continued in New Jersey—mostly in Monmouth County—until Governor William ordered an end to all hostilities on April 14, 1783.

Epilogue

When France and Spain joined the war, they prosecuted it in the areas of their economic interests. France focused particularly on the West and East Indies: the West Indies because they were a principal market for the slave trade in the Americas and the primary source of sugar and rum consumed in Europe and America; the East Indies because of the lucrative spice trade. Moreover, the French allowed the American colonies to use their ports in the West Indies as trade centers and havens to bring captured vessels. The island of St. Domingue (Haiti) and the Dutch island of St. Eustatius became essential channels for gunpowder and military supplies provided by the French and the Dutch.

France also sent six army battalions to the West Indies in November 1775 and another five battalions in October 1777. She had stationed 19 infantry battalions there by the summer of 1778, including eight at St. Domingue, which served as a base for deploying troops and ships to the other islands and to the coast of North America. The colony also raised two battalions of local volunteers, one white, the other free blacks, and had a militia of several thousand men. The island was a major naval base and provider of troops for operations in the war. France also had a sizable fleet in the area.

In summary, France provided 10.5 million livres in subsidies to the Congressional forces and some 35 million livres in loans during the American Revolutionary War. Jacques Necker, Finance Minister, enacted a *vingtième* (a 5 percent income tax) in 1776 to finance the military support for the Americans. He also made extensive use of borrowing to cover France's mounting deficits. When these still failed to keep pace with the financial demands, the comptroller tried to increase the royal treasury by increasing the efficiency of tax collectors (a very unpopular policy). As the national debt increased, Necker tried to maintain the trust of the financial community by publishing the budget. He listed the war expenses as nonrecurring costs and therefore was able to misleadingly report a surplus. Louis XVI dismissed Necker because he also listed the expenses of the royal court. But Necker's successors continued to borrow until the kingdom's credit was exhausted in 1786, thereby setting the stage for the French Revolution.

France actively joined the American Revolutionary War on June 17, 1778 when Admiral Keppel, leading 20 ships on a cruise out of Portsmouth, fell in with two French frigates and fired his guns to bring them to.

On the diplomatic front, the French continued to press for Spanish participation in the war. The Spanish, however, tried to play both sides and offered to join the British side in exchange for the return of Gibraltar. The British refused and Spain formally entered the war against Great Britain on June 21, 1779 but without recognizing the United States.

The Netherlands was drawn into war with Britain on December 20, 1780 but did not officially recognize the United States until April 19, 1782.

The war cost France 772,000,000 livres and she sent at least 61 warships, 31,497 seamen, and 12,680 soldiers to America. Of these 44,177 men, more than 5,040 perished as did many thousands of others, in campaigns around the world, to help procure American independence. At the end of the war, France and America continued to distrust each other and officers continued to bicker. France asked little for herself in the final negotiations. She hoped to get fishing rights in the Newfoundland fisheries and to regain territory she explored and settled on the western boundaries of America. She was disappointed on both counts. French fishing rights in Newfoundland remained substantially as they had been fixed by the Treaty of Utrecht 70 years earlier. In the West Indies, the islands captured by either party were restored. France might have claimed large advantages in India, but she obtained little more than some unimportant territory and some slight improvement in trade conditions. She gained no trade monopoly with America, not even any important part in it. Her position on the Continent was not materially strengthened by the American Revolution.

The important effect was on the French people themselves. The success of the American colonists in establishing a free government had a great influence upon the French mind during the years before the French Revolution. France had the satisfaction of humiliating an ancient rival, but she could not substantially weaken England's power. England remained an important factor in European politics. America remained neutral during both the French Revolution (1789–94) and the Haitian Revolution (1791–1804).

Tensions with France escalated into an undeclared war, called the "Quasi-War," which involved two years of hostilities at sea (1798–1800). The Convention of 1800 ensured that the United States would remain neutral in the Napoleonic wars and ended the French alliance with the United States. The two nations maintained generally quiet or cool relations until December 1835 when cordial relations resumed. French travelers to the United States were often welcomed in the name of Lafayette who made a triumphant American tour in 1824. Numerous political exiles found refuge in New York.

France was neutral during the American Civil War, 1861–65. The removal of Napoleon III in 1870, after the Franco-Prussian War, helped improve Franco–American relations. The U.S. Minister to France, Elihu B. Washburne, induced the small American population to provide much medical, humanitarian, and diplomatic support during the Siege of Paris, gaining much credit to the Americans. The grateful French people presented a gift to the United States in 1884: the Statue of Liberty. The copper statue was designed by French sculptor Frédéric Auguste Bartholdi. Gustave Eiffel, better known for the tower he erected in Paris, built its metal framework. The statue was dedicated on October 28, 1886. Many French people held the United States in high esteem, as a land of opportunity and as a source of modern ideas, from 1870 until 1918. Hundreds of American women traveled to France and Switzerland to obtain their medical degrees after 1870. Normal enrollments at French universities plunged during World War I and the government tried to attract American students. Thousands of American soldiers waiting to return to America after the war enrolled in university programs set up especially for them.

Charles Egbert Stanton, an officer in the United States Army and aide to General John J. Pershing, visited Lafayette's tomb in Paris and included the memorable expression "Lafayette, we are here!" in a speech he gave in Paris during World War I. During the interwar years, the two nations remained friendly. Beginning in the 1920s, American intellectuals, painters, writers, and tourists were drawn to French art, literature, philosophy, theatre, cinema, fashion, wines, and cuisine. Numerous writers such as William Faulkner, F. Scott Fitzgerald, Ernest Hemingway, and others were deeply influenced by their experiences of French life. Anti-Americanism developed in the 1920s but disappeared by the Allied invasion of Normandy and the liberation of Paris in World War II.

Appendix

Cargoes of Beaumarchais's ships sent to America

Amphitrite
(sailed from Le Havre for Dominica [Haiti] on December 14, 1776)

- 52 bronze guns (4- and 6-pounders), their carriages and fore-carriages, &c.;
- 20,160 4lb. cannon balls;
- 9,000 grenades;
- 24,000 pounds of lead balls;
- 2,900 spades;
- 239 iron shovels;
- 2,900 pickaxe mattocks;
- 500 rock picks;
- 484 pickheads;
- 1,000 mattocks;
- 300 hatchets;
- 1,500 bill-hooks;
- 5 miner's drills;
- 12 iron pincers;
- 10 pistols;
- 4 scoops (surgical instruments);
- 6 priming wires;
- 2 iron wedges;
- 4 pick-axes (sage-leaved);
- 15 crescent-shaped axes;
- 5 shears;
- 4 punches;
- 2 rammers;
- 6,132 muskets;
- 255,000 gun flints;

- 5,000 worms;
- 12,648 iron balls for cartridges;
- 345 grapeshot;
- 1,000lb. of tinder;
- 200 levers;
- 37 bales of tent covers;
- 12,000lb of gunpowder;
- 5 bales of blankets.
- 925 tents;
- clothing for 12,000 men;
- 5,700 stands of arms.

Mercure
(sailed from Nantes on February 4, 1777)

- 11,987 stands of arms;
- 1,000 barrels (50 tons) of gunpowder;
- 11,000 flints;
- 57 bales, 4 cases, and 2 boxes of cloth;
- 48 bales of woolens and linens;
- 9 bales of handkerchiefs;
- thread, cotton, and printed linens;
- 2 cases of shoes;
- 1 box of buttons and buckles,
- 1 case of sherry, oil etc.;
- 1 box lawn,
- 1 case of needles and silk neckcloths;
- caps, stockings, blankets, and other necessary articles for clothing the troops.

Seine
(sailed from Le Havre on February 19, 1777, captured off Martinique on Monday, April 5, 1777)

- 317 cases of muskets;
- 154 bales of tents or tent covers;
- 9 large pieces of bronze ordnance;
- clothing for 10,000 men and 10,000 tents;
- 2 barrels of flints;
- 2 barrels of gun worms;
- 100 hand spikes;
- 19 buckets;

- 359 bombs;
- 2 cast iron mortars;
- 17 sponges and rammers;
- 1,000lb. of matches;
- 1 beaked anvil;
- 1 vise,
- 6,000lb. of gunpowder;
- 10 cases of musket balls;
- 1 case containing sponges and bags for quick matches;
- 20 cases of tin or langrage;
- 43,600 tiles.

Amélie
(loaded by February 28, 1777; arrived Hispaniola [Haiti] on May 18)

- 19 bronze guns with their carriages & fore-carriages, &c.;
- 19 bronze guns without their carriages;
- 6,561 cannonballs;
- 288 bombs;
- 200 barrels of powder each of 100 pounds;
- 120 bars of lead;
- 100 spades;
- 100 mattocks;
- 20 cases of musket balls.

for the use of the artillery:

- 100lb. of old cart grease;
- 1 piece of camelot;
- 4lb. of thick wire;
- 200 needles;
- 2 reams of cartridge paper;
- and 4,900 flat tiles.

Comte de Vergennes/Thérèse
(sailed from Mindin to St. Domingue on April 26, 1777)

- between 60,000 and 70,000 livres of goods purchased by the American commissioners;
- stores for fitting out two 36-gun frigates.

Heureux/Flamand

(sailed from Marseilles to Martinique, destination New England on June 3, 1777)

- 50,000 lb. of refined sulfur;
- 40 Swedish-style bronze cannons, 4-pounders, with their equipment and carriages;
- 20 bronze mortars with their equipment;
- 20,000 4-pound balls;
- 3,000 grenades;
- 3,000 bombs;
- 20,000lb. of gunpowder
- 14,500 pioneers' implements;
- 8,300 entrenching tools;
- 269 miners' tools;
- 150,000 flints;
- 25,000lb. of lead in ball;
- 2,000lb. of match;
- 6,000 muskets with their bayonets;
- 1,000 officers' muskets with their bayonets;
- 500 pairs of pistols, trimmed in copper.

Listed as "44 Barrels of oil, 19 Slabs of marble, 5000 Packages of figs, 25 thousand of Soap and 2000 olives to put in oil."

Flamand (new name of *Heureux*)

(sailed for the West Indies on September 26, 1777; arrived at Portsmouth, New Hampshire on December 1, 1777)

- 25,000 muskets, saltpeter, etc.

Marie Catherine

(sailed from Dunkirk for Martinique on July 12, 1777)

- 34 bronze 4-pounders with their carriages;
- 16,872 cannonballs;
- 2,700 hand grenades.

Also shipped from Dunkirk about the same time:

- 66 large bronze cannons (12- to 32-pounders);
- about 60 fieldpieces (4-pounders) with their carriages and accoutrements.

Fier Roderigue (former French Navy frigate *Hippopotame*)
(preparing to sail from Rochefort on September 15, 1777)

- mounted 100 bronze cannons (4 33-pounders, 24 24-pounders, 20 16-pounders, 12 8-pounders, and 40 4-pounders);
- soldiers' ready-made clothing, of cloth and blankets, etc.

This matériel went a long way to equip the Continental Army. Congress authorized an army of 36 regiments or battalions, each consisting of 768 men (640 men at arms). They were formed into eight companies. The paper strength of the army in 1776 was 23,040 men at arms or 27,648, including officers, but the army was never at full strength.

The Continental Congress ordered each state to contribute one-battalion regiments in proportion to their population in 1777, and authorized Washington to raise an additional 16 battalions, increasing the army to 88 regiments or battalions. At full strength, this army would consist of 56,320 men at arms or a total of 67,584, including officers.

Abbreviations

Archives Nationales de France: Archives Nationales de France. Affaires de l'Angleterre et de l'Amérique. Paris: Ministère des Affaires Étrangères. Correspondance politique. Angleterre. Etats-Unis. France.

AJ: *The American Journal and General Advertiser.*

APS: American Philosophical Society, Philadelphia.

BEP: *The Boston Evening-Post and the General Advertiser.*

BF: Ben Franklin, *The Papers of Benjamin Franklin.*

BG: *The Boston-Gazette, and Country Journal.*

Boatner: Boatner, Mark M. *Encyclopedia of the American Revolution.*

BNA: British National Archives.

CC: *The Connecticut Courant, and Hartford Weekly Intelligencer.*

CG: *Connecticut Gazette.*

CG&UI: *The Connecticut Gazette; And The Universal Intelligencer.*

CJ: *The Connecticut Journal, and the New-Haven Post-Boy.*

CJWA: *Continental Journal*, published as *The Continental Journal, and Weekly Advertiser.*

CSCHS: *Collections of the South Carolina Historical Society.*

EJ: *The Essex Journal and New-Hampshire Packet.*

ExJ: *Exeter Journal*, published as *The Exeter Journal, or, New Hampshire Gazette.*

FJ: *Freeman's Journal*, published as *The Freeman's Journal, or New-Hampshire Gazette.*

GSSC: *Gazette of the State of South-Carolina.*

HCA: Great Britain. High Court of Admiralty.

IC: *The Independent Chronicle.*

IC&UA: *The Independent Chronicle and the Universal Advertiser*. Also *The New-England Chronicle*, published as *The Independent Chronicle and the Universal Advertiser.*

IG: *The Independent Gazetteer.*

IL: *The Independent Ledger and the American Advertiser.*

Latouche: Monaque, Rémi. *Latouche-Tréville, 1745–1804: l'amiral qui défiait Nelson.*

LCh: *London Chronicle.*

LG: *The London Gazette.*

MAG: *The Massachusetts Gazette or the Springfield and Northampton Weekly Advertiser.*

Marines: Smith, Charles R. *Marines in the Revolution.*

MAH: *The Magazine of American History.*

MG: *Dunlap's Maryland Gazette.*

MGGA: *The Massachusetts Gazette or the General Advertiser.*

MJ: *Maryland Journal or the Maryland Journal and Baltimore Advertiser.*

Montresor: Scull, G. D. *The Montresor Journals.*

Morningstars: Smith, Gordon Burns. *Morningstars of Liberty: the Revolutionary War in Georgia, 1775–1783.*

Morton : Beaumarchais, Pierre Augustin Caron de; Morton, Brian N.; Spinelli, Donald C. *Correspondance [de] Beaumarchais.*

MS: *Thomas's Massachusetts Spy or, American Oracle of Liberty.* Later, published as *Haswell's Massachusetts Spy or American Oracle of Liberty.*

NBBAS: O'Kelley, Patrick. *Nothing but Blood and Slaughter.*

NDAR: *Naval Documents of the American Revolution.*

NEC: *The New England Chronicle: or the Essex Gazette.*

NG: *The Newport Gazette.*

NHG: *The New-Hampshire Gazette, and Historical Chronicle.*

NJ Archives: *NJ Archives.*

NJG: *The New-Jersey Gazette.*

NM: *The Newport Mercury.*

NP: *The Norwich Packet and the Connecticut, Massachusetts, New-Hampshire, and Rhode-Island Weekly Advertiser.*

NYG: *The New York Gazette, And The Weekly Mercury,* (Gaine's *New* York *Gazette).*

NYGNA: *The New-York Gazetteer or Northern Intelligencer.*

NYJ: *The New-York Journal; or, The General Advertiser.*

PAG: *The Pennsylvania Gazette.*

PEP: *The Pennsylvania Evening Post.*

PG: *The Providence Gazette; and Country Journal.*

PJ: *Pennsylvania Journal.*

PL: *The Pennsylvania Ledger: Or The Virginia, Maryland, Pennsylvania, & New-Jersey Weekly Advertiser*. Also published as *The Pennsylvania Ledger: or the Philadelphia Market-Day Advertiser*.

PP: *Dunlap's Pennsylvania Packet or, the General Advertiser*.

Prensa: *Maryland Journal*, published as *La Prensa*.

RG: *The Royal Gazette*.

RNYG: *Rivington's New-York Gazetteer; Or, The Connecticut, Hudson's River, New-Jersey, and Quebec Weekly Advertiser*.

RAG: *The Royal American Gazette*.

RGG: *The Royal Georgia Gazette*.

RPAG: *The Royal Pennsylvania Gazette*.

RRG: *Rivington's Royal Gazette*.

SCAGG: *The South-Carolina and American General Gazette*.

SCG: *South-Carolina Gazette and General Advertiser*.

SCWA: *South-Carolina Weekly Advertiser*.

SCWG: *The South-Carolina Weekly Gazette*.

SG: *The Salem Gazette*.

TCG: *The Constitutional Gazette*.

VG: *The Virginia Gazette*.

Endnotes

Chapter 1

1 There seemed to be a possibility that Lord Chatham (William Pitt the Elder) might be asked to form a new government, in 1774 and early 1775, that would be receptive to the demands of the Americans.

2 Also spelled "de Laune" or "de Launes."

3 Doniol. vol. 1, pp. 402–419; Kite, pp. 57–61.

4 Letter from London to Comte de Vergennes, dated April 26, 1776 in Doniol. vol. 1, pp. 413–414. A letter from Arthur Lee dated June 21, 1776 stated that the British Army in America consisted of 40,000 men and a fleet of 100 ships, that they were well supplied with artillery and stores and that they had good officers and engineers. He also emphasized the difficulty of resisting such forces without assistance from France with officers, engineers, and large ships of war. RG 76, Records relating to French Spoliation Claims, 1791–1821; *Deane papers*. vol. 3, p. 297; Shewmake, p. 136.

5 *Deane papers*. vol. 1, p. 119.

6 Doniol places this document on May 1, 1776; Kite. vol. 2, p. 70.

7 Genet, George Clinton. "Beaumarchais' Plan to Aid the Colonies," in MAH. vol. 2, 1878, pp. 663–672; *Deane papers*. vol. 1, pp. 100–115; Shewmake, pp. 75–81.

8 Shewmake, pp. 38–39; Ferreiro, p. 50.

9 A livre or franc is equivalent to 20 sous and almost equal to 10 pence halfpenny sterling. An unskilled worker could make 1.5 livres/day.

10 Beaumarchais's plan was to use half of the 300,000,000 livres to rehabilitate the American paper money in gold and to use the remainder to purchase arms and munitions. He proposed purchasing gunpowder from the king's registrars for five sous a pound and billing the Americans for 20 sous a pound, the current market price. The return, paid in tobacco, could be sold for a substantial profit. Shewmake, pp. 77–78.

11 Loménie. vol. 2, p. 110.

12 Beaumarchais to Congress July 14, 1783, in Shewmake, pp. 403–409.

13 Loménie. vol. 2, p. 109.

14 Doniol. vol. 1, p. 373; Kite. vol. 2, pp. 78–83.

15 *Deane papers*. vol. 1, pp. 153–154; Shewmake, pp. 144–145.

16 ibid; Morton. vol. 3, p. 10.

17 *Deane papers*. vol. 1, pp. 159–161; Morton. vol. 3, p. 12; Shewmake, p. 148.

18 Dennery, Etienne, éd. *Beaumarchais* (Catalog of the 1966 exposition). Paris: Bibliothèque Nationale, 1966; MS, p. 327; Wharton. vol. 2, p. 129; U.S. House of Representatives, 20th Congress, First Session, Report no. 220, April 1828, pp. 24–25; Morton. vol. 2, pp. 241–244; Shewmake, p. 157.

19 Archives Nationales de France, 519, fol. 194; Stevens, p. 906; Morton. vol. 2, p. 265; Shewmake, p. 174; State Papers, House Document No. 111, appendix, 15th Congress, 1st session, pp. 23–24, NA; NDAR, 8:622–623.

20 Risch, Erna. *Supplying Washington's Army*. Washington, D.C.: Center of Military History, United States Army, 1981, p. 338.

21 "1 July 1777 (afternoon) Beaumarchais to Vergennes," Archives Nationales de France, 523, fol. 345; Stevens, pp. 240, 1559; Morton. vol. 3, p. 141.

22 Lord Stormont to Lord Weymouth, Paris, June 19, 1777, BNA, State Papers 78/302, pp. 366–369; NDAR. vol. 9, p. 411; Gabriel de Sartine to Charles Pierre Gonet, Commissary of Marine at Lorient. Versailles, November 22, 1777; NDAR. vol. 10, pp. 1015–1016; Lord Stormont to Lord Weymouth, Paris, June 19, 1777, BNA, State Papers 78/302, pp. 366–69; NDAR. vol. 9, p. 411.

23 A list of the ships at Portsmouth, New Hampshire May 22, 1777, BNA. Admiralty 1/487; NDAR. vol. 8, p. 1017; John Langdon to William Whipple, March 18, 1777. Captain J. G. M. Stone Private Collection, Annapolis; NDAR. vol. 8, pp. 140–141, 155–156; FJ. March 22, 1777; NDAR. vol. 8, p. 164; JCC. vol. 7, pp. 210, 211–212; NDAR. vol. 8, p. 235; Ferreiro, pp. 70–71; Washington papers. vol. 9, pp. 579–580; vol. 10, pp. 152–153.

24 Lord Stormont to Lord Weymouth. Paris, July 2, 1777. BNA. State Papers 78/305, 76; NDAR. vol. 9, p. 453.

25 Stevens, p. 241; *Maryland Journal*. Tuesday, May 27, 1777; NDAR. vol. 8, p. 1036n.

26 William Bingham to the Secret Committee of the Continental Congress. Saint Pierre, Martinique, Dec. 6, 1777. Library of Congress. Continental Congress Miscellany, Box 1780–1790; William Bingham to the Continental Congress Secret Committee. Saint Pierre, Martinique Dec. 28, 1777; NDAR. vol. 10, pp. 677, 821.

27 Archives Nationales de France. 523 fol. 23; Stevens, pp. 248, 1526; Morton. vol. 3, p. 102; Shewmake, p. 220; NDAR. vol. 8, pp. 406, 434, 727; BNA. Admiralty 1/487; NDAR. vol. 8, p. 1017; Charles Carroll of Carrollton to Charles Carroll, Sr. May 12, 1777. Carroll Papers. vol. 5, Maryland Historical Society; Intelligence regarding Martinique received from Arthur Pigott. BNA. State Papers 78/303, pp. 109–113; NDAR. vol. 9, p. 458.

28 NDAR. vol. 8, pp. 283–284; William Bingham to Silas Deane. St Pierre Mque March 21, 1777. *Deane Papers*. NDAR. vol. 8, p. 175; William Bingham to the American Commissioners in France. St Pierre Martinique April 26, 1777, *Deane Papers*. NDAR. vol. 8, pp. 450–452; Young's Prize List, April 30, 1777. NDAR. vol. 8, pp. 490–491.

29 Charles Carroll of Carrollton to Charles Carroll, Sr. May 12, 1777. Carroll Papers. vol. 5, Maryland Historical Society. William Carmichael to Charles W. F. Dumas. Paris, June 13, 1777; Wharton. vol. 11, pp. 337–339; NDAR. vol. 9, p. 396; William Bingham to the Continental Foreign Affairs Committee. St Pierre M/que October 13, 1777. RG 59, Records of the Department of State, Territorial Papers. vol. 1, October 13, 1777–Dec. 1811.

30 The Journal of the H.M.S. *Seaford*. BNA. Admiralty 51/880. NDAR. vol. 8, p. 280; Extract of a Letter from Granada, in the West Indies dated April 30, 1777. LCh. June 28 to July 1, 1777. NDAR. vol. 8, p. 489; See Young's Prize List, April 30, 1777. NDAR. vol. 8, pp. 490–491; NDAR. vol. 8, pp. 330–331; Vice Admiral James Young to Philip Stephens. May 2, 1777. BNA. Admiralty 1/310; NDAR. vol. 8, pp. 900–902. PJ. May 28, 1777, no. 1791, p. 2; NDAR. vol. 8, pp. 175–176, 226, 280 and note, 283–284 and 284 note, 450-452, 489 and note, 490–491, 537–538, 543–544 and 544 note, 570–571, 594–595, 622, 725–730, 900–901 and 901 note, 902–905. vol. 9, pp. 84 and note, 100–102 and 102 note. vol. 10, pp. 151–152 and 152 note, 677–678 and 678 note, 722–724, 821, 1130–1131 and 1131 note. PJ. May 14, 1777, no. 1789, p. 3; Philadelphia, May 10 Extract of a Letter from St. [Illegible] April 20, 1777, MJ. May 20, 1777. vol. IV, no. 185, p. 3; Philadelphia, May 14. CJ. May 28, 1777, no. 502, p. 2; PG. May 31, 1777. vol. XIV, no. 700, p. 2; MS. June 5, 1777. vol. VI, no. 318, p. 2; Extract of a Letter from St. Eustatia, April 20, 1777. VG. May 30, 1777, no. 1346, p. 2.

31 Wharton. vol. 2, pp. 276-277; Shewmake. p. 201; Stevens, no. 240, 306.

32 Beaumarchais to Silas Deane. Paris February 19, 1777. *Deane Papers*. NDAR. vol. 8, p. 595.

33 May 4, 1777 to Vergennes. Shewmake. p. 221; Morton. vol. 4, p. 312; Beaumarchais to Vergennes. March 7, 1777. Archives Nationales de France. 522 fol. 15; Stevens. 1445; Morton. vol. 3, p. 66; Shewmake, pp, 204–205; Archives Nationales de France. vol. 523, pp. 23–24; NDAR. vol. 8, pp. 817–818.

34 Continental Board of Admiralty to the Continental Navy Board of the Eastern Department, May 30, 1780, Miscellaneous, Papers of the Continental Congress, Papers Relating to Naval Affairs, Marine Committee Letter Book, 254, NA. Franklin papers. vol. 1, p. 299, www.franklinpapers. org; NDAR. vol. 9, p. 1001; Stevens. vol. 6, no. 574.

35 GSSC. Monday, May 12, 1777; NDAR. vol. 8, pp. 956–957.

36 Lord Stormont to Lord Weymouth. Paris May 21, 1777. BNA. State Papers, 78/302, 261–62; Joseph Hynson to Lieutenant Colonel Edward Smith. Paris, June 3, 1777; Stevens. no. 165; NDAR. vol.9, pp. 376–377; Philip Stephens to Vice Admiral Richard Lord Howe, June 6, 1777. BNA. Admiralty 2/1334; NDAR. vol. 9, p. 380.

37 Stevens. vol. 3, no. 306; The manifests were included in an intelligence report from Paul Wentworth to Lord Suffolk. Wentworth had the manifests by way of "MR. Ed--ds" i.e. Edward Bancroft; NDAR. vol. 10, pp. 999–1000; *Deane Papers*. NDAR. vol. 9, p. 450; Intelligence summary of French assistance to American naval vessels and privateers. BNA. State Papers 78/303, 99–101; NDAR. vol. 9, p. 455.

38 IC (Boston), Thursday, December 11, 1777. NDAR. vol. 10, pp. 667–668; Paul Wentworth to William Eden. London, c. Oct. 30, 1777. Auckland Papers. vol. 3, fol. 291–294; NDAR. vol. 10, p. 961; Stevens. no. 274.

39 Manifests of *Heureux*, *Amelia* and *Maria Catherine*. Stevens. vol. 3, no. 274, 306; NDAR. vol. 10, pp. 999–1000.

40 William Bingham to the Secret Committee of the Continental Congress. Saint Pierre, Martinique, Dec. 6, 1777. William Bingham to Nathaniel Shaw, Jr. Nov. 20, 1777, and Bingham to John Langdon, 27 Nov. 1777. NDAR. vol. 10, p. 677; Archives Nationales de France. vol. 523, 345–346; NDAR. vol. 9, p. 451.

41 Stevens. vol. 19, no. 1716; NDAR. vol. 10, pp. 886–887.

42 Beaumarchais to Vergennes. December 19, 1777. Archives Nationales de France. 526, no 101. Morton vol. 3, p. 231. Shewmake, p. 266, Stevens. vol. 3, no. 274.

43 Loménie. vol. 2, pp. 152–156; Morton. vol. 4, p. 284; Shewmake, p. 308.

44 March 23, 1778 to Congress. *Deane Papers*. vol. 2, pp. 428–431; Morton. vol. 4, pp. 91–94; Shewmake. pp. 298–300.

45 JCC. Saturday, June 5, 1779. vol. 13, pp. 690–692.

Chapter 2

1 Ferreiro. p. 39.

2 Ferreiro, pp. 57–58.

3 Morton and Spinelli, pp. 69, 75.

4 Ferreiro, p. 58.

5 Peltier-Dudoyer purchased a ship called *La Plaine de Léogane* on November 6, 1776 and renamed it the *Mercure*. Morton and Spinelli, p. 104.

6 http://www.delanglais.fr/Peltier/html/flotte.html, http://www.delanglais.fr/Peltier/html/jean.html

7 Morton and Spinelli, pp. 108, 219.

8 Paul Wentworth to the Earl of Suffolk, July 17, 1777, Stevens. vol. 2, no. 182; George Lupton to William Eden, August 20, 1777, Stevens. vol. 2, no. 187. vol. 19, no. 1751, 1752.

9   Morton and Spinelli. p. 230.

10   Ferreiro. p. 59.

11   JCC. vol. 7, pp. 92–93; *Deane papers.* vol. 3, p. 172; The American Commissioners: Contract with Jean-Joseph Carié de Montieu. BF. vol. 24. pp. 123–125; Stevens. vol. 3, no. 274.

12   Ferreiro, pp. 66–67.

13   Jonathan Williams, Jr. a grandnephew of Benjamin Franklin, spent most of the period from 1770 to 1785 in England and France, where he assisted Franklin with business affairs and served as a commercial agent for the Continental Navy in Nantes. He became Chief of Engineers of the Army Corps of Engineers, was the first superintendent of United States Military Academy, and was elected to the Fourteenth United States Congress.

In 1777, he had collected 80,000 stands of arms, pistols, swords, 300 bales of woolens, 80,000 uniforms, 50 tons of brass cannons from the French king's arsenals to be shipped in the fall in a ship under construction for Captain Nicholson. The cannons would be designated as copper bound to Martinique.

James Van Zandt alias George Lupton to William Eden. 20 Aug. 1777. Stevens. vol. 2, no. 187; Certification of a Bill of Exchange, Fri, Jan 1, 1779, BF. vol. 28, p. 323; From Chaumont: Promissory Notes, Fri, Jan 1, 1779, BF. vol. 28, p. 325.

14   Coudray brought 200 cannons, a quantity of ammunition and a number of gunners to St. Domingue to be transferred to smaller vessels and brought to America. The French also planned to send four Irish regiments in the French service. Stevens. vol. 3, no. 1372; From Jonathan Williams, Jr. Tue, Jan 12, 1779, BF. vol. 28, p. 373.

15   The Continental Congress appointed John Bondfield as the American commercial agent in Bordeaux in March 1778 shortly after France formally recognized the independence of the 13 colonies on February 6, 1778. This was the first known American diplomatic station in the world.

16   Farmers General was a group of financiers appointed by the king to manage certain taxes from 1697 to 1789. After the army, the Farmers General was the second largest employer in the country, bringing in more than half of the government's revenue. They operated up to 42 branches in the provinces, which, in turn, employed nearly 25,000 agents across the country.

17   BF. vol. 33, pp. liv–lv.

18   To John Bondfield, Mon, Sep 11, 1780, BF. vol. 33, p. 281; From Chaumont, Sat, Sep 16, 1780, BF. vol. 33, pp. 291–292; From John Bondfield, Tue, Sep 19, 1780, BF. vol. 33 p. 307; To John Bondfield, Fri, Sep 22, 1780, BF. vol. 33, p. 316.

19   From Jonathan Williams, Jr. Tue, Nov 7, 1780, BF. vol. 33, pp. 509–512.

20   Roberts, Priscilla H., and Richard S. Roberts. *Thomas Barclay (1728–1793): Consul in France, Diplomat in Barbary.* Bethlehem, Lehigh University Press, 2008. p. 136; The American Commissioners: Contract with Jean-Joseph Carié de Montieu. BF. vol. 24, pp. 123–125; From Guillaume Sabatier fils & Pierre Desprez (unpublished). Fri, Aug 29, 1783.

21   Ferreiro, p. 39; Rouzeau, L. Aperçus du rôle de Nantes dans la guerre d'indépendance d'Amérique (1775–1783). *Annales de Bretagne.* vol. 74, no. 2 (1967), pp. 217–278. http://www.persee.fr/doc/abpo_0003-91x_1967_num_74_2_2406.

22   Morton and Spinelli. p. 37; Beaumarchais to the Count De Vergennes, April 26, 1776. NDAR. vol. 4, p. 1066. Stevens. no. 1328; Count De Vergennes to Beaumarchais, April 26, 1776. Stevens. no. 1330; NDAR. vol. 4, pp. 1073–1074; Montaudouin Brothers to the Count de Vergennes. April 27, 1776. Stevens. no. 1331; NDAR. vol. 4, pp. 1074–1075; Bayard, Jackson, and Co. to Captain William Meston. *Public Advertiser*, London, April 11, 1776, NDAR. vol. 3, pp. 770–772; *Bristol Journal Extraordinary*, Monday, April 8, 1776.

23   Morton and Spinelli. pp. 39–40.

24 *Bristol Journal Extraordinary*, Monday, April 8, 1776. NDAR. vol. 4, pp. 1024–25, Extract of a
    Letter from Bristol, April 10, 1776. LCh. April 11 to April 13, 1776; NDAR. vol. 4, p. 1031.

25 Archard de Bonvouloir to Count de Guines. December 28, 1775. De Guines was the French
    ambassador to Great Britain. Doniol. vol. 1, pp. 287–292; NDAR. vol. 3, pp. 280–281; Lasseray.
    vol. 2, p. 638.

26 Hedges, James Blaine. *The Browns of Providence Plantations*. Providence: Brown University Press,
    1968. vol. 1, p. 229; George Washington to John Hancock. December 14, 1775. NDAR. vol.
    3, p. 94; General Washington to President of Congress. Force. Series 4. vol. 4, pp. 261–262;
    General Washington to Governour Cooke. Cambridge, December 14, 1775. Force. Series 4. vol.
    4, p. 264; Governour Trumbull to President of Congress. December 23, 1775. Force. Series 4.
    vol. 4, pp. 447–448; Thomas Wharton to Samuel Wharton. January 1, 1776. NDAR. vol. 3,
    p. 563; Richard Smith's Diary, Library of Congress. Tuesday Jan. 9. NDAR. vol. 3, p. 693; Dr.
    Barbeu-Dubourg to Vergennes. July 13, 1776, NDAR. vol. 6, pp. 475–476; Nicholas Brown to
    John Brown, December 11, 1775. Nicholas Brown Papers, John Carter Brown Library; NDAR.
    vol. 3, pp. 54–56.

27 Archard de Bonvouloir to Count de Guines, December 28, 1775. Doniol. vol. 1, pp. 266–269,
    287–292; NDAR vol. 3, pp. 279–285; Ferreiro. p. 52.

28 Silas Deane to the Committee of Secret Correspondence. August 18, 1776, in Force. 5th series
    vol. 1, p. 1011; Penet & Pliarne to Nicholas Brown, February 8, 1776. Nicholas Brown Papers,
    John Carter Brown Library; NDAR. vol. 3, pp. 1176–1177; Dr. Barbeu-Dubourg to Vergennes,
    May 31, 1776. Stevens. no. 566; NDAR. vol. 6, pp. 397–398; Ferreiro. p. 51.

29 Schaeper, Thomas J. *France and America in the Revolutionary Era: The Life of Jacques-Donatien
    Leray De Chaumont, 1725–1803*. Providence, Berghahn Books, 1995.

30 Hedges, James Blaine. *The Browns of Providence Plantations*. Providence: Brown University Press,
    1968. vol. 1 pp. 231–233.

31 ibid. vol. 1 p. 237; Nicholas Brown to Penet & Pliarne. April 23, 1776; Nicholas Brown Papers,
    John Carter Brown Library; NDAR. vol. 4, pp. 1215–1216.

32 Hedges, James Blaine. *The Browns of Providence Plantations*. Providence: Brown University Press,
    1968 vol. 1, p. 231.

33 ibid. vol. 1, pp. 236–237. Pliarne & Penet to Nicholas & John Brown. September 28, 1776;
    NDAR. vol. 6, pp. 617–618; Instructions of Nicholas & John Brown to Capt. Samuel Avery.
    Nicholas Brown Papers, John Carter Brown Library; NDAR. vol. 5, pp. 219–220; The Chevalier
    Cte. de Vraicourt. November 24, 1776. Force. Series 5. vol. 3, pp. 609–613.

34 Letter from Dr. Barbeu-Dubourg to Benjamin Franklin, June 10, 1776 in Force. Series 4 vol. 6,
    p. 781. Lasseray. vol. 2, pp. 510, 521.

35 *Deane papers.* NDAR. vol. 6, pp. 514–515.

36 Hedges, James Blaine. *The Browns of Providence Plantations*. Providence: Brown University Press,
    1968 vol. 1, p. 237.

37 Henry Laurens Papers, South Carolina Historical Society; NDAR. vol. 6, pp. 525–529.

38 To The Respectable Members Of The Secret Committee of the Province of New-York. Pliarne,
    Penet & Co. to the New-York Convention. Nantes, October 21, 1976. Force. Series 5. vol. 2,
    pp. 1146–1147; Penet & Pliarne to the Committees of Rhode Island, October 8, 1776. NDAR.
    vol. 6, pp. 1280–1281. Penet & Pliarne to the President of the Virginia Council. October 26,
    1776. Papers of Pliarne, Penet, Dacosta Freres & Co. 1776–1783, State Agents, Virginia State
    Library. NDAR. vol. 6, pp. 1425–1426; Nicholas Brown Papers, John Carter Brown Library;
    NDAR. vol. 6, pp. 524–525.

39 James Warren to Louis Poncet & Son. Bordeaux, December 3, 1776. Massachusetts Archives.
    vol. 151, pp. 3–4; Letters from the Board of War, 1776–1780. NDAR. vol. 7, pp. 355-356.

40 Massachusetts Board of War to Jacques Gruel & Co. Nantes. Massachusetts Archives. vol. 151, pp. 19–24, 44; Letters from the Board of War, 1776–1780. NDAR. vol. 7, pp. 1000–1002; The care taken to assure the arrival of at least one copy of this important letter is indicated by a notation, reading: "Origl by Capt Bartlet Copy by Capt Chapman Duplicate by Capt Adams Fourth by Capt Clarke Fifth by Capt Carver."

41 Massachusetts Board of War to Captain Jonathan Haraden. Massachusetts Archives. vol. 151, p. 415; Letters from the Board of War, 1776–1780. Massachusetts Archives. vol. 151, p. 416, NDAR. vol. 8, p. 105.

42 Massachusetts Board of War to Pliarne, Penet & Co. March 26, 1777. Massachusetts Archives. vol. 151, p. 61, Letters from the Board of War, 1776-1780. NDAR. vol. 8, p. 204; From Reculès de Basmarein & Raimbaux. Wed. Jun 4, 1777, BF. vol. 24, p. 116.

43 From Jacques-Barthélemy Gruel, Fri, Dec 25, 1778, BF. vol. 28, p. 281; Thomas J. Schaeper. Pierre Penet: French Adventurer in the American Revolution. *Daughters of the American Revolution Magazine.* CXVII (1983) pp. 854–856, Thomas Morris during his tenure as American commercial agent of Nantes had used him as his deputy. Benjamin Franklin to Patrick Henry, Fri, Feb 26, 1779, BF. vol. 28. pp. 611–612.

44 James Van Zandt alias George Lupton to William Eden. May 6, 1777 and June 4, 1777. Stevens. vol. 2, no. 154, 168; From Reculès de Basmarein & Raimbaux. Tue, Nov 18, 1777. BF. vol. 25, p. 172. They also made 40 expeditions, including the one that brought the Marquis de Lafayette to America. Reculès de Basmarein & Raimbaux to the American Commissioners. Sat, May 16, 1778. BF. vol. 26, pp. 472–474.

45 Albion, Robert Greenhalgh and Jennie Barnes Pope. *Sea Lanes in Wartime: The American Experience, 1775–1942.* W.W. Norton, 1942. p. 46; Castex, Robert. L'armateur de La Fayette, Pierre de Basmarein, d'après des documents inédits. *Revue des questions historiques.* series 3, no. 6 (Jan. 1925), p. 84.

46 Doniol vol. 2, p. 378. Lasseray. vol. 1, pp. 34, 190; Lafayette, Marie Joseph Paul Yves Roch Gilbert Du Motier marquis de. *Lafayette in the Age of the American Revolution: December 7, 1776–March 30, 1778.* Stanley J. Idzerda. Cornell University Press, 1977 pp. 84–85; Castex, Robert. L'armateur de La Fayette, Pierre de Basmarein, d'après des documents inédits. *Revue des questions historiques.* series 3, no. 6 (Jan. 1925), p. 91; James Van Zandt alias George Lupton to William Eden. 11 June 1777. Stevens. vol. 2, no. 171. vol. 3, no. 251.

47 Etat des expeditions maritimes faites par la Maison du Sr de Basmarein pour les Isles et la cote de Guinée et la Nouvelle Angleterre, s.d. 1779. Archives municipales de Bordeaux, 1 S 2. http://archives.bordeaux-metropole.fr/expositions/salle-recules-de-basmarein-raimbaux-et-compagnie-21/n:21; Information on Basmarein and the *Vengeance* is from Castex, Robert. "L'armateur de La Fayette, Pierre de Basmarein, d'après des documents inédits." *Revue des questions historiques.* series 3, no. 6 (Jan. 1925), pp. 112–15, 127; "Reculès de Basmarein & Raimbaux to the American Commissioners, before 16 May 1778," Founders Online, National Archives, last modified March 30, 2017, http://founders.archives.gov/documents/Franklin/01-26-02-0414; BF. vol. 26, pp. 472–474; Vigneaud, Jean-Paul. Bordeaux: des documents historiques sur La Fayette sauvés de la poubelle. www.sudouest.fr. October 25, 2013. Volo. James M. *Blue Water Patriots: The American Revolution Afloat.* Rowman and Littlefield, c.2006, pp. 232, 293; Albion, Robert Greenhalgh and Jennie Barnes Pope. *Sea Lanes in Wartime: The American Experience, 1775–1942,* W.W. Norton, 1942 p. 47; Journal of the House of Representatives of the United States, 1830–1831, Tuesday, February 1, 1831, p. 245; House of Representatives 21st Congress 2nd session Feb. 7, 1831 (doc. no. 98).

48 From Jean-Jacques de Lafreté, Thu, Feb 18, 1779, BF. vol. 28, p. 566.

49   From Jonathan Williams, Jr. Thu, Nov 5, 1778, BF. vol. 28, pp. 40–43; From George Washington to the United States Senate, May 28, 1794. Washington papers. Presidential series. vol. 16, p. 148.

50   The American Commissioners to Schweighauser, Sat, Sep 12, 1778, BF. vol. 28, p. 395.

51   Pierre-Augustin Caron de Beaumarchais to the American Commissioners, Sat, Feb 13, 1779, BF. vol. 28, p. 523.

52   John Bondfield to the American Commissioners, Thu, Nov 12, 1778, BF. vol. 28, p. 92. Gentlemen at Nantes to the American Commissioners Tue, Dec 15, 1778, BF. vol. 28, pp. 230–231.

53   The American Commissioners to Cornic, Veuve Mathurin & fils, Sat, Jan 2, 1779, BF. vol. 28, p. 326; The American Commissioners to Schweighauser, Sat, Jan 2, 1779, BF. vol. 28, p. 327; The American Commissioners to Benjamin Gunnison, Thu, Jan 14, 1779, BF. vol. 28, p. 380.

54   Jonathan Williams, Jr. to the American Commissioners, Sat, Jan 23, 1779, BF. vol. 28, p. 414.

55   To Schweighauser, Wed, Feb 17, 1779, BF. vol. 28, pp. 558–559.

56   To Schweighauser, Thu, Feb 25, 1779, BF. vol. 28, p. 602.

57   To Schweighauser, Thu, Aug 24, 1780, BF. vol. 33, pp. 225–227; From Schweighauser, Thu, Sep 7, 1780, BF. vol. 33, p. 261.

58   The American Commissioners to Jonathan Williams, Jr. Fri, Jul 10, 1778, BF. vol. 28, p. 69.

59   Titus Ogden to the American Commissioners, Mon, Jul 6, 1778, BF. vol. 28, p. 59; James Moylan to the American Commissioners, Fri, Jul 3, 1778, BF. vol. 28, p. 33.

60   The American Commissioners to Schweighauser, Mon, Jul 13, 1778, BF. vol. 28, p. 82.

61   James Moylan to the American Commissioners, Wed, Jul 29, 1778, BF. vol. 28, p. 62.

62   Puchelberg & Cie. to the American Commissioners, Lorient, August 24, 1778, BF. vol. 27, p. 292; Musco Livingston to the American Commissioners, Nantes, August 24, 1778, BF. vol. 27, p. 291; To Puchelberg & Co. Sun, Feb 13, 1780, BF. vol. 3, p. 478; Wharton, pp. 608–609; To William Hodgson, Sat, Feb 26, 1780, BF. vol. 31, p. 550; From Puchelberg & Cie. Wed, Apr 5, 1780, BF. vol. 32, pp. 215–216; From Puchelberg & Cie. Wed, Jun 28, 1780, BF. vol. 32, pp. 618–619; To Puchelberg & Cie. Mon, Jul 3, 1780, BF. vol. 33, p. 18; From Puchelberg & Cie. Mon, Jul 10, 1780, BF. vol. 33, pp. 55–56.

63   From Berubé de Costentin, Mon, Aug 24, 1778, BF. vol. 28, p. 293.

64   The American Commissioners to Schweighauser, Thu, Jul 9, 1778, BF. vol. 27, p. 63; To Desegray, Beaugeard fils & Cie. Sat, Oct 7, 1780, BF. vol. 33, p. 374.

65   From Desegray, Beaugeard fils & Cie. Sun, Oct 29, 1780, BF. vol. 33, pp. 472–473; From Desegray, Beaugeard fils & Cie. Thu, Nov 2, 1780, BF. vol. 33, p. 489; From Jonathan Williams, Jr. Tue. Nov 7, 1780. BF. vol. 33, pp. 509–512, The American Commissioners to Schweighauser, Sat, Jul 9, 1778, BF. vol. 27, p. 63.

66   James Van Zandt alias George Lupton.

67   Stevens. vol. 2, no. 187.

68   From Jonathan Williams, Jr. Tue, Sep 26, 1780, BF. vol. 33, pp. 335–336.

69   *Le commerce colonial de la France à la fin de l'Ancien Régime: L'évolution du régime de "l'Exclusif" de 1763 à 1789*. Publications de l'Université de Poitiers. Lettres et sciences humaines, 12. Paris: Presses Universitaires de France. 1972. vol. 2 pp. 682–683; From Lavaysse & Cie. Fri, Jul 30, 1779, BF. vol. 30, p. 173.

70   From John Diot & Co. Wed, Jan 12, 1780, BF. vol. 31, pp. 378–379, 484; To John Diot & Co. Thu, Jan 27, 1780, BF. vol. 31, pp. 412, 429, 463; To Gourlade and Moylan, Thu, Jan 27, 1780, BF. vol. 31, pp. 413–414.

71 Gourlade & Moylan to the American Commissioners, Wed, Dec 9, 1778, BF. vol. 28, p. 209. vol. 31, p. 518.

72 From Gourlade & Moylan, Mon, Feb 14, 1780, BF. vol. 31, pp. 485–486, 499, 515–516.

73 Stevens. vol. 20, no. 1799; Jonathan Williams, Jr. to the American Commissioners, Passy, 16 July 1778. BF. vol. 27. p. 112; S. and J.H. Delap to the American Commissioners, Sat, Jul 18, 1778, BF. vol. 27, p. 118.

74 Taverne Demont Dhiver to the American Commissioners, Mon, Feb 22, 1779, BF. vol. 28, p. 591.

75 The American Commissioners to Desegray, Beaugeard fils (unpublished) Thu, Jul 9, 1778.

76 Théodore Jauge to William Temple Franklin, Sat, Jul 4, 1778, BF. vol. 27, p. 48.

77 From Fleury & Demadières, Tue, Oct 10, 1780, BF. vol. 33, p. 403; From Fleury & Demadières (unpublished) Mon, Feb 17, 1783. From — Tessier (unpublished), Thu, Jul 23, 1778. From Josiah Darrell, Mon, Jan 25, 1779, BF. vol. 28, pp. 424–426; John Patterson to the American Commissioners, Tue, Dec 29, 1778, BF. vol. 28, p. 293.

78 *The French at Boston during the Revolution with particular reference to the French fleets and the fortifications in the harbor*, by Fitz-Henry Smith, Jr. Boston: privately printed, 1913 also published in the Bostonian Society Publications vol. 10. Boston: Old State House, 1913, pp. 29-34; Ferreiro, pp. 123-124. *In memoriam: citizen soldiers of Dracut, Mass. who served in the war of the American Revolution, 1775–1783*. Sons of the American Revolution. Old Middlesex Chapter. Lowell, Mass.?: publisher not identified, 1905? http://www.massar.org/docs/Early%20Publications/Citizen%20 Soldiers%20of%20Dracut,%20MA%20(1905).pdf.

79 Cressy, David. *Saltpeter: The Mother of Gunpowder*. Oxford: Oxford University Press, 2013 pp. 164, 169; William Duer to George Clinton. October 10, 1777; Smith, Paul Hubert and Ronald M Gephart. *Letters of Delegates to Congress, 1774–1789*. Washington: Library of Congress, 1976. vol. 8, p. 96; JCC. vol.9, p. 877. vol. 10, pp. 57, 109, 122, 15: 1152-4, 1164. This report is in the *Papers of the Continental Congress*, no. 147, I, folio 439, dated January 13. Orlando W. Stephenson. "The Supply of gunpowder in 1776." *The American Historical Review*. XXX (January 1925) page 277 shows that 478,250 pounds of saltpeter and 1,454,210 pounds of gunpowder were imported in 1776. See also Huston, James A. *The Sinews of War: Army Logistics, 1775–1953*. Washington, Office of the Chief of Military History, United States Army, 1966. p. 24; Lasseray. vol.1, pp. 82, 218–219; Smith, Robert F. "A veritable.. arsenal" of manufacturing: Government management of weapons production in the American Revolution by Robert F. Smith. Thesis/ dissertation. Ph. D. Lehigh University, 2008, pp. 14–17.

80 Lasseray. vol. 1, p. 82.
   • Mark Fouquet for his pay as Lieutenant of Artillery, from 17th November, 1777, to 17th Novr, 1779, being two years, the sum of .. 960
   • And for a gratuity for his services instructing different people in the several Eastern States in the art of powder making, agreeable to his contract with the Board of War, the sum of 3000 Livres tournois which he is to receive agreeable to an order of the Honble. Board of Treasury at the rate of 18 dollars continental money for every 5 Livres aforesaid making .. 10,80
   • The whole amounting to .. 11,760
   • That he has received from the Board of War on account of his pay .. 81
   • Which leaves a balance due to him of .. 11,679
   • That there is due to Nicholas Fouquet for his pay as Captain of Artillery from the 17th November, 1777, to the 17th November, 1779, being two years .. 1,200
   • That he has received of the Board of War on account of his pay .. 120
   • Which leaves a balance due to him of .. 1,080

- That there is due him for two years services instructing different people of the several Eastern States in the Art of Powder Making, agreeable to his Contract with the Board of War, and for which he expects to receive in Bills of Exchange on France the sum of six thousand Livres Tournois.
- That they have received the following sums for the payment of their expenses on the Road thro' the different States, which they are to be allowed agreeable to the instructions of the Board of War: .. Dollars.
- From the Board of War .. 100
- General Clinton, New York .. 100
- Governor Brown, Rhode Island .. 108
- Governor and Council, Massachusetts Bay .. 400
- do .. do .. , Portsmouth .. 800
- Amounting to .. 1,508

Which they received from the time they left York Town, February, 1778, and returned the latter end of September, 1779, during which time they travelled thro' the several Eastern States on the business upon which they were employed by the Board of War.

This report, dated October 5, 1779, is in the Papers of the Continental Congress, no. 136, III, folio 699.

That there is due to Mark Fouquet, for his pay as lieutenant of artillery, from 17th November, 1777, to 17th November, 1779, and for his services instructing different people in the eastern states, in the art of powder making, agreeable to his contract with the Board of War, a ballance of eleven thousand six hundred and seventy nine dollars.

That there is due to Nicholas Fouquet, for his pay as captain of artillery, from the 17th November, 1777, to 17 November, 1779, being two years, a ballance of one thousand and eighty dollars. And for his two years services instructing different people of the several eastern states in the art of powder making, agreeable to his contract with the Board of War, the sum of six thousand livres tournois:

Ordered, That the said accounts be paid.

Ordered, That the Board of Treasury prepare a set of bills of exchange, in favour of Captain Nicholas Fouquet, for six thousand livres tournois.

JCC. vol. 15, pp. 1154, 1165. vol. 27, p. 207n. See also the report in the *Papers of the Continental Congress*, no. 136, II, folio 59. Tuesday, October 12, 1779, JCC. vol. 15, pp. 1164-1165, *Papers of the Continental Congress*, no. 147, II folio 519; Thursday, January 15, 1778. JCC. vol. 10, p. 57, *Papers of the Continental Congress* no. 147, I folio 439 dated January 13.

81 47th Congress 1st session House of Representatives report no. 519 Heirs of Nicolas and Marc Antoine Fouquet. https://books.google.com/books?id=bE1HAQAAIAAJ&pg=PR436&lpg=PR436&dq=HEIRS+OF+NICOLAS+AND+MARC+ANTOINE+FOUQUET.&source=-bl&ots=CXJ3yt0RDh&sig=ZiGQDx0LyapWEdIU4vNl99l1Zmg&hl=en&sa=X&ved=0a-hUKEwiH0YrLvaHUAhXERSYKHWtYBUUQ6AEIKjAA#v=onepage&q=HEIRS%20OF%20NICOLAS%20AND%20MARC%20ANTOINE%20FOUQUET.&f=false.

To Benjamin Franklin from the Board of Treasury, October 16, 1779. BF. vol. 30, pp. 541–542. From Nicolas Fouquet, Wed, Aug 2, 1780. BF. vol. 33, p. 144. Franklin forwarded Fouquet's letter to Samuel Huntington, president of Congress, on August 9. It was read in Congress on February 22, 1781 and referred to the Board of War (JCC. vol. 19, p. 185). The Board of War also received a summary of testimonials from the various states where the Fouquets had worked. The report submitted by the Board of War on October 12, 1779 recommending payment beyond the sum mentioned in the contract can be found in JCC. vol. 15, pp. 1164–1165.

Chapter 3

1 Letter from Colonel Benedict Arnold to the Massachusetts Committee of Safety dated Crown Point, May 19, 1775. Massachusetts Archives. vol. 193, pp. 210, 211 in NDAR. vol. 1, pp. 364–367; PEP. vol. 1, no. 55 (May 30, 1775), p. 221; Ward. pp. 69–70.

2 There were four forts on the same site. Jacques de Chambly built the first wood fort in 1665 as a defense from Iroquois war parties on their way to Montréal. Two additional palisade forts were built before a stone fort was erected in 1709 to counter an impending British threat. The British captured the fort on September 1, 1760, ending French domination in the area. The fort was primarily a storage facility for the other British forts on the Richelieu River in September 1775. The British later developed a major military complex in the vicinity of the fort. The fort was abandoned in 1860 and is now restored according to the 1750 plans. It interprets the military and social history of the Richelieu Valley from 1665 to 1760.

3 PEP. vol. 1, no. 55 (May 30, 1775), p. 221; Ward. p. 69–70.

4 Extract of a letter from a Gentleman at Albany, September 2. BG, September 14, 1775.

5 Enys, John. "*The American Journals of Lt John Enys*" 1757–1818. Edited by Elizabeth Cometti. Syracuse, New York: Syracuse University Press, 1976, p. 16. www.ctssar.org/monthly_history/y1775september.htm.

6 CC. 563 (Aug. 10, 1775), p. 3; Journal of David Safford. CG, October 27, 1775, NDAR. vol. 2, p. 339.

7 Journal of David Safford. CG, October 27, 1775. NDAR. vol. 2, p. 339.

8 *A Narrative of the Captivity of Col. Ethan Allen*. Albany, 1814, pp. 15, 16; NDAR. vol. 2 p. 192.

9 ibid, pp. 16–28; NDAR. vol. 2, p. 196.

10 Peckham. p. 8; Trumbull. vol. 7, p. 149.

11 *Journals of Congress*. published by order of Congress. Yorktown Pennsylvania: printed by John Dunlap, Evans 15145, p. 226; Peckham. p. 8.

12 Trumbull. Loc. Cit.

13 ibid.

14 Extract of a letter from General Montgomery, dated Camp before St. Johns, October 20, 1775. PEP, v. 1, no. 123 (November 4, 1775), p. 506.

15 Trumbull. vol. 7, p. 150.

16 Extract of a letter from General Montgomery, dated Camp before St. Johns, October 20, 1775, PEP, v. 1, no. 123 (November 4, 1775), p. 506; RNYG. 134. (November 9,1775), p. 2, PEP. vol. 1, no. 123 (November 4, 1775) p. 506; PEP. vol. 1, no. 134 (November 30, 1775), p. 550; Essex Journal. vol. 2, no. 97 (Nov. 11, 1775), p. 2.

17 Extract of a letter from General Montgomery, dated Camp near St. Johns, November 3, 1775. CJ. 424 (November 29, 1775), p. 1.

18 ibid. Boatner, *Landmarks*. p.14.

19 PEP. vol. 1, no. 134 (November 30, 1775), p. 550; Peckham. p. 9.

20 Boatner, *Landmarks*, pp. 11–12.

21 Henry, John Joseph. *Account of Arnold's Campaign Against Quebec and of the hardships and sufferings of that band of heroes who traversed the wilderness of Maine from Cambridge to the St. Lawrence, in the autumn of 1775*. Albany: Joel Munsell, 1877. p. 74.

22 Journal of H.M. Sloop *Hunter*, Captain Thomas Mackenzie, BNA. Admiralty 51/466. NDAR. vol. 3, Henry, John Joseph. *Account of Arnold's Campaign Against Quebec and of the hardships and sufferings of that band of heroes who traversed the wilderness of Maine from Cambridge to the St. Lawrence, in the autumn of 1775*. Albany: Joel Munsell, 1877, pp. 80–81. Senter, Isaac. *The Journal of Isaac Senter, Physician and Surgeon to the Troops Detached From the American Army Encamped at*

Cambridge, Mass. on a Secret Expedition Against Quebec, Under the Command of Colonel Benedict Arnold, In September, 1775. Philadelphia: Published by the Historical Society of Pennsylvania. 1846, pp. 27–28.

23   Senter, Isaac. The Journal of Isaac Senter. *The Magazine of History with Notes and Queries.* Extra Number 42, 1915, pp. 72–144. (Eyewitness accounts of the American Revolution). New York: New York Times, Arno Press, 1969. p. 28; Henry, John Joseph. *Account of Arnold's Campaign Against Quebec and of the hardships and sufferings of that band of heroes who traversed the wilderness of Maine from Cambridge to the St. Lawrence, in the autumn of 1775.* Albany: Joel Munsell, 1877, pp. 90–91.

24   Boatner. *Landmarks*, pp. 11–12.

25   www.gov.pe.ca/photos/original/greatseal.pdf. http: //en.wikipedia.org/wiki/ Charlottetown,_Prince_Edward_Island.

26   Journal of H.M. Sloop *Hunter*, Captain Thomas Mackenzie, BNA. Admiralty 51/466; NDAR. vol. 3, p. 31.

27   ibid. Dearborn, Henry. *Revolutionary War Journals of Henry Dearborn, 1775–1783*, Edited by Lloyd A. Brown and Howard H. Peckham. New York: Da Capo Press, 1971. pp. 63–64; Senter, Isaac. *The Journal of Isaac Senter, Physician And Surgeon to The Troops Detached From The American Army Encamped At Cambridge, Mass. On A Secret Expedition Against Quebec, Under The Command of Col. Benedict Arnold, In September, 1775.* Philadelphia: Published by the Historical Society of Pennsylvania. 1846. pp. 30–31; Arnold, Isaac Newton. *The Life of Benedict Arnold, his Patriotism and his Treason.* Chicago, Jansen, McClurg & Co. 1880, pp. 98–100.

28   Extract of a letter from an officer under Colonel Arnold dated at Point aux Trembles (in Canada) November 21, 1775. PG. vol. 13, no. 631 (February 3, 1776), p. 1; NEC. vol. 8, no. 384 (November 30, 1775). PG. vol. 13, no. 631 (February 3, 1776), p. 1.

29   Dearborn, Henry. *Revolutionary War Journals of Henry Dearborn, 1775–1783*, Edited by Lloyd A. Brown and Howard H. Peckham. New York: Da Capo Press, 1971, p. 64.

30   ibid., pp. 66–74.

31   PEP, January 25, 1776; *New York Packet*, February 1, 1776; Moore. vol. 1, pp. 185–187; Arnold, Isaac Newton. *The Life of Benedict Arnold, his Patriotism and his Treason.* Chicago, Jansen, McClurg & Co. 1880, pp. 104–107; Dearborn, Henry. *Revolutionary War Journals of Henry Dearborn, 1775–1783*, Edited by Lloyd A. Brown and Howard H. Peckham. New York: Da Capo Press, 1971, pp. 66–74; Kemble, Stephen. *Journals of Lieutenant-Colonel Stephen Kemble, 1773–1789, and British Army Orders: General Sir William Howe, 1775–1778, General Sir Henry Clinton, 1778, and General Daniel Jones, 1778.* Prepared by New York Historical Society, Boston: Gregg Press, 1972, p. 66.

32   Journal of H.M. Sloop *Hunter*, Captain Thomas Mackenzie, BNA. Admiralty 51/466. NDAR. vol. 4, p. 316.

33   Roche, John F. Quebec Under Siege, 1775–1776: The "Memorandums" of Jacob Danford. *The Canadian Historical Review.* 50: 1969, pp. 68–85, 80.

34   NM, 923 (March 13, 1776), p. 2; CJ, 447 (March 8, 1776), p. 3.

35   Peckham. p. 14; Extract of a letter, dated in the Camp before Quebec, April 6, 1776. CJ. 447 (May 8, 1778), p. 3.

36   Peckham. p. 16; Haskell, Caleb. *Caleb Haskell's diary, May 5, 1775–May 30, 1776 a revolutionary soldier's record before Boston and with Arnold's Quebec expedition.* Newburyport, Massachusetts: W. Huse, 1881 *Proceedings of the Massachusetts Historical Society*, 2nd series. vol. II, p. 298; NDAR. vol. 4, pp. 1402–1404.

37   Journal of H.M. Sloop *Hunter*, Captain Thomas Mackenzie, BNA. Admiralty 51/466; NDAR. vol. 4, p. 1413.

38   Captain Charles Douglas, R.N. to Philip Stephens. *Isis* before Quebec, May 8, 1776. BNA. Colonial Office, 5/124, 46b, NDAR. vol. 4, pp. 1451–1452.

39 Journal of HMS *Surprize*, Captain Linzee. BNA. Admiralty 51/336, NDAR. vol. 4, p. 1454.

40 Journal of HMS *Surprize*, Captain Robert Linzee, BNA. Admiralty 51/336, NDAR. vol. 5, p. 42.

41 Journal of HM Sloop *Martin*, BNA. Admiralty 51/581, NDAR. vol. 5, pp. 59, 86.

42 Greenwood, pp. 25–26; Extract of a letter from Montréal, May 27, PEP. vol. 2, no. 230 (July 11, 1776), p. 343; Letter of Captain Charles Douglas to Philip Stephens, May 26, 1778. BNA. Admiralty 1/1706, NDAR. vol. 5, p. 260.

43 Brig. General Benedict Arnold to the Congressional Commissioners in Canada. PCC (Letters from General Officers), 162, 72, NA, NDAR. vol. 5, pp. 242–243; Extract of a letter from Montréal, May 27. PEP. vol. 2, no. 230 (July 11, 1776), p. 343; Greenwood, pp. 25–33.

44 Stedman, Charles. *The History of the Origin, Progress and Termination of the American War*. London: printed for the author, 1794, pp. 174–175. Greenwood, p. 119.

45 Journal of HM Sloop *Martin*. BNA. Admiralty 51/ 581, NDAR. vol. 5, p. 421; Letter from Captain Henry Harvey to Captain Charles Douglas. June 11, 1776. BNA. Colonial Office, 5/125, 15e, NDAR. vol. 5, p. 467; letter from General Sir Guy Carlton to Lord George Germaine, June 20, 1776. PEP. vol. 2, no. 273 (October 19, 1776), p. 523; Letter of Major Griffith Williams to Lord George Germain, June 23, 1776. *The Correspondence of King George the Third from 1760 to December 1783*. Sir John Fortescue, ed. London, 1927–1928. vol. 3, pp. 382–386, NDAR. vol. 5, pp. 692–694; Letter of Captain Charles Douglas to Philip Stephens, June 26, 1776. BNA. Colonial Office, 5/125, 15b, NDAR. vol. 5, pp. 747–750; Extract of a letter from Albany, dated June 12, 1776; PEP. vol. 2, no. 220 (June 18, 1776), p. 305; PEP. vol. 2, no. 228 (July 6, 1776), p. 337; Extract of a letter from Crownpoint, dated July 3, 1776, PEP. vol. 3, no. 233 (July 18, 1776), p. 233; EJ. vol. 3, no. 138 (August 23, 1776), p. 3; Cecil, Pierre. La Bataille de Trois- Rivières, 8 juin 1776. Histoire Québec. vol. 7, no. 1, pp. 3–4.

46 Letter from General Sir Guy Carlton to Lord George Germaine, June 20, 1776. PEP. vol. 2, no. 273 (October 19, 1776), p. 523.

47 NEC. vol. 2, no. 411 (July 4, 1776), p. 2; EJ. vol. 3, no. 131 (July 5, 1776), p. 3.

48 Peckham. p. 19.

49 Brigadier General Benedict Arnold to Major General Horatio Gates. Gates Papers, Box 4, New York Historical Society. NDAR. vol. 6, p. 925.

50 Kerr, W.B. "Nova Scotia in the Critical Years." *The Dalhousie Review*. vol. 12 (1932); Harvey, D. C. "Machias And the Invasion of Nova Scotia" *Annual Report of the Canadian Historical Association*, 1932; Clarke, Ernest. *The Siege of Fort Cumberland, 1776: an episode in the American Revolution*. Montréal & Kingston, London, Buffalo: McGill-Queen's University Press, 1995. p. 104.

51 Journal of Lieutenant Colonel Joseph Goreham, Proceedings at Fort Cumberland, BNA. Colonial Office, 217/52, Dominion (Public) Archives of Canada, Ottawa. 361; NDAR. vol. 7, p. 69; Clarke, Ernest. *The Siege of Fort Cumberland, 1776: an episode in the American Revolution*. Montréal & Kingston, London, Buffalo: McGill-Queen's University Press, 1995, pp. 137–138.

52 ibid. Clarke, Ernest. *The Siege of Fort Cumberland, 1776: an episode in the American Revolution*. Montréal & Kingston, London, Buffalo: McGill-Queen's University Press, 1995, pp. 109–110; Harvey, D.C. "Machias And the Invasion of Nova Scotia." *Annual Report of the Canadian Historical Association*, 1932.

53 EJ. 158 (January 9, 1777), p. 2; NHG. vol. 1, no. 33 (January 7, 1777), p. 4; *The New London Gazette*. vol. 14, no. 687 (January 10, 1777), p. 3.

54 ibid.

55 Clarke, Ernest. *The Siege of Fort Cumberland, 1776: an episode in the American Revolution*. Montréal & Kingston, London, Buffalo: McGill-Queen's University Press, 1995, pp. 111–114, 140–141; Journal of Lieutenant Colonel Joseph Goreham, Proceedings at Fort Cumberland,

BNA. Colonial Office, 217/52, 315, Dominion (Public) Archives of Canada, Ottawa, Photocopy; NDAR. vol. 7, p. 99; Webster. *The Forts of Chignecto. Shediac*, N.B.: Privately printed, 1930, pp. 116–122; Colonel Jonathan Eddy to The Massachusetts General Court, James Phinney Baxter, ed. *Documentary History of the State of Maine*. (Portland, 1910). vol. XIV, pp. 395–96; NDAR. vol. 7, p. 110; Sir George Collier to Captain George Dawson, H.M. Sloop *Hope*, BNA. Colonial Office, 217/52, 340–341, Dominion (Public) Archives of Canada, Ottawa, Photocopy; NDAR. vol. 7, p. 133; Harvey, D. C. "Machias And the Invasion of Nova Scotia" *Annual Report of the Canadian Historical Association*, s.l.: s.n. 1932.

56   Extract of a Letter from Plymouth, April 4, RGG, July 19, 1781, no. 125, p. 1.

57   New-York, Dec. 25. NYG. Dec. 25, 1780, no. 1523, p. 3; Charlestown, November 18, 1780. New-York, December 18. IL. Jan. 15, 1781. vol. III, no. 137, p. 2; New-York, December 5. CJ. Jan. 18, 1781, no. 690, p. 1.

58   Master's Log of HM Brig *Diligent*. BNA. Admiralty 52/1669; NDAR. vol. 7, p. 430.

59   Colonel John Allan's Journal in Kidder, Frederic. *Military Operations in Eastern Maine and Nova Scotia during the Revolution*. Albany: Joel Munsell, 1867. pp. 92–93.

60   ibid. pp.196–200; Peckham, pp. 35, 36; Letter from Colonel Alexr. Cambell. July 13, 1777. *Documentary History of the State of Maine, containing the Baxter Manuscripts*. James Phinney Baxter, ed. Portland, 1910 vol. 10, pp. 440–441.

61   Extract of a Letter from Gosport, Nov. 12. NYG. Feb. 2, 1778, no. 1371, p. 2; New-York, July 21. NYG, July 21, 1777, no. 1343, p. 3.

62   Best Account We Can at Present Obtain of an Affair That Engages the Attention of the Public. IL, June 22, 1778. vol. 1, no. 2, p. 3.

63   London, August 18. CJWA. Nov. 5, 1778, no. CXXVIII, p. 1.

64   www3.bc.sympatico.ca/charlotte_taylor/Folder1/aboriginal_peoples.htm. www3.bc.sympatico.ca/charlotte_taylor/Folder1/Wishart%20Period.htm.

65   Col. Allan's Dispatches Captured by the Enemy. Machias Oct 20, 1779 in Kidder, Frederic. *Military Operations in Eastern Maine and Nova Scotia during the Revolution*. Albany: Joel Munsell, 1867. p. 268; Peckham. p. 65.

66   Boston, August 10. IC&UA. Aug. 10, 1780. vol. XII, no. 624, p. 3. AJ, Aug. 16, 1780. vol. II, no. 73, p. 2. CJ. Aug. 17, 1780, no. 668, p. 3. PJ, Aug. 23, 1780, no. 1354, p. 3; Extract of a Letter, Taken in the *Mercury* Packet, Captain Dillon, from Thomas Irving, of London, to John. NJG. Aug. 23, 1780. vol. III, no. 139, p. 3; Boston, August 10. PEP. Aug. 29, 1780. vol. VI, no. 690, p. 103; Prensa. Sept. 5, 1780. vol. VII, no. 364, p. 2; Boston, August 7. NJG. Aug. 30, 1780. vol. III, no. 140, p. 2.

67   Hermione, pp. 222–223.

68   ibid.

69   Hattendorf. p. 98; PJ. Aug. 29, 1781, no. 1417, p. 2; PJ. Sept. 12, 1781, no. 1421, p. 2; Boston, August 10. CC. Aug. 21, 1781, no. 865, p. 3; Extract of a Letter from Boston, Dated August 5. FJ. Aug. 22, 1781, no. XVIII, p. 3; New Port, August 11. NM. Aug. 11, 1781, no. 1037, p. 3; Extracts from Rebel Papers. Boston, August 6. NYG. Aug. 13, 1781, no. 1556, p. 2; RAG. Aug. 14, 1781. vol. VII, no. CCCXCIX, p. 2; Boston, August, 9. MS. Aug. 16, 1781. vol. XI, no. 536, p. 2; Newport, August 11. NJG. Sept. 5, 1781. vol. IV, no. 193, p. 3; Boston, Aug. 27. BG. Aug. 27, 1781, no. 1409, p. 3; PP. Sept. 11, 1781. vol. X, no. 780, p. 2; Extract of a Letter from M De La Perouse, to M. De Barras, Dated July 23, 1781. CJWA. Aug. 30, 1781, no. CCLXXXVIII, p. 2; PEP. Sept. 10, 1781. vol. VII, no. 771, p. 145.

70   PJ. Aug. 22, 1781, no. 1413, p. 2; Boston, August 6. PJ. Aug. 29, 1781, no. 1417, p. 2; PJ. Sept. 12, 1781, no. 1421, p. 2; IL. Aug. 6, 1781. vol. IV, no. 167, p. 3; AJ. Aug. 8, 1781. vol. III, no. 151, p. 1; Paris, May 18. NYG. Aug. 6, 1781, no. 1555, p. 2; NJG. Aug. 22, 1781. vol. IV, no.

191, p. 2; AJ. Aug. 8, 1781, p. 1, NJG. Aug. 22, 1781, p. 2, Newport, August 11. NJG. Sept. 5, 1781. vol. IV, no. 193, p. 3; Boston, August 9. IC&UA. Aug. 9, 1781. vol. XIII, no. 708, p. 3; MS, Aug. 16, 1781. vol. XI, no. 536, p. 2; Extracts from Rebel Papers. Boston, August 6. NYG. Aug. 13, 1781, no. 1556, p. 2; RAG. Aug. 14, 1781. vol. VII, no. CCCXCIX, p. 2; Faibisy. PG. Aug. 11, 1781, p. 3, Hattendorf. p. 98; Boston, August 10. CC. Aug. 21, 1781, no. 865, p. 3; Extract of a Letter from Boston, Dated August 5. FJ. Aug. 22, 1781, no. XVIII, p. 3; New Port, August 11. NM. Aug. 11, 1781, no. 1037, p. 3; Boston, Aug. 27; BG; Aug. 27, 1781, no. 1409, p. 3; PP. Sept. 11, 1781. vol. X, no. 780, p. 2; Extract of a Letter from M De La Perouse, to M. De Barras, Dated July 23, 1781. CJWA. Aug. 30, 1781, no. CCLXXXVIII, p. 2; PEP. Sept. 10, 1781. vol. VII, no. 771, p. 145.

71   Boston, August 6. IL. Aug. 6, 1781. vol. IV, no. 167, p. 3; Paris, May 18. NYG. Aug. 6, 1781, no. 1555, p. 2; Extracts from Rebel Papers. Boston, August 6. NYG. Aug. 13, 1781, no. 1556, p. 2; Boston, August 23. AJ. Aug. 25, 1781. vol. III, no. 156, p. 2; CC. Aug. 28, 1781, no. 866, p. 3; Boston, August 27, IL, Aug. 27, 1781. vol. IV, no. 170.

72   CJWA. Aug. 16, 1781, no. CCLXXXVI, p. 3; Boston, Aug. 13. BG. Aug. 13, 1781, no. 1407, p. 3; Boston, August 9. AJ. Aug. 15, 1781. vol. III, no. 153, p. 2; NM. Aug. 18, 1781, no. 1038, p. 2; MS. Aug. 16, 1781. vol. XI, no. 536, p. 2; Boston, August 16. IC&UA. Aug. 16, 1781. vol. IV, no. 709, p. 3; MS, Aug. 23, 1781. vol. XI, no. 537, p. 2; PEP. Aug. 27, 1781. vol. VII, no. 767, p. 137. FJ. Aug. 29, 1781, no. XIX, p. 3; Boston, August 18. PP. Aug. 28, 1781. vol. X, no. 774, p. 2; A letter dated the [Illegible] instant, from an officer at Head-Quarters, Philipsburgh Says. PJ. Aug. 29, 1781, no. 1417, p. 2; New Port, August 11. NM. Aug. 11, 1781, no. 1037, p. 3; NJG. Sept. 5, 1781. vol. IV, no. 193, p. 3; Extracts from Rebel Papers. Boston, August 6. NYG. Aug. 13, 1781, no. 1556, p. 2; RAG, Aug. 14, 1781. vol. VII, no. CCCXCIX, p. 2.

73   Albany, September 16. NYGNA. Sept. 16, 1782. vol. I, no. 16, p. 3.

74   Extract of a Letter from Plymouth, November 22. RGG. Feb. 15, 1781, no. 103, p. 1.

75   Extract of a Letter from Edenburgh, June 4. PP. Sept. 11, 1781. vol. X, no. 780, p. 2; London, June 7. RGG. Sept. 27, 1781, no. 135, p. 3.

76   Boatner. *Landmarks.* p. 9.

Chapter 4

1   Williamsburg, April 27, PEP, May 7, 1776. vol. II, no. 202, p. 230; Williamsburg, April 26, MG. May 9, 1776. vol. XXXI, no. 1600, p. 3; Williamsburgh, (in Virginia), April 27, NYG, May 13, 1776, no. 1283, p. 3.

2   Extract of a Letter from New-York, August 12. PL. Aug. 17, 1776, no. LXXXII, p. 3.

3   Providence, June 22. NYG, July 1, 1776, no. 1290, p. 3; Providence, June 22. PEP. July 2, 1776. vol. II, no. 226, p. 329; PJ. July 3, 1776, no. 1752, p. 2; Providence, June 22. VG, July 20, 1776, no. 1302, p. 1.

4   Extract of a Letter from Portsmouth, July 17. NYG, Nov. 11, 1776, no. 1307, p. 1; Extract of a Letter from Plymouth Sound, Dated July 7, to a Gentleman in Bristol. NYG. Oct. 12, 1776, no. 1304, p. 3; London, July 29. IC. Oct. 24, 1776. vol. IX, no. 427, p. 2.

5   New-York, August 3. TCG. Aug. 3, 1776. vol. II, no. 106, p. 3; Extract of a Letter from Philadelphia, Dated August 1. NYJ. Aug. 8, 1776, no. 1753, p. 3; New-York, August 8 Extract of a Letter from Philadelphia, Dated August 3. MJ. Aug. 14, 1776. vol. III, no. 139, p. 1; Philadelphia, July 27. VG, Aug. 17, 1776, no. 1306, p. 1.

6   Newport, December, 2. MJ. Dec. 30, 1776. vol. III, no. 159, p. 2; Boston, December 5. VG, Jan. 10, 1777, no. 1327, p. 3.

7   Newbury-Port, Sept. 20. EJ. Sept. 20, 1776. vol. III, no. 142, p. 3; Extract of a Letter from New-York, September 14. CJWA. Sept. 26, 1776, no. XVIII, p. 2; Boston, September 26. CJ. Oct. 2, 1776, no. 468, p. 3; PEP. Oct. 5, 1776. vol. II, no. 267, p. 498; VG, Oct. 25, 1776, no. 1316, p. 2; Water town, Sept. 23. NM. Oct. 7, 1776, no. 947, p. 3.
8   *Whitehall Evening Post.* Thursday, November 14 to Saturday, November 16, 1776. NDAR. vol. 7, p. 744.
9   Pliarne & Penet to Nicholas and John Brown. Nicholas Brown papers. John Carter Brown Library. William Bell Clark. *Lambert Wickes, Sea Raider and Diplomat.* New Haven, 1932, PP, 98–99. Declaration of James Pratchell, master of the prize brick *La Vigne.* December 24, 1776. Franklin papers. 53 pt. 1, no. 27, NDAR. vol. 7, pp. 777, 780–781, 804–805; London. PJ. Mar. 26, 1777, no. 1782, p. 3; NDAR. vol. 7, pp. 777 and note, 780–781 and 781 note, 790–791, 804–805, 1308; Philadelphia, February 27. PEP. Feb. 27, 1777. vol. III, no. 320, p. 109; PJ. Mar. 5, 1777, no. 1779, p. 3; VG, Mar. 14, 1777, no. 1336, p. 2; Extract of a Letter from Bourdeax, Dated December 13, 1776. PEP. Mar. 6, 1777. vol. III, no. 323, p. 123; VG, Mar. 14, 1777, no. 111, p. 2.
10 NDAR. vol. 7, pp. 574–576.
11 New-York, January 22, 1777. RPAG. Mar. 3, 1778, no. 1, p. 3; MJ. Mar. 24, 1778. vol. V, no. 229, p. 1.
12 PEP. Thursday, February 27, 1777; Extract of a Letter from Philadelphia, Dated April 2d, 1777. CJWA. April 17, 1777, no. XLVII, p. 3; Boston, April 14. CC. April 21, 1777, no. 639, p. 3; Boston, April 17; PEP. April 29, 1777. vol. III, no. 345, p. 239; MJ. May 6, 1777. vol. IV, no. 182, p. 4; MG. May 6, 1777. vol. III, no. CVI, p. 2; Philadelphia. PEP. May 13, 1777. vol. III, no. 351, p. 262; Philadelphia, May 13. PP. May 13, 1777. vol. VI, no. 287, p. 3; Philadelphia, May 10, Extract of a Letter from St. [Illegible] April 20, 1777. MJ. May 20, 1777. vol. IV, no. 185, p. 3; VG, May 30, 1777, no. 1346, p. 2; Philadelphia, May 14. CC. May 26, 1777, no. 644, p. 2; CG&UI. May 30, 1777. vol. XIV, no. 707, p. 2.
13 Journal of HMS *Camilla*, Captain Charles Phipps. BNA, Admiralty 51/157. NDAR. vol. 7, pp. 1149–1150; *SCAGG.* Thursday, February 20, 1777; NDAR. vol. 7, pp. 1251; Captain George Keith Elphinstone, R.N. to Vice Admiral James Young. BNA, Admiralty 51/309; NDAR. vol. 7, pp. 1281; Vice-Admiral James Young to Philip Stephens. BNA, Admiralty 1/309; NDAR. vol. 8, pp. 68–70; NBBAS. vol. 1, p. 171; Charlestown, (South-Carolina) February 27. CJ. Mar. 26, 1777, no. 493, p. 3; Charlestown (S. C.) February 27, 1777. PEP. April 1, 1777. vol. III, no. 334, p. 179; MG. April 8, 1777. vol. II, no. CII, p. 2; PJ, April 9, 1777, no. 1784, p. 2.
14 NDAR. vol. 8, pp. 393–394, 1053–1063; HCA 32/397/2/1-36; New-York, April 21. NYG, April 21, 1777, no. 1330, p. 3.
15 NDAR. vol. 8, pp. 324–325 and 325 note, 395–396 and 396 note, 997 and note, 1053–1063.
16 Extract of a Letter from Portsmouth, April 25. CJWA. July 10, 1777, no. LIX, p. 2.
17 Captain John Jervis, R.N. to Philip Stephens. April 29, 1777. NDAR. vol. 8, pp. 799–800.
18 Captain John Jervis, R.N. to Philip Stephens. *Foudroyant*, at Sea. 1st May 1777. BNA, Admiralty 1/1987, 1, 50; NDAR. vol. 8, p. 807. Extract of a letter from Plymouth, May 4. *London Packet, or New Lloyd's Evening Post*, May 5 to May 7, 1777; NDAR. vol. 8, p. 816; Baltimore, October 7, Head Quarters. MJ. Oct. 7, 1777. vol. IV, no. 205, p. 3; Charles-town, August 28, 1777. PL. Oct. 10, 1777, no. XCVIII, p. 2; NDAR. vol. 8, pp. 807, 816. vol. 9, pp. 381–382, 390–391; Coker, pp. 91, 300; HCA 32/266/10/1-.
19 Extract of a Letter from France, Dated May 22, 1777. VG. Aug. 22, 1777, no. 134, p. 2; VG. Aug. 22, 1777, no. 1377, p. 1; Philadelphia, August 6. Extract of a Letter from an American Gentleman Paris, Dated May 13, 1777. VG, Aug. 22, 1777, no. 1377, p. 1.
20 NDAR. vol. 9, p. 7 and note, 123–124; Howe's prize list, 1777; HCA 32/320/2/1-19.
21 NDAR. vol. 8, p. 815. vol. 9, pp. 405–406, 415-416.

22   NDAR. vol. 9, pp. 406, 415 and note; HCA 32/298/16/1-11; Baltimore, October 7, Head Quarters. MJ. Oct. 7, 1777. vol. IV, no. 205, p. 3; Charlestown, (S. Carolina), September 11. CJ. Oct. 29, 1777, no. 524, p. 4.

23   Extract of a Letter from Cove of Cork, June 5. PEP. Oct. 14, 1777. vol. III, no. 410, p. 495.

24   NDAR. vol. 9, pp. 258–259; Howe's prize list, 1777.

25   Neeser, pp. 3–5; *The Pennsylvania Magazine of History and Biography*. vol. 22 pp. 481–482.

26   New-York, October 13. NYG, Oct. 13, 1777, no. 1355, p. 3.

27   NDAR. vol. 9, pp. 560 a. note, 561, 897 and note. vol. 10, pp. 15–16 and 16 note; Boston, September 8. MS. Sept. 11, 1777. vol. VII, no. 332, p. 2; CC. Sept. 15, 1777, no. 660, p. 2; Boston, Sept. 11. PEP. Sept. 23, 1777. vol. III, no. 408, p. 488; MJ. Sept. 30, 1777. vol. IV, no. 204, p. 2.

28   PJ. July 30, 1777, no. 1800, p. 2.

29   NDAR. vol. 11, pp. 971–975 and 976 note, 979–982.

30   NDAR. vol. 9, pp. 919–920, 920–921, 971. vol. 11, pp. 1173–1174 and 1174 note. Captain Nicholas Biddle to Robert Morris. *Papers of the Continental Congress, 1774–1789*. Washington: National Archives and Records Service, General Services Administration, 1971. (Letters Addressed to Congress, 1775–89), 1778. vol. II, pp. 241–243; NDAR. vol. 9, pp. 919–920; Baltimore, October 7 Head Quarters. MJ. Oct. 7, 1777. vol. IV, no. 205, p. 3; Charlestown (S. Carolina) September 11. PG, Oct. 18, 1777. vol. XIV, no. 720, p. 4; Charlestown, (S. C.) September 11. FJ, Nov. 1, 1777. vol. II, no. 21, p. 2; New-York, November 3. NYG, Nov. 3, 1777, no. 1358, p. 3; NDAR. vol. 9, pp. 919–920, 920–921, 971. vol. 11, pp. 1173–1174 and 1174 note.

31   Newbern, Sept. 19. VG. Oct. 10, 1777, no. 141, p. 1.

32   NDAR. vol. 9, pp. 986. vol. 10, p. 113. vol. 11, pp. 269–270 and 270 notes.

33   VG. 141 (March 10, 1777) p. 1; The following is an Extract of a Letter from the Rev. Mr. Hitchcock, Dated in Camp, Three Miles Above Stillwater, Sept. 21, 1777. CJWA. Oct. 9, 1777, no. LXXII, p. 3; a Letter from George Selech Silliman, to Mr. Israel Pebbins, Dated October 5, 1777. FJ, Oct. 11, 1777. vol. II, no. 18, p. 1; Hartford, October 14. CC. Oct. 14, 1777, no. 664, p. 2; October 9. CJ. Oct. 15, 1777, no. 522, p. 2; Charlestown, (S. Carolina) September 11. CJ. Oct. 29, 1777, no. 524, p. 4; Charlestown, (S. C.) September 11. FJ, Nov. 1, 1777. vol. II, no. 21, p. 2.

34   NDAR. vol. 10, pp. 875, 877, 895–897, 900 and note, 905, 906, 910–911 and 911 note, 912–913 and 913 note, 913–914 and 914 note, 914–915 and 915 note, 922, 925, 930 and note, 931–933 and 933 note, 933–934 and 934 note, 939 and note, 940–942, 946–947 and 947 notes, 960–963, 976–977 and 977 notes, 1014–1015, 1051–1054, 1060–1061, 1062–1063 and 1063 note, 1115, 1155–1156 and 1156 note. vol. 11, p. 133 and note; Morgan, William James. *Captains to the northward, the New England captains in the Continental Navy*. Barre, Mass. *Barre Gazette*, 1959, p.101; a Letter from George Selech Silliman, to Mr. Israel Pebbins, Dated October 5, 1777. FJ, Oct. 11, 1777. vol. II, no. 18, p. 1; Hartford, October 14. CC. Oct. 14, 1777, no. 664, p. 2.

35   Extract of a Letter from on Board the *Enterprize*, Man of War, Sir Tho, Rich, Dated Gibraltar, Octo. 23, NYG, Feb. 2, 1778, no. 1371, p. 2.

36   NDAR. vol. 10, pp. 875, 877, 895–897, 900 and note, 905, 906, 910–911 and 911 note, 912–913 and 913 note, 913–914 and 914 note, 914–915 and 915 note, 922, 925, 930 and note, 931–933 and 933 note, 933–934 and 934 note, 939 and note, 940–942, 946–947 and 947 notes, 960–963, 976–977 and 977 notes, 1014–1015, 1051–1054, 1060–1061, 1062–1063 and 1063 note, 1115, 1155–1156 and 1156 note; vol. 11, p. 133 and note; Morgan, William James. *Captains to the northward; the New England captains in the Continental Navy*. Barre, Mass. Barre Gazette, 1959, p.101; a Letter from George Selech Silliman, to Mr. Israel Pebbins, Dated

October 5, 1777. FJ; Oct. 11, 1777; Vol. II; no.18; p. 1. Hartford, October 14. CC. Oct. 14, 1777, no. 664, p. 2.

37   Extract of a Letter from on Board the *Enterprize*, Man of War, Sir Tho. Rich, Dated Gibraltar, Octo. 23. NYG, Feb. 2, 1778, no. 1371; p. 2.

38   NDAR. vol. 11, pp. 23–24 and 24 note, 29–30 and note, 58 and note, 112 and 113 note, 207 and notes.

39   NDAR. vol. 11, pp. 1060, 1112–1113 and 113 note.

40   NDAR. vol. 11, pp. 350 and note, 373–374 and 374 note, 374 and note, 374–375 and 375 note, 375 and note, 384 and note.

41   New-York, March 23. NYG. Mar. 23, 1778, no. 1378, p. 3; New-York, March 18. PL. Mar. 28, 1778, no. CXXXIX, p. 2.

42   Philadelphia. Extract of a Letter from a Gentleman on Board His Majesty's Ship *Emerald*, Dated in Hampton Bay. PEP. Mar. 30, 1778. vol. IV, no. 473, pp. 138, 140; RPAG. Mar. 31, 1778, no. IX, p. 3.

43   ibid.

44   ibid.

45   New-York, May 18. NYG. May 18, 1778, no. 1386, p. 3.

46   Newport, March 12. RPAG. April 7, 1778; Providence, March 21; CJ; April 8, 1778, no. 547, p. 2. vol. XI, p. 3.

47   London, March 9. PP, July 25, 1778, p. 2.

48   New-York, March 28. RPAG. April 14, 1778, no. XIII, p. 2; PEP. April 13, 1778. vol. IV, no. 479, p. 162.

49   Extract of a Letter from Barbadoes, Dated March 15. NYG. April 6, 1778, no. 1380, p. 5; New-York, April 23. RPAG. May 8, 1778, no. XX, p. 3; PEP. May 8, 1778. vol. IV, no. 488, p. 188.

50   New-York, March 28. RPAG. April 14, 1778, no. XIII, p. 2.

51   New York, March 28. PEP. April 13, 1778. vol. IV, no. 479, p. 162; RPAG. April 14, 1778, no. XIII, p. 2.

52   New-York, April 4, RG. April 4, 1778, no. 163, p. 3.

53   Kell. p. 64. Still, William N. *North Carolina's Revolutionary War Navy.* The O. Davis Sons, Inc. 1976. p. 24; NBBAS. vol. 1, pp. 194–95; Newbern, N. C. April 10, MG. May 5, 1778. vol. IV, no. CLVIII, p. 2.

54   New-York, April 13. Extract of a Letter from St. Augustine, Dated April 7, RG, May 9, 1778, no. 168, p. 3; RPAG. April 28, 1778, no. XVII, p. 3; New-York, April 23. RPAG. May 8, 1778, no. XX, p. 3; Extract of a Letter from Rhode-Island, Dated April 4. PL. April 29, 1778, no. CXLVIII, p. 2.

55   Boston, April 16, 1778. IC&UA. April 16, 1778. vol. X, no. 504, p. 3; Boston. April 16. CC. April 21, 1778, no. 691, p. 1; MS. April 23, 1778. vol. VIII, no. 364, p. 2.

56   New-York, April 23. RPAG. May 8, 1778, no. XX, p. 3; New-York, April 27. NYG. April 27, 1778, no. 1383, p. 3.

57   ibid. PEP. May 8, 1778. vol. IV, no. 488, p. 188.

58   New York, April 23. PEP. May 8, 1778. vol. IV, no. 488, p. 188.

59   New York, May 27. PEP. June 11, 1778. vol. IV, no. 494, p. 204.

60   New-York, May 25. NYG. May 25, 1778, no. 1387, p. 3.

61   New-York, May 18. NYG. May 18, 1778, no. 1386, p. 3

62   London, May 12, NYG, Aug. 17, 1778, no. 1400, p. 2.

63   ibid.

64   ibid.

65   Extract of a Letter from Lisbon, April 20. NYG. Aug. 10, 1778, no. 1399, p. 1.

66 Boston, May 21. CJ. May 27, 1778, no. 554, p. 3.
67 New-York, May 25. NYG. May 25, 1778, no. 1387, p. 3.
68 New York, May 27. PEP. June 11, 1778. vol. IV, no. 494, p. 204.
69 ibid.
70 The following Officers Are Amongst the Killed, in the Royal Army. NYG. July 6, 1778, no. 1393, p. 3; Philadelphia. PEP. Aug. 6, 1778. vol. IV, no. 514, p. 278.
71 New-York, July 14. RAG. July 14, 1778, no. LXXXVII, p. 3.
72 New-London, June 19. CJ. June 24, 1778, no. 558, p. 3; IC&UA. June 25, 1778. vol. X, no. 514, p. 2.
73 New-London, June 19. CJ. June 24, 1778, no. 558, p. 3.
74 Baltimore, Sept. 22, a Letter from His Most Christian Majesty to Count Darbaud, Dated Versailles, June 28, 1778. MG. Sept. 22, 1778. vol. IV, no. CLXXVIII, p. 3; Late European Intelligence. MS. Sept. 24, 1778. vol. VIII, no. 386, p. 1.
75 In a letter from a gentleman of the first character, directed to the Hon. Major General Heath, dated Philadelphia, July 12, 1778. Boston, July 20. IL. July 20, 1778. vol. I, no. 6, p. 3; CJWA. July 23, 1778, no. CXIII, p. 3; MS. July 23, 1778. vol. VIII, no. 377, p. 3; IC&UA. July 23, 1778. vol. X, no. 518, p. 3; ExJ. July 28, 1778. vol. I, no. 23, p. 1.
76 Philadelphia, July 25, MJ, July 28, 1778. vol. V, no. 248, p. 2. PEP. July 25, 1778. vol. IV, no. 509, p. 257.
77 Baurmeister, Carl Leopold. *Revolution in America: Confidential Letters and Journals, 1776—1784.* trans. and annotated by Bernhard A. Uhlendorf. New Brunswick: Rutgers University Press, 1957. p.189. *Documents Relating to the Revolutionary History, State of New Jersey.* Edited by William S. Stryker. Trenton: The John L. Murphy Publishing Co. 1901. Series 2. vol. 2, pp. 318. They also captured the British ship *Charlotte* and the snow *Bonnet* and their cargoes of indigo, tobacco, molasses, train oil, turpentine, tar, deerskins, mahogany and logwood. The cargoes went up for sale at Chester, Pennsylvania on the Delaware River on Wednesday, July 29, 1778. Baltimore July 28, MJ. July 28, 1778. vol. V, no. 248, p. 2.
78 MJ. July 21, 1778. vol. V, no. 247, p. 3; Philadelphia, July 18, PP. July 18, 1778, p. 3; PEP. July 18, 1778. vol. IV, no. 506, p. 246; New-York, July 25, RG. July 25, 1778, no. 190, p. 3.
79 Extract of a letter from Gosport, July 3; MS, Sept. 24, 1778. vol. VIII, no. 386, p. 1, NYG; Oct. 5, 1778, no. 1407, p. 1.
80 Hattendorf, pp. 4–5; The French fleet also captured a ship from New Providence (Nassau, Bahamas) bound to London, England and recaptured a French snow with dry goods which were coming up the Delaware River on Monday, July 6, 1778. New-York, July 25, RG. July 25, 1778, no. 190, p. 3; Hartford, July 21, CC. July 21, 1778, no. 704, p. 3; New-York, July 27, NYG. July 27, 1778, no. 1397, p. 3.
81 August 1. RG. Aug. 1, 1778, no. 192, p. 3; From Rivington's Royal Gazette. New-York, August 1; PP. Aug. 13, 1778, p. 2; PP. June 25, 1778, August 13, 1778; NBBAS. vol. 1, p. 202.
82 Late European Intelligence. Vienna (Germany), July 18. MS. Oct. 22, 1778. vol. VIII, no. 390, p. 1; Paris, July 17. PP. Oct. 27, 1778, p. 2; Paris, July 19. PP. Dec. 17, 1778, p. 2.
83 New-York, July 27. NYG. July 27, 1778, no. 1397, p. 3.
84 Kingston, (Jamaica), July 25. NYG. Dec. 7, 1778, no. 1416, p. 2.
85 Fremont-Barnes. vol. 4, p. 1279; Brest, 29 July, 1778. IL. Sept. 28, 1778. vol. I, no. 16, p. 2; NP. Oct. 5, 1778, no. 262, p. 3; Boston, September 28. CJ. Oct. 7, 1778, no. 573, p. 3; Boston, Sept. 21. IL. Sept. 21, 1778. vol. I, no. 15, p. 3; August 1. RG. Aug. 1, 1778, no. 192, p. 3.
86 Boston, Sept. 7. IL. Sept. 7, 1778. vol. I, no. 13, p. 2; Extract of Letter from Portsmouth, July 1. CJWA. Sept. 10, 1778, no. CXX, p. 2.
87 Boston, Sept. 21. IL. Sept. 21, 1778. vol. I, no. 15, p. 3; PP. Oct. 1, 1778, p. 2.

88 Kell, p. 68; Clark, Walter. *The State Records of North Carolina XIV–1779–'80*. Winston: Nash Brothers, 1896. p. 482; PP. November 7, 1778. NBBAS. vol. 1, p. 204.

89 A Letter from the French King to Count Orvilliers, Dated Versailles, August 1. IC&UA. Nov. 5, 1778. vol. XI, no. 533, p. 2.

90 London, August 11. NYG. Oct. 26, 1778, no. 1410, p. 2.

91 Providence, August 8. PG. Aug. 8, 1778. vol. XV, no. 762, p. 3; IC&UA. Aug. 13, 1778. vol. XI, no. 521, p. 2; NP. Aug. 17, 1778, no. 255, p. 3; NHG. Aug. 18, 1778, p. 2.

92 An Account the Late Occurrences at Rhode-Island. NYG. Aug. 17, 1778, no. 1400, p. 3.

93 New-York, Sept. 7. NYG. Sept. 7, 1778, no. 1403, p. 3; New London, August 7, PEP, Aug. 18, 1778. vol. IV, no. 519, p. 296.

94 Mackenzie. p. 590.

95 NYJ. September 7, 1778. Moore. vol. 2, pp. 84–86.

96 Extract of a letter from Lieutenant Carter, on board the *Defiance*, off the Start, Aug. 17. Prensa. Jan. 5, 1779. vol. VI, no. 275, p. 1.

97 Extract of a letter from Plymouth, August 17. Prensa. Jan. 5, 1779. vol. VI, no. 275, p. 1; Extract of a letter from Plymouth, August 17. Prensa. Jan. 5, 1779. vol. VI, no. 275, p. 1.

98 London, September 9. Prensa. Jan. 5, 1779. vol. VI, no. 275, p. 1; The following Paragraphs Are Taken from New York Papers. Paris, September 21. PEP. Jan. 14, 1779. vol. V, no. 564, p. 15.

99 Extract of a letter from Paris, August 22, Prensa. Jan. 5, 1779. vol. VI, no. 275, p. 1.

100 By Captain Yallet, Just Arrived Here from St. Eustatia, We Have Received the *St. Christopher's Gazette*. MJ. Dec. 22, 1778. vol. V, no. 273, p. 1; Late European Intelligence. MS. Jan. 21, 1779. vol. VIII, no. 403, p. 1.

101 Constantinople, (the Capital of Turkey), September 3. NYG. Dec. 21, 1778, no. 1418, p. 1.

102 Extract of a Letter from Dover, Sept. 8. NYG. Dec. 28, 1778, no. 1419, p. 2.

103 Charlestown, (South Carolina), August 19. PP. Nov. 7, 1778, p. 2.

104 Curious Paragraphs Taken from the *Halifax Gazette*. Halifax, September 29. CJWA. Oct. 29, 1778, no. CXXVII, p. 1; MS. Nov. 5, 1778. vol. VIII, no. 392, p. 4.

105 Allen, *Report of the Adjutant General of the State of New Hampshire for the Year Ending June 1, 1866*, Concord: George G. Jenks, 1866. vol. 2, p. 369.

106 Extract of a letter from Gibraltar, September 4. MJ. Dec. 22, 1778. vol. V, no. 273, p. 1; Extract of a Letter from Cape Francois, Dated Nov. 23. PJ. Jan. 6, 1779, no. 1810, p. 2; PP. Jan. 7, 1779, p. 3; Late European Intelligence. MS. Jan. 21, 1779. vol. VIII, no. 403, p. 1.

107 London, September 9. Prensa. Jan. 5, 1779. vol. VI, no. 275, p. 1.

108 Extract of a letter from the Groyne, September 9, 1778. MJ. Dec. 22, 1778. vol. V, no. 273, p. 1; PP. Jan. 2, 1779, p. 2; BG, Jan. 18, 1779, no. 1273, p. 2; PJ. Jan. 6, 1779, no. 1810, p. 2; Late European Intelligence. MS. Jan. 21, 1779. vol. VIII, no. 403, p. 1; Extract of a letter from the Groyne, September 9, 1778. MJ. Dec. 22, 1778. vol. V, no. 273, p. 1; PP. Jan. 2, 1779, p. 2; PJ. Jan. 6, 1779, no. 1810, p. 2; BG. Jan. 18, 1779, no. 1273, p. 2; London, October 3. CJ. Jan. 13, 1779, no. 587, p. 2; Late European Intelligence. MS. Jan. 21, 1779. vol. VIII, no. 403, p. 1.

109 By Captain Yallet, Just Arrived Here from St. Eustatia, We Have Received the *St. Christopher's Gazette*. MJ. Dec. 22, 1778. vol. V, no. 273, p. 1; Leghorn, Sept. 11. PEP. Jan. 1, 1779. vol. V, no. 561, p. 2; Late European Intelligence. MS. Jan. 21, 1779. vol. VIII, no. 403, p. 1.

110 Baltimore October 6. MJ. Oct. 6, 1778. vol. V, no. 258, p. 2; IL. Nov. 2, 1778. vol. I, no. 21, p. 2.

111 Extract of a Letter from Gosport, Sept. 25. NYG. Dec. 28, 1778, no. 1419, p. 2.

112 ibid. St. John's in Antigua, Nov. 25. Prensa. Jan. 5, 1779. vol. VI, no. 275, p. 1. The following paragraphs are taken from New York Papers. Paris, September 21. PEP. Jan. 14, 1779. vol. V, no. 564, p. 15. St. John's (in Antigua), Nov. 25, PG, Feb. 6, 1779. vol. XVI, no. 788, p. 2;

Boston, February 4, 1779. Boston, February 15; PG. Feb. 20, 1779. vol. XVI, no. 790, p. 3; NP, Feb. 15, 1779, no. 281, p. 3; Boston, February 11, 1779. IC&UA. Feb. 11, 1779. vol. XI, no. 547, p. 3.

113   Extract of a Letter from Gosport, Sept. 25. NYG. Dec. 28, 1778, no. 1419, p. 2; St. John's in Antigua, Nov. 25. Prensa. Jan. 5, 1779. vol. VI, no. 275, p. 1; The following Paragraphs Are Taken from New York Papers. Paris, September 21. PEP. Jan. 14, 1779. vol. V, no. 564, p. 15; St. John's (in Antigua), Nov. 25. PG. Feb. 6, 1779. vol. XVI, no. 788, p. 2; Boston, February 4, 1779. Boston, February 15. PG. Feb. 20, 1779. vol. XVI, no. 790, p. 3; NP. Feb. 15, 1779, no. 281, p. 3; Boston, February 11, 1779. IC&UA. Feb. 11, 1779. vol. XI, no. 547, p. 3; The following Paragraphs Are Taken from New York Papers. Paris, September 21. PEP. Jan. 14, 1779. vol. V, no. 564, p. 15.

114   MJ. Dec. 22, 1778. vol. V, no. 273, p. 1; Extract of a Letter from Gosport, Sept. 25. NYG. Dec. 28, 1778, no. 1419, p. 2; The following Paragraphs Are Taken from New York Papers. Paris, September 21. PEP. Jan. 14, 1779. vol. V, no. 564, p. 15.

115   By Captain Yallet, Just Arrived Here from St. Eustatia, We Have Received the *St. Christopher's Gazette*. MJ. Dec. 22, 1778. vol. V, no. 273, p. 1; London, October 3. CJ. Jan. 13, 1779, no. 587, p. 2; BG. Jan. 18, 1779, no. 1273, p. 2; NJG. Jan. 27, 1779. vol. II, no. 60, p. 2. Late European Intelligence. MS. Jan. 21, 1779. vol. VIII, no. 403, p. 1.

116   Extract of a Letter from Kinsale, July 21, PP, Oct. 20, 1781. vol. X, no. 796, p. 2; London, August 10. PP, Nov. 15, 1781. vol. X, no. 807, p. 1; Extract of a Letter from Cork, August 6;, NJG, Nov. 28, 1781. vol. IV, no. 205, p. 2.

117   By Captain Yallet, Just Arrived Here from St. Eustatia, We Have Received the *St. Christopher's Gazette*. MJ. Dec. 22, 1778. vol. V, no. 273, p. 1; Late European Intelligence. MS. Jan. 21, 1779. vol. VIII, no. 403, p. 1; Extract of a Letter from Madrid, Sept. 28. PP. Feb. 9, 1779, p. 2; Extract of a Letter from Gibraltar, Sept. 31. CJ. Feb. 10, 1779, no. 591, p. 2.

118   Pickering to the American Commissioners in France, 28 January 1779, in Franklin Papers, www.franklinpapers.org. Allen. *Report of the Adjutant General of the State of New Hampshire for the Year Ending June 1, 1866*, Concord: George G. Jenks, 1866. vol. 2, 369.

119   Extract of a Letter from Gibraltar, Sept. 31, CJ. Feb. 10, 1779, no. 591, p. 2.

120   Extract of a Letter from Deal, Oct. 1. PEP. Jan. 1, 1779. vol. V, no. 561, p. 3.

121   ibid.

122   Extract of a Letter from Gosport, Sept. 25. NYG. Dec. 28, 1778, no. 1419, p. 2; London, October 10. CJ. Feb. 10, 1779, no. 591, p. 2; Foreign Intelligence. London, October 10. PG. Feb. 13, 1779. vol. XVI, no. 789, p. 2; Trenton, February 10. NJG. Feb. 10, 1779. vol. II, no. 62, p. 3.

123   Extract of a Letter from Gosport, Sept. 25. NYG. Dec. 28, 1778, no. 1419, p. 2; Extract of a Letter from the Groyne, September 9. PP. Jan. 2, 1779, p. 2; PJ. Jan. 6, 1779, no. 1810, p. 2; Lloyd's book, October 2, 1778. MJ. Dec. 22, 1778. vol. V, no. 273, p. 1; Extract of a Letter from Plymouth, Sept. 20. PEP. Jan. 1, 1779. vol. V, no. 561, p. 3; Extract of a Letter from Cape Francois, Dated Nov. 23. PP, Jan. 7, 1779, p. 3; PJ. Jan. 6, 1779, no. 1810, p. 2; Extract of a Letter from Portsmouth, Sept. 30. NJG. Jan. 13, 1779. vol. II, no. 58, p. 1; Late European Intelligence, MS, Jan. 21, 1779. vol. VIII, no. 403, p. 1; London, October 10. CJ. Feb. 10, 1779, no. 591, p. 2; Foreign Intelligence. London, October 10, PG, Feb. 13, 1779. vol. XVI, no. 789, p. 2; Trenton, February 10. NJG. Feb. 10, 1779. vol. II, no. 62, p. 3.

124   Lloyd's book, October 2, 1778. MJ. Dec. 22, 1778. vol. V, no. 273, p. 1; Extract of a Letter from Plymouth, Sept. 20. PEP. Jan. 1, 1779. vol. V, no. 561, p. 3; Extract of a Letter from Cape Francois, Dated Nov. 23. PP, Jan. 7, 1779, p. 3. PJ. Jan. 6, 1779, no. 1810, p. 2; Extract of

a Letter from Portsmouth, Sept. 30. NJG. Jan. 13, 1779. vol. II, no. 58, p. 1; Late European Intelligence. MS. Jan. 21, 1779. vol. VIII, no. 403, p. 1.

125 New-York, Oct. 26. NYG. Oct. 26, 1778, no. 1410, p. 3.

126 Extract of a Letter from Portsmouth, Oct. 4. NYG. Dec. 28, 1778, no. 1419, p. 2; London, October 10. CJ. Feb. 10, 1779, no. 591, p. 2; Foreign Intelligence; London, October 10. PG. Feb. 13, 1779. vol. XVI, no. 789, p. 2; Trenton, February 10. NJG. Feb. 10, 1779. vol. II, no. 62, p. 3.

127 London, Oct. 10. NYG. Jan. 25, 1779, no. 1423, p. 2.

128 London, Oct. 10. CJ. Feb. 10, 1779, no. 591, p. 2.

129 Extract of a letter from Falmouth, October 11. CJ. Feb. 10, 1779, no. 591, p. 2; Trenton, February 10. NJG. Feb. 10, 1779. vol. II, no. 62, p. 3.

130 From *The London Gazette*. Nov. 14, Admiralty Office, Nov. 14, 1778. RAG. Feb. 25, 1779, no. CLII, p. 2.

131 Extract of a Letter from the Captain of the Mail Cutter *Privateer*, to his owners in London, Dated Falmouth, October 27. CJ. Feb. 10, 1779, no. 591, p. 2.

132 London, Oct. 10. NYG. Jan. 25, 1779, no. 1423, p. 2.

133 New-York, Oct. 26. NYG. Oct. 26, 1778, no. 1410, p. 3.

134 London, Oct. 10, NYG, Jan. 25, 1779, no. 1423, p. 2; New-London, Oct. 23. CJ. Oct. 28, 1778, no. 576, p. 3.

135 Extract of a Letter from the Musquito Shore, Dated October 20, 1778. RG. Mar. 20, 1779, no. 258, p. 3; Montego-Bay, January 9, 1779. PP. April 3, 1779, p. 3.

136 London, Oct. 10. NYG. Jan. 25, 1779, no. 1423, p. 2; London. PJ. Feb. 17, 1779, no. 1816, p. 2; Ireland before October 22, 1778. London, Oct. 10. NYG. Jan. 25, 1779, no. 1423, p. 2; New-York, Oct. 26. NYG. Oct. 26, 1778, no. 1410, p. 3; PJ. Feb. 17, 1779, no. 1816, p. 2; London, Oct. 10. NYG. Jan. 25, 1779, no. 1423, p. 2.

137 Extract of a Letter from Corke, October 22. CG&UI. Feb. 5, 1779. vol. XVI, no. 795, p. 3; CJ. Feb. 10, 1779, no. 591, p. 2; Extract of a Letter from Corke, October 22.

138 London, Oct. 10. NYG. Jan. 25, 1779, no. 1423, p. 2; New-York, November 2. NYG. Nov. 2, 1778, no. 1411, p. 3; London, Oct. 10, NYG, Jan. 25, 1779, no. 1423, p. 2.

139 London, Oct. 10. NYG. Jan. 25, 1779, no. 1423, p. 2; Extract of a Letter from Bristol, October 31. CG&UI. Feb. 5, 1779. vol. XVI, no. 795, p. 3; Extract of a Letter from Corke, October 22, CG&UI, Feb. 5, 1779. vol. XVI, no. 795, p. 3.

140 CJ. Feb. 10, 1779, no. 591, p. 2; London, October 31. Prensa. Feb. 16, 1779. vol. VI, no. 282, p. 1.

141 Extract of a Letter from the Captain of the Mail Cutter *Privateer*, to his owners in London, dated Falmouth, October 27. CJ. Feb. 10, 1779, no. 591, p. 2; London, Oct. 10. NYG. Jan. 25, 1779, no. 1423, p. 2; London. PJ. Feb. 17, 1779.

142 Extract of a Letter from the Captain of the Mail Cutter *Privateer*, to his owners in London, Dated Falmouth, October 27. CJ. Feb. 10, 1779, no. 591, p. 2; London, Oct. 10. NYG. Jan. 25, 1779, no. 1423, p. 2.

143 Extract of a Letter from Gosport, Nov. 18. NYG. Mar. 1, 1779, no. 1428, p. 2.

144 Extract of a Letter from Penzance, October 30. NYG. Feb. 22, 1779, no. 1427, p. 2; Smyrna, October 8. VG, April 2, 1779, no. 8, p. 1; PJ. April 14, 1779, no. 1204, p. 2.

145 Extract of a Letter from Penzance, October 30. NYG. Feb. 22, 1779, no. 1427, p. 2.

146 PP. April 15, 1779, p. 1; Philadelphia, April 16. Extracts from Several Letters of Good Authorities in Different Parts of France; PEP. April 16, 1779. vol. V, no. 590, p. 89.

147 Extract of a Letter from Brest, November 2. VG. April 24, 1779, no. 11, p. 2.

148 Extract of a Letter from a Gentleman of Antigua, to Aretas Akers, Esq. PJ. Feb. 10, 1779, no. 1819, p. 2; Hartford, February 16. CC. Feb. 16, 1779, no. 734, p. 3; CJ. Feb. 17, 1779, no. 592, p. 3; St. John's in Antigua, January 6. Prensa. Feb. 16, 1779. vol. VI, no. 282, p. 1.

149 Extract of a letter from Liverpool, November 6. London. RAG. Feb. 23, 1779, no. CLI, p. 1.

150 Extract of a Letter from Gosport, Nov. 18. NYG. Mar. 1, 1779, no. 1428, p. 2; Extract of a Letter from Paris, Nov. 18, 1778. PEP. Feb. 22, 1779. vol. V, no. 575, p. 46; New York, May 20. RAG. Mar. 20, 1779, no. CLXXVI, p. 3.

151 Baltimore, December 1. MJ. Dec. 1, 1778. vol. V, no. 269, p. 2; PG. Jan. 2, 1779. vol. XVI, no. 783, p. 2; Philadelphia, December 10. NP. Jan. 4, 1779, no. 275, p. 3.

152 The following is Taken from a Late New-York (City) Paper. Advices by the Pacquet. MS. Mar. 18, 1779. vol. IX, no. 411, p. 2.

153 St. John's in Antigua, Nov. 25. Prensa. Jan. 5, 1779. vol. VI, no. 275, p. 1; St. John's (in Antigua) Nov. 25. PG. Feb. 6, 1779. vol. XVI, no. 788, p. 2.

154 London, Nov. 28, NYG, Mar. 1, 1779, no. 1428, p. 2.

155 PJ. Dec. 30, 1778, no. 1809, p. 3; Philadelphia, December 30. IC&UA. Jan. 14, 1779. vol. XI, no. 543, p. 3.

156 New York, Dec. 28. PEP. Jan. 14, 1779. vol. V, no. 564, p. 16; PJ. April 14, 1779, no. 1204, p. 1.

157 Extract of a Letter from Bristol, Nov. 24, 1778. VG, April 24, 1779, no. 11, p. 2.

158 Extract of a Letter from Bermuda, Dec. 15. PG. Jan. 30, 1779. vol. XVI, no. 787, p. 3.

159 Camp at Coxheath Intelligence. PP. Dec. 17, 1778, p. 2.

160 Letter, Pickering to Franklin, 23 November 1778; Letter, Pickering to Franklin, 30 December 1778; Letter, Pickering to the American Commissioners in France, 28 January 1779; Letter, Pickering to Franklin, 22 December 1778; Letter, Pickering to Franklin, 30 December 1778; Letter, Pickering to Franklin, 23 December 1778; Letter, Peter Riou and Thomas Pickering to the American Commissioners, 23 December 1778, in Franklin Papers. www.franklinpapers.org.

161 ibid. London, Dec. 19. NYG. April 26, 1779, no. 1436, p. 2.

162 PJ. Jan. 13, 1779, no. 1311, p. 3; Boston, December 21. PP. Jan. 14, 1779, p. 3.

163 PP, April 15, 1779, p. 1; Philadelphia, April 16. Extracts from Several Letters of Good Authorities in Different Parts of France, PEP, April 16, 1779. vol. V, no. 590, p. 89; Extract of a Letter from Brest, November 2, VG, April 24, 1779, no. 11, p. 2; Extract from Several Letters, Written by Persons Who May be Depended on in Martinico. BG, April 26, 1779, no. 1287, p. 2.

164 PP, April 15, 1779, p. 1; Philadelphia, April 16. Extracts from Several Letters of Good Authorities in Different Parts of France, PEP, April 16, 1779. vol. V, no. 590, p. 89.

165 London. from the General Advertiser, Nov. 17, NYG, April 5, 1779, no. 1433, p. 2.

166 London, Dec. 22, NYG, Mar. 29, 1779, no. 1432, p. 2; PP, April 3, 1779, p. 3.

167 PP, April 15, 1779, p. 1; Philadelphia, April 16. Extracts from Several Letters of Good Authorities in Different Parts of France, PEP, April 16, 1779. vol. V, no. 590, p. 89.

168 Philadelphia, PP, April 15, 1779, p. 1.

169 New-London, June 24, IC&UA, July 1, 1779. vol. XI, no. 567, p. 2; Extract of a Letter from St. Eustatia Dated May 21, IL, July 5, 1779. vol. II, no. 56, p. 2; AJ, July 1, 1779. vol. I, no. XVI, p. 2; IL, July 5, 1779. vol. II, no. 56, p. 2; Boston, June 24, CJ, June 30, 1779, no. 611, p. 3; MS, July 1, 1779. vol. IX, no. 426, p. 2.

170 Philadelphia, March 31, CC, Mar. 30, 1779, no. 740, p. 4; PJ, Mar. 31, 1779, no. 1282, p. 3; MS, April 15, 1779. vol. IX, no. 415, p. 2; CJ, April 21, 1779, no. 601, p. 3.

171 St. Pierre, (Martinique) March 4. PP, April 24, 1779, p. 2; CJ, May 26, 1779, no. 606, p. 1.

172 ibid. Charlestown, April 21, VG, June 5, 1779, no. 17, p. 2; St. Pierre, (Martinique) March 4. By Tuesday's Western Post. Paris, (France) January 1, AJ, June 3, 1779. vol. I, no. XII, p. 2.

173 New-York, April 5, NYG, April 5, 1779, no. 1433, p. 3.

174   London, IL, May 31, 1779. vol. I, no. 51, p. 1. London, Dec. 19, NYG, April 26, 1779, no. 1436, p. 2.

175   ibid.

176   Memorial Presented Last Week to His Majesty by the Duke of Bolton, NYG, April 26, 1779, no. 1436, p. 2.

177   ibid.

178   PJ, June 9, 1779, no. 1291, p. 1.

179   Charlestown, Jan. 13, PEP, Mar. 1, 1779. vol. V, no. 577, p. 51; Prensa, Mar. 2, 1779. vol. VI, no. 284, p. 2.

180   London, Feb. 11, NYG, April 26, 1779, no. 1436, p. 3; Extract of a Letter from Portsmouth Feb. 5, CG&UI, May 27, 1779. vol. XVI, no. 811, p. 1.

181   London, Feb. 11, NYG, April 26, 1779, no. 1436, p. 3.

182   ibid. Extract of a Letter from Portsmouth Feb. 5; CG&UI, May 27, 1779. vol. XVI, no. 811, p. 1.

183   Memorial Presented Last Week to His Majesty by the Duke of Bolton, NYG, April 26, 1779, no. 1436, p. 2; Commodore Hyde Parker's fleet captured a French ship of 300 tons and 20 guns and 12 other vessels between November 27, 1778 and January 18, 1779.

184   New-York, January 28, RAG, Jan. 28, 1779, no. CXLIV, p. 3; Boston, January 28, PG, Jan. 30, 1779. vol. XVI, no. 787, p. 3; Extract of a Letter from Captain Alexander M' Pherson, of the Privateer Schooner *Experiment*, to His Agent in This City, NYG, Feb. 1, 1779, no. 1424, p. 3; New York, Jan. 27, PEP, Feb. 8, 1779. vol. V, no. 570, p. 36; PJ, Feb. 10, 1779, no. 1819, p. 3; Extract of a Letter from the Southward, CJWA, Jan. 21, 1779, no. CXXXIX, p. 3; CJWA, Jan. 28, 1779, no. CXL, p. 3; Boston, January 21, NP, Feb. 8, 1779, no. 280, p. 4; Boston, January 25, 1776, BG, Jan. 25, 1779, no. 1274, p. 3; NJG, Feb. 17, 1779. vol. II, no. 63, p. 2; Boston, January 28, 1779, IC&UA, Jan. 28, 1779. vol. XI, no. 545, p. 2; CJ, Feb. 3, 1779, no. 590, p. 3; CG&UI, Feb. 5, 1779. vol. XVI, no. 795, p. 4; PG, Jan. 30, 1779. vol. XVI, no. 787, p. 3; PG, Feb. 27, 1779. vol. XVI, no. 791, p. 2; PEP, Feb. 17, 1779. vol. V, no. 573, p. 41; PP, Feb. 18, 1779, p. 3; Boston, February 25, 1779, IC&UA, Feb. 25, 1779. vol. XI, no. 549, p. 3; Philadelphia, PJ, Feb. 3, 1779, no. 1814, p. 3; By the Boston Post, Boston, February 1, MS, Feb. 4, 1779. vol. VIII, no. 405, p. 3; IL, Feb. 22, 1779. vol. I, no. 37, p. 3; Boston, February 22, 1779, EJ, Mar. 2, 1779. vol. II, no. 54, p. 4; Prensa, Feb. 23, 1779. vol. VI, no. 283, p. 2; Boston, February 22, MS, Mar. 4, 1779. vol. VIII, no. 409, p. 4; Boston, February 25, PP, Mar. 16, 1779, p. 2; Newhaven, Feb. 24, PEP, Mar. 19, 1779. vol. V, no. 584, p. 66.

185   Extract of a Letter from Captain Alexander M' Pherson, of the Privateer Schooner *Experiment*, to His Agent in This City, NYG, Feb. 1, 1779, no. 1424, p. 3.

186   RG, Mar. 20, 1779, no. 258, p. 3; Montego-Bay, January 9, NYG, Mar. 22, 1779, no. 1431, p. 2; PJ, Mar. 31, 1779, no. 1282, p. 3.

187   Memorial Presented Last Week to His Majesty by the Duke of Bolton, NYG, April 26, 1779, no. 1436, p. 2; PJ, May 5, 1779, no. 1286, p. 2.

188   Philadelphia, February 25, PP, Feb. 25, 1779, p. 2; NJG, Mar. 3, 1779. vol. II, no. 65, p. 2; Philadelphia, Feb. 26, PEP, Feb. 26, 1779. vol. V, no. 576, p. 50; Philadelphia, February 22, Prensa, Mar. 2, 1779. vol. VI, no. 284, p. 2.

189   PJ, Mar. 24, 1779, no. 1821, p. 3; From the *Pennsylvania Advertiser*, of March 24, RG. April 3, 1779, no. 262, p. 2.

190   CJ, Feb. 10, 1779, no. 591, p. 2.

191   ibid.

192   PJ, Nov. 3, 1779, no. 1312, p. 1; Stockholm, February 10, PP, Nov. 4, 1779, p. 2; Paris, August 20, AJ, Dec. 2, 1779. vol. I, no. XXXVIII, p. 2.

193   ibid.

194 ibid.

195 ibid.

196 London, Feb. 11, NYG, April 26, 1779, no. 1436, p. 3; Extract of a Letter from Portsmouth Feb. 5, CG&UI, May 27, 1779. vol. XVI, no. 811, p. 1.

197 ibid.

198 PJ, Nov. 3, 1779, no. 1312, p. 1; Stockholm, February 10, PP, Nov. 4, 1779, p. 2; Paris, August 20, AJ, Dec. 2, 1779. vol. I, no. XXXVIII, p. 2.

199 New-York, February 15, NYG, Feb. 15, 1779, no. 1426, p. 3.

200 New-York, February 16, RAG, Feb. 16, 1779, no. CXLIX, p. 3; Hog-Neck Eleven O' Clock at Night, Feb. 1, 1779, PEP, Feb. 26, 1779. vol. V, no. 576, p. 48; New York, February 6, VG, Mar. 12, 1779, no. 5, p. 2.

201 Boston, February 15, IL, Feb. 15, 1779. vol. I, no. 36, p. 3, PJ, Mar. 3, 1779, no. 1818, p. 3.

202 Hartford, February 16, CC, Feb. 16, 1779, no. 734, p. 3; CJ, Feb. 17, 1779, no. 592, p. 3; IC&UA, Feb. 25, 1779. vol. XI, no. 549, p. 3; EJ, Mar. 2, 1779. vol. II, no. 54, p. 2; PEP, Mar. 10, 1779. vol. V, no. 581, p. 60; Boston, February 25, CJWA, Feb. 25, 1779, no. CXLIV, p. 3; PP, Mar. 16, 1779, p. 2; Extract of a Letter from a Gentleman at Hartford, Dated February 23d, 1779, IL, Mar. 1, 1779. vol. I, no. 38, p. 3; Boston, February 22 a Few Days Past Arrived in a Safe Port to the Eastward a Brick from Bermuda, by a Gentleman, Prensa, Mar. 23, 1779. vol. VI, no. 287, p. 3; Williamsburg, March 26, VG, Mar. 26, 1779, no. 7, p. 2.

203 London, Feb. 11, NYG, April 26, 1779, no. 1436, p. 3; Extract of a Letter from Portsmouth Feb. 5, CG&UI, May 27, 1779. vol. XVI, no. 811, p. 1.

204 Philadelphia, February 25. PP, Feb. 25, 1779, p. 2; Philadelphia, Feb. 26, PEP, Feb. 26, 1779. vol. V, no. 576, p. 50; Extract of a Letter from Bristol, Nov. 24, 1778, VG, April 24, 1779, no. 11,p. 2.

205 PJ, June 2, 1779, no. 1290, p. 2; London, Jan. 27, Prensa, June 8, 1779. vol. VI, no. 298, p. 3; London, CG&UI, June 10, 1779. vol. XVI, no. 813, p. 4.

206 London, March 20, Prensa, July 6, 1779. vol. VI, no. 302, p. 1; Charlestown, April 21, VG, June 5, 1779, no. 17, p. 2.

207 PP, April 8, 1779, p. 2; Extracts from Several Letter Written by Persons Who May be Depended on in Martinico, PEP, April 9, 1779. vol. V, no. 588, p. 82; BG, April 26, 1779, no. 1287, p. 2.

208 London, April 1, NYG, July 12, 1779, no. 1447, p. 2; PP, July 20, 1779, p. 2; Prensa. July 27, 1779. vol. VI, no. 305, p. 1; IL, Aug. 9, 1779. vol. II, no. 61, p. 1.

209 Extract of a Letter from Captain Reynolds, of His Majesty's Ship *Jupiter*, to Mr. Stephens, Plymouth, NYG, July 12, 1779, no. 1447, p. 2; Captain Douglass's Letter, Mentioned in the Foregoing, NYG, July 12, 1779, no. 1447, p. 2.

210 Paris, (France) May 27, PG, Sept. 4, 1779. vol. XVI, no. 818, p. 2; PJ, Sept. 15, 1779, no. 1305, p. 2; PP, Sept. 16, 1779, p. 2.

211 New-York, May 24, CJ, June 9, 1779, no. 608, p. 2; London, CG&UI, June 10, 1779. vol. XVI, no. 813, p. 4.

212 Extract of a Letter from Plymouth, April 27, RG, July 24, 1779, no. 294, p. 3; London, May 1, NYG, Aug. 2, 1779, no. 1450, p. 2.

213 ibid. Extract of a Letter from Liverpool, May 10, NYG, Aug. 9, 1779, no. 1451, p. 1.

214 London, May 1, NYG, Aug. 2, 1779, no. 1450, p. 2.

215 ibid.

216 Extract from Rivington's *New York Gazette*, CG, Aug. 11, 1779. p. 1; AJ, Sept. 9, 1779. p. 2.

217 From *London Gazette*. May 15 Whitehall, May 15, RAG, Aug. 12, 1779, no. CC, p. 2.

218 New-York, May 29, RG, May 29, 1779, no. 278, p. 3

219 From *London Gazette*. May 15 Whitehall, May 15, RAG, Aug. 12, 1779, no. CC, p. 2.

220 Providence, May 29, IL, June 7, 1779. vol. I, no. 52, p. 3.

221 London, July 1, NYG, Sept. 27, 1779, no. 1458, p. 1.

222 Philadelphia, PJ, June 9, 1779, no. 1291, p. 3.

223 London, CG&UI, June 10, 1779. vol. XVI, no. 813, p. 4.

224 Extract of a Letter from Gibralter, July 25, Brought by a Swedish Man of War, the *Mars*, PP, Nov. 27, 1779, p. 2; Extract of a Letter from Capt. John Hastie, of the Privateer *Hawke*, Belonging to Clyde, to the Owners, VG, Dec. 18, 1779, no. 45, p. 1; BG, Dec. 20, 1779, no. 1321, p. 2; London, August 30, IL, Dec. 20, 1779. vol. II, no. 80, p. 2; CC, Dec. 21, 1779, no. 778, p. 1; AJ, Dec. 23, 1779. vol. I, no. XLI, p. 1; London, September 2, CJ, Dec. 22, 1779, no. 634, p. 1.

225 The following Letters Were Found on Board of the Packet from Falmouth to New York, Taken by Capt. Taylor, PP, Aug. 21, 1779, p. 3; Extract of Another Letter from the Same Place, Aug. 14, IL, Sept. 13, 1779. vol. II, no. 66, p. 2; Philadelphia, August 31, AJ, Sept. 23, 1779. vol. I, no. XXVIII, p. 4.

226 Latouche, p. 86.

227 London, June 17, NYG, Sept. 6, 1779, no. 1455, p. 2.

228 London, June 19, NYG, Sept. 6, 1779, no. 1455, p. 1.

229 Latouche, pp. 86–88.

230 Extract of a Letter from Portsmouth, July 5, NYG, Sept. 27, 1779, no. 1458, p. 2.

231 London, June 17, NYG, Sept. 6, 1779, no. 1455, p. 2; Extract of a Letter from Portsmouth, July 5. NYG, Sept. 27, 1779, no. 1458, p. 2.

232 Philadelphia, July 6, Prensa, July 13, 1779. vol. VI, no. 303, p. 2.

233 Extract of a Letter, Et Sia, July 20, 1779, in Lat 46, Long. 15, from the Captain, NYG, Nov. 29, 1779, no. 1467, p. 2.

234 CJWA, Aug. 5, 1779, no. CLXXXVI, p. 2.

235 Philadelphia, July 29, VG, Aug. 14, 1779, no. 27, p. 2.

236 New York, Sept. 6, PEP, Sept. 18, 1779. vol. V, no. 629, p. 230.

237 Paris, Aug. 20. PP, Dec. 25, 1779, p. 1; CG&UI, Jan. 26, 1780. vol. XVII, no. 846, p. 1; AJ, Jan. 27, 1780. vol. I, no. XLVI, p. 2.

238 PJ, Nov. 3, 1779, no. 1312, p. 2; London, August 2. Extract of a Letter from the Hague, July 7, NJG, Nov. 3, 1779. vol. II, no. 97, p. 2; London, July 20. PP, Nov. 4, 1779, p. 2; London, August 21. PP, Nov. 27, 1779, p. 2; London, August 30, IL, Dec. 20, 1779. vol. II, no. 80, p. 2; London, September 3, VG, Dec. 25, 1779, no. 46, p. 2.

239 Corunna, August 4. PP, Feb. 26, 1780, p. 2; Genoa, July 10, NJG, Mar. 1, 1780. vol. III, no. 114, p. 3; Toulon, August 21, VG, Mar. 18, 1780, no. 58, p. 1; CC, Mar. 28, 1780, no. 792, p. 4; Spain, MS, April 13, 1780. vol. IX, no. 466, p. 4.

240 PJ, Nov. 3, 1779, no. 1312, p. 2; Extract of a Letter from Plymouth, Sunday Evening, August 22. PP, Nov. 4, 1779, p. 2; New York, November 8, PEP, Nov. 16, 1779. vol. V, no. 638, p. 249; London, August 2. Extract of a Letter from the Hague, July 7, NP, Nov. 16, 1779, no. 319, p. 2; London, August 2, IL, Nov. 22, 1779. vol. II, no. 76, p. 4; Extract of a Letter from Plymouth, September 1, 1779, VG, Nov. 27, 1779, no. 42, p. 1; NP, Dec. 28, 1779, no. 325, p. 1; London, September 8. PP, Jan. 6, 1780, p. 2; Extracts from English Papers, Dated in July and August Last. London, NJG, Jan. 19, 1780. vol. III, no. 108, p. 2.

241 Paris, le 4 septembre, NYG, 17 avril 1780, no. 1487, p. 2.

242 London, Aug. 7, NP, Dec. 28, 1779, no. 325, p. 1; NYG, Oct. 25, 1779, no. 1462, p. 3; Extract of a Letter from Plymouth, September 1, 1779, VG, Nov. 27, 1779, no. 42, p. 1; Extract of a Letter from Dover, to a Gentleman at Folkstone, Aug. 24, NYG, Nov. 15, 1779, no. 1465, p. 2; London. to the King's Most Excellent Majesty, VG, Dec. 4, 1779, no. 43, p. 1.

243 PP, Dec. 28, 1779, p. 2.

244 PJ, Nov. 3, 1779, no. 1312, p. 2; Extract of a Letter from Plymouth, Sunday Evening, August 22, PP, Nov. 4, 1779, p. 2.

245 Letter of September 2, 1779 to the Ministry of the Navy. Log of the *Hermione*, Archives Nationales de la Marine B4 158; Latouche, p. 98.

246 New York, Sept. 15, PEP, Sept. 29, 1779. vol. V, no. 630, p. 234; PJ, Oct. 6, 1779, no. 1308, p. 3; New-York, September 13, NYG, Sept. 13, 1779, no. 1456, p. 3.

247 London, Aug. 7, NYG, Oct. 25, 1779, no. 1462, p. 3; London. to the King's Most Excellent Majesty, VG, Dec. 4, 1779, no. 43, p. 1.

248 RG, Nov. 27, 1779, no. 330, p. 3; PJ, April 19, 1780, no. 1336, p. 1.

249 NBBAS. vol. 1 p. 309; PAG, October 20, 1779, March 22, 1780.

250 PJ, April 19, 1780, no. 1336, p. 1.

251 Extract of a Letter from Jamaica, June 12, NJG, Jan. 12, 1780. vol. III, no. 107, p. 2.

252 Charlestown (S. C.) September 4, VG, Oct. 9, 1779, no. 35, p. 2; Charlestown, (South-Carolina) Sept. 15, PP, Oct. 19, 1779, p. 2, PEP, Oct. 19, 1779. vol. V, no. 634, p. 241; PJ, Oct. 20, 1779, no. 1310, p. 2, IC&UA, Nov. 5, 1779. vol. XII, no. 585, p. 3; Charles town, Sept. 29, Prensa, Nov. 2, 1779. vol. VI, no. 319, p. 2; RG. Dec. 1, 1779, no. 331, p. 3; Dictionary of American Naval Fighting Ships http: //en.wikipedia.org/wiki/HMS_Ariel.

253 Extract of a Letter from Falmouth, September 10, PP, Dec. 30, 1779, p. 2; Extracts from Rebel Papers London, September 15, RAG, Jan. 18, 1780, no. CCXLV, p. 1; London, September 15, CG&UI, Feb. 9, 1780. vol. XVII, no. 848, p. 2.

254 Extract of a Letter from Pembroke, September 15, PP, Jan. 6, 1780, p. 2; Extract of a Letter from Bristol, Sept. 22, IC&UA, Jan. 13, 1780. vol. XII, no. 594, p. 1; Extract of a Letter from a Gentleman in Shields, to His Friend in Edinburg, September 20, VG, Jan. 15, 1780, no. 49, p. 2; Extract of a Letter from Newcastle, Dated September 20, AJ, Jan. 20, 1780. vol. I, no. XLV, p. 2; London, Sept. 25, IL, Jan. 24, 1780. vol. II, no. 85, p. 2; London, September 29, NP, Jan. 25, 1780, no. 329, p. 1; Extract of a Letter Dated St. Ives, in Cornwall, September 18, CG&UI, Jan. 26, 1780. vol. XVII, no. 846, p. 1; London, Sept. 10, IL, Feb. 21, 1780. vol. II, no. 89, p. 1.

255 Extract of a Letter from Edinburgh, September 15, PP, Jan. 6, 1780, p. 3; London, September 21, PP, Jan. 8, 1780, p. 2; London, September 25, AJ, Mar. 23, 1780. vol. II, no. 54, p. 1.

256 New-York, September 18, RG, Sept. 18, 1779, no. 310, p. 3.

257 Extract of a Letter from Edinburgh, September 15, PP, Jan. 6, 1780, p. 3; London, September 21, PP, Jan. 8, 1780, p. 2; London, September 25, AJ, Mar. 23, 1780. vol. II, no. 54, p. 1.

258 London, September 27, PP, Dec. 16, 1779, Supplement 1; Extract of a Letter from a Gentleman in Shields, to His Friend in Edinburgh, September 20, AJ, Jan. 20, 1780. vol. I, no. XLV, p. 1.

259 Extract of a Letter from Dover, September 24, PP, Dec. 18, 1779, p. 2; Extract of a Letter from a Gentleman in Shields, to His Friend in Edinburg, September 20, VG, Jan. 15, 1780, no. 49, p. 2; London, Sept. 25, IL, Jan. 24, 1780. vol. II, no. 85, p. 2; London, September 25, AJ, Jan. 27, 1780. vol. I, no. XLVI, p. 2; Extract of a Letter from Port-Glasgow, Sept. 23, PP, Dec. 18, 1779, p. 3; From *The London Gazette* of Sept. 25, Prensa, Dec. 28, 1779. vol. VI, no. 327, p. 2; Extract of a Letter from Port-Glasgow, Sept. 23, NJG, Jan. 5, 1780. vol. III, no. 106, p. 2; IL, Jan. 24, 1780. vol. II, no. 85, p. 2; Extract of a Letter from Port Glasgow, Sept. 25, VG, Jan. 15, 1780, no. 49, p. 2; AJ, Jan. 27, 1780. vol. I, no. XLVI, p. 3; London, September 28, CC, Feb. 1, 1780, no. 784, p. 4; Boston, March 9, MS, Mar. 16, 1780. vol. IX, no. 462, p. 3; PG, Mar. 18, 1780. vol. XVII, no. 846, p. 3; CG&UI, Mar. 22, 1780. vol. XVII, no. 854, p. 2; PEP, Mar. 27, 1780. vol. VI, no. 656, p. 34.

260 London, Sept. 25, Prensa, Feb. 29, 1780. vol. VII, no. 336, p. 1; Extract of a Letter from Portsmouth, September 9, PP, Jan. 1, 1780, p. 2.

261 Extract of a Letter from Deal, September 21, NHG, Jan. 29, 1780. vol. XXIV, no. 22012, p. 1.

262 London, September 27, PP, Dec. 16, 1779, Supplement 1.

263 PJ, Oct. 27, 1779, no. 1311, p. 1; Basseterre, (St. Christophe) Sept. 22, Prensa, Nov. 2, 1779. vol. VI, no. 319, p. 2; MS, Nov. 11, 1779. vol. IX, no. 445, p. 1.

264 Lloyd's List, Sept. 7, 1779, NYG, March 6, 1780 p. 1.

265 PJ, April 19, 1780, no. 1336, p. 1;

266 Jean Boudriot (*John Paul Jones and the Bonhomme Richard: a reconstruction of the ship and an account of the battle with H.M.S. Serapis.* English translation by David H. Roberts. Annapolis, Md.: Naval Institute Press, 1987. p. 82, thinks that Jones probably said, "I may sink, but I'm damned if I'll strike!".

267 John Henry Sherburne. *The life and character of John Paul Jones, a captain in the United States navy. During the revolutionary war.* New York: Adriance, Sherman & co. 1851, pp. 126–129 in Commager pp. 947–949.

268 Fanning, Nathaniel. *Fanning's narrative.* (Eyewitness accounts of the American Revolution). New York New York times 1968, c1912 pp. 47–48.

269 Boudriot, Jean. *John Paul Jones and the Bonhomme Richard: a reconstruction of the ship and an account of the battle with H.M.S. Serapis.* English translation by David H. Roberts. Annapolis, Md.: Naval Institute Press, 1987; Morison, Samuel Eliot. *John Paul Jones, a sailor's biography.* Boston: Little, Brown 1959; Schaeper, Thomas J. *John Paul Jones and the Battle off Flamborough Head: a reconsideration.* New York: P. Lang, 1989; Walsh, John Evangelist. *Night on fire: the first complete account of John Paul Jones's greatest battle.* New York: McGraw-Hill, c1978; Fremont-Barnes. vol. 1, pp. 105–107; Selesky. vol. 1, p. 82; Affidavit, CJWA, Dec. 30, 1779, no. CCII, p. 3; IL, Jan. 3, 1780. vol. II, no. 82, p. 4; PG, Jan. 8, 1780. vol. XVII, no. 836, p. 1; NP, Jan. 11, 1780, no. 327, p. 1; Extract of a Letter from Brest, Sept. 25, AJ, Jan. 6, 1780. vol. I, no. XLIII, p. 1; CC, Jan. 25, 1780, no. 783, p. 1; London, October 1, NJG, Feb. 9, 1780. vol. III, no. 111, p. 3; From the *Connecticut Courant*, Dated Jan. 25. London, October 1, Affidavit, RG, Feb. 12, 1780, no. 352, p. 3; Extract of a Letter from Amsterdam, Dated October 7, AJ, Jan. 6, 1780. vol. I, no. XLIII, p. 1; PG. Jan. 8, 1780. vol. XVII, no. 836, p. 1.

270 Extract of a Letter from Dover, September 24, PP, 1218, 1779 p. 2; PAG. 1222, 1779 P. 2.

271 New-York, Oct. 25, NYG, Oct. 25, 1779, no. 1462, p. 3.

272 PAG, Oct. 27, 1779; Hough, Franklin B. *The Siege of Savannah by the Combined American and French Forces under the command of General Lincoln and the Count D'Estaing in the Autumn of 1779.* Albany: J. Munsell, 1866, pp. 102–104, 143–144; Jones, Charles Colcock, Jr. *The siege of Savannah by the fleet of Count d'Estaing in 1779.* New York: New York Times 1968, pp. 23, 61–62; Cowan, Bob. The Siege of Savannah, 1779. *Military Collector and Historian.* XXVII: 2 (Summer 1975) p. 55; NBBAS. vol. 1, pp. 311–312; Extract of a Letter from Hartford, Octo. 25, CJWA, Oct. 28, 1779, no. CXCVIII, p. 3; Charles town, Sept. 29, Prensa, Nov. 2, 1779. vol. VI, no. 319, p. 2; Boston, October 23, NJG, Nov. 10, 1779. vol. II, no. 98, p. 2; Boston, October 25, PEP, Nov. 10, 1779. vol. V, no. 637, p. 248.

273 London, Novem. 1, NYG, Feb. 21, 1780, no. 1479, p. 2.

274 Extract of a Letter from Hartford, Oct. 25, CJWA, Oct. 28, 1779, no. CXCVIII, p. 3; Boston, October 25, PG, Oct. 30, 1779. vol. XVI, no. 826, p. 3; CC, Nov. 2, 1779, no. 771, p. 3; Extract of a Late Letter from an American Gentleman of Distinction in France, to a Friend in New-England, CJ, Nov. 3, 1779, no. 627, p. 3; Boston, October 23, NJG, Nov. 10, 1779. vol. II, no. 98, p. 2; Boston, October 25, PEP, Nov. 10, 1779. vol. V, no. 637, p. 248.

275 Extract of a Letter from a Merchant of Character, Dated L' Orient, October 20th, 1779, PP, Jan. 22, 1780, p. 3; VG, Feb. 12, 1780, no. 53, p. 2; Philadelphia, January 24, CJ, Feb. 16, 1780, no. 642, p. 2; Philadelphia, Jan. 26, PG, Feb. 19, 1780. vol. XVII, no. 842, p. 2.

276 Lloyd's List, Sept. 7, 1779, NYG, March 6, 1780, p. 1.

277 Latouche, pp. 101–103.

278 PJ, Mar. 8, 1780, no. 1330, p. 2.

279 London, Nov. 3, CJ, Mar. 8, 1780, no. 645, p. 4; London, Nov. 3, IL, Mar. 20, 1780. vol. II, no. 93, p. 2.

280 Extract of a letter from Weymouth, Nov. 4, Prensa, Feb. 29, 1780. vol. VII, no. 336, p. 1; London, November 4, NJG, Feb. 23, 1780. vol. III, no. 113, p. 2; London, Nov. 4, CC, Mar. 14, 1780, no. 790, p. 1; London, November 6, CJ, Mar. 15, 1780, no. 646, p. 4; British Intelligence from the New-York (City) Papers. London, November 4, MS, Mar. 16, 1780. vol. IX, no. 462, p. 1; London, September 25, AJ, Mar. 23, 1780. vol. II, no. 54, p. 1.

281 Extract of a Letter from Copenhagen, Nov. 9, IL, April 3, 1780. vol. II, no. 95, p. 2.

282 RG, Supplement, Nov. 10, 1779, no. 325, p. 3.

283 Lloyd's List, Sept. 7, 1779, NYG, March 6, 1780 p. 1.

284 ibid.

285 Extract of a Letter from Cork, Novem. 8, NYG, Feb. 21, 1780, no. 1479, p. 2; pp. Mar. 2, 1780, p. 2.

286 London, PP, Nov. 27, 1779, p. 1; August 30, NJG, Dec. 1, 1779. vol. II, no. 101, p. 2; Extract of a Letter from Capt. John Hastie, of the Privateer *Hawke*, Belonging to Clyde, to the Owners, VG, Dec. 18, 1779, no. 45, p. 1; London, August 30, IL, Dec. 20, 1779. vol. II, no. 80, p. 2; London, August 20, CC, Dec. 21, 1779, no. 778, p. 1; AJ, Dec. 23, 1779. vol. I, no. XLI, p. 1; London, September 2, CJ, Dec. 22, 1779, no. 634, p. 1.

287 PP, no.1230, 1779, p. 2.

288 London, October 29, NJG, Mar. 15, 1780. vol. III, no. 116, p. 2; Balch, Thomas. *The French in America during the war of independence of the United States, 1777–1783;* Thomas Balch, Thomas Willing Balch, Edwin Swift Balch, and others. Philadelphia, Porter & Coates, 1891–1895, Boston: Gregg Press, 1972, pp. 196–197; PAG. November 24, 1778. NBBAS. vol. 1 p. 356.

289 Extract of a Letter from Winchester, Dec. 11, VG, Mar. 25, 1780, no. 59, p. 2; Extract of a Letter from Portsmouth, December 13, NYG, April 24, 1780, no. 1488, p. 2; London, December 23, AJ, May 10, 1780. vol. II, no. 61, p. 1.

290 New- York, Jan. 3, NYG, Jan. 3, 1780, no. 1472, p. 3.

291 December 15, PG, April 8, 1780. vol. XVII, no. 849, p. 2; London, December 15, NP, April 11, 1780, no. 340, p. 2; Boston, December 13, BG, Dec. 13, 1779, no. 1320, p. 3; PG, Dec. 18, 1779. vol. XVI, no. 833, p. 2; By the Boston Post. Boston, December 20, MS, Dec. 23, 1779. vol. IX, no. 451, p. 2; Boston, Dec. 16, CJ, Dec. 29, 1779, no. 635, p. 2.

292 PJ, Dec. 15, 1779, no. 1318, p. 2; Extract of a Letter from Folkstone, August 27, NJG, Dec. 22, London, September 28, VG, Jan. 29, 1780, no. 51, p. 1.

293 Philadelphia, December 23, PP, Dec. 23, 1779, p. 3; CJ, Jan. 5, 1780, no. 636, p. 2; Baltimore, December 14, CC, Jan. 11, 1780, no. 781, p. 2; PG. Jan. 15, 1780. vol. XVII, no. 837, p. 3; Philadelphia, December 23, RG, Jan. 15, 1780, no. 344, p. 2; NYG, Jan. 17, 1780, no. 1474, p. 2; CG&UI, Jan. 19, 1780. vol. XVII, no. 845, p. 1; Philadelphia, Dec. 29, BG, Jan. 31, 1780, no. 1327, p. 2.

294 London, PJ, April 27, 1780, no. 1337, p. 2.

295 Extract of a Letter from the Groyne, NJG, Jan. 17, 1781. vol. IV, no. 160, p. 2.

296 Extract of a Letter from Genoa, Jan. 1, IL, May 1, 1780. vol. II, no. 99, p. 2.

297 Extract of a Letter from Havre De-Grace, Jan. 12, IL, May 1, 1780. vol. II, no. 99, p. 2.

298   Drinkwater, John. *A history of the late siege of Gibraltar: With a description and account of that garrison.* By a captain in the late Seventy-Second Regiment, or, Royal Manchester Volunteers. Philadelphia: Printed by William Spotswood, Front-Street, M.DCC.LXXXIX. 1789; New York, April 6, RAG, April 6, 1780, no. CCXLVIII, p. 3; New-York, April 6, NJG, April 19, 1780. vol. III, no. 121, p. 2; McGuffie, Tom Henderson. *The Siege of Gibraltar, 1779–1783.* Philadelphia, Dufour Editions, 1965; Russell, Jack. *Gibraltar besieged, 1779–1783.* London: Heinemann 1965 pp. 157–160. Fremont-Barnes. vol. 2, p. 510.

299   Philadelphia, January 27, PP, Jan. 27, 1780, p. 3.

300   Extracts of some Private Letters Brought by the Last Mails from Holland, NYG, May 1, 1780, no. 1489, p. 2.

301   Intelligence from Lloyd's List, PP, Jan. 20, 1781. vol. X, no. 700, p. 2.

302   New-York, May 1, NYG, May 1, 1780, no. 1489, p. 3; PJ, May 3, 1780, no. 1338, p. 3.

303   Savannah, (in Georgia), Feb. 10, NYG, May 1, 1780, no. 1489, p. 1.

304   Extract of a Letter from Rear Adm. Digby to Mr. Stephen Secretary to the Lords of the Admiralty, PEP, May 20, 1780. vol. VI, no. 667, p. 56; Extract of a Letter from Rear Admiral Digby, Mr. Stephens, Secretary to the Lords of the Admiralty, Dated on Board the Prince George at Sea, the 2d March, 1780, RG, May 6, 1780, no. 376, p. 3.

305   London, February 22, IC&UA, May 4, 1780. vol. XII, no. 610, p. 2; AJ, May 10, 1780. vol. II, no. 61, p. 2; MS, May 11, 1780. vol. X, no. 470, p. 1; PG. May 13, 1780. vol. XVII, no. 854, p. 1; PP, May 20, 1780, p. 2; The following Articles Are Taken from the Gazette of France, of March 7th, 1780, NJG, May 24, 1780. vol. III, no. 126, p. 2.

306   London, February 22, IC&UA, May 4, 1780. vol. XII, no. 610, p. 2.

307   ibid. MS, May 11, 1780. vol. X, no. 470, p. 1; PG. May 13, 1780. vol. XVII, no. 854, p. 1; Prensa. May 23, 1780. vol. VII, no. 348, p. 1; AJ, May 10, 1780. vol. II, no. 61, p. 2; PP, May 20, 1780, p. 2; The following Articles Are Taken from the Gazette of France, of March 7th, 1780, NJG, May 24, 1780. vol. III, no. 126, p. 2.

308   PJ, Sept. 6, 1780, no. 1356, p. 1.

309   Extract of a Letter from Dartmouth, March 21, NYG, May 29, 1780, no. 1493, p. 2.

310   Extract of a Letter from Leipsick, March 5, NYG, May 29, 1780, no. 1493; p. 2.

311   London, March 1, NYG, May 8, 1780, no. 1490, p. 2; Prensa. May 23, 1780. vol. VII, no. 348, p. 1.

312   London, March 1, NYG, May 8, 1780, no. 1490, p. 2; PEP, May 16, 1780. vol. VI, no. 666, p. 54; Prensa, May 23, 1780. vol. VII, no. 348, p. 1.

313   Extract of a Letter from Falmouth, March 20, NYG, May 29, 1780, no. 1493, p. 2.

314   Extract of a Letter from Penzance, March 23, NYG, May 29, 1780, no. 1493, p. 2.

315   NYG, Mar. 27, 1780, no. 1484, p. 3; Extract of a Letter from a Gentleman in South Carolina, Rebel House, 6 Miles from Charlestown, March 6, 1780, CG&UI, April 21, 1780. vol. XVII, no. 858, p. 3.

316   VG, April 1, 1780, no. 60, p. 2.

317   Extract of a Letter from Helstone, April 5, VG, Aug. 16, 1780, no. 76, p. 2.

318   Extract of a Letter from Glasgow, April 15, NYG, Aug. 14, 1780, no. 1504, p. 2; PJ, Sept. 27, 1780, no. 1359, p. 1.

319   Extract of a Letter from Waterford, May 12, NYG, Aug. 7, 1780, no. 1503, p. 2.

320   Extract of a Letter from Corke, April 6, NYG, July 3, 1780, no. 1498, p. 4.

321   PJ, Sept. 6, 1780, no. 1356, p. 1.

322   NYG, July 10, 1780, no. 1499, p. 2.

323   Extract of a Letter from Corke, April 6, NYG, July 3, 1780, no. 1498, p. 4.

324   Extract of a Letter from Harwich, April 28, NYG, July 10, 1780, no. 1499, p. 2; PJ, Sept. 27, 1780, no. 1359, p. 1.

325 London, April 27, NYG, July 17, 1780, no. 1500, p. 2; Extract of a Letter from Dover, April 24, NYG, July 3, 1780, no. 1498, p. 4; Boston, July 3, PEP, July 17, 1780. vol. VI, no. 679, p. 80.

326 Extract of a Letter from Dover, April 24, NYG, July 3, 1780, no. 1498, p. 4.

327 Extract of a Letter from Gibraltar, April 29, RG, July 15, 1780, no. 396, p. 3.

328 ibid.

329 Extract of a Letter from Corke, April 6, NYG, July 3, 1780, no. 1498, p. 4.

330 Extract of a Letter from Dover, May 1, NYG, July 10, 1780, no. 1499, p. 2; London, May 28, IL, Aug. 7, 1780. vol. III, no. 113, p. 1.

331 Boston, May 1, CJ, May 11, 1780, no. 654, p. 4; Amsterdam, May 4, IL, July 31, 1780. vol. III, no. 112, p. 4.

332 Amsterdam, May 4, IL, July 31, 1780. vol. III, no. 112, p. 4; AJ, Sept. 13, 1780. vol. II, no. 77, p. 1.

333 Extract of a Letter from Helstone, April 5, VG, Aug. 16, 1780, no. 76, p. 2.

334 Extract of a Letter from Rear-Admiral Gambler, to Mr. Stephens, Dated on Board the *Dunkirk*, at Plymouth, the 14th of May, 1780, NYG, July 31, 1780, no. 1502, p. 2.

335 New-York, Sept. 8, NYG, Sept. 11, 1780, no. 1508, p. 2; Paris, April 24, CG&UI, Oct. 17, 1780. vol. XVII, no. 884, p. 1.

336 Boston, May 25, PP, June 10, 1780, p. 2; Extract of a Letter from Trenton (New-Jersey) May 31, PG, June 10, 1780. vol. XVII, no. 858, p. 3.

337 Intelligence from Lloyd's List, PP, Jan. 20, 1781. vol. X, no. 700, p. 2, NJG, Jan. 24, 1781. vol. IV, no. 161, p. 2.

338 Extract of a Letter from Paris, July 2, NYG, Oct. 16, 1780, no. 1513, p. 2.

339 Boston, June 1, CJWA, June 1, 1780, no. CCXXII, p. 3; Boston, May 29, CG&UI, June 2, 1780. vol. XVII, no. 864, p. 2; PG. June 3, 1780. vol. XVII, no. 857, p. 3.

340 Intelligence from Lloyd's List, PP, Jan. 20, 1781. vol. X, no. 700, p. 2; NJG, Jan. 24, 1781. vol. IV, no. 161, p. 2.

341 Leghorn, June 7, PP, Sept. 26, 1780, p. 2; NYG, Oct. 2, 1780, no. 1511, p. 2; PG. Oct. 18, 1780. vol. XVII, no. 877, p. 2; CC, Oct. 24, 1780, no. 822, p. 1; Naples, June 6, CJ, Oct. 12, 1780, no. 676, p. 3.

342 Hermione. p. 166.

343 From the *Independent Chronicle*. Boston, May 18, RG, June 14, 1780, no. 387, p. 3; New-York, June 12, NYG, June 12, 1780, no. 1495, p. 3; New-York (City) June 10, PG, June 17, 1780. vol. XVII, no. 859, p. 3; Providence, June 14, AJ, June 14, 1780. vol. II, no. 66, p. 3; New York, June 10, AJ, June 21, 1780. vol. II, no. 67, p. 3; PJ, June 21, 1780, no. 1345, p. 3; PJ, June 28, 1780, no. 1346, p. 2; New-London, June 9. Providence, June 24, PG, June 24, 1780. vol. XVII, no. 860, p. 3; Newport, June 10, PP, June 27, 1780, p. 3; PP, July 4, 1780, p. 2; Boston, June 23, VG, July 12, 1780, no. 71, p. 2, NJG, June 28, 1780. vol. III, no. 131, p. 3.

344 Extract of a Letter from Aberdeen, PP, June 10, 1780, p. 4.

345 Extract of a Letter from Calais, June 12, NYG, Oct. 9, 1780, no. 1512, p. 2.

346 Intelligence from Lloyd's List, PP, Jan. 20, 1781. vol. X, no. 700, p. 2; NJG, Jan. 24, 1781. vol. IV, no. 161, p. 2.

347 New-York, July 3, NYG, July 3, 1780, no. 1498, p. 3.

348 Hattendorf, pp. 4–5.

349 Extract of a Letter from Guernsey, June 17, NYG, Oct. 9, 1780, no. 1512, p. 2; Intelligence from Lloyd's List, PP, Jan. 20, 1781. vol. X, no. 700, p. 2; NJG, Jan. 24, 1781. vol. IV, no. 161, p. 2.

350 Extract of a Letter from Falmouth, June 17, NYG, Oct. 9, 1780, no. 1512, p. 2.

351 Barneville. p. 230.

352 Barneville. p. 236.

353 Extract of a Letter from Cork, June 27, PP, Sept. 23, 1780, p. 2.

354 Extract of a Letter from Folkstone, June 25, NYG, Oct. 9, 1780, no. 1512, p. 2.

355 Extract of a Letter from Southampton, July 30, NYG, Oct. 16, 1780, no. 1513, p. 2.

356 Extract of a Letter from Lisbon, July 6, NYG, Oct. 16, 1780, no. 1513, p. 2.

357 Extract of a Letter from Dartmouth, July 4, PP, Sept. 26, 1780, p. 2; IL, Oct. 9, 1780. vol. III, no. 122, p. 2; NP. Oct. 10, 1780, no. 366, p. 3; MS, Oct. 19, 1780. vol. X, no. 493, p. 1; VG, Oct. 25, 1780, no. 86, p. 1; CJWA. Oct. 19, 1780, no. CCXLII, p. 3.

358 Barneville. p. 238.

359 Extract of a Letter Received from an Officer on Board the *Prudente* Frigate, Captain Walsgrave, NYG, Oct. 16, 1780, no. 1513, p. 2; From the *London Gazette,* July 22, Admiralty Office, July, 1780, PP, Nov. 7, 1780, p. 2; Admiralty Officer, July 1780, AJ, Dec. 16, 1780. vol. II, no. 90, p. 1.

360 Intelligence from Lloyd's List, PP, Jan. 20, 1781. vol. X, no. 700, p. 2; NJG, Jan. 24, 1781. vol. IV, no. 161, p. 2.

361 Extract of a Letter from Lisbon, July 6, NYG, Oct. 16, 1780, no. 1513, p. 2.

362 London, August 3, IL, Nov. 6, 1780. vol. III, no. 126, p. 4.

363 Extract of a Letter from Paris, July 2, NYG, Oct. 16, 1780, no. 1513, p. 2.

364 Extract of a Letter from Lisbon, July 15, NYG, Oct. 16, 1780, no. 1513, p. 4.

365 Newport, July 22, NP, Aug. 3, 1780, no. 357, p. 2; MS, Aug. 3, 1780. vol. X, no. 482, p. 3; NYG, Aug. 14, 1780, no. 1504, p. 3; PP, Aug. 22, 1780, p. 3.

366 Extract of a Letter from Plymouth, July 23, NYG, Oct. 16, 1780, no. 1513, p. 2.

367 ibid.

368 PJ, Nov. 29, 1780, no. 1368, p. 2; This Vessel Sailed the 29th June from New-London, Admiralty-Office, August 19, 1780, NJG, Dec. 13, 1780. vol. III, no. 155, p. 2

369 PJ, Nov. 1, 1780, no. 1364, p. 1; Hague, August 2, CJ, Nov. 23, 1780, no. 682, p. 3; Extract of a Letter from Nantz, August 1, PG, Jan. 10, 1781. vol. XVIII, no. 889, p. 3.

370 Admiralty Office, August 2, 1780, NYG, Oct. 16, 1780, no. 1513, p. 2.

371 PJ, Oct. 25, 1780, no. 1363, p. 3; Philadelphia, October 28, PP, Oct. 28, 1780, p. 3; Philadelphia, October 25. Extract of a Letter from Cadix, Aug. 16, 1780, NJG, Nov. 1, 1780. vol. III, no. 149, p. 3; Richmond, Nov. 4, VG, Nov. 4, 1780, no. 87, p. 2; From Cadix, August 17, CJ, Nov. 9, 1780, no. 680, p. 2.

372 London, August 21, MS, Dec. 14, 1780. vol. X, no. 501, p. 1.

373 Philadelphia, PJ, Nov. 29, 1780, no. 1368, p. 2; Boston, October 30. Extract of a Letter from an Officer of the Letter of Marque Ship *General Washington,* VG, Dec. 2, 1780, no. 91, p. 2.

374 PJ, Dec. 6, 1780, no. 1369, p. 1; Philadelphia, December 6. by the Brick *Duke of Lenster,* Captain Souder, from L' Orient, We Have the following Articles, Viz, NP, Dec. 26, 1780, no. 377, p. 1; London, August 22, CJ, Jan. 4, 1781, no. 688, p. 1.

375 London. Admiralty Office, August 26, 1780, RGG, Jan. 4, 1781, no. 97, p. 3.

376 Philadelphia, August 19, PP, Aug. 19, 1780, p. 3; Extract of a Letter, Taken in the *Mercury* Packet, Captain Dillon, from Thomas Irving, of London, to John, NJG, Aug. 23, 1780. vol. III, no. 139, p. 3; Philadelphia, IL, Sept. 18, 1780. vol. III, no. 119, p. 2; New York, September 21, Monday Evening Arrived the Schooner *Sukey,* Captain Harwood, in 10 Days, RAG, Sept. 21, 1780, no. CCCVII, p. 1.

377 London, August 22, AJ, Dec. 23, 1780. vol. II, no. 91, p. 1.

378 London. July 17, RG, Nov. 6, 1779, no. 324, p. 2.

379 ibid.

380   Newport, December, 2, MJ, Dec. 30, 1776. vol. III, no. 159, p. 2; Boston, December 5. VG, Jan. 10, 1777, no. 1327, p. 3.

381   London, September 19, NYG, Dec. 11, 1780, no. 1521, p. 2; Extract of a Letter from Portsmouth, Nov. 27, RGG, Feb. 15, 1781, no. 103, p. 1.

382   Extract of a Letter from Vice Admiral Arbutnot to Mr. Stephens, on Board the *Royal Oak*, at Sea, Oct. 17, 1780. RGG, Supplement. Feb. 1, 1781, no. 101, p. 1.

383   Boston, October 26, IC&UA, Oct. 26, 1780. vol. XIII, no. 635, p. 3; PG. Nov. 1, 1780. vol. XVII, no. 879, p. 2; PP, Nov. 14, 1780, p. 2; Boston, October 23, MS, Oct. 26, 1780. vol. X, no. 494, p. 2; Boston, October 17. CG. Oct. 31, 1780. vol. XVII, no. 886, p. 3; Boston, October 16, MS, Nov. 2, 1780. vol. X, no. 495, p. 1.

384   Tangier, August 30 1780, PP, Feb. 20, 1781. vol. X, no. 709, p. 2.

385   Extract of a Letter Received from an Officer on Board the *Prudente* Frigate, Captain Walsgrave, NYG, Oct. 16, 1780, no. 1513, p. 2.

386   Boston, Nov. 23, AJ, Nov. 25, 1780. vol. II, no. 87, p. 3; Extract of a Letter from Pool (in England) Found on Board the Prize Brick *Endeavor*, CG&UI, Nov. 28, 1780. vol. XVIII, no. 890, p. 2; Norwich, November 14, PP, Dec. 12, 1780, no. 688, p. 2.

387   Tangier, August 30 1780, PP, Feb. 20, 1781. vol. X, no. 709, p. 2; Paris, October 10, NM, Mar. 17, 1781, no. 1016, p. 1.

388   ibid.

389   Extract of a Letter from Leghorn, Oct. 10. RGG, Mar. 1, 1781, no. 105, p. 2; NYG, Mar. 5, 1781, no. 1533, p. 2.

390   Norwich, November 14, PP, Dec. 12, 1780, no. 688, p. 2.

391   Edinburgh, October 18. Extract of a Letter from Dublin, October 14, NP, Feb. 6, 1781, no. 383, p. 1.

392   ibid. New-York, October 16, NYG, Oct. 16, 1780, no. 1513, p. 3; The following Paragraph is Copied from the New-Jersey Journal, October 11, RG, Oct. 18, 1780, no. 423, p. 3.

393   Providence, Oct. 18, PG, Oct. 18, 1780. vol. XVII, no. 877, p. 3.

394   Extract of a Letter from Weymouth, Oct. 20, NYG, Feb. 5, 1781, no. 1529 p. 2.

395   ibid.

396   ibid.

397   Le Chevalier Yorke, RGG, Feb. 15, 1781, no. 103, p. 1; Hague, Nov. 21, NYG, Mar. 5, 1781, no. 1533, p. 2.

398   Providence, November 4, AJ, Nov. 4, 1780. vol. II, no. 84, p. 2; Boston, November 9, IC&UA, Nov. 9, 1780. vol. XIII, no. 637, p. 2; Boston, November 6, CG&UI, Nov. 14, 1780. vol. XVIII, no. 888, p. 3; Providence, Nov. 8, CJ, Nov. 16, 1780, no. 681, p. 3; Providence, October 25, PP, Nov. 21, 1780, p. 2; PJ, Nov. 22, 1780, no. 1367, p. 2; VG, Dec. 2, 1780, no. 91, p. 2; Boston, October 30, NJG, Nov. 29, 1780. vol. III, no. 153, p. 3.

399   Savannah, February 1, RGG, Supplement. Feb. 1, 1781, no. 101, p. 3.

400   London, PP, Oct. 31, 1780, p. 2.

401   PJ, June 30, 1781, no. 1400, p. 1.

402   London, September 16, RGG, Jan. 25, 1781, no. 100, p. 2.

403   Boston, Nov. 8, NYG, Feb. 19, 1781, no. 1531, p. 2; Admiralty Office, December 15, 1780, RGG, April 26, 1781, no. 113, p. 1.

404   Admiralty Office, December 15, 1780, RGG, April 26, 1781, no. 113, p. 1.

405   Savannah, February 1, RGG, Supplement. Feb. 1, 1781, no. 101, p. 3; London, Nov. 9, NYG, Feb. 19, 1781, no. 1531, p. 1.

406   RG, Nov. 11, 1780, no. 430, p. 3.

407 Letter from Captain Watt, of the *Pegasus*, in Yarmouth, Roads, to Mr. Stephens Nov. 22, 1780, NYG, Feb. 19, 1781, no. 1531, p. 2.

408 Extract of a Letter from Dover, Dec. 30, NYG, April 23, 1781, no. 1540, p. 2.

409 Extract of a Letter from Plymouth, Nov. 22, RGG, Feb. 15, 1781, no. 103, p. 1; Extract of a Letter from Lisbon, Oct. 20, NYG, Feb. 19, 1781, no. 1531, p. 2; Extract of a Letter from Annapolis, Jan. 22, IC&UA, Feb. 15, 1781. vol. XIII, no. 651, p. 3; Extract of a Letter from Williamsburg, Dated January 20, CJ, Feb. 15, 1781, no. 694, p. 2.

410 Boston, November 23, CG&UI, Nov. 28, 1780. vol. XVIII, no. 890, p. 2; NP. Dec. 5, 1780, no. 374, p. 3; Boston, Nov. 2, NJG, Dec. 13, 1780. vol. III, no. 155, p. 2; Boston, Nov. 6, NYG, Dec. 18, 1780, no. 1522, p. 2.

411 Extract of a Letter from Portsmouth, Nov. 27, RGG, Feb. 15, 1781, no. 103, p. 1.

412 Extract of a Letter from Lieut. Noble, of the *Expedition* Cutter, to Vice Admiral Evans, Dated St. Helen's Dec, 2, 1780, NYG, Mar. 5, 1781, no. 1533, p. 2.

413 Boston, October 30. Extract of a Letter from an Officer of the Letter of Marque Ship *General Washington*, VG, Dec. 2, 1780, no. 91, p. 2.

414 London, December 13. Extract of a Letter from Captain Charles Holmes Everitt, of His Majesty's Ship *Solebay*, NP, May 4, 1781, no. 396, p. 4, AJ, May 12, 1781. vol. III, no. 126, p. 1.

415 Extract of a Letter from Plymouth, Dec. 12, NYG, Mar. 26, 1781, no. 1536, p. 2.

416 ibid.

417 London, December 13. Extract of a Letter from Captain Charles Holmes Everitt, of His Majesty's Ship *Solebay*, NP, May 4, 1781, no. 396, p. 4, AJ, May 12, 1781. vol. III, no. 126, p. 1.

418 Extract of a Letter from Waterford, December 16, PP, May 5, 1781. vol. X, no. 730, p. 1; PP, June 14, 1781. vol. X, no. 742, p. 2.

419 Extract of a Letter from Faro, Dec. 16, RGG, May 17, 1781, no. 116, p. 1.

420 Extract of a Letter from Falmouth, Dec. 29, NYG, April 23, 1781, no. 1540, p. 2.

421 Extract of a Letter from Plymouth, Dec. 31, NYG, April 23, 1781, no. 1540, p. 2.

422 HCA 32/261/6/1-21; HCA 32/266/2/1-11.

470 His Majesty's Most Gracious Answer, RGG, May 10, 1781, no. 115, p. 1.

423 Extract of a Letter from Kinsale, Dec. 29, NYG, April 23, 1781, no. 1540, p. 2; London, PJ, May 2, 1781, no. 1390, p. 2; New-York, April 31, Prensa, May 8, 1781. vol. VIII, no. 399, p. 1; Extract of a Letter from Lord Mulgrane, Captain of the *Couragiue*, CJWA, Aug. 30, 1781, no. CCLXXXVIII, p. 3; PJ, Sept. 12, 1781, no. 1421, p. 3; Extract of a Letter from a Gentleman in Paris, 13th of May, 1781, PP, Sept. 13, 1781. vol. X, no. 781, p. 3.

424 Admiralty Office, January 10th, 1781, RG, May 12, 1781, no. 482, p. 2.

425 Summary of the Intelligence Brought by His Majesty's Ship *Cormorant*, Which We Are Informed, RG, April 25, 1781, no. 477, p. 3, New-York, April 21, FJ, May 2, 1781, no. II, p. 2.

426 Extract of a Letter from Corke, January 25, PP, July 2, 1781. vol. X, no. 750, p. 2.

427 New-York, January 17, RG, Jan. 17, 1781, no. 449, p. 2; From Rivington's New-York Gazette. New-York, January 17, NP, Feb. 6, 1781, no. 383, p. 1; London, October 9, CJ, Feb. 8, 1781, no. 693, p. 3.

428 Extract of a Letter from Kinsale, Dec. 29, NYG, April 23, 1781, no. 1540, p. 2.

429 Extract of a Letter from Waterford, Jan. 31, RGG, May 10, 1781, no. 115, p. 1; London, February 13, NYG, May 14, 1781, no. 1543, p. 2; Extract of a Letter from Portsmouth, Feb. 7, PP, May 26, 1781. vol. X, no. 736, p. 2.

430 Fish-Kill, March 1, NJG, Mar. 7, 1781. vol. IV, no. 167, p. 2.

431 PJ, May 30, 1781, no. 1394, p. 1.

432 FJ. May 30, 1781, no. VI, p. 2, PJ, May 30, 1781, no. 1394, p. 1; Extract of a Letter from Helvoetsluys, Feb. 12. NM. June 9, 1781, no. 1028, p. 1.

433 Extract of a Letter from London, Nov. 1, RG, Feb. 28, 1781, no. 461, p. 2; Charlestown, February 7, RGG, Supplement. Mar. 1, 1781, no. 105, p. 3.

434 Summary of the Intelligence Brought by His Majesty's Ship *Cormorant*, Which We Are Informed, RG, April 25, 1781, no. 477, p. 3.

435 FJ. May 30, 1781, no. VI, p. 2, PJ, May 30, 1781, no. 1394, p. 1; Extract of a Letter from Helvoetsluys, Feb. 12. NM. June 9, 1781, no. 1028, p. 1.

436 Newport, March 3, AJ, Mar. 7, 1781. vol. II, no. 107, p. 2; PG. Mar. 10, 1781. vol. XVIII, no. 897, p. 3; New-York, March 12, NYG, Mar. 12, 1781, no. 1534, p. 3; Extract of a Letter from a Gentleman at Philadelphia, February 21, CJWA, Mar. 15, 1781, no. CCLXIV, p. 3; Boston, March 19, IL, Mar. 19, 1781. vol. III, no. 146, p. 3; Boston, March 12, NYG, Mar. 26, 1781, no. 1536, p. 3; Extract of a Letter from a Gentleman in Newport, to His Friend in This town, Sunday, February 25, 1781, NHG, Mar. 5, 1781. vol. XXV, no. 1270, p. 2; Barneville. 254.

437 London, February 13, NYG, May 14, 1781, no. 1543, p. 2.

438 London, February 17, RGG, June 14, 1781, no. 120, p. 2.

439 St. Pierre, (Martinique) Feb. 15, 1781, PP, April 24, 1781. vol. X, no. 727, p. 2; FJ. April 25, 1781, no. I, p. 2; St. Pierre, (Martinigo) Feb. 15, 1781, BG, May 7, 1781, no. 1393, p. 2; CC, May 8, 1781, no. 850, p. 2; AJ, May 9, 1781. vol. III, no. 125, p. 1; NP. May 10, 1781, no. 397, p. 2; CJWA. May 10, 1781, no. CCLXXII, p. 1, IC&UA, May 10, 1781. vol. XIII, no. 663, p. 2; PG. May 12, 1781. vol. XVIII, no. 906, p. 4; By the Hartford Post. St. Pierre, (Martinico) Feb 15, MS, May 10, 1781. vol. XI, no. 522, p. 3; PJ, April 25, 1781, no. 1389, p. 2.

440 London. Feb. 27, FJ, July 4, 1781, no. XI, p. 2; Extract of a Letter from the Hague, Feb. 27, NYG, May 28, 1781, no. 1545, p. 2.

441 AJ, April 4, 1781. vol. III, no. 115, p. 2; Extract of a Letter from the First Lieutenant of an English Privateer That Was Taken by a French Frigate, PP, April 17, 1781. vol. X, no. 725, p. 1; Boston, March 29, NJG, April 18, 1781. vol. IV, no. 173, p. 2.

442 London, February 13, NYG, May 14, 1781, no. 1543, p. 2; Extract of a Letter from on Board the Monmouth, St. Jago Bay, April 24, NYG, Oct. 1, 1781, no. 1563, p. 1.

443 Extract of a Letter from Martinique, Dated March 4, NJG, May 2, 1781. vol. IV, no. 175, p. 2; Philadelphia, April 24, AJ, May 12, 1781. vol. III, no. 126, p. 2.

444 London, March 14, NYG, June 11, 1781, no. 1547, p. 2; London, RG, June 13, 1781, no. 491, p. 2.

445 New-York, March 19, NYG, Mar. 19, 1781, no. 1535, p. 3; NP. April 5, 1781, no. 392, p. 3; New York, March 20, RAG, Mar. 20, 1781, no. CCCLVII, p. 3; RG. Mar. 21, 1781, no. 467, p. 3; Portsmouth, March 8, 1781, CG&UI, April 6, 1781. vol. XVIII, no. 908, p. 2.

446 PJ, Aug. 25, 1781, no. 1416, p. 3; Extract of a Letter from Liverpool, March 13, RG, July 25, 1781, no. 503, p. 2.

447 Dublin, March 22, PP, June 19, 1781. vol. X, no. 744, p. 1.

448 Providence, March 31, NJG, April 18, 1781. vol. IV, no. 173, p. 3; Eller, Ernest McNeill, ed. *Chesapeake Bay in the American Revolution*. Centreville, MD: Tidewater Publishers, 1981. p. 466; Hattendorf, pp. 89–90; Barneville. 259–263.

449 Dublin, March 22, PP, June 19, 1781. vol. X, no. 744, p. 1.

450 London, April 6, IL, July 16, 1781. vol. IV, no. 163, p. 3; By Yesterday's Eastern Mail. London, April 6, AJ, July 18, 1781. vol. III, no. 145, p. 2.

451 *Relation de la Sortie de l'Escadre* Française *aux ordres du Ch^{er}. Destouches,* & *de l'affaire qui a eue lieu le 16 Mars 1781, d'entre-deux cette Escadre* le & *des celle Anglais, commandée par l'Amiral Arbuthnot;* Hattendorf, pp. 91; Barneville. 263–264.

452 Extract of a Letter from Kinsale, March 20, NYG, July 9, 1781, no. 1551, p. 2.

453 Extract of a Letter from Plymouth, March 28, NYG, July 9, 1781, no. 1551, p. 2.

454 ibid. London, March 29. East-India House, March 28, 1781, PG, June 9, 1781. vol. XVIII, no. 910, p. 1; London, March 29, CJ, July 12, 1781, no. 715, p. 4; CJWA, June 21, 1781, no. CCLXXVIII, p. 2; NP. June 21, 1781. vol. VIII, no. 403, p. 2; East-India House, March 27, 1781, PP, July 2, 1781. vol. X, no. 750, p. 2.

455 Extract of a Letter from Waterford, April 3, RG, June 23, 1781, no. 494, p. 2.

456 Providence, March 31, NJG, April 18, 1781. vol. IV, no. 173, p. 3.

457 Newport, March 31, AJ, April 4, 1781. vol. III, no. 115, p. 2; Extract of a Letter from the First Lieutenant of an English Privateer That Was Taken by a French Frigate, PP, April 17, 1781. vol. X, no. 725, p. 1; Boston, March 29, NJG, April 18, 1781. vol. IV, no. 173, p. 2.

458 Dublin, April, 3, PG, June 9, 1781. vol. XVIII, no. 910, p. 1; NP. June 21, 1781. vol. VIII, no. 403, p. 2; IL, June 25, 1781. vol. IV, no. 160, p. 4.

459 Extract from the Dispatches of Mons. Le Comte De Rochambault, Commander in Chief of the French Army in America, RG, June 20, 1781, no. 493, p. 2; Extract of a Letter from Paris, April 3, CJ, July 5, 1781, no. 714, p. 2; Paris, (France) April 3, PG, July 7, 1781. vol. XVIII, no. 914, p. 1; AJ, July 4, 1781. vol. III, no. 141, p. 1.

460 Lisbon, July 5. SG. Oct. 25, 1781. vol. I, no. 2, p. 3.

461 Admiralty Office, April 23, 1781, NYG, July 2, 1781, no. 1550, p. 2; RG. June 30, 1781, no. 496, p. 3; Paris, April 16, RAG, July 5, 1781. vol. VII, no. CCCLXXXVIII, p. 2; Extract of a Letter from Edinburgh, April 18, RGG, July 12, 1781, no. 124, p. 2.

462 Extract of a Letter from Hithe, March 20, RGG, July 19, 1781, no. 125, p. 1.

463 London, April 11, RGG, July 12, 1781, no. 124, p. 2.

464 New-York, April 18, RG, April 18, 1781, no. 475, p. 3; PJ, April 25, 1781, no. 1389, p. 2.

465 Cavalier. Clowes. vol. 3; Fremont-Barnes. vol. 3, pp. 1004–1005; Boston, August 16, IC&UA, Aug. 16, 1781. vol. IV, no. 709, p. 3; PG. Aug. 18, 1781. vol. XVIII, no. 920, p. 3; CJ, Aug. 23, 1781, no. 721, p. 2; MS, Aug. 23, 1781. vol. XI, no. 537, p. 2; Boston, August 18, PP, Aug. 28, 1781. vol. X, no. 774, p. 2; Boston, August 9, NJG, Aug. 29, 1781. vol. IV, no. 192, p. 2.

466 Extract of a Letter From Waterford, April 16, NYG, July 2, 1781, no. 1550, p. 1.

467 Hermione, p. 213.

468 Kingston, (Jamaica), April 21, NYG, June 4, 1781, no. 1546, p. 2.

469 By the *Carteret* and *Duke of Cumberland* Packets, Arrived Yesterday from Falmouth the Former with the April and the Latter with the May Mail, RAG, June 28, 1781. vol. VII, no. CCCLXXXVI, p. 3; a Letter from Captain Colins, of His Majesty's Ship *Aurora*, to Mr. Stephens, Dated in Mounts Bay, April 24, 1781, NYG, July 2, 1781, no. 1550, p. 2.

470 Extract of a Letter from Plymouth, Dated April 24, NYG, July 2, 1781, no. 1550, p. 2; By the *Carteret* and *Duke of Cumberland* Packets, Arrived Yesterday from Falmouth the Former with the April and the Latter with the May Mail, RAG, June 28, 1781. vol. VII, no. CCCLXXXVI, p. 3; Extract of a Letter from Falmouth, April 28, PP, July 12, 1781. vol. X, no. 754, p. 3.

471 By the *Carteret* and *Duke of Cumberland* Packets, Arrived Yesterday from Falmouth the Former with the April and the Latter with the May Mail, RAG, June 28, 1781. vol. VII, no. CCCLXXXVI, p. 3; Extract of a Letter from Paris, June 21, NYG, Oct. 1, 1781, no. 1563, p. 1.

472 By the *Carteret* and *Duke of Cumberland* Packets, Arrived Yesterday from Falmouth the Former with the April and the Latter with the May Mail, RAG, June 28, 1781. vol. VII, no. CCCLXXXVI, p. 3; Boston, July 5, CJ, July 12, 1781, no. 715, p. 2.

473 Boston, May 14, IL, May 14, 1781. vol. III, no. 154, p. 3; Boston, May 10, CJWA, May 17, 1781, no. CCLXXIII, p. 2; Extract of a Letter from Camp, April 27, 1781, IC&UA, May 17, 1781. vol. XIII, no. 664, p. 3; Extract of a Letter from a Gentleman in the Country to His

Friend in This town. NM. May 19, 1781, no. 1025, p. 3; Boston, May 14, PG, May 19, 1781. vol. XVIII, no. 907, p. 2; CJ, May 24, 1781, no. 708, p. 3; NYG, June 4, 1781, no. 1546, p. 3; NJG, June 6, 1781. vol. IV, no. 180, p. 2; Boston, May 21, MS, May 24, 1781. vol. XI, no. 524, p. 3; Boston, May 17. Extract of a Letter from a Gentleman of Note in Holland, NP, May 24, 1781, no. 399, p. 3.

474 PEP, May 25, 1781. vol. VII, no. 743, p. 85.

475 PJ, May 2, 1781, no. 1390, p. 3; Philadelphia, April 27, 1781, PEP, April 27, 1781. vol. VII, no. 734, p. 68; Extract of a Letter from Amiens, February 6, 1781, to a Gentleman in This City, PP, April 28, 1781. vol. X, no. 728, p. 3; NJG, May 2, 1781. vol. IV, no. 175, p. 3; CC, May 15, 1781, no. 851, p. 2; NP. May 17, 1781, no. 398, p. 3; Extract of a Letter from a Gentleman of Credit in Holland, to His Correspondent in This City, January 23, 1781, AJ, May 19, 1781. vol. III, no. 128, p. 2; Philadelphia, May 2, FJ, May 2, 1781, no. II, p. 2.

476 By the *Carteret* and *Duke of Cumberland* Packets, Arrived Yesterday from Falmouth the Former with the April and the Latter with the May Mail, RAG, June 28, 1781. vol. VII, no. CCCLXXXVI, p. 3; Extract of a Letter from Plymouth, April 28, PP, July 12, 1781. vol. X, no. 754, p. 3; Extract of a Letter from Edinburgh, April 28, NYG, July 23, 1781, no. 1553, p. 2.

477 PJ, July 18, 1781, no. 1405, p. 2; Boston, July 5, IC&UA, July 5, 1781. vol. XIII, no. 703, p. 3; CJ, July 12, 1781, no. 715, p. 2; MS, July 12, 1781. vol. XI, no. 531, p. 2; PP, July 17, 1781. vol. X, no. 756, p. 3; Boston, July 21. NM. July 7, 1781, no. 1032, p. 2; Boston, June 28, NJG, July 18, 1781. vol. IV, no. 186, p. 2.

478 Extract of a Letter from Youghall, May 2, PP, Oct. 23, 1781. vol. X, no. 797, p. 1; Dublin, May 12, CJ, Nov. 8, 1781, no. 732, p. 4.

479 London, May 8, RGG, Supplement. Aug. 9, 1781, no. 128, p. 1.

480 Admiralty-Office, May 11, PP, Aug. 18, 1781. vol. X, no. 770, p. 2.

481 PJ, Aug. 22, 1781, no. 1413, p. 3; PJ, Aug. 4, 1781, no. 1410, p. 6; Baltimore, August 28, Prensa, Aug. 23, 1781. vol. VIII, no. 417, p. 2; following Account is Handed Us by a Gentleman Just Arrived from Cape Francois, and May be Depended on as Authentic, NJG, Aug. 29, 1781. vol. IV, no. 192, p. 3; Extract of a Letter from a Gentleman at Alexandria, September 5th, 1781, NHG, Sept. 29, 1781. vol. XXV, no. 1300, p. 2; New-York, August 1, NYG, Aug. 6, 1781, no. 1555, p. 1; From Rivington's Royal Gazette, August 8, NJG, Aug. 22, 1781. vol. IV, no. 191, p. 3; Paris, May 18, FJ, Aug. 22, 1781, no. XVIII, p. 2; Paris, May 15. NM. Sept. 8, 1781, no. 1041, p. 2.

482 London, May 8, RGG, Supplement. Aug. 9, 1781, no. 128, p. 1; Extract of a Letter from Plymouth, May 13, PP, Aug. 18, 1781. vol. X, no. 770, p. 2.

538 Extract of a Letter from Penzance, May 15, NYG, June 11, 1781, no. 1547, p. 2.

483 From Late New-York Papers. New-York, July 25, PP, Aug. 7, 1781. vol. X, no. 765, p. 2.

484 Kingston, (Jamaica) May 19, RGG, July 26, 1781, no. 126, p. 1.

485 Extract of a Letter from Newcastle, May 19, NYG, Aug. 27, 1781, no. 1558, p. 2; PP, Sept. 8, 1781. vol. X, no. 779, p. 2; Savannah, May 31, RGG, May 31, 1781, no. 118, p. 2.

486 Extract of a Letter from Paris, June 16, NYG, Oct. 1, 1781, no. 1563, p. 1.

487 Extract of a Letter from Falmouth, May 22, NYG, Sept. 3, 1781, no. 1559, p. 2.

488 London, May 14, PP, Sept. 13, 1781. vol. X, no. 781, p. 1.

489 Extract of a Letter from Cork, May 26, PP, Sept. 11, 1781. vol. X, no. 780, p. 2.

490 PJ, Oct. 6, 1781, no. 1428, p. 1; Extract of a Letter, Paris, June 21, RGG, Nov. 1, 1781, no. 140, p. 2; London, June 28, PEP, Sept. 12, 1781. vol. VII, no. 772, p. 147; PP, Sept. 13, 1781. vol. X, no. 781, p. 3; Admiralty-Office, June 19. Extract of a Letter from Captain Fanshaw, of the Egmont, to Mr. Stephens, NJG, Sept. 19, 1781. vol. IV, no. 195, p. 1.

491 Kingston, (Jamaica) May 19, RGG, July 26, 1781, no. 126, p. 1; Kingston, (Jamaica), May 24, RG, Aug. 1, 1781, no. 505, p. 3; Kingston, (Jamaica) June 2, NYG, Aug. 6, 1781, no. 1555, p. 1; PP, Aug. 11, 1781. vol. X, no. 767, p. 3.

492 Admiralty Office, May 30, 1781, RG, Aug. 8, 1781, no. 507, p. 2.

493 PJ, Sept. 1, 1781, no. 1418, p. 2.

494 Admiralty-Office, June 14, 1781, NYG, Oct. 1, 1781, no. 1563, p. 1.

495 Extract of a Letter from Falmouth, June 5, NYG, Oct. 1, 1781, no. 1563, p. 1; Admiralty-Office, June 9, 1781, NYG, Oct. 1, 1781, no. 1563, p. 1.

496 RGG, July 26, 1781, no. 126, p. 4; Kingston, (Jamaica) June 2, NYG, Aug. 6, 1781, no. 1555, p. 1; PP, Aug. 11, 1781. vol. X, no. 767, p. 3; From New York Papers. London, PEP, Aug. 10, 1781. vol. VII, no. 762, p. 123; Montego-Bay, (Jamaica) June 9, PP, Aug. 11, 1781. vol. X, no. 767, p. 3; IL, Sept. 3, 1781. vol. IV, no. 171, p. 2.

497 PJ, Aug. 1, 1781, no. 1409, p. 2; Halifax, June 19, NP, July 19, 1781. vol. VIII, no. 407, p. 3; CJWA. July 19, 1781, no. CCLXXXII, p. 1, CG&UI, July 20, 1781. vol. XVIII, no. 923, p. 3; RG. Aug. 8, 1781, no. 507, p. 3; From the *Nova-Scotia Gazette*, July 3. Basseterre, RG, Aug. 22, 1781, no. 511, p. 2.

498 Extract of a Letter from Hartlepool, June 20, PP, Oct. 9, 1781. vol. X, no. 792, p. 2.

499 RG, June 30, 1781, no. 496, p. 3; Admiralty Office, April 23, 1781, NYG, July 2, 1781, no. 1550, p. 2.

500 Extract of a Letter from Paris, June 21, NYG, Oct. 1, 1781, no. 1563, p. 1.

501 Extract of a Letter from Aldborough, in Suffolk, June 21, NYG, Oct. 1, 1781, no. 1563, p. 2.

502 Hermione, pp. 219 – 220.

503 London, July 10, NYG, Oct. 1, 1781, no. 1563, p. 3.

504 Extract of a Letter from Penzance, Cornwall, July 22, RG, Oct. 20, 1781, no. 528, p. 1.

505 Providence, June 30, CG&UI, July 6, 1781. vol. XVIII, no. 921, p. 3.

506 RG, June 30, 1781, no. 496, p. 3.

507 PJ, Aug. 22, 1781, no. 1413, p. 3.

508 Extract of a Letter from Cork, July 26, PP, Nov. 13, 1781. vol. X, no. 806, p. 2.

509 RG, July 4, 1781, no. 497, p. 2; PJ, July 14, 1781, no. 1404, p. 3; New-York, July 2, NYG, July 2, 1781, no. 1550, p. 3; New-York, July 3, RAG, July 3, 1781. vol. VII, no. CCCLXXXVII, p. 3; IL, July 23, 1781. vol. IV, no. 164, p. 3.

510 PJ, Sept. 15, 1781, no. 1422, p. 2.

511 RG, July 14, 1781, no. 500, p. 3; PJ, July 25, 1781, no. 1407, p. 2; New-York, July 4, RGG, Supplement. Aug. 30, 1781, no. 131, p. 3.

512 Extract of a Letter from Brest, July 19, RG, Oct. 13, 1781, no. 526, p. 3; London, July 18, PP, Oct. 20, 1781. vol. X, no. 796, p. 2.

513 Extract of a Letter from Kinsale, July 21, PP, Oct. 20, 1781. vol. X, no. 796, p. 2; London, August 10, PP, Nov. 15, 1781. vol. X, no. 807, p. 1; Extract of a Letter from Cork, August 6, NJG, Nov. 28, 1781. vol. IV, no. 205, p. 2.

514 Extract of a Letter from Cork, July 26, PP, Nov. 13, 1781. vol. X, no. 806, p. 2.

515 PJ, Oct. 20, 1781, no. 1432, p. 1; Extract of a Letter from Penzance, Cornwall, July 22, RG, Oct. 20, 1781, no. 528, p. 1; Extract of a Letter from Portsmouth, July 23. NJG, Oct. 31, 1781. vol. IV, no. 201, p. 3.

516 Admiralty-Office, August 21, 1781, PP, Nov. 13, 1781. vol. X, no. 806, p. 2.

517 Extract of a Letter from Limerick, July 26, PP, Nov. 8, 1781. vol. X, no. 804, p. 2.

518 Extract of a Letter from Cork, July 26, PP, Nov. 13, 1781. vol. X, no. 806, p. 2.

519 Extract of a Letter from Limerick, Aug. 4, PP, Nov. 17, 1781. vol. X, no. 808, p. 1; London, August 10, PP, Nov. 15, 1781. vol. X, no. 807, p. 1; Extract of a Letter from Cork, August 6, NJG, Nov. 28, 1781. vol. IV, no. 205, p. 2.

520 ibid.

521 PJ, Oct. 20, 1781, no. 1432, p. 1; London, July 18, PP, Oct. 20, 1781. vol. X, no. 796, p. 2.

522 Extract of a Letter from Berwick, August 4, PP, Nov. 15, 1781. vol. X, no. 807, p. 2; London, CJ, Dec. 6, 1781, no. 736, p. 2.

523 PJ, Aug. 15, 1781, p. 2; New London, August 3, CG&UI, Aug. 3, 1781. vol. XVIII, no. 925, p. 3; MS, Aug. 9, 1781. vol. XI, no. 535, p. 3; New-London, July 27, CJ, Aug. 9, 1781, no. 719, p. 4; Norwich, Aug. 2, PEP, Aug. 14, 1781. vol. VII, no. 763, p. 128; Boston, August 9, PP, Aug. 21, 1781. vol. X, no. 771, p. 3; NJG, Aug. 29, 1781. vol. IV, no. 192, p. 2; PJ, Nov. 10, 1781, no. 1438, p. 1; Extract of a Letter from Limerick, Aug. 4, PP, Nov. 17, 1781. vol. X, no. 808, p. 1.

524 PJ, Aug. 29, 1781, no. 1417, p. 1; Extract of a Letter from Limerick, Aug. 4, PP, Nov. 17, 1781. vol. X, no. 808, p. 1.

525 ibid.

526 London, RG, Oct. 13, 1781, no. 526, p. 2.

527 ibid.

528 London, August 10, PP, Nov. 15, 1781. vol. X, no. 807, p. 1.

529 London. Admiralty-Office, August 28, 1781, RGG, Nov. 29, 1781, no. 144, p. 1.

530 Extract of a Letter from a Loyalist in Philadelphia, to His Friend in This City, Dated August 13th, 1781, RG, Aug. 18, 1781, no. 510, p. 3.

531 Bristol, August 22, PP, Oct. 30, 1781. vol. X, no. 800, p. 2.

532 RG, Aug. 25, 1781, no. 512, p. 3; New-York, August 23, NYG, Aug. 27, 1781, no. 1558, p. 2; Between August 11 and 22, 1781. New-York. August 22, PP, Aug. 28, 1781. vol. X, no. 774, p. 2; Savannah, September 6, RGG, Sept. 6, 1781, no. 132, p. 2, September 11, 1781. p. 2.

533 PJ, Dec. 1, 1781, no. 1444, p. 2.

534 Boston, August 27, IL, Aug. 27, 1781. vol. IV, no. 170, p. 3; Prensa. Sept. 25, 1781. vol. VIII, no. 421, p. 1; Yesterday's Eastern Mail. Boston, August 27, AJ, Aug. 29, 1781. vol. III, no. 157, p. 1.

535 Kingston, (Jamaica) August 11, RGG, Dec. 27, 1781, no. 148, p. 2; Salem, Dec. 27, PEP, Jan. 22, 1782. vol. VIII, no. 803, p. 10.

536 New-York, September 12, RGG, Oct. 18, 1781, no. 138, p. 1.

537 FJ, Dec. 26, 1781, no. XXXVI, p. 3; London, PJ, Dec. 22, 1781, no. 1450, p. 3.

538 New-York. August 22, PP, Aug. 28, 1781. vol. X, no. 774, p. 2.

539 PJ, Aug. 22, 1781, no. 1413, p. 3; London, May 14, NJG, Aug. 29, 1781. vol. IV, no. 192, p. 2.

540 RG, Sept. 8, 1781, no. 516, p. 3; Philadelphia, August 25, NJG, Sept. 5, 1781. vol. IV, no. 193, p. 3.

541 Extract of a Letter from Gen. Masson, to Governor Rutledge, Camp, St. Stephens, August 6, 1781, PG, Sept. 22, 1781. vol. XVIII, no. 925, p. 3.

542 London, August 2, RGG, Nov. 22, 1781, no. 143, p. 3.

543 New-York, September 10, NYG, Sept. 10, 1781, no. 1560, p. 3.

544 September 22. Extract of a Letter from Madrid, Aug. 21. SG. Dec. 14, 1781. vol. I, no. 9, p. 2.

545 London, September 29, BEP, Dec. 15, 1781. vol. I, no. 9, p. 3; CC, Jan. 1, 1782, no. 884, p. 2; PAG, Jan. 2, 1782, p. 2.

546 Philadelphia, Sept. 1, PP, Sept. 1, 1781. vol. X, no. 776, p. 3; Philadelphia, August 25, NJG, Sept. 5, 1781. vol. IV, no. 193, p. 3; Philadelphia, September 4, Prensa, Sept. 11, 1781. vol. VIII, no. 419, p. 1.

547   FJ, Sept. 19, 1781, no. XXII, p. 3; Boston, September 6, IC&UA, Sept. 6, 1781. vol. XIV, no. 680, p. 3; MS, Sept. 13, 1781. vol. XI, no. 540, p. 2; Worcester, September 9, MS, Sept. 6, 1781. vol. XI, no. 539, p. 3; Boston, September 3, PEP, Sept. 17, 1781. vol. VII, no. 774, p. 151; PP, Sept. 18, 1781. vol. X, no. 783, p. 2; New-York, September 24, NYG, Sept. 24, 1781, no. 1562, p. 2; New-York, September 12, RGG, Oct. 18, 1781, no. 138, p. 1; Boston, August 27, Prensa, Sept. 25, 1781. vol. VIII, no. 421, p. 1; Boston, September 6, MS, Sept. 13, 1781. vol. XI, no. 540, p. 2.

548   PJ, Sept. 15, 1781, no. 1422, p. 2; Extract of a Letter from Greenock, August 24, RGG, Nov. 22, 1781, no. 143, p. 3.

549   RG, Sept. 8, 1781, no. 516, p. 3; New-York, September 10, NYG, Sept. 10, 1781, no. 1560, p. 3.

550   Providence, September 15, PG, Sept. 15, 1781. vol. XVIII, no. 924, p. 3; MS Supplement, Sept. 20, 1781. vol. XI, no. 541, p. 3.

551   New-York, September 10, NYG, Sept. 10, 1781, no. 1560, p. 3.

552   Selesky. vol. 1, pp. 206–210; Fremont-Barnes. vol. 1, pp. 218–221; Clowes. vol. 3. Dull, John R. *The French Navy and the American Revolution: a Study of Arms and Diplomacy, 1774–1787.* Princeton, NJ: Princeton University Press, 1975; Gardiner. James, William. *The British Navy in Adversity: A Study of the War of American Independence.* 1926. Reprint, New York: Russell and Russell, 1970; Larrabee, Harold A. *Decision at the Chesapeake.* New York: Clarkson N. Potter, 1964; Mackesy. Mahan, Alfred T. *The Influence of Sea Power upon History, 1660–1783.* 1890. reprint, New York: Dover, 1987; Palmer, Michael A. *Command at Sea: Naval Command and Control Since the Sixteenth Century.* Cambridge, MA: Harvard University Press, 2005; Rodger, N.AM. *The Command of the Ocean: A Naval History of Britain, 1649–1815.* New York and London: Norton, 2004; Syrett, David. *The Royal Navy in American Waters, 1775–1783.* Aldershot, UK: Scholar Press, 1989; Tilley, J. A. *The Royal Navy in the American Revolution.* Columbia: University of South Carolina Press, 1987; PP, Nov. 29, 1781. vol. XI, no. 813, p. 2; Providence, September 15, PG, Sept. 15, 1781. vol. XVIII, no. 924, p. 3; MS Supplement, Sept. 20, 1781. vol. XI, no. 541, p. 3; New-London, Sept. 10, CJ, Sept. 20, 1781, no. 725, p. 2; Boston, September 20, IC&UA, Sept. 20, 1781. vol. XIV, no. 682, p. 3; Extract of a Letter from Williamsburgh, September 9, 1781, PP, Sept. 20, 1781. vol. X, no. 784, p. 3; New-York, September 24, NYG, Sept. 24, 1781, no. 1562, p. 2; New-London, September 14, NJG, Sept. 26, 1781. vol. IV, no. 196, p. 2.

553   PJ, Jan. 2, 1782, no. 1453, p. 2; Extract of a Letter from Liverpool, Oct. 6, NYG, Dec. 24, 1781, no. 1575, p. 2.

554   New-York, September 10, NYG, Sept. 10, 1781, no. 1560, p. 3.

555   PJ, Dec. 15, 1781, no. 1448, p. 2; London, September 11, PP, Dec. 13, 1781. vol. XI, no. 819, p. 2.

556   Hermione, pp. 233–234.

557   PJ, Dec. 12, 1781, no. 1447, p. 3; Extract of a Letter from a Gentleman in Cadix, September 11, 1781, PP, Dec. 11, 1781. vol. XI, no. 818, p. 3; Baltimore February 5, MJ, Feb. 5, 1782. vol. IX, no. 440, p. 2; Foreign Intelligence. London, November 20, PP, Feb. 26, 1782. vol. XI, no. 851, p. 2; Fort-Royal, (Grenada) Feb. 14, NJG, Mar. 27, 1782. vol. V, no. 222, p. 2; London, January 8, RG, Mar. 6, 1782, no. 567, p. 2.

558   Boston, September 20, IC&UA, Sept. 20, 1781. vol. XIV, no. 682, p. 3; Providence, September 22, PG, Sept. 22, 1781. vol. XVIII, no. 925, p. 3.

559   Extract of a Letter from Dover, October 4, PG, Jan. 12, 1782. vol. XIX, no. 941, p. 2.

560   Extract of a Letter from St. Mary's Scilly, Sept. 27, RGG, Dec. 27, 1781, no. 148, p. 1.

561   ibid.

562 London, September 29, BEP, Dec. 15, 1781. vol. I, no. 9, p. 3; CC, Jan. 1, 1782, no. 884, p. 2; PAG. Jan. 2, 1782, p. 2.

563 PJ, Sept. 29, 1781, no. 1426, p. 2.

564 London, Oct. 2, NYG, Jan. 7, 1782, no. 1577, p. 2.

565 From the East-India Office, Sept. 27, 1781, PP, Jan. 5, 1782. vol. XI, no. 829, p. 2.

566 PJ, Dec. 26, 1781, no. 1451, p. 3; London, Oct. 18, NYG, Jan. 7, 1782, no. 1577, p. 3; Kaminkow, p. 220.

567 Extract of a Letter from Plymouth, Oct. 5, NYG, Dec. 31, 1781, no. 1576, p. 2; PJ, Oct. 13, 1781, p. 2; Extract of a Letter from Plymouth, Oct 14, NYG, Jan. 21, 1782, no. 1579, p. 2.

568 PJ, Dec. 26, 1781, no. 1451, p. 3; London, October 3, MJ, Feb. 12, 1782. vol. IX, no. 441, p. 2; From the *Freeman's Journal*, Dated Philadelphia Feb. 6, RG, Feb. 13, 1782, no. 561, p. 2; From *Rivington's New-York Royal Gazette*, January 9. Dublin, October 16, PP, Jan. 19, 1782. vol. XI, no. 835, p. 3; IL, Feb. 11, 1782. vol. IV, no. 196, p. 2.

569 Baltimore, October 16, MS, Nov. 8, 1781. vol. XI, no. 548, p. 3; *Norwich Packet*, p. 3. vol. IX, no. 422

570 Extract of a Letter from Torbay, October 16, NYG, Jan. 21, 1782, no. 1579, p. 2.

571 London, Oct. 18, NYG, Jan. 7, 1782, no. 1577, p. 3; London, October 2, RG, Jan. 12, 1782, no. 552, p. 1; London, PP, Jan. 31, 1782. vol. XI, no. 840, p. 2; London, Oct. 18, NYG, Jan. 7, 1782, no. 1577, p. 3; London, October 2, RG, Jan. 12, 1782, no. 552, p. 1; London, PP, Jan. 31, 1782. vol. XI, no. 840, p. 2.

572 NBBAS: vol. 3, pp. 379–380; Lewis, James A. *Neptune's Militia: The Frigate South Carolina during the American Revolution.* Kent, Ohio, Kent State University Press, 1999. pp. 45–46. Gruber, Ira D. "The Final Campaign of the American Revolution: Rise and Fall of the Spanish Bahamas." *Journal of Southern History.* vol. 58, no. 4, 1992. p. 114.

573 List of Prizes Taken by the Squadron of the Count De Grasse, in the Chesapeake, FJ, Oct. 24, 1781, no. XXVII, p. 3.

574 Boston, November 19, IL, Nov. 19, 1781. vol. IV, no. 182, p. 3.

575 Latouche, p. 123.

576 Extract of a Letter from Waterford, Nov. 5, PP, Feb. 23, 1782. vol. XI, no. 850, p. 2.

577 Extract of a Letter Dated Antwerp. Oct. 18, IL, Feb. 25, 1782. vol. IV, no. 199, p. 3; Extract of a Letter from Madrid, October 6, NP, Mar. 7, 1782, no. 439, p. 1.

578 PJ, Dec. 8, 1781, no. 1446, p. 3; New-York, Dec. 1. NM, Dec. 22, 1781, no. 1056, p. 3; PJ, Dec. 15, 1781, no. 1448, p. 3; New-York, November 30, PP, Dec. 13, 1781. vol. XI, no. 819, p. 3.

579 PJ, Dec. 26, 1781, no. 1451, p. 3; New-York, December 17. Extract of a Letter, London, Oct. 1, 1781, NYG, Dec. 17, 1781, no. 1574, p. 3.

580 Extract from the *London Gazette*, Dated Saturday 19th January, 1782, PP, Mar. 16, 1782. vol. XI, no. 859, p. 3; Captain Stirling's Letter, Giving an Account of the Loss of His Majesty's Ship *Savage.* Lancaster, Sept. 23, 1781, PP, Mar. 21, 1782. vol. XI, no. 861, p. 2; Clowes. vol. 3; Gardiner, Ireland, Bernard. *Naval warfare in the age of sail.* London: Collins, 2000; James, William. *The naval history of Great Britain: during the French Revolutionary and Napoleonic wars.* Mechanicsburg, PA: Stackpole, 2003; James, William. *The British Navy in Adversity: A Study of the War of American Independence.* 1926. Reprint, New York: Russell and Russell, 1970; Syrett, David. *The Royal Navy in American Waters, 1775–1783.* Aldershot, UK: Scholar Press, 1989; Fremont-Barnes. vol. 4, p. 1279. London. Admiralty-Office, December 18, 1781, PP, Mar. 14, 1782. vol. XI, no. 858, p. 1; London, PJ, Mar. 16, 1782, no. 1474, p. 2; The following Are the Terms Proposed by the Dutch Ministry, Appointed to Treat with the Russian Ambassador. SG. April 11, 1782. vol. I, no. 26, p. 2; MS, April 11, 1782. vol. XII, no. 571, p. 3; Philadelphia,

April 3. MS, April 18, 1782. vol. XII, no. 572, p. 3; Salem, April 4, SG, April 4, 1782. vol. I, no. 25, p. 3; New-London, March 12, MS, April 4, 1782. vol. XII, no. 570, p. 3.

581   PJ, Dec. 29, 1781, no. 1452, p. 3.

582   Extract of a Letter from Clyde, Dec. 26, NYG, April 8, 1782, no. 1590, p. 2.

583   Chatham, February 23, MS, Feb. 28, 1782. vol. XI, no. 564, p. 3.

584   London, January 8, RG, Mar. 6, 1782, no. 567, p. 2.

585   London, January 8, 1782, RG, April 13, 1782, no. 578, p. 3.

586   London, August 13, PG, Nov. 2, 1782. vol. XIX, no. 983, p. 1; New-York, October 16, PP, Oct. 22, 1782. vol. XI, no. 953, p. 2; We Have Received the Leiden Papers to August 20, PG, Oct. 26, 1782. vol. XIX, no. 982, p. 3; From *Rivington's Royal Gazette*. New York October 12, MJ, Oct. 29, 1782. vol. IX, no. 478, p. 2.

587   New-York, January 23, RG, Jan. 23, 1782, no. 555, p. 3.

588   London, Jan. 24, NYG, April 22, 1782, no. 1592, p. 2; NJG, May 1, 1782. vol. V, no. 2; London, Jan. 24. IC. May 2, 1782. vol. XIV, no. 714, pp. 2, 27; London, January 20, SG, May 2, 1782. vol. I, no. 29, p. 2.

589   PJ, Jan. 26, 1782, no. 1460, p. 2; New-York, PP, Jan. 26, 1782. vol. XI, no. 838, p. 3; Philadelphia, February 6, FJ, Feb. 6, 1782, no. XLII, p. 3; From the *Freeman's Journal*, Dated Philadelphia Feb. 6, RG, Feb. 13, 1782, no. 561, p. 2; Philadelphia, Feb. 6, CC, Feb. 19, 1782, no. 891, p. 2.

590   Foreign Intelligence. Oviedo, February 20, PP, May 23, 1782. vol. XI, no. 888, p. 1.

591   New-London, March 15, CJ, Mar. 28, 1782, no. 752, p. 3; Salem, April 4, SG, April 4, 1782. vol. I, no. 25, p. 3; New-London, March 12, MS, April 4, 1782. vol. XII, no. 570, p. 3; New-London, March 22, SG, April 18, 1782. vol. I, no. 27, p. 4.

592   Paris, February 18, NYG, May 6, 1782, no. 1594, p. 1.

593   PJ, Mar. 2, 1782, no. 1470, p. 2; New-York, February 18, PP, Mar. 2, 1782. vol. XI, no. 853, p. 2; New York February 18. MJ. Mar. 12, 1782. vol. IX, no. 445, p. 2; New-York, Feb. 23, NP, Mar. 21, 1782, no. 441, p. 2; New-York, April 22, NYG, April 22, 1782, no. 1592, p. 3.

594   Foreign Intelligence. London, November 20, PP, Feb. 26, 1782. vol. XI, no. 851, p. 2; The following Improvement in the Mariner's Compass is Proposed to Those Who Are Interested in the Use of That Valuable Instrument, NJG, Mar. 13, 1782. vol. V, no. 220, p. 2.

595   New-London, May 31, CG&UI, May 31, 1782. vol. XIX, no. 968, p. 3.

596   New-London, March 29, CG&UI, Mar. 29, 1782. vol. XIX, no. 959, p. 3; Boston, April 8, IL, April 8, 1782. vol. IV, no. 205, p. 3; Boston, April 12, SG, April 11, 1782. vol. I, no. 26, p. 3.

597   Extract of a Letter from Gosport, March 11, PP, May 7, 1782. vol. XI, no. 881, p. 3; London March 1, MG, May 16, 1782. vol. XXXVII, no. 1844, p. 1.

598   Foreign Intelligence. London, March 16, IG, June 8, 1782, no. 9, p. 2.

599   Prizes Arrived Here since Our Last, RG, April 6, 1782, no. 576, p. 3; New-York, April 3, PP, April 13, 1782. vol. XI, no. 871, p. 3.

600   London, March 28, PP, July 4, 1782. vol. XI, no. 906, p. 2; IG. July 6, 1782, no. 13, p. 3; London, March 26, NJG, July 17, 1782. vol. V, no. 238, p. 2.

601   Richmond, April 6, PP, April 16, 1782. vol. XI, no. 872, p. 3; CJ, May 2, 1782, no. 757, p. 1.

602   PJ, April 17, 1782, no. 1483, p. 2; New-York, April 8, NYG, April 8, 1782, no. 1590, p. 3; New-York, April 12, SG, April 26, 1782. vol. I, no. 28, p. 3; IC&UA, April 26, 1782. vol. XIV, no. 713, p. 3.

603   London, NYG, April 8, 1782, no. 1590, p. 2.

604   ibid.

605   New-York, April 16, NYG, April 15, 1782, no. 1591, p. 3.

606 Baltimore April 16, MJ, April 16, 1782. vol. IX, no. 450, p. 2; PEP, April 22, 1782. vol. VIII, no. 817, p. 41; RG, May 4, 1782, no. 584, p. 3; Richmond, (Virginia) April 16, PG, May 4, 1782. vol. XIX, no. 957, p. 3; By the Hartford Post. Richmond, (Virginia) April 16, MS, May 2, 1782. vol. XII, no. 574, p. 3.

607 London, PP, April 16, 1782. vol. XI, no. 872, p. 2; London, December 14, MJ, April 23, 1782. vol. IX, no. 451, p. 1.

608 London, April 23, FJ, July 31, 1782. vol. II, no. LXVII, p. 2; New York July 24, MJ, Aug. 6, 1782. vol. IX, no. 466, p. 1.

609 Admiralty-Office, April 30, 1782, NP, Aug. 15, 1782 p. 1.

610 PP, Aug. 6, 1782. vol. XI, no. 920, p. 3; PP, June 1, 1782. vol. XI, no. 892, p. 2; SG. June 13, 1782. vol. I, no. 35, p. 4; Kingston, (Jamaica), SG, June 13, 1782. vol. I, no. 35, p. 4; By the *Hartford Post*, MS, June 13, 1782. vol. XII, no. 580, p. 2.

611 House of Commons, PJ, July 24, 1782, no. 1511, p. 2; London, August 9, NYG, Oct. 21, 1782, no. 1618, p. 2; From the *London Gazette*, April 27, PG, Aug. 3, 1782. vol. XIX, no. 970, p. 4.

612 New York July 24, MJ, Aug. 6, 1782. vol. IX, no. 466, p. 1.

613 New-York, July 15, NYG, July 15, 1782, no. 1604, p. 3.

614 Weymouth, May 15, PP, Aug. 6, 1782. vol. XI, no. 920, p. 3; Extract of a Letter from Gosport, May 24, PP, Aug. 13, 1782. vol. XI, no. 923, p. 2.

615 Charlestown, (S. Carolina) July 3, NP, Sept. 12, 1782, no. 466, p. 4; By the *Hartford Post*. Charlestown, (South-Carolina) July 6, MS, Sept. 19, 1782. vol. XII, no. 594, p. 2; Salem, September 19, SG, Sept. 19, 1782. vol. I, no. 49, p. 3; NHG. Sept. 21, 1782. vol. XXVI, no. 1351, p. 3; Boston, September 23, BG, Sept. 23, 1782, no. 1465, p. 3; Boston, September 26, CJWA, Sept. 26, 1782, no. CCCXLV, p. 3.

616 PJ, June 28, 1780, no. 1346, p. 2; PJ, July 12, 1780, no. 1348, p. 3; BG. June 19, 1780, no. 1347, p. 3; Boston, June 12, IL, June 12, 1780. vol. II, no. 105, p. 3; Boston, June 8, MS, June 15, 1780. vol. X, no. 475, p. 2; NJG, June 28, 1780. vol. III, no. 131, p. 3; Boston, May 29, PP, June 24, 1780, p. 2; Newport, June 10, PP, June 27, 1780, p. 3; NJG, June 28, 1780. vol. III, no. 131, p. 3; Providence, June 28, AJ, June 28, 1780. vol. II, no. 68, p. 3; Boston, June 19, NP, June 22, 1780, no. 351, p. 3; Boston, June 15, CJ, June 22, 1780, no. 660, p. 3; Boston, June 23, VG, July 12, 1780, no. 71, p. 2; PP, July 4, 1780, p. 2; Boston, June 15, NJG, July 5, 1780. vol. III, no. 132, p. 2.

617 American News. Salem, June 20, PP, May 11, 1782. vol. XI, no. 883, p. 5; PP, July 9, 1782. vol. XI, no. 908, p. 3; Salem, June 20, SG, June 20, 1782. vol. I, no. 36, p. 3; NHG. June 22, 1782. vol. XXVI, no. 1338, p. 3, IL, June 24, 1782. vol. V, no. 216, p. 3; BEP. June 22, 1782. vol. I, no. XXXVI, p. 3; Boston, June 24, BG, June 24, 1782, no. 1452, p. 3; Boston, June 20, MS, June 27, 1782. vol. XII, no. 582, p. 2.

618 Paris, July 4, SG, Sept. 19, 1782. vol. I, no. 49, p. 4; Paris, (France) July 6, MS, Sept. 19, 1782. vol. XII, no. 594, p. 2; July 6. Extract of a Letter from Count De Guichen, to the Marquis De Castries, Secretary of State for the Marine, PG, Sept. 21, 1782. vol. XIX, no. 977, p. 2; PP, Sept. 24, 1782. vol. XI, no. 941, p. 2; FJ. Sept. 25, 1782. vol. II, no. LXXV, p. 3; NYG, Oct. 7, 1782. vol. I, no. 19, p. 2; NJG, Oct. 9, 1782. vol. V, no. 250, p. 1; Extract of a Letter from a Merchant in Nantz, Dated July 16, 1782, IC&UA, Oct. 3, 1782. vol. XV, no. 761, p. 3; CG&UI, Oct. 4, 1782. vol. XIX, no. 986, p. 2; PEP, Oct. 14, 1782. vol. VIII, no. 867, p. 152; By the *Hartford Post*. Philadelphia, Sept. 10, MS, Oct. 3, 1782. vol. XII, no. 596, p. 3.

619 Extract of a Letter from Edward Pellow, Esquire, Commanding His Majesty's Ship the *Artois*, PP, Oct. 24, 1782. vol. XI, no. 954, p. 1.

620 Salem, August 15, MS, Aug. 29, 1782. vol. XII, no. 591, p. 2.

621   PJ, Oct. 12, 1782, no. 1533, p. 2; Extract of a Letter from Dublin, June 13, NYG, Oct. 7, 1782, no. 1616, p. 2.

622   London, June 25, NYG, Sept. 30, 1782, no. 1615, p. 2.

623   PJ, July 31, 1782, no. 1513, p. 2; New-York, July 15, NYG, July 15, 1782, no. 1604, p. 3; From *Rivington's Royal Gazette*, Dated New-York, July 17, PP, July 27, 1782. vol. XI, no. 916, p. 2.

624   House of Commons, PJ, July 24, 1782, no. 1511, p. 2.

625   PJ, Oct. 9, 1782, no. 1532, p. 2; London, June 15, NM, Aug. 30, 1782, no. 1092, p. 2; Salem, September 19, SG, Sept. 19, 1782. vol. I, no. 49, p. 3; NHG, Sept. 21, 1782. vol. XXVI, no. 1351, p. 3; Philadelphia Paper of the 4th Instant, Contains the following Comical Anecdote, IL, Sept. 23, 1782. vol. V, no. 229, p. 3; Boston, September 23, BG, Sept. 23, 1782, no. 1465, p. 3.

626   MS, Sept. 5, 1782. vol. XII, no. 592, p. 1; New-York, August 3, RG, Aug. 3, 1782, no. 611, p. 3; PP, Aug. 8, 1782. vol. XI, no. 921, p. 3; IG. Aug. 10, 1782, no. 18, p. 3; MJ. Aug. 13, 1782. vol. IX, no. 466, p. 2; BEP. Aug. 24, 1782. vol. I, no. XLV, p. 4; New York July 24, MJ, Aug. 6, 1782. vol. IX, no. 466, p. 1; Philadelphia, August 7, FJ, Aug. 7, 1782. vol. II, no. LXVIII, p. 3; New-York, August 1, CC, Aug. 13, 1782, no. 916, p. 3; New-York, August 1, IC&UA, Aug. 15, 1782. vol. XIV, no. 754, p. 3; London, May 28. MAG. Aug. 20, 1782. vol. I, no. 15, p. 2; York, August 2, MG, Aug. 20, 1782. vol. I, no. 15, p. 2; Providence, August 10, PG, Aug. 10, 1782. vol. XIX, no. 971, p. 3.

627   St. John's, Antigua, July 20, NYG, Sept. 9, 1782, no. 1612, p. 2.

628   London, May 28. MAG. Aug. 20, 1782. vol. I, no. 15, p. 2; Boston, August 12, PEP, Aug. 27, 1782. vol. VIII, no. 854, p. 124. Extract of a Letter from New [Illegible]. MAG. Aug. 27, 1782. vol. I, no. 16, p. 3; Boston, NJG, Aug. 28, 1782. vol. V, no. 244, p. 2.

629   London, August 9, MS, Nov. 14, 1782. vol. XII, no. 602, p. 1.

630   Philadelphia, August 21, FJ, Aug. 21, 1782. vol. II, no. LXX, p. 3.

631   Extract of a Letter from [Illegible] April 18, RAG, Oct. 22, 1782. vol. VIII, no. DXXIII, p. 3.

632   MS, Sept. 5, 1782. vol. XII, no. 592, p. 1; Boston, August 29, CJWA, Aug. 29, 1782, no. CCCXLI, p. 3.

633   London, Aug. 30, NYG, Oct. 28, 1782, no.1619, p. 3.

634   Salem, October 17. NYGNA. Nov. 4, 1782. vol. I, no. 23, p. 3.

635   Extract of a Letter from Torbay, October 16, NYG, Jan. 21, 1782, no. 1579, p. 2.

636   Extract of a Letter from Margate. Sept. 2, 1783, NYG, Nov. 4, 1782, no. 1620, p. 2;

637   PJ, Sept. 18, 1782, no. 1526, p. 3; Philadelphia, Sept. 19, PP, Sept. 19, 1782. vol. XI, no. 939, p. 3; Philadelphia Sept. 18, MJ, Sept. 24, 1782. vol. IX, no. 473, p. 3; Boston, September 26, CJWA, Sept. 26, 1782, no. CCCXLV, p. 3; Boston, September 23, CG&UI, Sept. 27, 1782. vol. XIX, no. 985, p. 3; PG. Sept. 28, 1782. vol. XIX, no. 978, p. 3; CC, Oct. 1, 1782, no. 923, p. 2; Trenton, October 2, NJG, Oct. 2, 1782. vol. V, no. 249, p. 3; Boston, September 23, MS, Oct. 3, 1782. vol. XII, no. 596, p. 4; Boston, September 23, CJ, Oct. 3, 1782, no. 779, p. 3; New-York, September 23, PP, Oct. 3, 1782. vol. XI, no. 945, p. 3; New York, Sept. 28, PEP, Oct. 4, 1782. vol. VIII, no. 864, p. 146; By Order of the Honorable Lieut. General Leslie, PG, Oct. 5, 1782. vol. XIX, no. 979, p. 3; New-York, October 9, RG, Oct. 9, 1782, no. 630, PP, Oct. 15, 1782. vol. XI, no. 950, p. 2; New-York, September 28, CG&UI, Oct. 11, 1782. vol. XIX, no. 987, p. 1; New York, Sept. 23. MAG. Oct. 15, 1782. vol. I, no. 23, p. 2; NM. Oct. 19, 1782, no. 1099, p. 2; SG. Oct. 24, 1782. vol. II, no. 54, p. 2; Kingston, (Jamaica) November 23. SCWA. April 9, 1783. vol. I, no. 8, p. 2.

638   The reports of Latouche and Vallongue on the loss of the *Aigle* are in the Archives Nationales de la Marine 84 185, 202 and 278. Monaque, Rémi. *Latouche-Tréville, 1745–1804: l'amiral qui défiait Nelson*. Paris: SPM, 2000 pp. 164–168; Biron, Armand-Louis de Gontaut, duc de. *Memoirs of the Duc de Lauzun*. (Eyewitness accounts of the American Revolution). New York:

New York Times, Arno Press, c1969 p. 218; New-London, Sept. 13, CC, Sept. 17, 1782, no. 921, p. 3.

639   London. from the *Courier De L'Europe*, November 22, 1782, PP, Mar. 1, 1783. vol. XII, no. 1009, p. 2.

640   Extract of a Letter from Cadix, Sept. 9, 1782, NYG, Feb. 3, 1783, no. 1633, p. 2.

641   August 29, RAG, Dec. 3, 1782. vol. VIII, no. DXXXV, p. 1.

642   London, September 24, PP, Dec. 5, 1782. vol. XI, no. 972, p. 2.

643   MS, Sept. 19, 1782. vol. XII, no. 594, p. 2.

644   Extract of a Letter from Captain Moulton, of the *True Love*, (One of the Jamaica Fleet), FJ, Jan. 8, 1783. vol. II, no. XC, p. 3.

645   PJ, Oct. 2, 1782, no. 1530, p. 3; New-York, September 30, NYG, Sept. 30, 1782, no. 1615, p. 3; New-York, September 23, PP, Oct. 3, 1782. vol. XI, no. 945, p. 3.

646   London, November 2, IG, Feb. 22, 1783, no. 65, p. 2.

647   New-York, October 5, RG, Oct. 5, 1782, no. 629, p. 3; New-York, October 3, NYG, Oct. 7, 1782, no. 1616, p. 2; New-York, October 4, PP, Oct. 12, 1782. vol. XI, no. 949, p. 3; Philadelphia, Oct. 5. MAG. Oct. 29, 1782. vol. I, no. 25, p. 2.

648   Latouche, pp. 101–103.

649   October 19. Extract of a Letter from Paris, Oct. 10, NYG, Dec. 23, 1782, no. 1627, p. 2.

650   Philadelphia, December 26, 1782, PEP, Jan. 6, 1783. vol. IX, no. 886, p. 2.

651   Lucia Gazette. Carenage (St. Lucia) Nov. 2, PP, Feb. 18, 1783. vol. XII, no. 1004, p. 2.

652   London, October 28, IG, Feb. 4, 1783, no. 60, p. 3; NJG, Feb. 12, 1783. vol. VI, no. 268, p. 2; London, October 15. NYGNA. Feb. 17, 1783. vol. I, no. 38, p. 2.

653   London. from the *Courier De L'Europe*, November 22, 1782, PP, Mar. 1, 1783. vol. XII, no. 1009, p. 2.

654   Extract of a Letter from Captain Kempthorn, Commander of His Majesty's Pacquet Boat the *Antelope*, Dated Port L'Orient, Octo. 21, PP, Jan. 23, 1783. vol. XI, no. 993, p. 2.

655   PJ, Mar. 15, 1783, no. 1574, p. 1.

656   London. List of Fleet under Lord Howe, RG, Nov. 20, 1782, no. 642, p. 2; London, September 10, CG&UI, Dec. 13, 1782. vol. XIX, no. 996, p. 4.

657   London. from the *Courier De L'Europe*, November 22, 1782, PP, Mar. 1, 1783. vol. XII, no. 1009, p. 2.

658   London, December 28, NYG, Mar. 31, 1783, no. 1641, p. 2.

659   Extract of a Letter from Lisbon, Dec. 3, NYG, Mar. 31, 1783, no. 1641, p. 2.

660   London, RG, Dec. 7, 1782, no. 647.

661   PJ, Feb. 22, 1783, no. 1568, p. 3; New-York, February 13, NYG, Feb. 17, 1783, no. 1635, p. 3.

662   Extract of a Letter from Liverpool, Dec. 28, NYG, Mar. 31, 1783, no. 1641, p. 2.

663   New-York, January 8, NYG, Jan. 13, 1783, no. 1630, p. 1; New-York, January 7, PP, Jan. 14, 1783. vol. XI, no. 989, p. 3.

664   PJ, Jan. 29, 1783, no. 152, p. 2; New-York, Jan. 22, RG, Jan. 22, 1783, no. 660, p. 3; PP, Jan. 28, 1783. vol. XI, no. 995, p. 2; New-York, January 22, SG, Feb. 13, 1783. vol. II, no. 70, p. 2; PG. Feb. 15, 1783. vol. XX, no. 998, p. 3; CJ, Feb. 20, 1783, no. 799, p. 2.

665   PJ, Sept. 20, 1783, no. 1627, p. 2.

666   New-York, Jan. 22, CJ, Feb. 20, 1783, no. 799, p. 2.

667   From the *Royal Gazette*, New-York, January 15, NJG, Jan. 29, 1783. vol. VI, no. 266, p. 3; From a Spanish Paper, October 30, 1782, IG, Feb. 1, 1783, no. 59, p. 3; New-York, Jan. 22, CJ, Feb. 20, 1783, no. 799, p. 2.

668   Philadelphia, February 1, IG, Feb. 1, 1783, no. 59, p. 3; NJG, Feb. 5, 1783. vol. VI, no. 267, p. 3.

669　PJ, Jan. 29, 1783, no. 152, p. 2; New-York, Jan. 22, RG, Jan. 22, 1783, no. 660, p. 3; PP, Jan. 28, 1783. vol. XI, no. 995, p. 2; SG. Feb. 13, 1783. vol. II, no. 70, p. 2; PG. Feb. 15, 1783. vol. XX, no. 998, p. 3.

670　Philadelphia, March 27, PP, Mar. 27, 1783. vol. XII, no. 1020, p. 3; PJ, Mar. 1, 1783, no. 1570, p. 2, p. 5. Extract of a Letter from Basseterre, Guadaloupe, to a Gentleman at Baltimore, in Maryland, Jan. 27, PP, Mar. 4, 1783. vol. XII, no. 1010, p. 2; PP, Mar. 11, 1783. vol. XII, no. 1013, p. 3; New-York, February 19, CG&UI, Mar. 7, 1783. vol. XX, no. 1008, p. 2; Chatham, March 5, MS, Mar. 20, 1783. vol. XIII, no. 620, p. 3.

671　New-York, February 25, CG&UI, Mar. 7, 1783. vol. XX, no. 1008, p. 3.

672　PJ, Mar. 1, 1783, no. 1570, p. 6; RG, Mar. 1, 1783, no. 671, p. 3; New-York, March 1, PP, Mar. 6, 1783. vol. XII, no. 1011, p. 2; New-York, February 19, CG&UI, Mar. 7, 1783. vol. XX, no. 1008, p. 2.

673　Providence, March 8, PG, Mar. 8, 1783. vol. XX, no. 1001, p. 3; IL, Mar. 17, 1783. vol. V, no. 254, p. 3; New Port, March 8, NM, Mar. 8, 1783, no. 1119, p. 3; Philadelphia, March 15, IG, Mar. 15, 1783, no. 71, p. 2.

674　*American News.* New-York, March 5, IG, Mar. 11, 1783, no. 70, p. 3.

675　PJ, Mar. 29, 1783, no. 1578, p. 3.

676　St. Christophers, February 12, 1783, PP, April 3, 1783. vol. XII, no. 1023, p. 3.

677　PJ, April 9, 1783, no. 1781, p. 3; New-York, April 2, PP, April 8, 1783. vol. XII, no. 1025, p. 2.

Chapter 5

1　CJ. vol. LXXI (October 2, 1777) p. 4; Copy of a letter from General Sir William Howe to Lord George Germain, dated head-quarters, Germantown, October 4, 1777. LG, *Extraordinary*, MS (March 12,1778) VIII: 358, p. 13.

2　Selesky. vol. I, pp. 101–106; Fremont-Barnes. vol. I, pp. 129–133; André, John. *Major André's Journal: Operations of the British Army under Lieutenant Generals Sir William Howe and Sir Henry Clinton June 1777 to November 1778.* Tarrytown, NY: William Abbatt, 1930, New York Times & Arno Press, 1968; Black, Jeremy. *War for America: the Fight for Independence.* Stroud, UK: Alan Sutton, 1991; Canby, Henry S. *The Brandywine.* New York: Farrar and Rinehart, 1941; Carrington, Henry B. *Battles of the American Revolution 1775–1781, Including Battle Maps and Charts of the American Revolution.* New York: Promontory Press, 1974, originally published in 1877 and 1881; Conway, Stephen. *The War of American Independence, 1775–1783.* London: Arnold, 1995; Ewald, Johann. *Diary of the American War: A Hessian Journal,* Captain Johann Ewald, Translated and edited by Joseph P. Tustin. New Haven and London: Yale University Press, 1979; Greene, Francis V. *The Revolutionary War and the Military Policy of the United States.* New York: Scribner, 1911; Higginbotham, Don. *The War of American Independence: Military Attitudes, Policies, and Practice, 1763–1789.* New York: Macmillan, 1971; Lengel, Edward G. *General George Washington, A Military Life.* New York: Random House, 2005; Mackesy. Reed, John F. *Campaign to Valley Forge: July 1, 1777–December 19, 1777.* Philadelphia: University of Pennsylvania Press, 1965; Smith, Samuel Stelle, *The Battle of Brandywine.* Monmouth Beach, NJ: Philip Freneau Press, 1976; Taafe, Stephen. *The Philadelphia Campaign, 1777–1778.* Lawrence, KS: University Press of Kansas, 2003. Townshend, Joseph. *The Battle of Brandywine.* 1846, New York: New York Times, 1969; Ward. pp. 341–354; *Continental Journal.* LXXI (October 2, 1777), p. 4; Copy of a letter from General Sir William Howe to Lord George Germain, dated head-quarters, Germantown, October 4, 1777. *The London Gazette, Extraordinary; The Massachusetts Spy: Or, American Oracle of Liberty* (March 12,1778) vol. VIII, no. 358, p. 13.

3   Montresor. p. 474.

4   *Documents Relating to the Revolutionary History, State of New Jersey.* Edited by William S. Stryker. Trenton: The John L. Murphy Publishing Co. 1901. Series 2. vol. 2, p. 129; Stewart, Frank J. *Salem a Century Ago.* Salem, NJ: Salem Standard and Jerseyman, 1934. vol. 3, pp. 47, 65, 76–77, 81; Sickler, Joseph Sheppard. *The History of Salem County, New Jersey.* Salem, NJ: Sunbeam Publishing Company, 1937. p. 146.

5   Sparks. *Writings of Washington* pp. v, 368 in Tower, Charlemagne. *The Marquis de la Fayette in the American Revolution.* 2nd ed. Philadelphia: J.B. Lippincott Co. 1901. vol. I, p. 327.

6   Selesky. vol. 1, pp. 55–56; Fremont-Barnes. vol. 1, pp. 83–84; Gottschalk, Louis. *Lafayette joins the American Army.* Chicago: University of Chicago Press, 1937; Jackson, John W. *With the British Army in Philadelphia, 1777–1778.* San Rafael, Calif.: Presidio Press, 1979; Lengel, Edward G. *General George Washington, A Military Life.* New York: Random House, 2005; Nelson, Paul David. *General James Grant: Scottish Soldier and Royal Governor of East Florida.* Gainesville: University Press of Florida, 1993; Nelson, Paul David. *Sir Charles Grey, First Earl Grey: Royal Soldier, Family Patriarch.* Madison, NJ: Fairleigh Dickinson University Press, 1996; Montresor, pp. 492–493; Taaffe, Stephen R. *The Philadelphia Campaign, 1777–1778.* Lawrence, KS: University Press of Kansas, 2003.

7   Martin, Joseph Plumb. *Private Yankee Doodle, being a narrative of some of the adventures, dangers, and sufferings of a Revolutionary Soldier,* edited by George F. Scheer, originally published in Hallowell, Me. 1830, anonymously. (Republished, Boston, 1962); *A narrative of some of the adventures, dangers and sufferings of a Revolutionary soldier.* (Eyewitness accounts of the American Revolution). New York: New York Times, 1968. pp. 132–133.

8   Selesky. vol. 2, pp. 733–740; *An Account of the Action from Brandywine to Monmouth: A Seminar on the Impact of the Revolutionary War on the Delaware Valley.* Philadelphia: Council of American Revolutionary Sites, 1997; Fremont-Barnes. vol. 3, pp. 806–810; André, Major John, *Major Andre's Journal: Operations of the British Army under Lieutenant Generals Sir William Howe, and Sir Henry Clinton, June 1777, to November 1778,* edited by Henry Cabot Lodge, Boston, 1902, Tarrytown, NY: William Abbatt, 1930; Black, Jeremy. *War for America: the fight for independence.* Stroud, UK: Alan Sutton, 1991; Blanco, Richard L. ed. *The War of the Revolution, 1775–1783: an encyclopedia.* New York: Garland Pub. 1993; Carrington, Henry B. *Battles of the American Revolution 1775–1781, including battle maps and charts of the American Revolution.* New York: Promontory Press, 1974, originally published in 1877 and 1881; Clinton. Conway, Stephen. *The War of American Independence, 1775–1783.* London: Arnold, 1995; Ewald; Higginbotham, Don. *The War of American Independence: Military Attitudes, Policies, and Practice, 1763–1789.* New York: Macmillan, 1971; Lengel, Edward G. *General George Washington, A Military Life.* New York: Random House, 2005; Lundin, Leonard. *Cockpit of the Revolution.* Princeton: Princeton University Press, 1940; Mackesy; Smith, Samuel Stelle. *The Battle of Monmouth.* Monmouth Beach, NJ: Philip Freneau Press, 1964; Stryker, William Scudder. *The Battle of Monmouth.* Port Washington, NY: Kennikat Press, 1927, 1970; Ward. pp. 576–586; Wood, W. J. *Battles of the Revolutionary War, 1775–1781.* Chapel Hill, NC: Algonquin, 1990.

9   Alberts, Robert. *George Rogers Clark and the Winning of the Old Northwest.* Washington, DC: National Park Service, 1975. Ward, pp. 850–865.

10   Mackenzie. vol. 2, p. 230; *Historic and Architectural Resources of Tiverton, Rhode Island: a preliminary report.* Providence: Rhode Island Historical Preservation Commission, 1983, p. 10; Mays; Stember, Sol. *The Bicentennial Guide to the American Revolution.* Saturday Review Press: New York, distributed by Dutton, 1794, s.l.: New York Times and Arno Press, 1969; NYJ. September 7, 1778; Moore. vol. 2, pp. 84–86; Providence, August 8, PG, Aug. 8, 1778. vol. XV, no. 762,

p. 3; IC&UA, Aug. 13, 1778. vol. XI, no. 521, p. 2; NP. Aug. 17, 1778, no. 255, p. 3; NHG. Aug. 18, 1778, p. 2; BG. Aug. 17, 1778, no. 1251, p. 2.

11 NYJ. September 7, 1778; Moore. vol. 2, pp. 84–86.

12 Burgan, Michael. *George Rogers Clark: American General* (Revolutionary War Leaders). New York: Chelsea House, 2001; Gelbert, Doug. *American Revolutionary War Sites, Memorials, Museums, and Library Collections: A State-By-State Guidebook to Places Open to the Public.* McFarland: Jefferson, NC, c.1998; Harding, Margery Herbling. *George Rogers Clark and his Men: military records, 1778–1784.* s. l.: Kentucky Historical Society, 1981; Lowell, Harrison H. *George Rogers Clark and the War in the West.* Lexington: University Press of Kentucky, 1976; Nester, William R. *Frontier War for American Independence.* Mechanicsburg, PA: Stackpole, 2004; Quaife, Milo Milton, ed. *The Conquest of the Illinois by George Rogers Clark.* Carbondale: Southern Illinois University Press, 2001; Scheer, George F. and Hugh F. Rankin. *Rebels and Redcoats.* Cleveland and New York: World Publishing Co. 1957; Starkey, Armstrong. *European and Native American Warfare, 1675–1815.* Oxford, UK: Routledge, 1998; Ward, pp. 850–865.

13 Hamilton, Henry. *Henry Hamilton and George Rogers Clark in the American Revolution with the Unpublished Journal of Lieut. Gov. Henry Hamilton.* Edited by John D. Barnhart. Crawfordsville, IN: R. E. Banta, 1951, pp. 189–192.

14 Ripley, pp. 233–234; Moultrie. vol. 2, pp. 3–5; Lipscomb, Terry W. *South Carolina Revolutionary Battles*: Part II (Names in South Carolina. vol. XXI (Winter 1974). South Carolina Historical Society, 1974. p. 25; NBBAS. vol. 1 pp. 299–300.

15 Selesky. vol. 2, pp. 1116–1120; Fremont-Barnes. vol. 4, pp. 1212–1214; Clinton; Dawson, Henry B. *The Assault on Stony Point, by General Anthony Wayne, July 16, 1779.* Morrisania, NY: Henry B. Dawson, 1863; Johnston, Henry P. *The Storming of Stony Point on the Hudson, Midnight, July 15, 1779: Its Importance in the Light of Unpublished Documents.* New York: James T. White, 1900; Nelson, Paul David. *Anthony Wayne: Soldier of the Early Republic.* Bloomington: Indiana University Press, 1985; Palmer, David R. *The River and the Rock: The History of Fortress West Point, 1775–1783.* New York: Greenwood, 1969; Skarsky, I. W. *The Revolution's Boldest Venture: The Story of "Mad Anthony" Wayne's Assault on Stony Point.* Port Washington, NY: Kennikat Press, 1965; Stillé, Charles J. *Major-General Anthony Wayne and the Pennsylvania Line in the Continental Army.* Philadelphia: Lippincott, 1893; Ward; Wildes, Harry Emerson. *Anthony Wayne: Trouble Shooter of the American Revolution.* New York: Harcourt, Brace, 1941.

16 NBBAS. vol. 1, p. 309; PAG. October 20, 1779, March 22, 1780.

17 Moultrie. vol. 2, p. 34; Morningstars. vol. 1, pp. 166–167.

18 PEP. vol. V. no. 635, October 26, 1779, p. 243.

19 Journal of the Garrison Regiment von Knoblauch, 1776–84. *Hessian Documents of the American Revolution.* Morristown National Historical Park.

20 Boatner. p. 192; Hough, Franklin Benjamin, ed. *The siege of Charleston by the British fleet and army, under the command of Admiral Arbuthnot and Sir Henry Clinton, which terminated with the surrender of that place on the 12th of May, 1780.* Albany, J. Munsell, 1867. p. 151; Hayes, John T. *The Saddlebag Almanac.* January 1997. vol. V, pp. 87, 91–92; Jones, Charles Colcock, ed. and tr. *The Siege of Savannah in 1779, as described in two contemporaneous journals of French officers in the fleet of Count d'Estaing.* Albany, N. Y. J. Munsell, 1874. p. 15; NBBAS. vol. 1, p. 310.

21 Jones, Charles Colcock. *The siege of Savannah by the fleet of Count d'Estaing in 1779* (Eyewitness accounts of the American Revolution). New York: New York Times, 1968, pp. 18–23, 28–29; Jones, Charles C. Jr. *The History of Georgia.* Boston: Houghton, Mifflin and Company, 1883. vol. II, p. 388; Lawrence, Alexander A. *Storm over Savannah: the story of Count d'Estaing and the siege of the town in 1779.* Athens: University of Georgia Press, 1951. p. 158; McCall, Hugh. *The History of Georgia, containing brief sketches of the most remarkable events up to the present day,*

1784. Savannah: Seymour & Williams, 1811, Atlanta, Cherokee Pub. Co. 1969, 1909. vol. II, p. 255; RRG. no. 334, Dec. 11, 1779; Dawson, Henry B. *Battles of the United States by Sea and Land*. New York: Johnson, Fry, & Company, 1858, pp. 562–569; CJ, 631 (December 1, 1779), p. 3; CG&UI, XVII: 838, p. 3.

22 Davies. vol. XVII, pp. 242–243; PAG. November 10, 1779, December 15, 1779, December 20, 1780; Hough, Franklin Benjamin, ed. *The siege of Charleston by the British fleet and army, under the command of Admiral Arbuthnot and Sir Henry Clinton, which terminated with the surrender of that place on the 12th of May, 1780*. Albany, J. Munsell, 1867. Spartanburg, SC: Reprint Company, 1975, pp. 151–152; Lawrence, Alexander A. *Storm Over Savannah, the Story of Count d'Estaing and the Siege of the town in* 1779. Athens: University of Georgia Press, 1951, pp. 116–117; NBBAS. vol. 1, p. 353; Muster rolls of Capt. Thomas French's company in Clark, Murtie June. *Loyalists in the Southern Campaign of the Revolutionary War*. Baltimore: Genealogical Publishing Co. Inc. 1981. vol. 3, pp. 10–14; Colonel John White to General Benjamin Lincoln, 2 October 1779, in Albert Sidney Britt Jr. et al. eds. *Selected Eighteenth Century Manuscripts*. Savannah: The Society of Colonial Wars in the State of Georgia, 1980, pp. 53–54, taken from Collection no. 859 (1), Georgia Historical Society, Savannah, Georgia. Account of the Ogeechee capture in (Charleston) *Gazette of the State of South Carolina*, 6 October 1779; "Anecdote," *The (Fort Hawkins, GA) Messenger*, 2 June 1823, White, George. *Historical Collections of Georgia*. New York: Pudney & Russell, 1855, Baltimore: Genealogical Pub. Co. 1969, pp. 367–369; Lee, Henry. *Memoirs of the War in the Southern Department of the United States*. ed. Robert E. Lee. New York: University Publishing Company, 1869, pp. 144–145; Thompson, Maurice. "A Boy's Strategy." *Atlanta Constitution Junior*. 17 November 1895; Morningstars. vol. 1, pp. 167–168.

23 Selesky. vol. II, pp. 1035–1040. Fremont-Barnes. vol. IV, pp. 1124–1130. Campbell, Colin, ed. *Journal of an Expedition against the Rebels in Georgia in North America under the Orders of Archibald Campbell, Esquire, Lieutenant Colonel of His Majesty's 71st Regiment, 1778*. Darien, GA: Ahantilly, 1981; Coleman, Kenneth. *The American Revolution in Georgia*. Athens: University of Georgia Press, 1958; Commager; Jones, Charles Colcock, Jr. *The siege of Savannah by the fleet of Count d'Estaing in 1779*. New York: New York Times 1968; Kennedy, Benjamin, ed. *Muskets, Cannon Balls, and Bombs: Nine Narratives of the Siege of Savannah in 1779*. Savannah, GA: Beehive, 1974; Lawrence, Alexander A. *Storm Over Savannah, the Story of Count d'Estaing and the Siege of the town in* 1779. University of Georgia Press, 1951; Searcy, Martha Condray. "General Robert Howe and the British Capture of Savannah in 1778." *Georgia Historical Quarterly*. 36 (December 1952): 303–327; Ward. pp. 688–694. Wilson, David K. *The Southern Strategy: Britain's Conquest of South Carolina and Georgia, 1775–1780*. Columbia: University of South Carolina Press, 2005; Major Alexander MacDonald of Kinlochmoidart, 71st Highlanders, to his wife Susannah (Campbell of Airds) MacDonald, Savannah. November 6, 1779, in the Robertson MacDonald of Kinlochmoidart Papers, MS3945, folios 58–59, National Library of Scotland. Edinburgh, Scotland; Duc De Castries, *Papiers de Famille* (Paris: Editions France-Empire, n. d.), 378. Benjamin Lincoln Collection 416 (September–October 1779) in the Domestic Collection of the Library of Congress, Washington, D. C. The Benjamin Lincoln Papers (13 reels of microfilm) Collection 488; Letter to the editor. *(Savannah) Daily Georgian*. August 8, 1835; Moses Buffington to Peter Buffington Sr. Savannah. December 8, 1779, in Albert Sidney Britt, Jr. et al. eds. *Selected Eighteenth Century Manuscripts*. Savannah: The Society of Colonial Wars in the State of Georgia, 1980. pp. 54–55, taken from Collection no. 101(1). Georgia Historical Society. Savannah, Georgia; John Jones to Polly Jones. October 7, 1779, in *Muskets, Cannon Balls, & Bombs, Nine Narratives of the Siege of Savannah in 1779*, ed. and trans. Benjamin Kennedy. Savannah: Beehive Press, 1974, pp. 16, 19, 152; Jones, Charles C. Jr. *The Life and Services of*

the Honorable Maj. Gen. Samuel Elbert of Georgia. Cambridge: The Riverside Press, 1887. p. 35; Journal of the Siege of Savannah from the *Royal Georgia Gazette.* November 18, 1779, in SCAGG. December 10, 1779; Stevens, William Bacon. *A History of Georgia.* Philadelphia, PA, 1859. vol. 2, p. 228; Lawrence, Alexander A. *Storm Over Savannah, the Story of Count d'Estaing and the Siege of the town in 1779.* University of Georgia Press, 1951. p. 102; Testimony of John Were at the court-martial of General Robert Howe, *Proceedings of a General Court Martial, Held at Philadelphia for the Trial of Major General Howe, Dec. 7, 1781.* Philadelphia, 1782 reprinted in Collections of the New York Historical Society 1879 (New York, 1880) p. 230; Orders for attack in Order Book of John Faucheraud Grimke. *South Carolina Historical and Genealogical Magazine.* 17 (January 1916): 85–86; Gordon, William. *The History of the Rise, Progress, and Establishment, of the Independence of the United States of America.* New York, NY, 1789. vol. 3, p. 33; GSSC; November 18, 1777. Duc De Castries. *Papiers de Famille.* Paris: Editions France-Empire, n. d. p. 378; Johnston, Elizabeth Lichtenstein. *Recollections of a Georgia Loyalist.* 1901 reprinted Spartanburg, SC: The Reprint Company, 1972. p. 62; CJ, December 29, 1779. Reuber, Johannes. *Diary of a Hessian Grenadier of Colonel Rail's Regiment.* trans. Bruce E. Burgoyne (privately printed, Johannes Schwalm Historical Association, Inc. n. p. n. d.), (from a copy of the diary of Johannes Reuber in the possession of Kennery Jones, Worcester, MA). p. 39; Major Alexander MacDonald to his wife Susannah MacDonald, Savannah. November 6, 1779. Edinburgh, Scotland. National Library of Scotland. British Journal of the siege of Savannah, 3 September–25 October 1779, in the Francis Rush Clark papers, Collection no. 2338 (III) in the Sol Feinstone Collection of the David Library of the American Revolution. Washington Crossing, Pennsylvania; Morningstars. vol. 1 pp. 168–174.

24   "Account of the Siege of Savannah, from a British Source." *Collections of the Georgia Historical Society.* Savannah: Braid & Hutton, 1901. vol. 5, pt. 1, p. 138; Hough, Franklin Benjamin, ed. *The siege of Charleston by the British fleet and army, under the command of Admiral Arbuthnot and Sir Henry Clinton, which terminated with the surrender of that place on the 12th of May, 1780.* Albany, J. Munsell, 1867. Spartanburg, SC: Reprint Company, 1975 pp. 45, 78–79; NBBAS. vol. 1, p. 354.

25   Charlestown, (South Carolina) Sept 22, PEP, Oct. 26, 1779. vol. V, no. 635, p. 243; Charles town, Sept. 29, Prensa, Nov. 2, 1779. vol. VI, no. 319, p. 2; Charlestown (South-Carolina), Sept. 22, NJG, Nov. 3, 1779. vol. II, no. 97, p. 2; New-York, October 25, PP, Nov. 4, 1779, p. 3; Charlestown, September 29, NP, Nov. 16, 1779, no. 319, p. 3; Charlestown, Sept. 29, CC, Nov. 16, 1779, no. 773, p. 2; Charlestown (S. C.), Sept. 29, CJ, Nov. 17, 1779, no. 629, p. 1; Charlestown (S. C.), Sept. 29, PG, Nov. 20, 1779. vol. XVI, no. 829, p. 2; Charlestown, September 29, RG, Dec. 1, 1779, no. 331, p. 3.

26   Clark, George Rogers. *George Rogers Clark Papers 1771–1781.* James, Alton James, ed. Springfield, Illinois State Historical Library, 1912. Collections of the Illinois State Historical Library vol. VIII, pp. cxxxiii–cxxxiv.

27   Peckham. p. 77.

28   Funk, Arville, L. *Revolutionary War Era in Indiana.* Corydon, IN: ALFCO Publications, 1975, pp. 17–20.

29   http: //petite-fort. tripod.com/Fort_History.htm. Funk, Arville, L. *Revolutionary War Era in Indiana.* Corydon, IN: ALFCO Publications, 1975, pp. 21–22.

30   Peckham. p. 80.

31   Boatner; Kinnaird, Lawrence. "The Spanish Expedition Against Fort St. Joseph in 1781, A New Interpretation." *Mississippi Valley Historical Review.* vol. 19 (September 1932), pp. 173–191.

32   Galvez, Bernardo de. "Diary of The Operations Against Pensacola," translated by Gaspar de Cusachs New Orleans, LA. *The Louisiana Historical Quarterly.* 1 (January, 1917) p. 52.

33 RG, no. 498 (July 7, 1781), p. 2.

34 Fleming, Thomas. Bernardo de Gálvez, "The Forgotten Revolutionary Conquistador Who Saved Louisiana." *American Heritage*. vol. 33, no. 3 (April/May), 1982, p. 38.

35 Rush, Nixon Orwin. *The battle of Pensacola, March 9 to May 8, 1781, Spain's final triumph over Great Britain in the Gulf of Mexico*. Tallahassee, Florida: State University, 1966, pp. 57–58.

36 Peckham. p. 84; Galvez, Bernardo de. "Diary of the Operations Against Pensacola," translated by Gaspar de Cusachs. New Orleans, LA. *The Louisiana Historical Quarterly*. vol. 1 (January, 1917), p. 67; Worcester, Donald E. trans. "Miranda's Diary of the Siege of Pensacola, 1781." *The Florida Historical Society Quarterly*. vol. 29 (January, 1951), pp. 176–177.

37 AJ. vol. III, no. 145 (July 18, 1781), p. 1; PG. vol. XVIII, no. 916, p. 2; Morningstars. vol. 1, p. 245.

38 Blanco, Richard L. ed. *The War of the Revolution, 1775–1783: an Encyclopedia*. New York: Garland Pub. 1993; Boatner; Purcell, L. Edward, and Sarah J. Purcell. "Battle of Spencer's Tavern." *Encyclopedia of Battles in North America, 1517 to 1916*. New York: Facts on File, Inc. 2000; Facts on File, Inc. *American History Online*. www.factsonfile.com; Simcoe, John Graves. *Simcoe's Military Journal. A History of the Operations of a Partisan Corps Called the Queen's Rangers, Commanded by Lieut. Col. J. G. Simcoe, During the War of the American Revolution*. New York: Bartlett & Welford, 1844, New York: New York Times, Arno Press. Eyewitness Accounts of the American Revolution. 1968.

39 Ward, Christopher. The War of the Revolution. New York: Macmillan, 1952.

40 Washington, George. *The Diaries of George Washington, 1748–1799*. Boston, New York: Houghton Mifflin Company, Kraus Reprint Co. 1925, 1971. vol. II, pp. 231–233.

41 Ward. pp. 881–882.

42 IC&UA. vol. XIII, no. 706 (July 26, 1781), p. 2; Bolton, Robert. *The History of the Several towns, Manors, and Patents of the County of Westchester from its First Settlement to the Present Time*. New York: Chas. F. Roper, 1881. vol. 2, pp. 621–622.

43 Rice, Howard C, Jr. and Anne S. K. Brown. *The American Campaigns of Rochambeau's Army 1780, 1781, 1782, 1783*. Princeton: Princeton University Press, Providence: Brown University Press, 1972. vol. 1, pp. 32, 132, 248–251.

44 Journal of HM Galley *Dependence*. BNA. Admiralty 51/4159–Captain's Log no. 4159 Part 3 (1777), p. 59; Rice, Howard C, Jr. and Anne S.K. Brown. *The American Campaigns of Rochambeau's Army 1780, 1781, 1782, 1783*. Princeton: Princeton University Press, Providence: Brown University Press, 1972. vol. 1, pp. 34–35, 248–251.

45 Peckham. p. 88.

46 Mackenzie. vol. 2, p. 568; Lossing, Benson John. *The Pictorial Field-book of the Revolution, or, Illustrations, by Pen and Pencil, of the History, Biography, Scenery, Relics, and Traditions of the War for Independence*. New York, Harper & Brothers 1860 vol. II. Chapter XXIII.

47 PEP. vol. VII, no. 758 (July 27,1781), p.115.

48 RG, no. 470 (March 31, 1781) p.2; NYG (March 31, 1781), no. 1537 (April 2, 1781), p. 2.

49 Letter to Gov. Franklin, from Lt. Col. Upham of the Associated Loyalists, and commandant at Lloyd's Neck, dated Fort Franklin, July 13. *The Scots Magazine*. vol. 43, no. MDCCLXXXI. p. 469.

50 Thacher, James. *Military Journal of the American Revolution*. Hartford: Hurlbut, Williams & Company, 1862, pp. 280–281; *The Freeman's Journal: or, The North-American Intelligencer*. vol. XXVII (October 24, 1781) p. 2; CJ. vol. CCXCVI (October 5, 1781), p. 3.

51 Tarleton, Banastre. *A History of the Campaigns of 1780 and 1781 in the Southern Provinces of North America*. London: T. Cadell, 1787, s.l.: The New York Times & Arno Press, 1968, pp. 376–381;

Ewald, pp. 329–330; Thacher, James. *Military Journal of the American Revolution*. Hartford: Hurlbut, Williams & Company, 1862, pp. 280–281.

52 Minutes of Occurrences respecting the Siege and Capture of York in Virginia, extracted from the Journal of Colonel Jonathan Trumbull, Secretary to the General, 1781. In *Proceedings of the Massachusetts Historical Society*. Boston: the Society. vol. 14 (1875–76), pp. 331–338; Ewald. p. 334.

53 Popp, Stephen. *Popp's Journal, 1777–1783*; J.C. Rosengarten, ed. *Pennsylvania Magazine of History and Biography*. vol. 26 (1902), p. 41.

54 van Cortlandt, Philip. Autobiography of Philip van Cortlandt. *Magazine of History and Biography*. vol. 22 (1898), p. 294.

55 Martin, Joseph Plumb, *Private Yankee Doodle, Being a Narrative of Some of the Adventures, Dangers, and Sufferings of a Revolutionary Soldier*. edited by George F. Scheer, originally published in Hallowell, ME 1830, anonymously (Republished, Boston, 1962). *A Narrative of Some of the Adventures, Dangers and Sufferings of a Revolutionary Soldier*. Eyewitness accounts of the American Revolution. New York: New York Times, 1968, pp. 234–235.

56 *The Norwich Packet and the Weekly Advertiser*. vol. IX, no. 423 (November 15, 1781), p. 3; Feltman, William. *The Journal of Lieut. William Feltman, of the First Pennsylvania Regiment, 1781–82, including the march into Virginia and the Siege of Yorktown*. Philadelphia: Henry Carey Baird for the Historical Society of Pennsylvania, 1853. Eyewitness Accounts of the American Revolution. New York: The New York Times & Arno Press, 1969. p. 21.

57 Thacher, James. *Military Journal of the American Revolution*. Hartford: Hurlbut, Williams & Company, 1862, pp. 283–287. Tarleton, Banastre. *A History of the Campaigns of 1780 and 1781 in the Southern Provinces of North America*. London: T. Cadell, 1787, s.l.: The New York Times & Arno Press, 1968, pp. 388–389.

58 Selesky. vol. 2, pp. 1291–1308; Fremont-Barnes. vol. 4, pp. 1382–1392. Alden, John R. *The South in the Revolution, 1763–1789*. Baton Rouge: Louisiana State University Press, 1957; Billias, George A. ed. *George Washington's Generals and Opponents: Their Exploits and Leadership*, 1964. reprint, New York: Da Capo, 1994; Bosnal, Stephen. *When the French Were Here*. Garden City, NY: Doubleday, 1945; Breen, Kenneth. "A Reinforcement Reduced: Rodney's Flawed Appraisal of French Plans, West Indies 1781." In *New Interpretations in Naval History: Selected Papers from the Ninth Naval History Symposium*. Edited by William R. Roberts and Jack Sweetman. Annapolis, MD: Naval Institute Press, 1991; Breen, Kenneth. "Sir George Rodney and St. Eustatius in the American War: A Commercial and Naval Distraction, 1775–1781." *Mariner's Mirror*. vol. 84 (May 1998), pp. 192–203; Buchanan, John. *The Road to Guilford Courthouse*. New York: John Wiley and Sons, Inc. 1997; Chidsey, Donald B. *Victory at Yorktown*. New York: Crown, 1962; Chávez, Thomas E. *Spain and the Independence of the United States*. Albuquerque: University of New Mexico Press, 2002; Clowes. Davis, Burke. *The Campaign that Won America: The Story of Yorktown, 1781*. New York: Dial, 1970; Dull, John R. *The French Navy and the American Revolution: a study of arms and diplomacy, 1774–1787*. Princeton, NJ: Princeton University Press, 1975; Ellis, Joseph J. *His Excellency George Washington*. New York: Knopf, 2004; Fleming, Thomas J. *Beat the Last Drum: The Siege of Yorktown, 1781*. New York: St. Martin's, 1963; Flexner, James Thomas. *George Washington in the American Revolution*. Boston: Little Brown, 1968; Flexner, James Thomas. *Washington: The Indispensable Man*. New York: Mentor, 1979; Fortescue, John. *The War of Independence: The British Army in North America, 1775–1783*. London: Greenhill, 2001; Fortescue, Sir John William. *A History of the British Army*. 2nd ed. London: Macmillan and Company, 1911; Freeman, Douglas Southall. *George Washington, a biography*. New York: Scribner, 1948–1957; Gottschalk, Louis. *La Fayette and the Close of the American Revolution*. Chicago: University of Chicago Press, 1942; Greene, Jerome A. *The Guns of Independence: The Siege of Yorktown, 1781*. New York: Savas Beattie, 2005;

Griffith, Samuel B. *The War for American Independence: From 1760 to the Surrender at Yorktown in 1781*. Champaign: University of Illinois Press, 2002; Johnston, Henry P. *The Yorktown Campaign and the Surrender of Cornwallis, 1781*. New York: Eastern Acorn Press, 1981; Ketchum, Richard M. *Victory at Yorktown: The Campaign that Won the Revolution*. New York: Henry Holt, 2004; Larrabee, Harold A. *Decision at the Chesapeake*. New York: Clarkson N. Potter, 1964; Leckie, Robert. *George Washington's War: The Saga of the American Revolution*. New York: Harper Perennial, 1993; Lewis, Charles Lee. *Admiral de Grasse and American Independence*. Annapolis, MD: Naval Institute Press, 1945; Lewis, James A. "Las Damas de la Havana, El Precursor, and Francisco de Saavedra: A Note on Spanish Participation in the Battle of Yorktown." *The Americas*. vol. 37 (July 1981), pp. 83–89; Mackesy. Mahan, Alfred T. *The Influence of Sea Power upon History, 1660–1783*. Boston: Little Brown, 1890; Morrill, Dan L. *Southern Campaigns of the American Revolution*. Baltimore: The Nautical & Aviation Publishing Company of America n.d.; Morrissey, Brendan. *Yorktown 1781: The World Turned Upside Down*. Oxford: Osprey, 1997; Padron, Francisco Morales, ed. *Journal of Don Francisco Saavedra de Sangronis*. Gainesville: University of Florida Press, 1989; Pybus, Cassandra. "Jefferson's Faulty Math: The Question of Slave Defections in the American Revolution." *William and Mary Quarterly*. vol. 62 (April 2005), pp. 243–264; Rice, Howard C, Jr. and Anne S.K. Brown. *The American Campaigns of Rochambeau's Army 1780, 1781, 1782, 1783*. Princeton: Princeton University Press, Providence: Brown University Press, 1972; Sands, John O. *Yorktown's Captive Fleet*. Charlottesville: University Press of Virginia, 1983; Skaggs, David Curtis. "Decision at Cap Français: Franco-Spanish Coalition Planning and the Prelude to Yorktown." In *New Interpretations in Naval History: Selected Papers from the Thirteenth Naval History Symposium*. Edited by William M. McBride. Annapolis, MD: Naval Institute Press, 1998; Syrett, David. *The Royal Navy in American Waters, 1775–1783*. Aldershot, UK: Scholar Press, 1989; Thayer, Theodore G. *Yorktown: Campaign of Strategic Options*. Philadelphia: Lippincott, 1975; Tilley, J. A. *The Royal Navy in the American Revolution*. Columbia: University of South Carolina Press, 1987; Urwin, Gregory J. W. "Cornwallis and the Slaves of Virginia: New Look at the Yorktown Campaign." In *ACTA: International Commission of Military History. XXVIII Congress: Coming to the Americas*. Edited by John A. Lynn. Wheaton, IL: United States Commission on Military History and the Cantigny First Division Foundation, 2003; Ward. pp. 886–. Washington, George. *The Diaries of George Washington*. Edited by Donald Jackson. Charlottesville: University Press of Virginia, 1976–1979; Whitridge, Arnold. *Rochambeau: Neglected Founding Father*. New York: Collier Books, 1965; Wickwire, Franklin, and Mary Wickwire. *Cornwallis: The American Adventure*. Boston: Houghton Mifflin, 1970; Wickwire, Franklin, and Mary Wickwire. *Cornwallis and the War of Independence*. London: Faber and Faber, 1971; Willcox, William B. "The British Road to Yorktown: A Study in Divided Command." *American Historical Review*. vol. 52 (October 1946) pp. 1–35; Willcox, William B. *Portrait of a General: Sir Henry Clinton in the War of Independence*. New York: Knopf, 1964; Wood, W. J. *Battles of the Revolutionary War, 1775–1781*. Chapel Hill, NC: Algonquin, 1990.

59 Damon, Allan L. "A Melancholy Case." New York. *American Heritage: the magazine of history*. vol. 21, no. 2 (February, 1970), pp. 92–94.

Bibliography

Allen, Gardner Weld. *A Naval History of the American Revolution*. Boston and New York: Houghton Mifflin Company, The Riverside Press Cambridge, 1913.

Allen, Gardner Weld. *Massachusetts privateers of the Revolution*. Boston: The Massachusetts Historical Society, 1927.

Almon, John and Pownall, Thomas. *The Remembrancer, or impartial repository of public events*. London: J. Almon, 1775–1784.

Beaumarchais, Pierre Augustin Caron de; Morton, Brian N.; Spinelli, Donald C. *Correspondance [de] Beaumarchais*. Paris: A.-G. Nizet, 1969– 1978.

Boatner, Mark M. *Encyclopedia of the American Revolution*. 3d ed., New York: McKay, 1980.

Boatner, Mark Mayo. *Landmarks of the American Revolution*. 2nd ed. Library of Military History. Detroit: Charles Scribner's Sons, 2007.

Cavalier, Roderick. *Admiral Satan: the life and campaigns of Suffren*. London: Tauris, 1994.

Claghorn, Charles Eugene. *Naval officers of the American Revolution: a concise biographical dictionary.* Metuchen, N. J.: Scarecrow Press, 1988.

Clinton, Henry. *The American Rebellion: Sir Henry Clinton's Narrative of His Campaigns, 1775–1782, with an appendix of original documents*. Edited by William B. Willcox. New Haven: Yale University Press, 1954.

Clowes, William Laird. *The Royal Navy: a history from the earliest times to 1900*. London: Chatham, 1996. 7 vols.

Commager, Henry Steele. *The spirit of 'seventy-six; the story of the American Revolution as told by participants*. edited by Henry Steele Commager and Richard B. Morris. New York: Harper & Row, 1967.

Davies, K. G. *Documents of the American Revolution 1770–1783*. (Colonial Office Series) Shannon: Irish University Press, 1972.

Deane, Silas; Isham, Charles. *The Deane papers…* 1774–[1790]. Edited by Charles Isham. New York: New-York Historical Society, 1887–1890.

Doniol, Henri. *Histoire de la Participation de la France à l'établissement des États-Unis d'Amérique. Correspondance diplomatique et documents*. Paris: Imprimerie nationale, 1886 1892.

Ewald, Johann. *Diary of the American War: A Hessian Journal*. Translated and edited by Joseph P. Tustin. New Haven and London: Yale University Press, 1979.

Faibisy, John D. "A Compilation of Nova Scotia Vessels Seized During the American Revolution and Libelled in the New England Prize Court." in *Naval Documents of the American Revolution*, X, 1201–1210.

Ferreiro, Larrie D. *Brothers at Arms: American Independence and the Men of France & Spain Who Saved It*. Alfred A. Knopf, 2016.

Force, Peter. *American archives: consisting of a collection of authentick records, state papers, debates, and letters and other notices of publick affairs, the whole forming a documentary history of the origin and progress of the North American colonies; of the causes and accomplishment of the American revolution; and of the Constitution of government for the United States, to the final ratification thereof. In six series*. Washington, 1837–1853.

Franklin, Benjamin, et al. *The Papers of Benjamin Franklin*. New Haven: Yale University Press, 1959. http://franklinpapers.org/franklin//

Fremont-Barnes, Gregory and Richard Alan Ryerson, eds. *The Encyclopedia of the American Revolutionary War: a political, social, and military history*. Santa Barbara, CA: ABC-CLIO, 2006.

Gardiner, Robert, ed. *Navies and the American Revolution, 1775–1783*. London: Chatham, 1996.

Greenwood, John. *The Revolutionary Services of John Greenwood of Boston and New York, 1775–1783*. Edited from the original manuscript with notes by his grandson Isaac J. Greenwood. New York: The De Vinne Press, 1922.

Hattendorf, John B. *Newport, the French Navy, and American Independence*. Newport: The Redwood Press, 2005.

Hermione: Log of the *Hermione*. Captain Louis René Madeleine Le Vassor de Latouche-Tréville. Archives Nationales de la Marine, Paris. B4 158. Published as Journal de la frégate du Roi l'*Hermione* de 32 canons (extraits) Commandée par M. de La Touche, Lieutenant de Vaisseau. La campagne, commencée le 23 janvier 1780, finie le 26 fevrier 1782. in Tott François de, et al. *Deux Voyages Au Temps De Louis Xvi, 1777-1780: La Mission Du Baron De Tott En Égypte En 1777-1778 Et Le Journal De Bord De L'Hermione En 1780*. Presses Universitaires De Rennes, 2005.

James, William. *The naval history of Great Britain: during the French Revolutionary and Napoleonic wars*. Mechanicsburg, PA: Stackpole, 2003.

Kaminkow, Marion and Jack, *Mariners of the American Revolution*. Baltimore: Magna Carta Book Company, 1967.

Kell, Jean Bruyere. *North Carolina's Coastal Carteret County During the American Revolution, 1765–1785, A Bicentennial Project of the Carteret County Bicentennial Commission*. Era Press, 1975.

Kite, Elizabeth Sarah. *Beaumarchais and the War of American Independence*. Boston, R. G. Badger 1918.

Loménie, Louis de. *Beaumarchais et Son Temps: études sur la société en France au XVIIIe siècle d'après des documents inédits*. Paris: Michel Lèvy Frères, Éditeurs, 1858.

MacKenzie, Frederick. *Diary of Frederick MacKenzie, Giving a Daily Narrative of his Military Services as an Officer of the Regiment of Royal Welsh Fusiliers during the years 1775–1781 in Massachusetts, Rhode Island, and New York*. Cambridge, Mass.: 1930; (Eyewitness accounts of the American Revolution). New York: New York Times, 1968, c1930.

Mackesy, Piers. *The War for America, 1775–1783*. Lincoln: University of Nebraska Press, 1993.

Mays, Terry M. *Historical Dictionary of the American Revolution*. Lanham, MD: Scarecrow Press, 1999.

Monaque, Rémi. *Latouche-Tréville, 1745–1804: l'amiral qui défiait Nelson*. Paris: SPM, 2000.

Moore, Frank. *Diary of the American Revolution: from Newspapers and Original Documents*. New York: Charles Scribner; London: Sampson Low, Son & Co., 1890.

Moultrie, William. *Memoirs of the American Revolution so far as it related to the States of North and South Carolina and Georgia*. New York, 1802; (Eyewitness accounts of the American Revolution). New York: New York Times, 1968.

Naval documents of the American Revolution. William Bell Clark, editor; with a foreword by President John F. Kennedy and an introd. by Ernest McNeill Eller. Washington: Naval History Division, Dept. of the Navy: For sale by the Supt. of Docs., U.S. G. P. O., 1964.

Neeser, Robert Wilden. *Letters and papers relating to the cruises of Gustavus Conyngham: a captain of the Continental Navy, 1777–1779*. Port Washington, N. Y.: Kennikat Press, 1970.

O'Kelley, Patrick. *Nothing but Blood and Slaughter*. Booklocker.com, 2004.

Parker, John C. *Parker's Guide to the Revolutionary War in South Carolina: battles, skirmishes and murders*. Patrick, S. C.: Hem Branch Publishing, 2009.

Paullin, Charles Oscar, *The Navy of the American Revolution*, Cleveland: The Burrows Brothers Company, 1906.

Peckham, Howard Henry. *The Toll of Independence: engagements & battle casualties of the American Revolution.* edited by Howard H. Peckham. Chicago: University of Chicago Press, 1974.

Ripley, Warren. *Battleground: South Carolina in the Revolution.* Charleston, SC: Evening Post, 1983.

Scull, G. D. *The Montresor Journals.* ed. and annotated by G. D. Scull: [New York, Printed for the Society, 1882]; July 1, 1777, to July 1, 1778.

Selesky, Harold E., editor in chief. *Encylopedia of the American Revolution*, 2nd ed. Detroit: Charles Scribner's Sons, 2007.

Shewmake, Antoinette. *For the Good of Mankind: Pierre-Augustin Caron de Beaumarchais political correspondence relative to the American Revolution.* Lanham, MD: University Press of America, 1987.

Smith, Charles R. *Marines in the Revolution.* Washington, DC: Government Printing Office, 1975.

Smith, Gordon Burns. *Morningstars of Liberty: the Revolutionary War in Georgia, 1775–1783.* Milledgeville, Ga: Boyd Publishing, 2006.

Stevens, B. F. *Facsimiles of Manuscripts in European Archives Relating to America, 1773–1783.* London, 1889–98. 25 vols.

Trumbull, Benjamin. *Trumbull's Journal of the Expedition against Canada.* Collections of the Connecticut Historical Society. Hartford: the Society, 1899.

Ward, Christopher. *The War of the Revolution.* New York: Macmillan, 1952.

Wharton, Francis, ed. *Revolutionary Diplomatic Correspondence of the United States.* Washington: GPO, 1889. 6 vols.

Index